W9-DEP-106

# FRANCHISING
# IN EUROPE

*Edited by Martin Mendelsohn*

CASSELL

053202|        179173

**Cassell Plc**
Wellington House       387 Park Avenue South
125 Strand             New York, NY 10016-8810
London WC2R 0BB        USA

© Martin Mendelsohn and contributors 1992

All rights reserved. No part of this publication may be
reproduced or transmitted in any form or by any means,
electronic or mechanical including photocopying, recording
or any information storage or retrieval system, without
prior permission in writing from the publishers.

First published in hardback 1992
This paperback edition first published 1993
Reprinted 1996

**British Library Cataloguing-in-Publication Data**
A catalogue record for this book is available from the British Library.

ISBN 0-304-32812-X

Typeset by Colset Private Limited, Singapore

Printed in Great Britain by Bookcraft (Bath) Ltd, Midsomer Norton, Avon

# CONTENTS

053202

179173

# CHAPTER 1
# INTRODUCTION

*Martin Mendelsohn*

Franchising is a method of marketing goods and services which has proved remarkably successful in something like 80 countries worldwide. Once the concept is understood and adopted by the business community in any country the rate of growth which is then achieved is quite startling. Spain is a good example of what can be achieved, with growth from a negligible franchise community in 1986 when it joined the European Community to approximately 200 franchisors and 20 000 franchised outlets estimated for 1990.

The technique of franchising did not derive from one moment of inventiveness by an imaginative individual. It evolved from the solutions developed by businessmen in response to the problems with which they were confronted in their business operations.

It may be said that at the beginning of this century driving and drink (but not alcoholic) were the catalysts for franchising activity, followed by a trickle of developments until the 1930s, when Howard Johnson started his famous chain in the USA, and the 1940s and 1950s, which saw the birth of so many of the modern giants of the franchising community.

During these distinct phases different categories of franchising emerged and involved all levels in the chain from manufacturer to consumer. Thus we find franchise arrangements between:

1    Manufacturer and retailer

2    Manufacturer and wholesaler

3    Wholesaler and retailer

4    Retailer and retailer

Each of these categories can be identified clearly.

1    *Manufacturer and retailer*. This category was that which emerged from the development of the car industry. In *Automobile Franchise Agreements* the author Charles Mason Hewitt identifies the problems with which the car manufacturers were confronted as:

'(1) Some rapid means of acquiring retail outlets requiring a minimum of attention, outlay and fixed expense;

(2) Some means of making their cars conveniently available for consumer inspection in advance of purchase on a nationwide basis;

(3) Some means of coping with the repair problem;

(4) Some means of coping with the off season storage problems;

(5) Some means of acquiring a ready market for their goods without having fixed legal commitments for delivery; and

(6) Some means of acquiring cash on delivery or even in advance if possible.'

The solution to these problems was the franchised automobile dealer.

It was not until the 1930s that franchising was introduced in the USA to the business of petrol stations, which also come within this category.

2   *Manufacturer and wholesaler.* This category came into existence probably a little earlier than the adoption of franchising by the car industry when soft drink manufacturers established the practice of franchising their bottling factories. Briefly, what they did (and indeed still do) was to grant the right within a defined area to use a concentrate or syrup manufactured by, and of course obtained from, them. The bottler's functions include making up and bottling the drink, using the manufacturer's syrups and in accordance with the manufacturer's requirements, and distributing the resulting products. Prime examples of this category are Coca-Cola, Pepsi-Cola and Schweppes.

3   *Wholesaler and retailer.* This category is not so easy to identify but the franchising technique which enables wholesalers to secure outlets for products and maximize the use of storage and distribution facilities has been used with profit in such areas as automotive products, drug stores and hardware stores.

4   *Retailer and retailer.* This category comprises what were the initial business format franchises. It developed from the establishment of a retail operation which is successful and which is then expanded by the use of the franchise method of marketing. This category resulted from the Howard Johnson initiative of the 1930s which grew into the explosion of the 1950s which saw the birth of the now great market leaders including McDonald's, Kentucky Fried Chicken, Burger King, Dunkin' Donuts, Pizza Hut, Holiday Inn, Travelodge and Sheraton.

The growth and development of all these categories of franchise resulted from the provision of a common solution to common problems. It is perhaps convenient to summarize what business format franchising is and why the parties to a franchise and the consumer benefit from the relationship.

Franchising, that is to say the business format franchise, involves the following characteristics:

1  The development by the franchisor of a successful business format which is operated under a trade mark, trade name (service mark) or other form of branding.

2  The grant by the franchisor of the right to the franchisee, permitting the franchisee to trade using that business format under the trade mark, trade name or other form of branding.

3  The franchisor provides to the franchisee a range of services which are calculated to ensure so far as is practicably possible that the franchisee will enjoy the same or a greater degree of success as the franchisor has achieved. These services will include:

(a)  the application of developed criteria for the selection and identification of trading sites

(b)  guidance to the franchisee to assist in obtaining occupation rights to the site, complying with zoning laws, preparation of plans for layouts, shopfitting and refurbishment and general assistance in the evaluation of the correct level and mix of stock and in the opening launch of the business

(c)  the training of the franchisee in the operation of the business format and the provision of a manual with detailed operational instructions

(d)  the training of the franchisee in any methods of manufacture or preparation which may be appropriate

(e)  the training of the franchisee in methods of accounting, business controls, marketing and merchandising

Having established the franchisee in business the franchisor then offers continuing services for which a fee is payable. The fee (often called a royalty or a management services fee) is paid in return for continuing services rendered. These continuing services usually include:

(a)  operational back-up

(b)  updating of the operational manual

(c)  marketing and promotional support

(d)   advertising on a national or regional basis with funds contributed by franchisees

(e)   standards and performance monitoring

(f)   research and development

(g)   in appropriate cases the benefits of the bulk purchasing power which the network commands

In short the franchisee benefits by having support services available which no individual self-employed trader could command and at a price which makes economic sense.

4     In negotiating the grant of the franchise the franchisor will explain to the prospective franchisee why his concept system and branding merit an investment.

5     The franchisee is required to make a substantial capital investment from his own resources so as to provide both commitment and motivation.

6     The franchisee's ownership and day-to-day involvement in the operation of his business strengthens his commitment and motivation and tends to ensure that the business is exploited to the maximum advantage. The value of the consumer as a customer is reflected by the way in which the franchisee interests himself in his customers' needs.

7     The consumer benefits from dealing with what appears to be a multiple network, but as it is in multiple ownership he is in reality dealing with an owner.

As a boost to growth, franchising provides a powerful alternative to ownership of one's own outlets.

1     The growth is achieved by using the manpower and capital resources of others and can thus be more rapid. That, of course, was the way in which the motor manufacturers solved the problems to which I referred earlier.

2     The commitment and interest of the franchisee, together with the risks he runs, tend to ensure that standards are maintained and that performance is better.

3     The customer gets a better service by dealing with an owner instead of a less interested manager and staff.

The franchisor and franchisee present to the market-place a powerful partnership (not in the legal sense) which is calculated to produce profit for both by providing the consumer with:

1    A uniform branded product at each outlet.

2    A high quality of product and service.

3    A committed and interested local owner.

The franchisee joins the network and pays the price because:

1    He wants to buy into the success of the franchisor.

2    He wants to belong to a 'club' and not be out on his own.

3    He wants the comfort of knowing that the initial and continuing services will be available to him.

The franchisor selects his franchisees with certain basic requirements in mind:

1    He will wish to be satisfied that the franchisee's financial resources are adequate.

2    He will have to make a judgment that the franchisee:

   (a)  has the commitment

   (b)  has the ability to accept the responsibilities and stress of self-employment

   (c)  has the ability to run the business in accordance with the established format

The reputable franchisor cannot run the risk for itself or the franchisee that the franchisee will not be able to make a success of the business.

   In examining the growth of franchising one must start in the USA, not only because it was the cradle of modern franchise development, but also since it is the largest market-place for franchising systems. It is undoubtedly the largest exporter of franchising systems despite the great advances which have been made in other countries, notably Canada, Japan, Australia, France, Germany and the United Kingdom. Franchising in some form exists in over 80 countries and that number will continue to grow although in many cases the number of franchise systems will be very small. Table 1.1 illustrates the level of franchising activity in various countries for which information is available.

**Table 1.1**

|                                | Number of franchisors | Number of outlets | Sales in US $bn |
|--------------------------------|-----------------------|-------------------|-----------------|
| Australia (1987–1988)          | 184                   | 10 303            | 4.12            |
| Austria (1988)                 | 30                    | 1 363             | N/A             |
| Belgium (1987)                 | 77                    | 4 045             | 3.2             |
| Canada (1987)                  | 1000                  | 45 000            | 51.69           |
| Denmark (1989)                 | 60                    | 500               | N/A             |
| Federal Republic of Germany (1987) | 180               | 9 000             | 5.41            |
| France (1988)                  | 675                   | 29 698            | 16              |
| Italy (1988)                   | 197                   | 11 500            | 3.36            |
| Japan (1988)                   | 619                   | 102 397           | 44.30           |
| Netherlands (1988)             | 248                   | 8 332             | 5.76            |
| Norway (1988)                  | 120                   | 850               | 0.48            |
| Republic of Korea              | 33                    | 337               | 0.25            |
| Sweden (1988)                  | 60                    | 1 000             | 2.4             |
| United Kingdom (1990)          | 379                   | 18 260            | 7.57            |
| United States of America (1988) | 2177                 | 368 458           | 190.1           |

Source: Various, including National Franchise Associations, European Franchise Federation, International Franchise Association, Australian Government Survey
*Note*: these figures exclude sales of cars, trucks and gasoline, and soft drink bottlers.

As the 1992 implementation of the Single European Act approaches, the world of franchising is trying to assess the opportunities. The American franchise companies are considering whether, because of their 'Fortress Europe' fears, they should accelerate their plans to expand operations into the EC. There are franchisors in other countries who will also be viewing Europe 1992 with mixed feelings of opportunity and risk. The relaxation of the grip of communism in Eastern Europe, with the opportunities for business which that presents, adds to the difficulty in making choices not only for the non-EC franchisor but also for the franchisor within the EC which is considering expansion beyond its national borders.

What difference will the 1992 concept, and the elimination of barriers which it promises, make to international franchising activities? In using the expression 'international', one includes trade between member states of the EC. For all practical purposes, 1992 will not make that much difference to the rate of growth of international franchising, except to the extent that activity is stimulated by the publicity which has been given to the concept and the encouragement given by the Commission and governments of the member states to business interests.

There certainly does seem to be an increased interest throughout the franchising community in international expansion. However, that interest has been developing over the last few years at an ever-increasing pace which owes nothing to 1992 and it may be difficult to know whether the reason for any franchisor's international growth is part of that trend or attributable to the interest generated by the perceived benefits which will flow from the 1992 single market reality.

It may indeed be said that, 1992 apart, if the 1940s and 1950s in the USA were the years when franchising made its first significant thrust into the US domestic market-place, the 1980s and 1990s will be looked back upon as the years when international franchising made a similar impact on the world market-place.

The formula upon which franchise development is based involves a blend of complementary skills and resources. The franchisor, with its established name, trade mark or service mark and the associated goodwill coupled with a developed business format system combines with the franchisee with financial and man-power resources coupled with, one hopes, ambition, some entrepreneurial skills and commitment. At its best the combination is remarkably successful.

This formula lends itself to the development of a network on an international as well as a domestic scale since the system has built into it the mechanism for converting the individual with no business experience or skills into a business person with the specialist business and technical skills in all the relevant aspects which are necessary to conduct the franchised business.

In taking franchise operations across national borders many problems exist, which will continue to arise in intra-EC member states' activity post-1992:

1    We do not speak the same language in all EC member states.

2    We have different national characteristics, we are different as people in likes, dislikes and lifestyle.

3    Our cultures differ.

4    Our habits and customs differ.

5    Business methods and attitudes are different.

6    Despite harmonization, national laws having an effect on franchising will differ, e.g. real estate laws.

These factors all combine to make it essential for franchisors to ensure that their concept is adapted to cope with the differences which exist; manuals have to be rewritten in the local language, and the system fine-tuned by pilot operations to ensure that what has been successful in one of the national markets will succeed in the new market. It is unlikely that prospective franchisees will purchase a franchise in, say, Spain merely because the franchisor has achieved success in, say, the Republic of Ireland – they will wish to see success demonstrated in Spain before they are convinced.

Franchisors will be concerned that the French government has introduced laws which will have an impact not only on franchising but also on other business methods. At a time when barriers are being removed it does not seem to make sense to create a new one. Nor does there seem to be a case for introducing legislation in 11 other member states because one state has its own internal difficulties.

The adoption by the European Franchise Federation (EFF) of a Code of Ethics (see Appendix C) has enabled some uniformity of approach to be adopted. However, the member associates of the EFF have agreed that national variations within the overall spirit of the code should be permitted.

The possibility of increasing interest in legislative restraints will be a cause of concern to those engaged in franchising, particularly where existing legal remedies are adequate to cope with fraudulent practices. What is needed is a far higher level of education about what franchising is and what are the pitfalls. One of the recurrent themes one hears is the claim by franchisees that they should be guaranteed success because that is what franchising is. Franchising, of course, is nothing of the sort but it does offer a new business a better chance of success than would otherwise be the case. What is often overlooked is that in franchising the franchisor provides the franchisee with the basic tools to enable him to run the business. The degree of success or failure is invariably affected by the franchisees' attitude, commitment and ability. Given this, some will do exceptionally well, some will achieve an acceptable average level of performance and some will experience problems. This is simply because not all will be the same in attitude, commitment and ability.

If one of the results of 1992 will be creation of laws throughout the EC because one member state experiences difficulties, the effect can only be inhibiting on the development of new franchise opportunities through the cost of compliance resulting in a restriction of the growth of this sector to the advantage of the larger and better-established businesses.

International franchising can have many rewards, but the rewards will only be commensurate with the thoroughness with which the franchisor prepares to take this giant step. In the same way as one is cautioned against franchising prematurely in the domestic market-place just because a franchisee is there, one is also to be cautioned against franchising prematurely on an international basis. The pitfalls are just as great and the risk that someone will steal a franchisor's ideas and know-how, and establish better rights to them in the other territory than the franchisor can establish, is much greater.

Business format franchising in Europe in systems numbers and numbers of outlets is lagging far behind the USA on a comparable basis, bearing in mind the population figures. To catch up with the US market's present numbers the EC will need to increase franchisor numbers by 1277 and outlets by a staggering 374 360. If the EC franchise community has the potential to catch up with the USA, then the level of franchise activity in the EC will be extensive over the next few years.

With such an apparent growth prospect in view, it is not surprising that 1992 is exciting foreign franchisors. The promotion of 1992 and the single market is clearly encouraging all segments of commerce, including franchisors, to consider intra-EC growth. The question is whether European franchisors who have been significantly slow to export their franchises will now market themselves so effectively throughout the EC and indeed other parts of the world that the EC will become a net exporter of franchise systems and outlets instead of the net importer which it has been for so long.

This book has been written by franchise lawyers from each of the member states of the EC, eleven of whom are members of the EuroFranchise Lawyers' Group. All effort has been made to deal with the same issues and in the same order to assist readers in locating information. However, it has not been possible completely to achieve this since in some countries the law has developed on such a basis that the lines of demarcation are different. With so many contributors whose first language is not English it will be appreciated that each chapter will reflect the style of the author and the manner which he or she has selected for the expression of his or her system's particular concepts.

The editor hopes that it has been possible to ensure that each contribution clearly explains the concepts and issues. The responsibility for any failing in this respect is accepted by the editor.

# CHAPTER 2
# EUROPEAN OVERVIEW AND EC COMPETITION LAWS

*Martin Mendelsohn*

## OVERVIEW

Franchising in Europe (the European Community) has been actively growing for many years. In some member states the size of the franchise community and its maturity is quite impressive. Up-to-date statistical information is not readily available for all member states and in many of those for which it is available one has to rely on what are best estimates by franchise associations based upon information supplied by members and their knowledge of non-members. Table 2.1 summarizes the information currently available (drawn from Table 1.1).

Table 2.1

| Country | Number of franchises | Number of outlets |
|---|---|---|
| Belgium (1987) | 77 | 4 045 |
| Denmark (1989) | 60 | 500 |
| Federal Republic of Germany (1987) | 180 | 9 000 |
| France (1988) | 675 | 29 698 |
| Italy (1988) | 197 | 11 500 |
| Netherlands (1988) | 248 | 8 332 |
| United Kingdom (1990) | 379 | 18 260 |

Source: Various, including franchise associates and European Franchise Federation

For all this activity in franchising in Europe, there is a long way to go before franchising has the effect on the market-place which it has had in the USA. Even a country like Australia, with its limited population numbers, is able to boast 13.9 franchisors per million population compared with 8.4 per million in the USA. Canada, again with a relatively modest population, claims some 1000 franchisors with 45 000 outlets. Although Canada's figures probably reflect its proximity to the USA, without a widespread acceptance of franchising and its success in operation these results would not be achieved.

European franchising benefits from having available a level of knowledge and learning about franchising which did not exist in the USA at a similar level of franchise development there. Most member states have a franchise association which provides a focal point for franchising as well as promoting ethical conduct among franchisors. The European Franchise Federation (a federation of European franchise associations) has recently agreed with members a uniform Code of Ethics to be adopted, with local adjustments, by all national associations. The text of the code is set out in Appendix C of this book together with, by way of example, the adjustments adopted by the British Franchise Association. Readers should contact the relevant national association to ascertain whether any local adjustments to the code have been adopted and, if so, what they are.

As the reader will appreciate, apart from France, there are no specific franchise laws in any member states of the EC although the general body of commercial laws has varying impact in each state. In France, franchising, together with all licensing transactions, is affected by a law adopted early in 1990, which requires precontractual disclosure. The expected regulations containing the detailed requirements have not been published as at the end of October 1990, although Gérard Sautereau has, in the chapter on France, provided information relating to the latest draft of the regulations which was available at that time.

## COMPETITION LAWS

The European Commission, by its adoption of a block exemption regulation for categories of franchise agreements, has laid down the first legislation for franchising (albeit limited to competition law) in Europe and the first formal legal definition of franchising. The events which led to the adoption of the block exemption regulation commenced with litigation in Germany.

The brief facts are that Pronuptia de Paris GmbH (a subsidiary of the French company Pronuptia de Paris SA) had granted three exclusive franchises to Firma Pronuptia de Paris Irmgard Schillgalis for Hamburg, Oldenburg and Hanover. The case reached the European Court of Justice (CJEC) after Pronuptia de Paris GmbH had successfully sued at first instance for non-payment of franchise fees. The defendant appealed to the Oberlandesgerich, which held that the contract was void because it infringed the provisions of Article 85(1) of the Treaty of Rome. There had been no notification of the agreement under the provisions of Regulation 17. In an astonishing judgment, the West German court held that, substantially, all common franchising contractual provisions were anti-competitive under Article 85(1). Had the CJEC followed the German court's reasoning, franchising would have been virtually outlawed in Europe. The only provisions which emerged unscathed were:

1    A suggested retail price clause (provided that the franchisor does not enforce its price suggestion as fixed prices)

2    A non-competition clause prohibiting the franchisee from competing
     directly with the franchisor for a period of one year from termination of the
     agreement

Among specific provisions held to be invalid were:

1    The requirement that advertising by the franchisee should have the prior
     approval of the franchisor and that the advertising should comply with the
     general methods and standards of the franchisor

2    The requirement that the franchisee design her shop to conform with the
     brand image of the franchisor and to devote the shop primarily to the sale of
     bridal fashion items

3    The requirement that the franchisee purchase supplies of products from the
     franchisor or an authorized supplier

4    The requirements that the franchisee should sell the franchised products
     only in shops approved by the franchisor

5    The requirements relating to the equipping and fitting-out of the shop,
     training of staff, sales techniques, purchasing and marketing

EC competition law, out of which the case arises, is derived from Article 85 of the
Treaty of Rome, which provides as follows:

> '1   The following shall be prohibited as incompatible with the Common
>      Market: all agreements between undertakings, decisions by associa-
>      tions of undertakings and concerted practices that may affect trade
>      between Member States and which have as their object or effect the
>      prevention, restriction or distortion of competition within the Com-
>      mon Market, and in particular those which:
>
> > (a)   directly or indirectly fix purchase or selling prices or any other
> >       trading practices or other trading conditions;
> >
> > (b)   limit or control production, markets, technical development or
> >       investment;
> >
> > (c)   share markets or sources of supply;
> >
> > (d)   apply dissimilar conditions to equivalent transactions with other
> >       trading parties, thereby placing them at a competitive disadvant-
> >       age;
> >
> > (e)   make the conclusions of contracts subject to acceptance by the
> >       other parties of supplementary obligations which, by their nature

> or according to commercial usage, have no connection with the
> subject of such contracts.'

Paragraph 2 of Article 85 spells out the consequences of offending against paragraph 1.

> '2  Any agreements or decisions prohibited pursuant to this Article shall
> be automatically void.'.

This provision does not mean that the whole agreement, which contains provisions that offend against Article 85(1), is void, but only those severable parts which are prohibited. The effect of the provisions is a matter for national law. In some countries the 'blue pencil' principle would apply, but in some others the parts rendered void could be so fundamental to the contract as a whole that the contract is wholly defeated. Paragraph 3 of Article 85 provides machinery for the Commission to grant exemption.

> '3  The provisions of para 1 may, however, be declared inapplicable in
> the case of:
>
> (i)   any agreement or category of agreements between undertakings;
>
> (ii)  any decision or category of decisions by associations of under-
>       takings; or
>
> (iii) any concerted practice or category of concerted practices.
>
> which contribute to improving the production or distribution of goods
> or to promoting technical or economic progress, while allowing con-
> sumers a fair share of the resulting benefit, and which does not:
>
> (a)   impose on the undertakings concerned, restrictions that are not
>       indispensable to the attainment of those objectives; or
>
> (b)   afford such undertakings the possibility of eliminating competi-
>       tion in respect of a substantial part of the products in question.'

Most franchise systems should qualify for exemption under Article 85(3) but the following factors should be noted:

1  Only the Commission has power to grant exemption under the provision. No court considering competition law issues can give exemption under this provision.

2  No exemption can be given by the Commission unless the agreement is notified to it as provided in Regulation 17, which contains the procedure for dealing with exemptions.

In the past, the Commission, in cases where large numbers of agreements are notified, has adopted regulations granting exemption to all agreements in a particular category (block exemption regulations) provided that, so far as provisions having a competition law impact are concerned, the agreements comply with the regulation. An example of a block-exemption regulation is Regulation 67/67, covering exclusive dealing supply agreements (this relation was cited in Pronuptia, but the court held that it did not apply). It has since been replaced by Regulations 83/83 and 84/83.

### Questions raised by the appeal

The decision of the Oberlandesgericht was appealed by the franchisor to the Bundesgerichtshof, which referred the following questions to the European Court of Justice under Article 177 of the Treaty:

1    Is Article 85(1) of the EEC Treaty applicable to franchise agreements such as the contracts between the parties, which have as their object the establishment of a special distribution system whereby the franchisor provides to the franchisee, in addition to goods, certain trade names, trade marks, merchandising material and services?

2    If the first question is answered in the affirmative, is Regulation No. 67/67/EEC of the Commission of 22 March 1967 on the application of Article 85(3) of the Treaty to certain categories of exclusive dealing agreements (block exemption) applicable to such contracts?

3    If the second question is answered in the affirmative:

   (a)  Is Regulation 67/67/EEC still applicable if several undertakings which, though legally independent, are bound together by commercial ties and form a single economic entity for the purposes of the contract, participate on one side of the agreement?

   (b)  Does Regulation 67/67/EEC, and in particular Article 2(2)(c) thereof, apply to an obligation on the part of the franchisee to advertise solely with the prior agreement of the franchisor and in a manner that is in keeping with the latter's advertising, using the publicity material supplied by him, and in general to use the same business methods? Is it relevant in this connection that the franchisor's publicity material contains price recommendations which are not binding?

   (c)  Does Regulation 67/67/EEC, and in particular Articles 1(1)(b), 2(1)(a) and 2(2)(b) thereof, apply to an obligation on the part of the franchisee to confine the sale of the contract goods exclusively or at least for the most part to particular business premises specially adapted for the purposes?

(d) Does Regulation 67/67/EEC, and in particular Article 1(1)(b) thereof, apply to an obligation on the part of the franchisee who is bound to purchase most of his supplies from the franchisor to make the rest of his purchases of goods covered by the contract solely from suppliers approved by the franchisor?

(e) Does Regulation 67/67/EEC sanction an obligation on the franchisor to give the franchisee commercial, advertising and professional support?

The following answers have been given by the CJEC:

'1 The compatibility of distribution franchise contracts with Article 85(1) depends on the clauses contained in those contracts and on the economic context in which they have been included.

2 Clauses that are indispensable for the purpose of preventing the know-how provided and the help given by the franchisor from benefiting competitors do not constitute restrictions of competition within the meaning of Article 85(1).

3 Clauses that institute controls indispensable for the preservation of the identity and reputation of the network symbolized by the sign do not constitute restrictions of competition within the meaning of Article 85(1).

4 Clauses that result in a sharing of markets between franchisor and franchisees or between franchisees constitute restrictions of competition within the meaning of Article 85(1).

5 The fact that the franchisor may communicate to the franchisee indicative prices does not constitute a restriction of competition provided that as between the franchisor and the franchisees or between the franchisees there is no concerted practice with a view to the effective application of these prices.

6 Distribution franchise contracts which contain clauses leading to market sharing between franchisor and franchisee or between franchisees are liable to affect trade between member states.

Regulation 67/67 does not apply to distribution franchise contracts such as those that have been examined in the context of the present proceedings and accordingly the third question did not require a reply.'

The replies as well as some of the conclusions reached in the main text of the judgment provide some useful guidance but also leave many questions unanswered.

The court stated that it has only pronounced on 'distribution franchise contracts by virtue of which the franchisee undertakes to sell certain goods in a shop which carried the franchisor's sign'. Service franchises which predominate are not considered, nor are those where a franchisee manufactures under the direction of the franchisor. In the course of its decision, the court has provided much encouragement for franchising.

The court recognized that franchising is *sui generis* and that distribution franchising contracts differ from other traditional distribution systems and sales concession systems and acknowledged that 'such a system, which allows the franchisor to share its success, does not itself jeopardise competition'.

The court recognized that a franchisor should, without fear of the application of Article 85(1), be entitled:

1    To protect his know-how and the information provided in training and in support services

2    To take measures to preserve the identity and the reputation of the branding – the trade name

3    To impose obligations on the franchisee to apply the business methods of the franchisor and to make use of the know-how that has been provided

but only by provisions in the contract which are indispensable for these purposes.

The court provided examples of the sort of provisions which are permitted for this purpose. The examples are:

1    In-term and post-term covenants restraining the franchisee from opening a similar business which would compete with members of the network

2    The prohibition of the transfer of the business without the consent of the franchisor

3    The obligation imposed on the franchisee not to sell the products except at a location furnished and decorated according to the franchisor's instructions

4    The requirements as to the position of the premises

5    The restriction on the ability of the franchisee to transfer to other premises

6    The control over the goods to be offered at each location by specifying the franchisor or nominated suppliers as the purchasing source provided a franchisee is not prevented from acquiring those goods from other franchisees

7    The control by the franchisor over the nature of the franchisee's advertising

The court came down heavily against:

1   What it describes as market-sharing between franchisor and franchisee or between franchisees that it also regards as capable of affecting trading between member states

2   Clauses which limit the franchisee's freedom to determine his own prices – recommended prices are permitted provided that as between franchisor and franchisee or between franchisees there is no concerted practice with a view to the effective application of those prices

Following the decision of the CEJC the European Commission issued five decisions exempting franchise agreements notified by Yves Rocher, Computerland, Charles Jourdon, Service Master and Pronuptia.

The Block Exemption Regulation was adopted by the European Commission for categories of Franchise Agreements on 30 November 1988 effective from 1 February 1989. The Regulation presents two separate challenges to practitioners who advise in relation to franchise agreements and who draft them. The first is to consider whether any changes should be made to existing agreements and the second is to decide whether and to what extent the Regulation will affect one's draft documents in the future.

There are some fundamental principles of EC competition law which should be considered. For example, does the franchise benefit from the EC de Minimis Notice?[1] Many franchisors may well consider that their system is able to do so but there will always be reservations since one cannot judge growth rates of a business which may overtake the turnover test and it can often be very difficult conclusively to determine how the Commission will define the market.

The issue of whether or not the agreement affects trade between member states seems to have been conclusively determined in relation to distribution franchise contracts by the European Court of Justice in the Pronuptia judgment[2] where it states:

> '36 . . . (d) Clauses which result in a sharing of markets between franchisor
> and franchisees or between franchisees constitute restrictions of competi-
> tion within the meaning of Article 85(1)
> (f) Distribution franchise contracts which contain clauses leading to
> market sharing between franchisor and franchisees or between franchisees
> are liable to affect trade between member states'

It seems clear that exclusive rights granted by a franchisor to franchisees and location clauses which oblige the franchisee to carry on the business only from an identified address constitute restrictions on competition, as does a provision restricting the franchisee's area of active exploitation of his franchise. Since most franchise agreements use one of these approaches it is likely, following the court's statement of the law, that in those cases trade between member states will be affected.

Although the court in paragraph 36(f) (see above) refers to distribution franchise contracts, it seems that the Commission takes the view that for all practical competition rules purposes there is no distinction to be drawn between such contracts and service franchise contracts.[3]

Whether one is considering drafting a new agreement or reviewing an existing agreement the same considerations will apply. There are two initial questions to ask:

1    Is (or will) the agreement (be) restrictive of competition under Article 85(1) of the Treaty?

2    If the answer to that question is yes, will the agreement be able to benefit from the block exemption regulation?

The first question is answered so far as franchise agreements are concerned by the judgment of the European Court of Justice in the Pronuptia case when it identified the grant of exclusive territorial rights, the tieing of products and price fixing as being restrictive of competition under Article 85(1). It also pointed out that restrictions on the disclosure or use of know-how and confidential information and for the protection of the franchisor's branding and the imposition of the use of systems are not restrictive of competition insofar as they are essential for their protection from competition or preservation as the case may be.

The Commission has identified in the Regulation those provisions regarded as restrictive of competition under Article 85(1). Exemption is granted pursuant to Article 1.1 to franchise agreements entered into between two undertakings which include one or more of the following restrictions:

1    The grant of exclusive territorial rights, which can include the franchisor agreeing not to supply its goods to third parties in the territory.

2    The imposition of a location clause restricting the franchisee to operating from premises specified in the contract.

3    A prohibition against a master franchisee concluding agreements with third parties outside the contract territory.

4    A prohibition against the franchisee seeking customers outside the contract territory. This prohibition is likely to affect mobile franchises more than those which are tied to premises.

5    An obligation on the franchisee not to manufacture, sell or use in the course of the provision of services, goods competing with the franchise; where the

subject of the franchise is to sell or use in the course of the provision of services both certain types of goods and spare parts or accessories thereof, this obligation may not be imposed in respect of these spare parts or accessories.

This list includes the provisions most frequently seen in franchise agreements which can be regarded as restrictive of competition.

In answering the second question it is necessary to review the definitions of franchising and franchise agreements in the Regulation[4] which provide their own checklist:

1    Is there a franchise agreement to which two undertakings are parties?

In many cases where the franchisee is a small proprietorial company the franchisor will require that the principal shareholders and directors join in the franchise agreement to guarantee its performance by the franchisee and to protect the franchisor's know-how. It seems that if such shareholders and directors are not undertakings (as that expression is interpreted) they can be parties to the contract without difficulty. If the shareholders and directors are undertakings for competition law purposes they would probably be regarded as the same unit as the franchisor.

2    Does the franchisor possess industrial and intellectual property rights relating to trade marks, trade names, shop signs, utility models, designs, copyrights, know-how or patents, which are to be exploited for the resale of goods or the provision of services to end users?

3    Are goods sold or services provided to end users? If the franchisee is a manufacturer or wholesaler not dealing with end users the Regulation cannot apply.

Manufacturing agreements are described by the Commission in the Regulation[5] as industrial agreements which are manufacturing licences based upon patents and/or technical know-how combined with trade mark licences. The Commission did not include franchising at wholesale level since it lacked experience in that field.[6] The terms of the definition clearly do not include such categories of franchise.

4    Does the agreement contain the following elements:

    (a)   the grant by one undertaking to another of the right to exploit a franchise for marketing specified goods and/or services?

(b)   a direct or indirect financial consideration? (This wording in the defini-
       tion recognizes that apart from initial fees and continuing franchise fees
       (management services fees) a franchisor may receive indirect financial
       rewards (e.g. mark-up on product sales).

(c)   obligations relating to at least:

       (i)    the use of a common name or shop sign? and

       (ii)   the uniform presentation of layout design and decor of premises?
              and/or

       (iii)  in those cases where the franchisee is mobile (i.e. the franchisee
              travels to customers rather than the reverse) a uniform design and
              appearance of the vehicles used? and

       (iv)   the communication by the franchisor to the franchisee of know-
              how? and

       (v)    the provision of continuing commercial or technical back-up ser-
              vices by the franchisor?

(d)   a package of non-patented practical information comprising the fran-
       chisor's know-how resulting from its experience and testing?

(e)   the franchisor's know-how as a body or in the precise configuration and
       assembly of its components is not generally known or easily accessible?

(f)    that know-how is of importance for the sale of goods or the provision of
       services to end users?

(g)   that know-how at the date of the agreement is useful to the franchisee by
       being capable of improving its performance or by helping it to enter a
       new market?

(h)   the know-how being described in detail; is there, for example, an opera-
       tional manual or manuals?

If all these elements are present then there are a franchise and a franchise agreement which satisfy the definition in the Regulation.

Technical compliance is not sufficient; there must be reality. Franchising is a
method of marketing goods and services and as such and on the basis of its structure is a member of a family of related transactions involving the manufacture
and distribution of goods and the provision of services. Many of the features of
these transactions are to be found in franchising arrangements and there are

similarities between the provisions of the agreements which are used by the whole family. One should not expect to be able to blur the differences in order to benefit from the franchising exemption when the reality of the transaction is different from franchising. This Regulation will not benefit those who only pay 'lip service' to its qualifying provisions while disguising the true nature of their transaction.

One then has to consider the effect which the provisions of the Regulation have on the terms of the franchise agreement. These are considered by category.

### Territorial restrictions

1   The grant by the franchisor of exclusive territorial rights, coupled with undertakings by the franchisor not to appoint another franchisee or itself to carry on business within the territory, is permitted.[7]

2   The franchisor may also undertake not to supply goods manufactured by it, to its specification or bearing its trade mark to third parties within the territory allocated to the franchisee.[7]

3   The franchisee may be restricted to trading only from the premises identified in the contract (i.e. a location clause).[8]

4   The franchisee should also be permitted to move to alternative premises with the franchisor's consent. The franchisor cannot withhold its consent to such a move if the alternative premises match the franchisor's normal criteria for trading premises.[9]

5   The franchisee can be prohibited from soliciting or touting for custom from those whose residence is or business premises are outside any allocated territory but the franchisee cannot be required to refuse to do business with a non-solicited customer from outside the territory.[10]

6   A master franchisee can be prohibited from selling franchises outside his territory.[11]

While the issue of exclusivity so far as Article 85(1) is concerned has been dealt with in the Regulation, the commercial considerations, which have given rise to many difficulties in practice, remain. There also remains, for the time being, the fact that the grant by a franchisor of exclusive rights will, where there are two or more parties to the franchise agreement who carry on business in the UK, inevitably lead to the application of the Restrictive Trade Practices Act 1976 to the agreement. This latter consideration will cease to be relevant when the proposed revised UK competition laws, now the subject of a White Paper, are implemented in the near future. There may also be competition law considerations in other EC member states which have to be taken into account.

The commercial considerations revolve round the difficulties, particularly in the early stages of the development of a franchised business, of fairly defining a

053202

territory. The tendency is to allocate an area which is too large. Many franchisors who have tried to establish exclusive territories have created problems for themselves by having unexploited areas and an inability to force the franchisee to expand his business to fill the demand which has been created for the goods or services offered by the franchised network. The impact of such a situation affects franchisees as well as franchisors since there is an open invitation to others to provide the facilities which the network is not supplying. The obvious solution of establishing performance targets, allowing for the effect of inflation on true growth, is also not so easy to achieve. It is not a separate issue since the performance capability of any territory which is allocated must be related to the correct assessment of its potential, giving the franchisee the necessary scope for establishing and developing his business without inhibiting the growth of the franchised network. If the franchisor cannot fairly define the territory it is unlikely to be able to establish fair and realistic performance criteria to apply throughout the term of the contract. The ability to grant exclusive territorial rights without adverse competition law consequences will not affect the commercial considerations and while location clauses will continue to be used widely there may not be an increase in the grant of exclusive territorial rights.

### Goods the subject of the franchise

The franchisee can be prohibited from manufacturing, selling or using in the course of the provision of services, goods competing with the franchisor's goods (i.e. goods produced by the franchisor or according to its instructions and/or bearing the franchisor's name or trade mark).[12] The obvious course for franchisors to adopt would be to ensure that all goods involved in the franchised business should be manufactured by the franchisor or to its instructions or bearing the franchisor's branding. In some cases this is done but in many cases it will not be possible. A strongly branded product may just not be available for 'own brand' labelling or the range and volume of products involved may make it impracticable to arrange.

Without prejudice to the above, the franchisor must not refuse, for reasons other than protecting the franchisor's industrial or intellectual property rights, or maintaining the common identity and reputation of the franchised network, to designate as authorized manufacturers third parties proposed by the franchisee.

The franchisee can be required so far as is necessary to protect the franchisor's industrial or intellectual property rights or to maintain the common identity and reputation of the franchise network:

1   To sell, or use in the course of the provision of services, exclusively goods which match minimum objective quality specifications laid down by the franchisor[13]

2   To sell, or use in the course of the provision of services, goods manufactured only by the franchisor[14]

3    To sell, or use in the course of the provision of services, goods manufactured by nominated third parties where it is impracticable owing to the nature of the goods which are the subject matter of the franchise to apply objective quality specifications[14]

4    To sell the goods only to end users, other franchisees and others within the manufacturer's distribution network[15]

5    To use his best endeavours to sell the goods[16]

6    To offer for sale a minimum range of goods[16]

7    To achieve minimum sales targets and plan orders in advance[16]

8    To keep minimum stocks[16]

9    To provide customer and warranty services[16]

10   To honour guarantees whether the goods have been obtained from the franchisor, nominated suppliers, other franchisees or other distributors of the goods which carry similar guarantees in the common market[17]

The franchisee cannot be prevented from:

1    Buying the goods from other franchisees or other distributors thereof[18]

2    Fixing his own prices, although the franchisor may recommend prices.[19] It should be noted that the Commission can withdraw the benefit of the exemption given by the Regulation if 'franchisees engage in concerted practices relating to sale prices of the goods or services which are the subject matter of the franchise'.[20] In view of this provision franchisors should prohibit such concerted practices in the franchise agreement so that action may be taken to require the practice to be discontinued or enable the agreement to be terminated

3    Obtaining spare parts or accessories for the franchisor's goods other than from the franchisor[21]

4    Supplying goods or services to non-solicited end users because of their place of residence[22]

The provisions relating to products taken as a whole indicate that the position on tied supplies of goods may be summarized as follows:

179173

1    The franchisee can be required to sell or use in the provision of services only franchisor's goods (as defined) and no others. This requirement cannot be imposed in respect of accessories or spare parts for these goods.

2    The franchisee must be permitted to obtain franchisor's goods from other franchisees or other distributors of such goods.

3    Insofar as it is necessary to protect the franchisor's industrial or intellectual property rights or to maintain the common identity and reputation of the franchised network, the franchisor can require the franchisee:

   (a)   only to sell goods obtained from nominated suppliers where it is impracticable owing to the nature of the goods to formulate objective quality specifications

   (b)   to sell exclusively goods which match minimum objective quality specifications laid down by the franchisor

4    The franchisee cannot be prevented from obtaining supplies of goods of a quality equivalent to those offered by the franchisor without prejudice to (1) and (3a) above.

The combined effect of (3) and (4) is that the franchisee may be obliged to deal in goods supplied by a nominated supplier where it is impracticable to formulate objective quality criteria. In the Pronuptia case[2] the Court gave two examples to illustrate what this means. The first was the nature of the products, such as fashion goods (not a surprise since the case involved a fashion goods franchise), and the second was where the cost of monitoring compliance with the specification would be too expensive as could be the case if there were a large number of franchises.

If one wished to take advantage of either or both examples it is probably sensible to use the opposition procedure under the Regulation,[23] given that the agreement otherwise complies with its requirements.

To resolve these issues (apart from any others which may be relevant) the following questions will have to be addressed:

1    Is what is proposed necessary to protect the franchisor's industrial or intellectual property rights or to maintain the common identity and reputation of the franchised network?

2    Is it impracticable to formulate objective quality criteria by reason of:

   (a)   the nature of the goods; or

(b)  the cost of monitoring compliance in the light of the numbers of sup-
     pliers involved?

There has been much commentary, particularly in the USA, over the 'nature of
the goods' provision which it is said *inter alia* prevents a fast food operation from
nominating which particular brand of beverage should be served by franchisees.
A case can be made that a franchisor should be able to nominate brands of
product as it is necessary to maintain the common identity of the network. It is
also suggested that a case can be made, as it was for fashion goods, that it can be
impracticable to formulate objective quality criteria where subtle variations of
flavour and consumer taste are involved.

### Competition

The franchisor can require the franchisee:

1   Not to manufacture, sell or use in the course of the provision of services
    goods which compete with the franchisor's goods. This requirement cannot
    be extended to spare parts and accessories for such goods.[24]

2   Insofar as it is necessary to protect the franchisor's industrial or intellectual
    property rights or to maintain the common identity and reputation of the
    franchised network not to engage directly or indirectly in any similar busi-
    ness in a territory where the franchisee would compete with:

    (a)  a member of the franchised network; or

    (b)  the franchisor

    at all during the agreement and for a reasonable period not exceeding one
    year after the agreement ends in the territory where the franchisee has
    exploited the franchise.[25] This prohibition can extend to non-solicited cus-
    tomers who reside or have their place of business outside the franchisee's
    allocated territory.

3   Insofar as it is necessary to protect the franchisor's industrial or intellectual
    property rights or to maintain the common identity and reputation of the
    franchised network not to acquire financial interests in the capital of com-
    petitors which would give the franchisee power to influence the economic
    conduct of the competitor.[26]

It is understood that the Commission takes the view that 'power to influence'
means power to compel by agreement or weight of voting. There is unlikely to be
a problem in practice if the business in which the investment is made is a listed
company. However, if it is a small proprietorial company there is a great

temptation for the investing franchisee to influence the economic conduct of the business by the power of his knowledge derived from the franchisor's know-how, if the business encounters difficulties. The franchisee may be prohibited from being personally involved in the conduct of a competing business in which he has invested.

## Know-how
The franchisor is entitled to protect its know-how and can impose an obligation on franchisees:

1   Not to use the know-how other than for the purpose of exploiting the franchise, during or after the end of the agreement but only until the know-how becomes generally known or easily accessible other than by breach of an obligation by the franchisee[27]

2   Not to disclose the know-how to third parties during or after the termination of the agreement[28]

3   To require staff of the franchisee to keep confidential the know-how imparted to them to enable them to discharge their duties as employees of the franchisee

## General matters
1   The franchisor must oblige the franchisee to indicate his status as an independent undertaking. This is, in any event, quite a frequent requirement in franchise agreements.[29]

2   Insofar as is necessary to protect the franchisor's industrial or intellectual property rights or to maintain the common identity and reputation of the franchised network, the franchisee can be required to make advertising contributions and not to advertise unless the nature of such advertising shall have been approved by the franchisor.[30]

3   The franchisor must not prohibit the franchisee from challenging the validity of the industrial or intellectual property rights which form part of the franchise. However, if a franchisee does mount such a challenge the franchisor can provide for the termination of the agreement.[31]

4   The Regulation contains a list,[32] which is not intended to be exhaustive, of typical franchise contract clauses which are not considered to be restrictive of competition and are thus permissible without any qualifications. They do not call for any special comment.

It should be understood that as EC competition law stands the conduct of the parties can be investigated to see whether, in practice, they are behaving in a manner which contravenes the requirements of the Regulation. This is recognized in the Regulation[33] which provides that the franchisor must not use its right:

(a)   to inspect the location (or vehicle)

(b)   to veto a move to new premises or

(c)   to withhold consent to an assignment of the franchisee's rights and obligations under the franchise agreement (i.e. sell the business)

for reasons other than:

(a)   protecting the franchisor's industrial or intellectual property rights

(b)   maintaining the common identity and reputation of the franchise network, or

(c)   verifying that the franchisee is performing his obligations under the agreement

5   The franchisor can require franchisees to introduce modifications of the franchisor's commercial methods.[34]

## RECENT PROPOSED DEVELOPMENT

The European Commission has prepared a draft directive on the liability of suppliers of services. It is not yet clear what will be the outcome of the consideration of the draft by the EC member states. The implications for franchisors are clear. The draft directive which, if adopted, would require all EC member states to introduce legislation to give effect to its terms, seeks to impose upon franchisors joint and several liability with master franchisees and franchisees for the supply of services for 'danger to the health and physical integrity of persons or the physical integrity of moveable or immoveable property, which were the subject of a service, arising out of or in the performance of a service'.

*Notes*

1 Commission Notice of 3 September 1986 on Agreements of Minor Importance (OJ C231/2).

2 Pronuptia de Paris v. Schillgalis (161/84) [1986] 1 CMLR 414.

3 Commission Decision 88/604 EEC, Service Master (OJ No L. 332 3.12.88p. 38) paragraph 6.

4 The definitions of 'franchise' and 'franchise agreement' contained in Article 1(3) of the Block Exemption Regulation are here reproduced for ease of reference (the complete text of the Regulation is found in Appendix B).

'3    For the purposes of this Regulation:

(a) "franchise" means a package of industrial or intellectual property rights relating to trade marks, trade names, shop signs, utility models, designs, copyrights, know-how or patents, to be exploited for the resale of goods or the provision of services to end users;

(b) "franchise agreement" means an agreement whereby one undertaking, the franchisor, grants the other, the franchisee, in exchange for direct or indirect financial consideration, the right to exploit a franchise for the purposes of marketing specified types of goods and/or services; it includes at least obligations relating to:

   – the use of a common name or shop sign and a uniform presentation of contract premises and/or means of transport;
   – the communication by the franchisor to the franchisee of know-how;
   – the continuing provision by the franchisor to the franchisee of commercial or technical assistance during the life of the agreement;

(c) "master franchise agreement" means an agreement whereby one undertaking, the franchisor, grants the other, the master franchisee, in exchange for direct or indirect financial consideration, the right to exploit a franchise for the purposes of concluding franchising agreements with third parties, the franchisees;

(d) "franchisor's goods" means goods produced by the franchisor or according to its instructions, and/or bearing the franchisor's name or trade mark;

(e) "contract premises" means the premises used for the exploitation of the franchise or, when the franchise is exploited outside those premises, the base from which the franchisee operates the means of transport used for the exploitation of the franchise ("contract means of transport");

(f) "know-how" means a package of non-patented practical information, resulting from experience and testing by the franchisor, which is secret, substantial and identified;

(g) "secret" means that the know-how, as a body or in the precise configuration and assembly of its components, is not generally known or easily accessible; it is not limited in the narrow sense that each individual component of the know-how should be totally unknown or unobtainable outside the franchisor's business;

(h) "substantial" means that the know-how includes information which is of importance for the sale of goods or the provision of services to end users, and in particular for the presentation of goods for sale, the processing of goods in connection with the provision of services, methods of dealing with customers, and administration and financial management; the know-how must be useful for the franchisee by being capable, at the date of conclusion of the agreement, of improving the competitive position of the franchisee, in particular by improving the franchisee's performance or helping it to enter a new market;

(i) "identified" means the know-how must be described in a sufficiently comprehensive manner so as to make it possible to verify that it fulfils the criteria of secrecy and substantiality; the description of the know-how can either be set out in the franchise agreement or in a separate document or recorded in any other appropriate form.'

5 Commission Regulation (EEC) No 4087/88 of 30 November 1988 on the application of Article 85(3) of the Treaty to categories of franchise agreement paragraph (4) of the preamble.
6 Ibid. paragraph (5) of the preamble.
7 Ibid. Article 2(a).
8 Ibid. Article 2(e).
9 Ibid. Articles 3(2)(i) and 8(e).
10 Ibid. Articles 2(d) and 8(c).
11 Ibid. Article 2(b).
12 Ibid. Article 2(e).
13 Ibid. Article 3.1.(a).
14 Ibid. Article 3.1.(b).
15 Ibid. Article 3.1.(e) and 4(a).
16 Ibid. Article 3.1.(f).
17 Ibid. Article 4(b).
18 Ibid. Article 4(a).
19 Ibid. Article 5(e).
20 Ibid. Article 8(d).
21 Ibid. Article 2(e).
22 Ibid. Article 5(g) and 8(c).
23 Ibid. Article 6.
24 Ibid. Article 1(e).
25 Ibid. Article 3(c).
26 Ibid. Article 3(d).
27 Ibid. Article 3.2.(d) and 5(d).
28 Ibid. Article 32(a).
29 Ibid. Article 4(c).
30 Ibid. Article 3(g).
31 Ibid. Article 5(f).
32 Ibid. The list is contained in Article 3.2.
33 Ibid. Article 8(e).
34 Ibid. Article 3.2.(f).

# CHAPTER 3
# TECHNIQUES FOR INTERNATIONAL EXPANSION

*Martin Mendelsohn*

## PRELIMINARY CONSIDERATIONS

In reaching the decision to 'go international' with a franchise operation, a number of factors will have to be considered. Many of them are not peculiar to the franchise system. They are factors which would have to be considered whether or not franchising was involved.

Even if one is not considering the introduction of a franchise into an existing domestic operation, the possibility that the business may best be expanded overseas by the franchise method of marketing should be considered. This approach has been adopted by some with advantage.

The first consideration is the protection of industrial and intellectual property rights and this must be given attention even before the actual decision is taken to develop the business through franchising. The franchisor is developing and acquiring many industrial and intellectual property rights. The principal visible right will be the trade mark and/or trade name under which the business is conducted. These rights will all need the widest possible protection. With this in mind, the possibility of going international must be considered long before the decision to do so is actually taken.

It should be borne in mind that success breeds imitators, and in international terms there are those territories in which it is possible to register a mark in respect of a name which it is not intended to exploit, except for the purpose of requiring the true owner of the name, when he enters that territory, to pay a large sum in order to buy the rights to his own name.

It is, therefore, sensible at the earliest possible moment to review one's international intentions so that enlightened decisions can be made about whether, and if so where, to register trade marks and/or service marks for future use at the appropriate time.

There is an additional factor to consider, which is that it is often found that what is a very successful mark in one country is a complete disaster in another. There have also been cases in which a successful and inoffensive mark in one language turns out to be, in the language of a foreign country, a derogatory or even an indecent word.

It is important, therefore, to establish an international registration programme as soon as possible after it is appreciated that there is international scope for the development of the business. It is desirable to obtain advice from those who practise in the field of international trade marks (be they lawyers or trade mark agents), but it should be remembered that in some cases failure to use the mark for a given period of time might lead to a loss of rights in favour of those who are aware of the way in which money can be made out of the exploitation of other people's names.

Apart from the trade mark/service mark elements of the industrial and intellectual property rights, there can also be (although this is much more rare in a franchise situation) a patent to be protected. Patent registration requirements are very much more stringent than those for trade marks in that normally there is a very limited period within which patents can be applied for and registered. If, therefore, a patent is involved, proper professional advice should be sought immediately.

Apart from the formal methods of registration which are available for trade marks and patents, the other industrial and intellectual property rights, such as know-how, ideas and trade secrets, are not normally protectable by any form of registration. The protection of these rights depends upon contractual terms entered into between those who own them and those who enter their employment or into licensing arrangements with them.

There is also the question of copyright. Very often the franchisor owns the copyright in much of the printed material which is produced for the purpose of the franchise scheme. Methods and effectiveness of copyright protection in the various jurisdictions in which it is intended to expand should be explored. Additionally, appropriate steps should be taken to ensure that the copyright in any translations which have to be prepared in the language of the territory into which one is franchising should remain vested in the franchisor and should not be allowed to pass, for example, to a franchisee who may have the responsibility for arranging the translation.

Having chosen the international route, one is then faced with a number of interrelated evaluations, the handling of which will depend upon the method chosen for expansion.

## METHODS OF INTERNATIONAL EXPANSION

There are a number of different approaches to international development which are commonly in use. These include:

1    Company-owned *only* operations

2    Direct franchising

3    The establishment of a branch operation

4    The establishment of a subsidiary

5    The establishment of an area developer

6    The grant of master franchise rights

7    The entry into of a joint venture

Let us examine each in turn.

## Company-owned only operations

In such a case the company would decide not to franchise in the target territory but only to establish its own operations. In order to do this the company would have to possess the manpower and financial resources to establish and sustain the operation. A successful company-owned network would, of course, provide the basis for the future use of the franchise marketing method for growth if a change of course was considered desirable.

## Direct franchising

This involves the franchisor in entering into a franchise agreement with each individual franchisee and providing the basic support directly. As a technique it is normally limited in scope since the further away the franchisor is from the target territory the more difficult it becomes to serve franchisees. Very often direct franchising, combined with the establishment of branches or subsidiaries, can provide tax advantages.

The use of the direct franchising method also makes the franchisor vulnerable to a failure to recognize the differences which exist between the territory of origin of the system and the target territory.

## The establishment of a branch operation

This may be set up in the following circumstances:

1    The franchisor may be operating its own outlets.

2    The franchisor is franchising direct into the target territory and has established a branch operation to service franchisees.

3    The branch has been established as a regional base to provide services to franchisees within the region.

Whether or not a branch is established may well be affected by fiscal or legal considerations rather than the business need to have a presence in the territory. These considerations may lead the franchisor to follow the next course available to it, the establishment of a subsidiary.

## The establishment of a subsidiary
The establishment of a subsidiary may fulfil any of four functions:

1 The franchisor could be franchising directly from its territory into the target territory and will use the subsidiary to service franchisees.

2 The franchisee may grant master franchise rights to the subsidiary and the subsidiary will be either opening its own operations or sub-franchising or both.

3 The subsidiary may be involved with a joint venture partner.

4 The subsidiary may be used as a regional base either to provide services to franchisees in the region or to master franchisees in the region.

The service which the branch or subsidiary would provide would be similar in nature and would cover the whole range of franchisor services, including, as the network develops, a training facility.

## The establishment of an area developer
This may involve one of two basic approaches:

1 An arrangement in which the developer is given the right to open a multiple number of outlets to a predetermined schedule and within a given area. This is the most common.

2 An arrangement in which the developer is given the right to establish to a predetermined schedule and within a given area a combination of his own outlets and sub-franchised outlets. In the USA, by the use of this sort of system, some networks achieve a phenomenal growth rate of many hundreds of outlets each year.

## The grant of master franchise rights
This form of arrangement has many of the characteristics of the area development agreement. The area developer will undoubtedly have the right to a part of a country. The master franchisee will usually have the exclusive right within a country either to open its own outlets or to sub-franchise or to do both. The master franchisee in essence stands in the shoes of the franchisor in the country and is, to all intents and purposes, the franchisor of the system in that country.

The franchisor has to consider a number of points:

1 The difficulties in identifying and selecting the right master franchisee.

2 The need to have a strong home base to sustain the demands.

3    The diversion of manpower and financial resources from the domestic operations. It should be noted that it will always take more people and cost more money than one would expect.

4    The time factor – it will always take much longer than one expects.

The problems which arise when the franchisor feels it has no alternative but to terminate are many and varied. It is likely that the franchisor will inherit problems since termination will result either from the master franchisee having done its job badly or because it is not doing very well.

### The entry into of a joint venture

This involves the franchisor in establishing a joint company with another company or person within the territory, and the exploitation of the territory either by means of operations owned by the joint venture, as by sub-franchising, or a combination of both.

## COMMON PITFALLS

There is a pattern of problems which give rise to difficulties. However, before considering them, prime consideration must be given to whether or not the franchisor has a sufficiently well-developed domestic business upon which to base his international growth.

There are examples of franchisors who, with less than five operations (mainly company-owned with a negligible infrastructure, particularly in terms of trained personnel), confidently feel that they have valuable names and business systems which should be exported. Quite apart from the self-evident fact that they have not established the viability and thus the value of what it is that they wish to sell, they certainly have nothing of value to offer in international terms so far as their name and their ability to support an overseas operation is concerned.

A small franchisor will find that the development of his domestic operation will take up all the time of his manpower and all his financial resources. If he believes that the 'rewards' of international development are either a panacea for the ills of the business, or likely to provide a large cash injection, he could be in for a rude shock.

The successful development of an international network takes as much meticulous planning and patient building up as a national network. The early rewards for the franchisor (front-end payments) have to be repaid with services of value if the venture is to have a prospect of success. A healthily developed international franchise can and will take some time to 'go on stream' with positive cash flow and profitability.

It is essential in most cases, before expanding into the international marketplace, to have a strong well-established home-based business with a wide range of trained and experienced senior staff. Some members of the staff should be given prime responsibility for international expansion and have the freedom to devote the whole of their time and attention to the task, rather than relying on them to be produced when required. Without a unit dedicated to international activities there will always be an excuse that staff should be retained in expanding domestic operations. This will result in the neglect of the international operations.

It must be recognized that it is essential for the franchisor to be able to provide operational support. It is a mistake to try to overload the front-end fee element. Indeed, some figures which have been quoted would place such a heavy 'cost of money' burden on the sub-franchisor or other partner in the target territory that a successful launch and development would be jeopardized.

There are many franchisors, including household names, who have experienced great difficulties in seeking to establish international operations. Many of their problems have arisen from five factors:

1   An insufficiently strong home-based business

2   Our unwillingness to devote resources exclusively to international development

3   An unwillingness or inability to devote sufficient financial resources to the effort

4   An unwillingness or inability to devote sufficient manpower resources

5   An inability to recognize the amount of time it will take to become established and profitable

The degree of underestimation by companies of the last three factors can vary from between half to one third, and it is as well to recognize the potential difficulties in order to be able to plan to overcome them. Another problem is experienced in identifying the right local partner (sub-franchisor or joint venture partner) or staff.

It may seem strange, but there is no doubt whatever that whenever businessmen decide to 'go international' with their franchise schemes, they drop their guard and forget the normal diligent measures which they would take in their own country to ensure that the person with whom they are dealing is what he purports to be. This lapse only leads to a failure to achieve any forward progress, and the venture often turns out to be a costly failure as well. Why it is that businessmen are more trusting of people in a foreign country than they would be in their own is something of a mystery, but it is a phenomenon which exists and which has been experienced repeatedly. Obviously, it must be avoided.

Sensible franchisors take great care when selecting franchisees for their network. Even greater care must be taken when the franchisee will be a sub-franchisor and will have an entire country entrusted to him.

Full recognition has to be given to the fact that the successful home operation will probably be unknown in the target territory. The incoming franchisor will be in the position of being a foreigner trying to convince those in the country in which he is trying to introduce his system that his operation will work there. The franchisor must acknowledge that there are different social and cultural attitudes and lifestyles in foreign countries which could necessitate a rethink of his operation. For example, the similarity between the language spoken in the USA and the UK should not be allowed to delude a US franchisor into believing that the UK market is the same as that in his home country.

Apart from the legal considerations, which are dealt with elsewhere in this work, there are other factors to be considered, such as the:

1    Availability of suitable property

2    Cost of rental of property

3    Labour practices and costs

4    Availability of suitable equipment

5    Availability of product supplies

6    Ability to remit profits

and the many other operational considerations (specific to the particular business) which have to be borne in mind. In practice, the only way to resolve these issues is by establishing pilot operations to evaluate and fine-tune the system to the requirements of the target territory.

From the business point of view the ideal position may thus be summarized as follows:

1    Establish a strong home base which can adequately support the additional burdens of international expansion.

2    Do not overvalue and thus overprice the franchise opportunity.

3    Establish a pilot operation and prove the system works in the target territory.

4    Recognize and come to terms with the differences in social attitudes, culture, taste and lifestyle.

5    Choose carefully those with whom one will establish a working relationship.

6    Be patient. Do not underestimate the time it will take to enjoy the fruits of international operations.

7    Do not underestimate the drain on financial and manpower resources which
     going international will involve.

## CONTRACTUAL ARRANGEMENTS

We now come to the contractual arrangements. There are three types of agreement which should be considered:

1    The unit agreement

2    The area development agreement

3    The master franchise agreement

There is a common thread throughout these agreements since they all fundamen-
tally deal with similar issues. The unit agreement is found in all transactions since
it is common practice even where there is an area development agreement or a
master franchise agreement to require the completion of an agreement for each
individual franchised unit.

The sorts of provisions one might expect in each of these types of agreement
are briefly summarized.

### The unit agreement
*Identification of rights*  Identify the franchisor's industrial and intellectual property rights, e.g. trade marks, service marks, know-how, system.

### Grant of rights

1    Territory – whether or not there will be a territory allocated and if so
     whether exclusive or non-exclusive.

2    Location – no territorial rights; rights limited to premises identified in the
     agreement.

3    Extent of rights to use the franchisor's industrial and intellectual property,
     including the franchisor's system.

*Term*  The length of the agreement can be affected by national laws, particularly
if there is a product tie. In many cases franchisors grant rights to franchisees to
call for extensions (or renewals) of the franchise agreement.

*Franchisor's services*  These fall into two categories:

1    Initial services – calculated to cover all aspects of assisting the franchisee in
     starting up his business, including: training, premises selection and fitting

out, assistance with leasing, overcoming any zoning laws restrictive of the use of premises, staff training, stock (inventory) selection, merchandising, opening and launch assistance.

2    Ongoing services – the franchisor maintains a range of services to assist the franchisee in trading successfully and in remaining competitive in the market-place. These services will include: ongoing training for franchisee and staff, market research, product and service research, development and market testing, accounting and management advisory support, 'hands-on' assistance through field support staff, auditing and promotion (to which franchisees contribute), bulk purchasing benefits and quality controls.

*Payment of fees* Franchisors commonly receive income from a franchised network on two bases:

1    Initial fees – often franchisors will charge an 'entry fee' which may be a mark-up on the cost of the provision of initial services or alternatively will identify an initial franchisee fee as a separate payment.

2    Ongoing fees – commonly called 'royalties' because the method of calculation is invariably a percentage of the franchisee's gross sales. These fees are also frequently called 'management services fees', which in the context of a unit franchise agreement is more descriptive of the nature of the fees.

In addition to these fees there are other opportunities for franchisors to receive income from other sources, e.g. mark-up on product sales, kickbacks or rebates from suppliers to the network of goods and services, income from leasing of real estate. It is rare to find franchisors who receive payments from all of these sources.

*Franchisee's obligations* These will normally be coupled with controls on operational activities. The franchisee will be required to operate the franchisor's system as described in an operational manual. The franchisee will accept obligations which enable the franchisor to ensure that operational standards are maintained.

*Sale of business* The agreement will set out the basis upon which the franchisee may sell the franchised business. There will usually be conditions to ensure that the franchisor retains control over who are its franchisees.

*Termination and consequences of termination* The circumstances in which rights of termination may be exercised will be detailed. It is usual to provide an opportunity to remedy breaches prior to the exercise of a right to terminate. The consequences of termination are usually quite drastic, requiring the franchisee to cease the franchised business, not to trade from the premises or within the territory in a competitive business, to cease using the franchisor's know-how and system and to de-identify the premises so that they no longer resemble the franchisor's business.

*Other boiler plate provisions* These are usual in commercial transactions and will be found in most franchise agreements.

## The area development agreement

The development agreement provides the framework for the area developer to become the owner and operator of a multiple number of franchised outlets. The developer will require protection in the form of exclusive rights for the territory and the franchisor will require the developer to exploit the territory to the fullest extent possible and within a realistic time frame.

The arrangements which will be embodied in the agreement will be calculated to deal with the essential issues which arise when the developer undertakes the commitment and the franchisor places exploitation of a large territory in the hands of the developer.

The area development agreement is essentially a form of option ('development right'), frequently with the characteristics of a put and call option. Upon each exercise of the development right the franchisor and the area developer will enter into a unit agreement.

The development agreement will contain detailed provisions in relation to the development programme and the procedure for selecting and approving locations, as well as the detailed business infrastructure to be established by the area developer. The area developer will have to undertake certain central obligations in terms of business organization and functions. His senior staff will have to undergo specific training, and it is likely that the franchisor would require that the person to be appointed managing director (general manager) will have to be approved by the franchisor and to have passed the franchisor's training course. In addition it is not uncommon to find a requirement that the managing director (general manager) should have a minimum equity stake in the business.

There are a number of problems to be considered in structuring the arrangements:

1   What is to be the number and density of the outlets?

2   Are exclusive or non-exclusive rights to be granted?

3   Will the area developer be limited to opening the number of outlets agreed upon in the contract, or will he be permitted to open more? If so, on what basis?

4   What degree of transferability will there be? Will the area developer be permitted to dispose of his right to develop the area? That would be unusual as most franchisors would expect an area developer to complete the development schedule before seeking to sell the business.

5    To what extent will the area developer be permitted to dispose of individual units without affecting the development right and on what conditions? The issue is not whether the area developer can sell individual units, but whether he can do so before he has fully developed the territory (as required by the contract) or if he does so thereafter, must he replace the outlet sold with another – if so, on what terms?

When one considers the problems of termination of these arrangements, the position becomes even more difficult. There are three possible component parts to terminate:

1    The development right

2    The total development agreement

3    Individual unit agreements

Let us consider each in turn.

**The development right** This would normally be capable of termination in the event of a failure to perform the development schedule. If the area developer has exclusive rights, should he merely lose his exclusivity? Whether or not he has exclusive rights, should he lose the right to continue to exploit the development schedule in the future? If so, are there ways in which he may be able to protect himself against a slower rate of progress than he has planned? One should remember that the franchisor will attach great importance to the maintenance of the development schedule and may feel that the failure to do so would operate too much to the detriment of the development of the network in the target territory. Whichever way the franchisor decides to approach the problem there is no clear answer. At the worst the franchisor would have parallel systems being operated by the original area developer and one subsequently appointed. The practical problems which can arise in such circumstances where there are in essence two developers within a given territory may lead some franchisors to require that the defaulting developer's agreement should be capable of being terminated for a failure to sustain the development schedule.

**The total development agreement** This would apply to failure by the developer to observe and perform the 'non-development right' provisions in the development agreement, i.e. the detailed infrastructure referred to earlier. One would normally expect that such failure would not lead to termination unless the developer had been given an opportunity to put matters right. However, given that, despite warnings and in the face of a failure to remedy the default, the franchisor terminates the agreement, one would expect such termination to bring the development agreement to an end, including the development right. This would have to be the case, since if the general provisions relating to the area developer's business structure are ignored it would be futile to permit him to continue to develop by opening further units. Similarly, such a breach would also be expected to lead to a position where the individual unit agreement would also be capable of being terminated since the business structure, designed to provide the basis for the supervision and control of those units, would not be in existence.

*Individual unit agreements*  One might expect that there could be problems with individual units which could lead to termination of the agreement relating to such a unit. Whether or not that termination should affect the main agreement must depend upon:

1    Why the agreement is terminated

2    How many of such agreements are terminated within any given period of time

3    Whether or not the breach of the individual unit agreement involved a sufficiently serious breach of the main agreement

One then has to consider what should be the consequences of termination of each of these three agreements.

1    Does the loss of the development right affect the continued operation of the individual outlets, and if not can the developer still apply to open new outlets, but independently of the development arrangement? What would be the consequences if he did?

2    If the whole of the development agreement is terminated should the individual unit agreement also be in jeopardy?

3    One would also expect that all the normal consequences of termination of a franchise agreement would be equally applicable. In cases where the franchisor has an option to purchase on termination, the scale of the business to be purchased could cause problems for him because the amount of money involved could be considerable.

### The master franchise agreement
The master franchise agreement reflects the commercial bargain which has been struck by the franchisor with the sub-franchisor to:

1    Introduce the franchisor's system to the target territory

2    Evaluate the viability of the system in the target territory

3   Equip the sub-franchisor to become the franchisor in the target territory

4   Develop the growth of the system in the target territory

5   Result in the sub-franchisor providing the full range of franchisor's ongoing
    services to sub-franchisees in the target territory

It should be understood that in these transactions the aspirations of the parties
and balance of negotiating power will vary from case to case, as well as the skill,
financial resources, knowledge and experience of the prospective sub-franchisor.

*Structure of the master franchise agreement*   The master franchise agreement will
have to accommodate the issues which the commercial discussions will have confronted. In many of these issues, there is no such thing as the right answer since
these agreements, unlike unit agreements, are all negotiated.

The principal issues to be dealt with in negotiating and preparing the master
franchise agreements insofar as they have not been dealt with above are as
follows:

1   The rights to be granted

2   Territory

3   Exclusivity

4   Performance schedule

5   Franchise fees

6   Withholding taxes

7   Training

8   Sale of business

9   Default issues

10  Choice of law-venue selection

We shall now look briefly at each of these subjects in turn.

*The rights to be granted*   These will always include the use of the franchisor's trade
marks, service marks, trade names, goodwill, know-how, confidential information, copyright material and all the usual elements which one finds in franchise

transactions. The length of the term for which the rights are granted must also be specified.

By nature, one should be seeking to establish a long-term relationship. Sub-franchisees will wish to have the comfort of a realistic length of term in the unit agreements with probably right or expectations of renewal. The master franchise agreement must be long enough to accommodate the ability of the sub-franchisor to grant realistic terms to his sub-franchisees. The sub-franchisor will wish to have a long enough term to make the investment worthwhile and to see that he will benefit from the future growth of the business which he will be building, using his financial and manpower resources.

If franchisor and sub-franchisor are both happy with the relationship from the financial, business, and personal point of view then there is no real reason why it should not continue indefinitely.

*Territory* As is the case with operators of individual units who seek the comfort of territorial rights, most sub-franchisors also seek the widest possible territorial rights. In fixing the extent of the territory to be exploited by the sub-franchisor, regard clearly has to be paid to the franchisor's overall international marketing strategy and how each of the individual sub-franchisors will fit into the pattern of that strategy.

Ideally, the territory should be one in which the sub-franchisor has the knowledge, experience and capacity to cope. One of the reasons for master franchise agreements is to have the sub-franchisor stand in the shoes of the franchisor in relation to the market-place. It somewhat defeats the object of the exercise if territories are granted of such a nature and/or extent that the sub-franchisor is not capable of achieving proper exploitation.

*Exclusivity* Most sub-franchisors would wish to have exclusive rights to the territory which is allocated to them. This enables them to invest with the comfort of knowing that they will be the sole exploiters of the opportunity in the territory. Exclusivity is normally tied to performance criteria and can be lost if these criteria are not met. This can lead to practical problems if one has a network which is being developed by a sub-franchisor who fails after a period of time to meet the performance schedules.

In practical terms, the loss of exclusivity without the loss of the continuing right to grant further sub-franchises raises issues similar to those discussed above in relation to area development agreements.

*Performance schedule* The agreement of a performance schedule which sets out the projected annual and cumulative rates of growth of the network in the target territory is a common feature of these agreements. Indeed, without it, the franchisor would not have the confidence that a commitment exists which should result in the proper exploitation of the territory. Unless a sub-franchisor is prepared to accept a realistic performance schedule for the establishment of operational units, the master franchise route can lose some of its attractions. The performance schedule is obviously of great importance where exclusive rights are granted because this is the franchisor's insurance policy against under-exploitation.

There are practical difficulties in establishing performance schedules. It may not be possible at the time that the contract is being negotiated to have an accurate idea, or sufficiently accurate knowledge, to enable the parties to judge what would be an achievable rate of expansion. One thing that is certain is that the franchisor's expectations are likely to be on the optimistic side, while those of the sub-franchisor will be on the pessimistic side. However, most sub-franchisors will prepare business plans in the process of deciding whether or not to take the opportunity on board and these must include some assessment of the growth rate which the business is capable of achieving. Otherwise, the sub-franchisor would not be able to make a balanced business judgment about whether or not to go into the proposition, and the level of resources which would need to be committed to it.

### Franchise fees
#### Front-end fees
One of the most difficult questions to come to terms with in the negotiation of a master franchise agreement is how much should the franchisor receive for:

1    The grant of the rights

2    The transfer of know-how

3    Setting up the sub-franchisor in the territory

If this was an easy question to answer, it would not cause the problems with which one is so often confronted. Indeed, there are many franchisors whose expectations are such that any would-be sub-franchisors are frightened off. There are instances in which unrealistic figures have been agreed only to be resented by the sub-franchisor when he realizes that he cannot make money at all, or, at least, sufficiently quickly to justify the high level of the initial cost.

It seems that there are a number of factors which could be taken into account when trying to calculate what would be a proper level of front-end charge by a franchisor. The degree of importance to be attached to each will differ from country to country, depending upon the practices to be found in each. The factors are:

1    The actual cost to the franchisor of dealing with the sub-franchisor; setting him up; and proving that the concept works within the target territory.

2    How much it would cost, and how long it would take the sub-franchisor to

acquire the requisite know-how and skills to operate a similar business in his territory.

3    The value of the territory as estimated by the franchisor.

4    The estimated aggregate amount of the initial franchise fees which could be charged by the sub-franchisor to his sub-franchisees in the development of the network in the territory.

Franchisors who are based in those countries where high initial fees are charged to franchisees tend to have much higher expectations under the latter two factors, and, therefore, demand far more than may be considered realistic in the target territory. As the medium- to long-term interests of the franchisor probably are best served by having well-motivated and successful sub-franchisors, this type of attitude has to be reconsidered.

The first two factors are probably the more sensible avenues of approach. The timing of payments may differ, and, in some cases, an agreement of a sensible up-front figure may enable the parties to agree some sort of sharing arrangement in respect of the initial franchise fees which are received from sub-franchisees as they are established.

*Continuing fees (royalties)*

These are normally calculated on the aggregate amount of the gross network sales to the ultimate consumer. The level at which they are fixed obviously has to provide the franchisor with a good economic reason to be involved, but it must be appreciated that these payments represent a straight deduction from the gross income of the sub-franchisor, and that if they are too high, the sub-franchisor will not be able to run his business profitably. In such circumstances, the network will not be given the proper support and cannot succeed.

There may be exchange control requirements to be complied with in some countries. The mere fact that exchange control permission has been obtained does not necessarily mean that payments can be made with any degree of regularity because payments can be delayed administratively by the country's central bank when it assess the total outflow of funds from the country during any particular month.

If, by reason of exchange controls, currency conversion cannot take place, provision should be made in the agreement to establish what will be the alternative.

**Withholding taxes** In dealing with the payment provisions in the contract, the way in which the payments will be treated and characterized in both the franchisor's country and the target territory should be considered.

Any double-taxation agreement which exists should also be examined to ensure that if the franchisor wishes to receive payments which are free of withholding tax, this can be done so far as possible. Provision should be made in the contract to enable the franchisor to obtain the benefit of any double-taxation agreement by the provision of evidence of payment in the target country in such form as may be necessary to enable the relief to be claimed (see Chapter 4).

*Training* The degree of training support will, of course, vary from case to case. However, many franchisors find it sensible, particularly in the early stages, to ensure that both the sub-franchisor's staff and the sub-franchisees and their staff are trained at the franchisor's domestic training facility. There are many who find that the quality of training at the domestic base just cannot be reproduced and, even though there have to be changes made to accommodate local requirements, this degree of training is essential.

One would expect that the contract would contain the details of how, and how many of, the sub-franchisor's team will be trained and are to be identified by their job title.

In appropriate cases, it may be that the franchisor will provide an opening crew for the first few units which are established in the target territory. This crew will provide on-site training for the sub-franchisor's staff. Normally, the training is provided free of charge, but the sub-franchisor and his sub-franchisees would be expected to pay all their expenses relating to getting to and from the training site, and their subsistence and other expenses during the course of the training. The intensity of training and support which is given during the piloting stage in the target territory can, in some cases, be quite high. The agreement would also provide for the sub-franchisor to establish his own training facilities in the course of time, and for the franchisor to provide the necessary back-up and training aids to enable this to be done.

*Trade marks and other industrial and intellectual property rights* This has been dealt with above.

*Sale of the business* The master franchise agreement will have to contain provisions dealing with the basis upon which the agreement may be assigned and the sub-franchisor's business sold.

The basic principles are the same as those which apply to the sale of a franchised business by a sub-franchisee. However, there are some differences in detail because the level of investment will inevitably be much greater, and the skills which the purchaser will require will not be the same as those which are required for the operation of a franchised unit.

A purchaser of sub-franchisor's business will have to demonstrate not only his financial capacity, but also his ability to understand the franchise system and to manage the business of a sub-franchisor. The criteria to be applied should be specified as should any conditions which are considered appropriate.

*Default issues* An area of prime concern to the franchisor will be the degree to which the sub-franchisor monitors and controls the quality and standards which are achieved by his sub-franchisees. One must not lose sight of the fact that the sub-franchisees are trading using the franchisor's know-how and systems and are benefiting from the goodwill associated with the name.

It is the franchisor who is running the risk of events occurring which are adverse to his interests. The sub-franchisor is the custodian of those interests in his territory. Provision should be made in the agreement for the policing of those standards, but if all else fails, the franchisor has to have remedies. These would obviously be built around default provisions in the contract.

A terminating event would usually be any default under the agreement of which the franchisor has given notice to cure and which remains uncured after a fixed period of time, which may be as much as 30 or 60 days.

Money defaults may be treated more seriously with a shorter period of notice. Quality control defaults may need the longer period in order for the default to be put right because it may involve enforcing rights against another. The failure by the sub-franchisor to ensure that his sub-franchisees comply with the terms of their contracts is a serious issue, but one which may require reasonable time to cure.

There will, as in most commercial agreements, be provision for termination in the event of insolvency, bankruptcy, or liquidation.

Consideration will also have to be given to whether the sub-franchisor is to have the right to terminate the agreement, and in what circumstances. In some cases, the sub-franchisor is given the right to terminate in the event of the insolvency, bankruptcy, or liquidation of the franchisor.

The consequences of termination are usually drastic. In brief terms, one would expect that the sub-franchisor will lose the right to continue, will have to de-identify his business, and be bound by effective post-term restraints on competition and the use of the franchisor's know-how (see comments above). There are other considerations and one of the most important is, of course, what is to happen to the network of sub-franchisees?

1 Will the franchisor be entitled to take them over?

2 Will the franchisor be obliged to take them over?

3 Will the sub-franchisor be able to make a virtue out of termination and claim payment of a sum of money by way of compensation for 'the takeover of his business'?

4 Will the franchisor, now that he has terminated the sub-franchisor for good cause, want to take over what could be a badly run network of disgruntled sub-franchisees, who are intent on making difficulties, and be faced with considerable expense to put the business right? Rather than the sub-franchisor expecting to be paid something (as mentioned above) should he,

on the contrary, be liable to pay the franchisor for the costs the latter will have to face in coping with the problems which he will inherit?

5    What is to happen to any property (including leases) which the sub-franchisor has acquired for leasing or sub-leasing to the sub-franchisees, and which may have a capital value which the franchisor cannot afford to pay?

The issues are many and varied, and the list given is far from complete, but will serve to indicate the complexity of this particular subject.

*Choice of law (venue selection)*  All international contracts should specify the law to be applied to the contract, and the venue for the resolution of disputes. Consideration should also be given to whether the parties wish to have disputes referred, or capable of being referred, to arbitration.

# CHAPTER 4
# TAX CONSIDERATIONS

*Manzoor G. K. Ishani*

The purpose of this chapter is to consider some general aspects of taxation as they may apply to international franchising transactions. Although a detailed examination of the tax consequences of various types of international franchise transactions is not within the scope of this chapter, the issues discussed are nevertheless relevant. The importance of having an efficient tax structure in any international franchise transaction should not be overlooked. However, that is not to say that the transaction and structure should be driven by tax-efficient considerations. Rather, attention should be paid to this aspect of the transaction with a view to ensuring, so far as is possible and reasonably practicable, that the benefits which are intended to flow to the parties from the transaction are not eroded by taxation more than need be the case.

Given the limited scope of this chapter, it is of course imperative that expert advice is taken on any specific matter.

Franchisors will be concerned to minimize the incidence of taxation on their proposed foreign franchise transactions. In particular, franchisors will be keen to:

1   Minimize the incidence of tax in the country into which they are proposing to franchise

2   Minimize or defer taxes in their own country

3   Minimize or avoid withholding taxes

4   Maximize any benefits to be derived from tax credits

5   Maximize any advantage offered by any double-taxation treaty between their own country and the country into which they propose to franchise

There are a number of key tax issues which a franchisor will need to consider when contemplating granting a franchise to a foreign franchisee.

1   How will any franchise fees be treated for tax purposes? Will they be treated as royalty income or commercial profits, active income or passive income, initial fees or services fees?

2      If and to the extent that payment for the provision by the franchisor of goods
       and/or services is treated differently for taxation purposes, to what extent is
       it desirable to break these up and to attribute to each of them a separate con-
       sideration, thereby taking advantage, wherever possible, of a lower tax rate?
       For example, continuing franchise fees could be split into three different
       categories:

       (a)   royalty payments for the use of the franchisor's intellectual property
             rights

       (b)   management services fees for the back-up and support which the fran-
             chisor is usually obliged to provide to the franchisee

       (c)   marketing and promotions fees in consideration of the franchisor
             making available to the franchisee artwork, publicity material and so on

       In many countries, such as Canada, the Netherlands and Switzerland, sums
       paid for tangible assets such as plant and property will usually, but not
       always, be set off against tax. Other countries treat such payments slightly
       differently so that, for example, in the USA such payments are usually
       deductible or amortizable for tax purposes, over the term of the franchise
       contract.

3      Should the franchisor have a permanent establishment in the country into
       which he is proposing to sell a franchise? Does he need to have any form of
       presence and, if so, is it more tax-efficient to establish that presence directly
       or through some form of agency or a wholly owned subsidiary?

4      Would it be more efficient to route the franchise through a foreign company
       which is established in a low-tax country?

5      What is the likely impact upon the proposed transaction of any customs and
       excise duties, value added taxes, purchase and/or sales taxes?

6      Is the grant of a franchise to a foreign franchisee itself a taxable event?

7      If a franchise is granted at arm's length and to an unconnected party, does
       that prevent future reallocations of income to the franchisor for tax
       purposes?

The above analysis, of course, becomes much more complex if the franchisor
intends to franchise in several different countries.

Most franchise transactions usually provide for the payment by the franchisee to the franchisor of two types of fees; initial franchise fees and continuing

franchise fees. Initial franchise fees are usually payable at the commencement of the transaction and are usually required by the franchisor to be paid in consideration of the franchisor providing goods and/or services, such as training, equipment packages, assistance to the franchisee in setting up an initial unit, assistance in adapting its system for the country in which it is proposing to franchise and so on. Sometimes initial franchise fees also include a sum which represents payment to the franchisor for the grant to the franchisee of the right to a particular territory.

As far as possible, most franchisors will seek to treat the receipt of these payments as capital (rather than income), as in most jurisdictions receipts of capital enjoy privileged rates of taxation.

One should examine closely the nature of the franchisor's business. It may very well be that the franchisor's business is that of selling franchises, in which case the initial franchise fees received by him may well be treated as income, although it is arguable that receipts from the sale of rights to a particular foreign territory should not be treated as such. In many international franchise transactions the way in which the initial franchise fee is structured, and the timing of its payment, is not always simple or straightforward. Where the payment of the initial franchise fee, or a part of it, is geared towards the performance of the franchisee (for example, related directly to the achievement by the franchisee of targets specified in a development schedule so that payments are made to the franchisor upon the opening of each outlet), there may be a tendency for such payments to be treated as income in the hands of the franchisor and not capital as in the case of 'one-off' payments. In the UK such an arrangement could give rise to tax problems. In such circumstances specialist tax advice should first be sought.

The second most common source of revenue for a franchisor in an international franchise transaction is the payment by a franchisee of continuing fees during the term of the franchise agreement. These present little difficulty so far as their tax treatment is concerned. Generally these amounts will be received by franchisors as trading income and will be treated by revenue authorities as deductible expenses of the franchisee. The main complication which seems to arise most commonly when considering the payment of continuing franchise fees is that of the application of withholding taxes to such payments. Whether or not any such payments will be subject to a withholding tax varies from country to country, and will essentially depend upon the nature of the payments made.

One of the most common ways of minimizing exposure to withholding taxes is by the use, where available, of double-taxation treaties between the franchisor's country and that of the franchisee, which provide for little or no withholding taxes to be levied. In the absence of a suitable treaty, it may be appropriate for the franchisor to divorce himself further from his franchisee by interposing between them a third party to whom the franchisor grants rights and who, in turn, grants rights to the franchisee. The relationship between the franchisor and the intermediary need not be at arm's length; indeed, in many such arrangements the intermediary is a subsidiary of the franchisor. In such an arrangement it is usually necessary for the intermediary to be based in a country which provides favourable tax treatment as regards withholding taxes and as regards taxes on royalties/continuing franchise fees generally.

It has long been the tradition to use the Netherlands for this purpose. The Netherlands is regarded as ideal because it imposes no withholding tax on royalties/continuing franchise fees and treats favourably royalties/continuing franchise fees which 'flow through' the intermediary from the franchisee to the franchisor, under the so-called 'royalty spread' ruling (see below). Furthermore, the Netherlands has double-taxation treaties with more countries than most other countries which provide for minimal withholding taxes on royalties.

Under the royalty spread ruling, it is usually possible to agree with the Dutch tax authorities that the Dutch intermediary company will be subject to a minimal taxable profit (calculated on a sliding scale, so that the higher the turnover, the lower the percentage minimum tax profit). In these cases it is the usual practice for the Dutch intermediary company to retain the full amount of the royalty spread, thereby enabling the Dutch intermediary to pay the relevant taxes and local expenses.

Although a number of other countries have provisions which enable similar rulings to be obtained, they do not all have quite the extensive network of double-taxation treaties with other countries as the Netherlands. In some cases, such as the Netherlands Antilles, their double-taxation treaties specifically provide that where particular local tax advantages are being sought other benefits such as reduced withholding taxes will not apply.

For some time now, there has been a trend amongst revenue authorities to limit treaty abuse by limiting the extent to which reliefs can be obtained by the use of double-taxation treaties. The concept of discouraging treaty shopping is not new. The oldest example is probably Switzerland where, for a number of years, the concept of treaty abuse has been recognized by its domestic law under which the provisions of Swiss double-taxation treaties can be prevented from applying if the Swiss tax authorities consider that their network of treaties is being abused.

One common scheme used by franchisors to minimize or to defer taxes in their own countries on dividends and/or royalties/continuing franchise fees is for such payments to be made to an intermediary established in a tax haven country and to accumulate such payments there. However, a number of countries have increasingly become aware of this scheme and have adopted legislation which provides that passive income of a controlled foreign company can be attributed back to the parent in the relevant country and treated as its income and which therefore becomes subject to tax on a current basis. Some countries also now have similar rules in respect of passive income, which apply where an individual controls the two companies in question.

Franchisors should not overlook the possibility of maximizing the use of foreign tax credits on royalties/continuing franchise fee income. Franchisors should ensure that where such payments are subject to withholding taxes, the

income is received in the hands of a company which can use the tax credits associated with it. It does not necessarily have to be the franchisor, but it must be a
company which has sufficient income to ensure that the credit is utilized. This
emphasizes the need for serious consideration to be given to the international
group structure of the franchisor.

The relationship between franchisor and franchisee is also important when
considering taxation. In most cases, the relationship between the two will be at
arm's length; however, in many international franchise transactions there is a
much closer connection between franchisor and franchisee. There may be a joint
venture between the two, there may be some form of partnership arrangement, or
the franchisor may be a shareholder and investor in the franchisee.

In some cases such an arrangement is designed to last only for a limited
period of time to enable the franchisee to set up and open the initial outlets. In
such circumstances the payment of an initial franchise fee and continuing franchise fees, and the distribution of profits and dividends should be kept distinct and
separate, or any favourable tax treatment of one or more categories of payments
may be lost.

Even where the parties are independent and at arm's length, problems can
arise if a franchisor has a number of franchisees in one country. If such a
franchisor has a presence in that country, depending upon the terms of any
relevant double-taxation treaty, he may be held to have a permanent establishment or other taxable presence in the franchisee's country. Franchisors should, as
far as possible, avoid this occurring. The safest way of ensuring that a franchisor
is not exposed to a claim of taxation by the revenue authorities of the franchisee's
country is for the franchisor to make sure that he has no presence in the franchisee's country or, where such presence is essential, that it is kept to a minimum.

Some franchisors have used the instrument of financing to minimize taxes
arising from international transactions. Here again, the Netherlands seems to be
a special favourite in that a Dutch company can be a useful intermediary. It is
possible (subject to satisfying certain conditions) for a Dutch finance company to
agree with the Dutch Inspector of Taxes that a special Dutch ruling be applied to
it, under which it will be taxed on between $\frac{1}{4}$ % and $\frac{1}{8}$ % of the outstanding capital
of its loans. When one considers the fact that the Netherlands does not impose a
withholding tax on interest and given what was said earlier about the extensive
network of double-taxation treaties between the Netherlands and other countries,
the benefits of using a Dutch finance intermediary rather than a franchisee paying
interest direct to a franchisor become apparent. However, all is not plain sailing.
Some countries limit the availability of such benefits by a reference to gearing
ratios and by restricting the amount of debt which a company may have relative
to the amount of its equity. Falling foul of such rules could prove to be an
expensive exercise because any interest paid may cease to become a tax-
deductible expense and may be treated as a distribution instead.

As can be seen, structuring a tax-efficient international franchising transaction can be complex. In some cases the advantages are more apparent than real.

What is undoubtedly true is that in considering any international franchise structure the commercial considerations must be paramount and the structure, once
the commercial considerations have been established, should, where possible, be
adjusted to take advantage of such special tax privileges and incentives as may be
available. It is not often possible to predict with any degree of certainty how a
particular international franchise transaction will develop. A balance has to be
struck between the benefits which a franchisor can reasonably be expected to reap
over a given period of time and the costs of setting up a structure to achieve that
result.

In the final analysis, it matters not how elaborate a franchisor's scheme is for
its international franchise operations, and there is little point in establishing a
network of companies and/or a presence in all the right countries so that the
correct answers can be given to all the tax-led questions, thereby enabling the
franchisor to achieve the desired tax objective in theory, if in practice the franchisor fails to realize the real benefits intended to be derived from the transaction
contemplated.

# CHAPTER 5
# BELGIUM

*André Lombart*

## AN OVERVIEW OF FRANCHISING IN BELGIUM

Franchising is undergoing a period of rapid growth in Belgium. It has been used for many years in the country, as is shown by the fiftieth anniversary of the network of a franchisor in the food distribution trade. However, it is only since the early 1980s that its development has been of any significance. According to the latest figures available, those for 1988, Belgium hosts 82 franchisors, who share 3102 franchisees, accounting in total for an annual turnover of over BF 100 billion. In recent years, this growth has also witnessed a change in attitudes towards franchising. The change is particularly apparent in two ways:

1   The second-largest Belgian concern, GB-INNO-BM S.A. (plc), has carried out a major part of its diversification by franchising, including as a master franchisee. Today, it occupies the market through the use of a dozen names, such as Quick, Christiaensen, Pizza Hut, Pearle Vision and Auto 5. The GB-INNO-BM group's turnover in 1989 was of BF 296 billion, 25% of which resulted from franchise networks. This corporate strategy, intentionally directed towards franchising, has attracted the attention of other Belgian companies. Thus franchising, traditionally restricted to the development of small and medium-sized companies, now appeals increasingly to large concerns, which contributes to the growing credibility of this marketing method.

    The main Belgian and foreign banks operating in Belgium have set up means of financing specifically designed for franchising, and have trained their staff to appreciate and deal with the problems of franchising. The analysis capabilities which these banks display at the financing stage lead to a safer, healthier franchise sector, as riskier ventures cannot obtain bank financing.

2   Belgian franchisors are now exporting their franchise formulae (Quick, Christiaensen, Watchwatch, Jeff de Bruges) whereas they earlier limited their network to Belgian territory. The success of such exports has reinforced the interest in franchising. Parallel to this change in attitudes, the Belgian

market has remained receptive towards foreign concepts. This phenomenon may be accounted for in several ways:

(a)  The Belgian consumer is often multicultural. Most Belgians speak two even three languages, and this multicultural tendency is reinforced by the presence of businessmen and civil servants from all European countries.

(b)  Communication networks allow the Belgian consumer to tune into about 25 different television channels from eight European countries. He watches the adverts, which are sometimes for brand names that are not distributed in Belgium.

The Belgian legal system is barely protectionist, and thus investment in Belgium is quite easy, particularly if done via a franchise.

The Belgian government, though conscious of the positive influence of franchising on trade, distribution and self-balanced economic growth has, up to now, stuck to the non-interventionist rule which guides the Belgian economy. Several draft laws on franchising have been submitted to parliament by individual members, but none has been passed so far. However, the Belgian government is presently considering the need for an Act containing a disclosure obligation, such as already exists in France ('loi Doubin').

The Association Belge de la Franchise has approximately 30 members, all franchisors, but has since 1990 decided to try and open its ranks to the members' franchisees.

## STRUCTURE OF BELGIAN VENTURES

A franchisor who decides to develop his business in Belgium will do so by granting a franchise directly or through a master franchise agreement to a franchisee in Belgium, by establishing a branch in Belgium or by creating a separate Belgian company.

A foreign company may prefer to establish only a branch in Belgium rather than creating another legal entity, but must appreciate that the Belgian branch will be submitted to Belgian taxes and to Belgian commercial law requirements. For example, it will have to obtain a registration number at the Register of Commerce and keep accounts in conformity with Belgian law; a manager will have to be appointed in Belgium, the annual accounts and the by-laws of the company published in the Annexes of the *Moniteur Belge* (Belgian Official Journal); statutory information will be displayed on all the company's documents (letters, bills, and so on); the company must have a 'tax on value added' number in order to commence business activities.

If the franchisor decides to create a separate Belgian company, he will have to choose the type of company which is most suitable for his business needs. The Belgian law on companies defines six types of companies with legal personality and two types of associations without legal personality. The general partnership (société en nom collectif), the limited partnership (société en commandite simple), the public company (société anonyme), the limited partnership with shares (société en commandite par actions), the private company (société privée à responsabilité limitée) and the co-operative company (société coopérative) are the six companies with legal personality (Article 2 of the Commercial Law). The two associations without legal personality are the temporary association (association momentanée) and the association in participation (association en participation) (Article 3 of the Commercial Law). We will only consider for our purposes the three most common types of companies in Belgium, which are the public company, the private company and the co-operative company.

The aim of this chapter is to give the reader only an overview of Belgian company law, so, when creating a company, it will be necessary to be advised by a Belgian lawyer.

### The public company

The public company is the type of company best suited to big businesses. The public companies are the major economic agents in Belgium. This company is characterized by the limitation of liability of shareholders to their contribution in the capital of the company, and it is also the only Belgian company with freely negotiable shares, which makes it easy to leave or join it.

A public company may issue capital or beneficiary shares (i.e. a share in the profit only). Shares are either registered ('nominatives') or transferable to the bearer ('au porteur').

*Formation of a company: formal requirements* The by-laws of a company must be drafted by a notary. An important number of provisions need to be included in the by-laws, for example name, duration (if not unlimited), capital, registered statutory office, corporate objects, etc. All these conditions are described in the Law on Companies, Article 30.

Once drafted, the by-laws are subject to a rule of publicity. They are published in the form of extracts in the Annexes of the *Moniteur Belge* and deposited at the commercial court of the area where the registered office of the company is to be located.

Prior to the legal creation of any company, the founders are empowered to act on its behalf during its formation (this applies to other types of Belgian companies). Hence they need not delay the start of business activities while complying with all the formal and statutory requirements.

Once a company is set up, all the undertakings of the founders on behalf of the company will be taken over by the company itself. However, if a company is never incorporated, its founders will remain contractually liable.

*Statutory requirements* A company must have at least two shareholders who may be individuals or companies.

The minimum capital of a public company is BF 1 250 000. At the time of incorporation:

1    The capital must be entirely subscribed.

2    The shares issued for a cash consideration must be paid up at no less than 25% of their nominal or par value.

3    The capital must be paid up to BF 1 250 000.

If shares are issued for a consideration other than in cash, the consideration must be transferred in full within five years of incorporation.

Furthermore, a financial plan (plan financier) must be established by the company and given to the notary who is to draft the by-laws. In this plan, the founders of the company have to justify that the amount of the capital of the company is sufficient for the company to develop its activities for two years at least.

This plan needs to be drafted very carefully by the founders, because if the company is declared bankrupt in the first three years of its activities, the founders may be liable for all or part of the company's debts if the amount of the capital was obviously too low (at the time of formation) to enable the company to develop its activities for at least two years.

A well-written plan will certainly contribute to the success of the company, and is often required by banks as a condition for the granting of credit.

***Directors' appointments, duties and responsibilities*** The board of directors (conseil d'administration) is the main entity of a public company but not the only one. The others are the assembly of shareholders (assemblée générale) and statutory auditors (commissaires).

At a general meeting, the assembly of shareholders elects at least three directors and the statutory auditors, and then approves the annual accounts, the management report and the audit report. This meeting is held at least once a year. Most of the decisions of the general assembly of shareholders are taken by a majority vote of all shareholders present or represented at the meeting. Qualified majorities are required for such things as the modification of the by-laws of the company, the increase or decrease of the capital and early dissolution.

Statutory auditors must be members of the Belgian Institute of Public Accountants (Institut des Réviseurs d'entreprises). Their duty is to control and audit the accounts of the company; they have important powers but may not interfere with the management of the company. Each year, they prepare a substantial report on the operations of the company which is submitted to the shareholders at the annual meeting of the shareholders.

There must be statutory auditors in public as well as in private companies but there is an exception in favour of small companies (companies not exceeding more than one of the following limits):

1   50 employees

2   Balance sheet total of BF 70 million

3   Turnover of BF 145 million

In these small companies, the control may be exercised by each shareholder.

### Appointment of directors

As has already been said, directors are elected by the general assembly of shareholders for a maximum of six years but may be re-elected. They are removable (at any time) by a decision of a majority of the shareholders.

### Duties

The board of directors has very extensive powers: it does everything that is necessary for the realization of the company's objectives except for the decisions reserved by law or the by-laws to the general assembly of shareholders. The board of directors may delegate the daily management of the company to one of its members, who will be the managing director (administrateur délégué) or to non-member persons who will then be general managers (directeur général).

### Liability

Directors are contractually liable to the company for their negligence in the administration of the company. They are also jointly liable for the losses resulting from any violation of the by-laws or of the law. Although directors always act on behalf of the company, they may be declared liable for all or part of the company's debts if their serious negligence has contributed to the bankruptcy of the company.

### The private company (société privée à responsabilité limitée)

The private company is the most widespread type of company in Belgium and is most appropriate for small businesses. Many rules which have been described for a public company may be transposed here to the private company, with the following differences.

The shares of a private company are all registered and are not easily negotiable.

The transfer of shares to a third party (not an existing shareholder) needs to be approved by a majority of the shareholders owning at least three-quarters of the capital of the company. As the shares are all registered, the transfer is made by transcription in the Register of Shares. The private company may only issue capital shares.

A private company may not issue debentures.

*Formation of a company: formal requirements* These are the same as for a public company (notary, publication, and so on).

*Statutory requirements* Not so long ago a minimum of two shareholders was required. But the law of 14 July 1987, applicable since 1 September 1987, has created a second type of private company, the one-person private company (société privée à responsabilité limitée unipersonnelle). The rules applying to this one-person company are exactly the same as the rules applying to a private company, with two restrictions:

1    Only an individual (no company) may create this type of company.

2    One person may create only one company.

The minimum capital of the private company is BF 750 000, of which at least BF 250 000 must be paid up at the time of incorporation (plus the contributions in kind plus one-fifth of the contributions in cash).

*Managers' appointments, duties and responsibilities* As in a public company, there is a general assembly of shareholders and statutory auditors, who act following the same rules as the public company ones. However, there are no directors. Their function is taken over by the manager(s).

*Appointment*
The company is managed by one or more managers. A manager is often appointed in the by-laws. If not, he will be elected by the general assembly of the share-holders. A manager who is appointed in the by-laws may only be removed by a vote of three-quarters of the shareholders if he has committed a serious act of negligence.

*Duties and liability*
The powers and the liability of a manager are the same as those of the directors of a public company. The only difference concerns the case of bankruptcy. As we have seen, the directors of the public company may have to pay the company's debts if they are guilty of serious negligence. The same rule applies to 'big' private companies but not to private companies with a turnover of less than BF 25 million and total assets of less than BF 15 million.

### The co-operative company (la société coopérative)
The purpose of this type of company would be, in the mind of our legislator, to serve its members rather than to make profits. But, in practice, the co-operative company closely resembles public or private companies. It is characterized by

more freedom in the elaboration of by-laws of the company, in the administration of the company, etc.

There are only a couple of articles governing the co-operative companies in the corporate laws that are obligatory. Most of the articles of the law apply only if nothing else is stated in the contract (by-laws). The shareholders of the co-operative company are jointly liable and their liability is unlimited unless the by-laws state the opposite (which is often the case). It is impossible to transfer shares to persons who are not already shareholders (except if stated otherwise in the by-laws of the company).

*Formal requirements at the formation of the company* These are not as numerous as for the two first types of companies. The by-laws may be stipulated in a private document (without the intervention of a notary) but need to be published as extracts in the Annexes of the Belgian Official Journal.

*Statutory requirements* These provide that companies may be members of a co-operative company as well as individuals but there must be at least three shareholders in a co-operative company.

There is no *statutory* minimum capital in a co-operative company but the minimum capital of the company must be stated in its by-laws. This minimum capital does not have to be paid up at any time. Though based upon this minimum, the capital is *variable* during the life of the company (this is the major difference from the first two types of companies analysed).

The number of shareholders can vary at any time with the admission or removal of members. There is no obligation to provide a financial plan in a co-operative company. Thus shareholders will not be liable for the debts of the company if the initial estimate of minimum capital is too low.

*Directors' appointments, duties and responsibilities* If nothing is stated in the by-laws, a co-operative company is managed by a single director. Civil law governs the question of his liability.

Control of the company accounts is carried out by statutory auditors (as in private and public companies). Statute does not lay down specific voting rules for the general assembly of shareholders. If the by-laws of the company are silent on the matter, shareholders have equal voting rights.

The Act of 20 July 1991, as implemented by the Royal Decree of 10 October 1991, which came into force on 1 November 1991, has profoundly modified the co-operative company, though the principles set out above remain valid.

## Conclusion

To conclude this section on the structures of Belgian companies, it is important to summarize the advantages and disadvantages of the three most common types of companies. Although public and private companies are the traditional type of company, the co-operative company has experienced a real boom in recent years. The figures reproduced in Table 5.1 speak for themselves. Though in 1984 only

**Table 5.1 Number of companies created each year**

|                    | 1984 | 1985 | 1986 | 1987 | 1988 |
|--------------------|------|------|------|------|------|
| Public company     | 2804 | 1840 | 3701 | 4990 | 6607 |
| Private company    | 9933 | 8457 | 6999 | 7545 | 6787 |
| One-person company |      |      |      | 538  | 2845 |
| Co-operative company | 600 | 1279 | 3334 | 5662 | 8424 |

Source: B. Coupe, 'Faillites et créations de sociétés par forme juridique', *Bull. A.C.*, Namur, 1989 no. 2, p. 6, cited M. Coipel, 'Evolution du paysage des personnes morales de droit privé', *Chroniques de droit à l'usage du Palais*, T. VII, Story-Scientia, 1989.

600 co-operative companies were created, in 1988 there were 8424 new co-operative companies, that is, more than public and private companies (for the first time). This is the result of the advantages of this type of company (no minimum capital, easy constitution, no control of contributions in kind, no specific rules for liability of the founders and directors, etc.).

But one must remember that the shares may not be transferred to non-members. In addition, banks and suppliers are more suspicious towards this type of company.[1]

## LEGAL CONSIDERATIONS

### Introduction
As is the case is most EC countries, Belgium has no specific legislation on franchising. The Ministry of National Commerce is presently considering the need for specific legislation of franchising, and consulting with franchising professionals. However, it is unlikely that such legislation will be adopted in the near future.

Thus, franchising is mainly governed by the general principles of the Belgian Civil Code, particularly those relating to contracts and obligations. In certain cases, the Act of 1961 on exclusive sales concessions may be applicable, or at least referred to (see Section 3.10). The existence of a direct link of subordination between the franchisor and the franchisee may, in extreme cases, cause the requalification of the franchise agreement into an employment agreement, thus allowing the judge to apply labour law to the parties' dispute.

Apart from national legislation, Belgium is also greatly influenced by the definitions and principles set out in the EC block exemption regulation which extend beyond competition law considerations.

Finally, many contracts refer expressly to the European Code of Ethics, which has been adopted by the Belgian Franchise Association. It is also very likely that the courts will consider this Code as the expression of generally recognized usages of the trade.

## Pyramid selling

Pyramid selling is prohibited in Belgium by the Law on Business Practices of 14 July 1971,[2] Article 52. This article states that it is forbidden to organize sales using the 'snowball' method (or any similar method) or to participate in such sales. The 'snowball method' consists, in particular, in offering products to the general public and allowing a member of it to hope that he will receive this product free of charge, or for an amount of money inferior to its real value, on condition that he brings these products to the attention of third parties, in exchange for payment, introduction to a trading scheme, coupons or any other titles.

The definition of pyramid selling is very broad and authorizes no exceptions. The infringement of this law is a criminal offence (Article 63 of the Law on Business Practices). The initiator and participants of such a trading scheme will also be liable in tort.

The reason for prohibiting pyramid selling is that the increase in the number of sellers is such a dominant feature that the market will reach its saturation point very quickly and it will no longer be possible to sell the products. The last members of the trading scheme would become the victims of the pyramid selling.

Pyramid selling is not franchising and no case of pyramid selling has yet appeared in a Belgian franchise.

In the distribution sector, the Brussels Court of Appeal has recently held that Article 52 of the Law on Business Practices was applicable to a producer + distributor + sub-distributor + local-distributor network whose fee structure was held to be pyramidal.[3]

In this case, known as the 'Home and Family Products' case, the court found that the system made it mathematically impossible for an appointed distributor to carry on business if he did not find sub-distributors who, themselves, would not be able to survive if they did not find local distributors. Thus the system was only viable if it kept building up towards its saturation point, where it inevitably collapsed. The facts of this case were the following.

The object of the 'Home and Family Products' company was the sale and distribution of cleaning products. The company developed a network of three categories of independent distributors to sell these products.

1    The local distributor paid a registration fee, allegedly for training and marketing material, and could then buy products from the direct distributor and sell them to consumers with a profit of 25% of retail price.

2    The direct distributor had to pay an amount of between BF 55 000 and 75 000; he bought his products directly from the company with a price reduction of 40% of retail price. He had the choice to sell the product either to consumers (with a profit of 40% of retail price) or to the local distributor (with a profit of 15% of retail price).

3    The general distributor had to recruit at least one direct distributor. He

bought the products from the company with a price reduction of 50% of retail price and sold them to the consumer or direct distributor.

The scheme which has been described is a little different from the one of Article 52 of the Law on Business Practices, but the article also condemns any similar scheme. Consequently, the Court of Appeal fined the participants, but only one of them was sentenced to imprisonment.

## Competition law

There is no one general Belgian law on the protection of competition, but there are many rules contained in different laws, as for example:

1    The Law on Business Practices of 14 July 1971[2]

2    The Law on Protection against Abuse of Economic Power of 27 May 1960[4]

3    The Law on Exclusive Concessions, of Sale of 27 July 1961[5]

4    The Law on Economic Regulation and Prices of 22 January 1945[6]

The consequence is that the various laws approach the competition problem from different points of view. The Law on Business Practices contains a number of rules preventing unfair competition. The Law on Protection against Abuse of Economic Power attacks restrictions of competition due to an abuse of power.[7]

***The Law on Business Practices of 14 July 1971***[2]   This Law concerns the distribution of goods and services. It provides that a person dealing in the course of a business (tradesman) should give a consumer specific information as to prices, the quantities, the name and composition of products and by prescribing rules concerning commercial publicity, etc. The Law also regulates certain trade practices, such as sales at a loss, clearance sales, tied sales, itinerant sales, public sales, pyramid selling, etc. More generally, the Law prohibits any act contrary to principles of fair trading by which a tradesman interferes with the professional interests of one or more other tradesmen (Article 54). This Article 54 and the Law on Business Practices in general have been frequently applied by the Belgian courts.

The effectiveness of the Law is principally due to its sanctions. The infringement of any article is a criminal offence if it is accomplished in bad faith. But the effectiveness of the Law is reinforced by its introduction of a new type of remedy: the 'action en cessation', in case of violation of the Law. Any victim of an act of unfair trading (apart from certain exceptions) may apply to the President of the Commercial Court to order the cessation of the act. After a very swift procedure, the president may satisfy the request by ordering that the tradesman or company cease the unfair activities. The cessation order is often accompanied by an order for an 'astreinte', which is a (usually significant) non-compliance penalty which the defendant will have to pay to the plaintiff for each breach of the cessation order.

***The Law on Protection against Abuse of Economic Power of May 1960[4]*** This Law is in keeping with European competition law, but, unlike European law, it contains no rule intended to prevent the concentration of businesses. The only purpose of this Law is to prevent the *abuse* of economic power.

Economic power is defined in Article 1 as the power that an individual or company acting alone or a group of persons acting together have within the Belgian territory to exercise a predominant influence on the supply of goods or capital, or on the price or the quality of goods or services. Article 2 defines *abuse* as the ability of one or more persons (possessing economic power) to affect the general interest by practices distorting or restricting normal competition or restricting the economic freedom of the producers, distributors or consumers, or the development of production or exchanges.

A long procedure needs to be followed in order to establish the existence of an abuse of economic power. An inquiry is made by commissaires who investigate cases of abuse of economic power. If they find an abuse of economic power, they refer the case to the Council of Economic Litigations, which gives its opinion to the Minister of Economic Affairs. The Minister decides whether there has been an abuse or not. In a case of abuse, he gives recommendations to the parties. If the parties do not follow those recommendations, they may be ordered to do so by virtue of a Royal Order.

This Law has not been applied often, because of its very long and inefficient procedure. In fact, only one case is known where measures were taken by virtue of a Royal Order against an Abuse of Economic Power.[8]

Contrary to most other European countries, and the EC, which have rather strict competition law, Belgian law is not able to deal effectively with the abuse of economic power. Therefore, the Minister of Economic Affairs drafted a Bill on Economic Competition (31 July 1986).[9] The Bill has been approved by the government recently, but still needs to be voted on by parliament (Senate and House of Representatives), and this has not yet been done. This Bill is in keeping with European competition law and some of its articles are very similar to Articles 85 and 86 of the Treaty of Rome. It will give more power to the Minister of Economic Affairs in order to combat the abuse of economic power, so the passing of this Bill into law would be a step forward in the development of an effective Belgian competition law.

***Contractual clauses and other practices restricting competition*** Consideration is given below to clauses which are likely to be found in a franchise agreement.

The *exclusive supply clause* is in widespread use in franchise agreements. Under this type of clause, the franchisee has to buy his supplies from the franchisor (or from a particular distributor or importer) and may not obtain them from another distributor of goods or services. This clause is valid under Belgian law unless, of course, it falls under the application of the European competition law; that is, unless it affects trade in the EC (see the chapter on EC competition law).

It happens quite often that the franchisor grants *exclusive territorial rights* to the franchisee and this is perfectly legal in Belgium (again, see restrictions under European competition law).

The *non-competition* clause prohibits the franchisee from setting up a competing business during the franchise agreement or after its termination. This non-competition clause must be limited in time in order to be valid under Belgian law.

Franchisors often establish the *sale prices* of goods (or services) or minimum prices by contract. This clause is valid in Belgium unless its purpose is unlawful (if, for example, the clause is intended to increase prices). But the franchisee will have to fix his prices in conformity with the Law on Economic Regulation and Prices of 22 January 1945. This Law prohibits the sale of goods on the market at a price above the 'normal' price (but 'normal' price is not defined in the Law); the same Law also authorizes the Minister of Economic Affairs to fix maximum prices for certain products.

### Liability of franchisor

As in Belgium there is no legislation regulating franchising obligations, there are no specific statutes defining the franchisor's liability. One must thus refer to general principles and distinguish contractual liability from quasi-contractual liability.

*Contractual liability* Most cases on franchisor's liability are contractual liability cases. In the absence of relevant legislation on the duties of the franchisor, one must refer to the contractual clauses.

The liability of the franchisor will vary greatly, depending on the undertakings the franchisor has given in the franchise contract. However, the question of the liability of the franchisor is often raised in the context of an allegation of non-performance of the franchise system.

When computing an unexpectedly low return, the franchisee is likely to invoke the absence or the weakness of know-how, the faulty organization of the network, the absence of efficient services (lack of assistance, defective advertising support, defective selection) and, if it has been chosen by the franchisor, the faulty selection of the location. These different elements often turn out in practice to differ widely when one compares the actual returns recorded by the franchisee with the provisional elements provided by the franchisor before the signature of the contract. The franchisor will generally counter that the system is not open to criticism and the low returns of the franchisee are due to the franchisee's own defective management and failure to operate properly the franchisor's system. The judges will have to determine where the fault lies.

Very few cases are actually published on the subject, as many franchising contracts include arbitration clauses to ensure some confidentiality of the decision. Furthermore, many disputes are amicably resolved.

*Quasi-contractual liability* As for any other person, the franchisor remains liable towards parties for any acts he carries out. To the author's knowledge, there are no cases where the liability of the franchisor has been established in respect of acts carried out by one of his franchisees.

## Industrial and intellectual propriety

*Trade marks* Belgium implemented the uniform Benelux trade mark law with the law of 30 June 1969. This sets up a uniform protection of trade marks of products for the whole of Benelux (Belgium, the Netherlands, Luxembourg). The system was extended to service marks as from 1 January 1987. Thus by a single registration, one can obtain protection throughout the whole of the Benelux territory. The protection of trade marks afforded by this uniform law thus depends on a preliminary registration: no registration, no protection. Following registration, protection is afforded for a period of ten years, as long as the fees are paid. Trade mark registrations may, however, be renewed as many times as required.

At the time of registration, there is in Benelux no preliminary enquiry for pre-existing trade mark rights. Protection is thus only afforded subject to the rights resulting from a preceding registration by a third party and it is up to the applicant to carry out the required searches and appreciate the validity of his registration. Furthermore, Belgium has also become a member of the Madrid Agreement and it is possible to apply for international registration and to request its extension for the Belgian territory.

Finally, the trade mark rights are extinguished in the event of there being no 'normal' use of the trade mark on the Benelux territory, in the absence of any valid reason, either by the owner or by a licensee, for either the three years following the application for registration or for an uninterrupted period of five years.

*Patents* Since the Law of 24 May 1854 on patents, amended in 1984, Belgium has adopted a system for the protection of exclusive but temporary rights for any discovery or improvement which may be exploited as an item of industry or commerce. Protection also presupposes the registration of patents by the patent office, with protection assured for a period of 20 years. Thereafter, the discovery becomes an item of public knowledge.

*Designs* (**Dessins et modèles**) Belgium has become a member of the convention of Benelux on dessins et modèles since the law of 1 December 1970. Protection is also founded on a preliminary application for registration which is valid for five years from the date of application. It may, however, be renewed for two successive periods of five years upon payment of the renewal tax.

***Know-how*** The protection of know-how is not recognized in any specific manner in Belgian law. In some cases, if there is an original creation, know-how may be protected by copyright.

In addition, settled and prudent case law has in some cases accepted the concept of parasitism, i.e. the tradesman who takes an idea of his competitor, saving on all the research, testing and perfecting procedures, will be guilty of parasitism. Such a practice may be considered as contrary to honest business usage. The tradesman who suffers a loss due to the practice may apply for the immediate cessation of such a practice or fines. This application is brought before the President of the Tribunal de Commerce under the provisions of the law on trade practices and the provisions of the 'cessation' application.

## Real estate and leasing

One of the most sensitive points in the setting-up of a franchise network in Belgium is that of the compatibility of the franchisor's and the franchisees' rights in the business. The franchisee will often be the lessee of the buildings in which the business is being carried on. The Law of 1951 on business leases provides efficient protection of the lessee's interest. Hence, even if the franchisor himself rents the buildings and sub-leases thereafter to his franchisee, the latter will very often, at the time when the franchise contract comes to an end, be able to invoke the protection of the 1951 Law to continue to use the buildings.

The rights of a lessee under a business lease may be summarized as follows:

1    The duration of the lease must be at least nine years except in the case of sub-leases where the sub-lease may be given a duration coinciding with the length of principal lease.

2    The lessee has the right to request the renewal of the lease three times. The lessor may not refuse this renewal except in specific situations defined by the law (e.g. desire to occupy the building himself or have it occupied by his family, desire to demolish the building and to rebuild it).

3    If the lessee can terminate the lease every three years, the lessor may only terminate if the lease terms provide for the lessor's right to renounce; even in the latter case, he may only use this option to renounce in precise legally defined situations (e.g. desire to occupy the building himself or by his family, desire to demolish the building and rebuild it).

4    The lessee may always dispose of his rights under the lease to a third party, and if the disposal is made at the same time as the disposal of the business, the disposal is effective despite any clauses to the contrary in the lease.

5    Of course, the judge may rescind the lease and deprive the lessee of these rights if he is in breach of his obligations.

It is also very difficult for the franchisor to retain control over the network's sales outlets. When a franchisee leaves a network, it will often be difficult for the franchisor to retain the sales point by having a new franchisee to run it. One must search for alternative solutions by, for example, making use of an option or preemption rights allowing the franchisor to buy back the business from the franchisee at the end of the contract terms.

## Foreigners working and establishing businesses in Belgium

Belgium has always been open to foreigners who wish to set up a business or professional activity on its territory. Foreigners who wish to work in Belgium must, however, have obtained either a work permit if they are employees, or a 'professional card' if they are self-employed, to show they have obtained the necessary professional qualifications in their country of origin. This type of permit is, however, no longer required for nationals of EC member states.

The facilities available to most foreign workers are, moreover, excellent, since Brussels as the site of the EC Commission has long been accustomed to the presence of many foreign executives. Structural facilities (press, cultural activities, sports, schools) are now being run and afford the best possible welcome to foreign workers.

## Employment laws
### The agreement
#### Writing
It is in the interests of the employer to draft the contract before taking on the worker. In the absence of a written document, the worker is presumed to be employed under the terms of an indefinite-term contract for which there is no trial period.

#### Type of contract
The employment contract may be either for a definite term for a precisely defined job or for an indefinite term. The principle is that the employer or employee may not conclude two successive employment contracts for a definite term if there has not been between these two definite-term contracts an interruption attributable to the worker except if the employer proves that these contracts will be justified by the nature of the work or other legitimate reasons. The relevant exceptions are rarely accepted by the courts.

#### A trial period may be inserted in the contract
A trial period clause will be void if it has not been concluded in writing and signed by the worker before the beginning of his employment.

1    Duration of trial period:

   (a)   Workers: 7 days minimum, 14 days maximum

(b)  Employees: 1 month minimum, 6 months or 1 year maximum

depending on whether gross annual salary does not exceed or exceeds BF 88 200 as at 1 January 1990.

2     Advantage: a reduction in the notice period (see below)

*Special rules*
Special rules exist for other types of contracts:

1     Part-time contract

2     Student contract

3     Replacement contract

4     Interim contract

### Principal modes of severance
*Dismissal with notice*
The dismissal must be notified in a written form:

1     Dated

2     Signed

3     Indicating the starting date and duration of notice

4     Complying with language regulations

Dismissal by employer is:

1     By postal registered delivery

2     By process server certificate (exploit d'huissier)

Resignation by employee is:

1     By postal registered letter

2     By process server certificate

3     By remittance of written document to employer (signature of duplicate by employer).

Notice by registered letter is deemed to be delivered the third day following the date of postage; the other modes of notification are effective immediately.

For employees whose gross salary does not exceed BF 735 000, the duration of notice period is as follows:

1    Dismissal by employer: At least three months if length of service does not exceed five years. This notice period increases by three months for each new period of five years length of service.

2    Resignation by employee: Six weeks if the employee's length of service does not exceed five years, three months if the employee's length of service does exceed five years.

For employees whose gross salary does exceed BF 735 000, duration of the notice period depends on length of service, age, salary and office; the minimum legal requirements have to be respected.

The maximum notice period which must be observed by the employee is 4½ months or six months according to whether gross annual salary exceeds or does not exceed BF 1 470 000. For workers, the duration of notice period is 28 days when the notice is given by the employer, and 14 days when it is given by the worker. The notice periods are doubled in the case of workers having at least 20 years' uninterrupted length of service with the same firm.

In principle, the notice is effective from the first day of the month which follows the month of the notice (employees), and the Monday which follows the week of notice (workers).

One must check whether a reduced notice period is applicable (example: contractual trial period in the contract, use of the exception for the contracts of workers who do not have more than six months' length of service in the firm.

*Dismissal with indemnity*
The dismissal must be notified in a written document:

1    Dated

2    Signed

3    Indicating the amount of indemnity

There is no prescribed manner of notification, but the advised manner is by postal registered delivery.

The date of severance of the contract can be fixed by the person who severs the contract.

*Immediate severance for a serious ground without indemnity or notice period*

1    *Serious ground.* Any serious fault which makes it definitely and immediately impossible to continue employment relations (for example, theft, assault and battery).

2    *Appreciation.* In case of dispute, the courts decide on the seriousness of the grounds.

3    *Proof.* The person who has drafted the contract must prove the existence of a serious ground and the lawfulness of the procedures. All the elements of proof must be obtained before carrying out the dismissal.

4    *Notification.* The notification must be given within the three clear days which follow the discovery of the existence of a serious ground (preferably by registered letter). The disclosure of the serious grounds must be given within the three clear days which follow the dismissal (registered letter, delivery of the written documents and signature of the other party on the duplicate, process server certificate).

*Protection against dismissal*
Certain special rules or precautions must be observed or taken when any of the following protected workers are dismissed:

1    Trade union representative, actual or substitute

2    Actual or substitute member of the Security and Hygiene Committee of the Workers' Council or the non-elected candidate

3    Pregnant women

4    Enlisted or re-enlisted worker

5    Worker with conscientious objector status

6    Assistant on training vacation

7    Assistant on career vacation

8    Assistant carrying out a political mandate

9    Security chief

The dismissal may only be carried out on grounds that are connected with capability or conduct of the worker or that are based on running requirements of the firm, of the establishment or of the service.

In default, the dismissal may be considered as abusive (sanction: a sum equal to six months' salary must be paid by the employer).

One must also consider the special dismissal procedures provided for in the collective agreements of the joint commission on which the firm depends.

## Foreign investment

Just as for physical persons or companies, Belgium also warmly welcomes foreign investors. There are no restrictions and any investment contemplated by a foreign company may be done without any preliminary permit.

## Other significant issues

The Law of 27 July 1961 regulates the unilateral rescission of indefinite-term exclusive sales concessions. This Law defines a sales concession as being any agreement by which a licensor reserves to one or more licensees the right to sell in their own name and on their own account the products that the licensor makes or distributes. The Law applies to any concession satisfying this condition if it is exclusive or quasi-exclusive, or when the licensor imposes on the licensee important duties which are connected with the concession in a strict and definite manner and for which the fee is such that the licensee would suffer a severe loss in case of rescission of the concession (Article 1). One may notice that many franchise systems are based on the resale, exclusively by the franchisee, or products made or distributed by the franchisor, and thus may come within the terms of the above Law.

The Law only applies to concessions with an indefinite term in matters which concern the consequences of rescission. However, franchise contracts are often concluded for a definite term. Nevertheless, the Law specifies that when the agreement has been renewed twice, any further renewal is deemed to be for an indefinite term. Any agreement regulated by the Law may only be brought to an end upon a reasonable notice period or just indemnity to be determined by the parties at the time of the rescission of the contract, except for the case of serious breach by one of the parties. In the absence of agreement of the parties, the judge will consider equitable rules and in default he will consult usages of the trade.

The length of the notice period or the size of the indemnity depend on several criteria and more particularly the length of collaboration between the two parties and the relative size of the concession in the global turnover of the licensee. In certain cases, these indemnities have reached considerable sums and it is thus important to approach the matter carefully. Furthermore, if the concession was rescinded by the licensor on grounds other than serious breach by the licensee or if the licensee brings the contract to an end because of a serious fault of the licensor, the licensee may be awarded a further indemnity, computed by taking the following into consideration:

1   An important increase in clients brought in by the licensee and who are retained by the licensor after the rescission of the contract

2    The expenses which the licensee has incurred in order to run the concession
     and which will profit the licensor after the rescission of the contract

3    The payments which the licensee owes to personnel whom he is forced to
     dismiss, due to the rescission of the sale concession

Finally, we must state that if the concession has effects on the whole or part of the
Belgian territory, the party who has suffered loss will be able, despite any clause
to the contrary, to bring a suit before the Belgian courts and request the application of statutory Belgian laws. However, recently the tribunals have conceded
that in the case of a contract between business from two member states of the EC
and which contains clauses attributing competence to another state, a Belgian
judge must decline competence despite the fact that the Law on sale concessions is
statutory.

## Termination

Apart from the particular law on exclusive concessions, there are more specific
regulations concerning the rescission of a franchise contract and one must apply
the general principles of the law on obligations and refer to the contractual
clauses. The party who has suffered loss due to a wrongful rescission of the contract will, of course, be able to demand just compensation. It must be stated that
the rescission of the contract may only be obtained by judicial decision, in the
absence of an express clause. Recent case law, however, tends to indicate that in
contracts where the parties are in close contractual relations, which is without
doubt the case in a franchise contract, the rescission clause must be considered as
implied.

# TAX AND FINANCIAL CONSIDERATIONS

## Tax rates

Companies in Belgium are subject to corporation tax at a rate of 41% (39%).
However, if the taxable income of the company does not exceed BF 14 800 000,
(BF 13 000 000), the company will be subject to the reduced following rates:

1  From 0 to 1 000 000              29% (28%)
2  From 1 to 3 600 000              37% (36%)
3  From 3 600 000 to 14 800 000     43% (41%)
   (13 000 000)

N.B. The figures shown in brackets represent the thresholds and rates applicable
as from the 1992 tax year.

   Furthermore, companies which distribute a dividend representing more
than 13% of their capital cannot benefit from the reduced rates.

Individuals are subject to scaled income tax according to the following tranches and rates:

1  From 0 to 230 000              25%
2  From 230 000 to 305 000       30%
3  From 305 000 to 435 000       40%
4  From 435 000 to 1 000 000     45%
5  From 1 000 000 to 1 500 000   50%
6  From 1 500 000 to 2 500 000   52.5%
7  Above 2 500 000               55%

The single person's allowance is BF 176 000 and for married couples BF 139 000 for each spouse.

As far as unearned income is concerned, individuals can make use of a deduction of 25% on any dividend.

There is no wealth tax in Belgium.

**What income is taxable?**
Companies are subject to corporation tax on any profits within the world, including dividends, royalties and interest.

International tax treaties provide for the income obtained from a fixed establishment situated in the contracting states to be free from Belgian taxes.

Belgian dividends of foreign origin received by companies are not subject to the taxable tranches up to a limit of 90% (85% for financial companies) on condition that the individuals are the result of a long-term investment. This allowance is not, however, applicable when the dividends are paid out by companies established in countries with advantageous tax rates by holdings or by financing institutions or by financing companies subject to a particular fiscal treatment.

If the financial transfers consist of unearned income of foreign origin (dividends of a non-permanent participation, fees, etc.) which outside Belgium have been subject to taxation at source similar to Belgian income tax, this unearned income gives rise to the right for the Belgian company to be subject to flat rate foreign taxation (qfie) equal to 15/85 of the net unearned income.

Most usual professional expenses are deductible.

Losses can be set off and carried forward indefinitely.

Non-resident companies are taxed on the profits made by fixed branches or establishments located in Belgium.

Individuals are taxed on their worldwide income subject to exemptions provided for in international conventions against double taxation.

There are advantageous tax schemes for foreign executives of foreign companies who have been temporarily placed in Belgium. These executives may deduct from their gross salary those private expenses which the employer undertakes to pay.

Capital gains are in principle taxed at the usual rate. There are, however, many exceptions providing either for reduced rates (19.5% for corporations and 16.5% for individuals) and even exoneration when the price received for the sale of an asset is fully used to buy another asset in Belgium. Capital gains made on the transfer of shares and bonds are also not taxable, except when the sale is made to a foreign company.

## TVA (VAT)

TVA is charged on individuals or companies whose activities consist in carrying out habitually and independently the delivery of goods or the provision of services.

Import activities are subject to the tax; those of export are, in principle, not taxable.

The general TVA rate is 19% but there are other special TVA rates as follows:

1   6% on essential products and food products, and on services of a social or cultural nature

2   17% on real estate

3   25% on luxury products, e.g. vehicles, jewellery

4   8% additional tax on the 25% rate for certain luxury products

## Other taxes

A contribution tax of 0.5% is payable on the capital of the company when it is created or when its capital is increased.

Transfers of land give rise to a transfer tax of 12.5% on the value of the land.

Finally, the customs policy of Belgium is essentially determined by the EC and its institutions.

## Social security obligations

Any person who employs salaried workers must be affiliated to or contact the following bodies:

1   National social security office (ONSS). The employer must declare any personnel who work for him and contribute the following to the ONSS:

    (a)  the 'worker' social contributions: the employer pays these out of the employees' salary (12.07% of gross salary).

    (b)  the 'employer' social contributions, which vary according to the status of the worker (employee or 'manual worker'), and the number of

workers occupied by the business (as of 1 April 1990, vary between 32.46%
and 40.26% of gross salary).

2    Child benefit fund (Caisse d'allocations familiales).

3    Holiday fund (except if the employer has only employee personnel).

4    Industrial injury insurance fund.

5    Interim medical service.

6    Inland revenue.

The employer must also deduct income tax from the salary paid to workers and
pay it to the inland revenue. Apart from these compulsory affiliations, the
employer may be affiliated to a 'social management office' which will carry out
the main duties imposed on employers in social matters.

**Investment incentives**
There are several incentives, which it would be lengthy to list. Furthermore, these
regulations are very different. One should, however, mention the characteristic
institution of co-ordination centres, which might well apply to networks of
franchises.

Belgium has set up a fiscal scheme which is most advantageous for the
headquarters called 'centre de coordination'. The co-ordination centres may be
constituted either in the form of a branch office or, what is more often the case in
practice, in the form of a subsidiary. The centres must belong to a multinational
group satisfying certain size criteria and certain turnover criteria, i.e. consolidated capital and reserves exceeding BF 1 billion and a minimum consolidated
turnover of BF 10 billion.

The concern must be multinational:

1    It must own subsidiaries in at least four different countries.

2    It must own foreign funds representing at least BF 500 million or 20% of the
     group's own consolidated funds.

3    Its turnover outside Belgium must be at least BF 5 billion or 20% of the
     consolidated turnover.

The centre's aim must be exclusively the development and the centralization
of activities of two types:

1    The provision of administrative support services (advertising, provision and

collection of information, scientific research, accounting centralization services, etc.)

## 2  Financial activities

The centre is not allowed to hold participating shares of another company.

Finally, the centre must employ in Belgium the equivalent of at least ten full-time employees on the expiry of a delay of two years, starting from the beginning of its activities.

This scheme appears to be most useful to a franchisor, since Belgium constitutes, according to several international experts, the ideal site for the establishment of headquarters. Such groups as American Express, General Motors, Coca-Cola, Philips, Renault, Shell and Sheraton have established their centres of co-ordination in Belgium.

Let us now examine the fiscal advantages of the scheme.

The co-ordination centre is taxed at the normal rate of 39% applied at a fixed threshold computed on part of its expenses. Thus, some expenses are not taken into account for the purpose of the taxable income. These will be financial costs and several items of personal expenditure.

In principle the fixed threshold which will be applied is equal to the percentage which the centre uses in its relations with the firms of the group, or, in the absence of such a group percentage, 8%.

In order to encourage the centres to deposit their excess liquid assets in Belgium, the withholding tax is not payable on the income from deposits made by the co-ordination centres. Likewise, in order to allow the centre to perform its role as financial centre of the international groups, the withholding tax is not payable out of dividends, interest or fees paid or attributable to the co-ordination centres. Furthermore, the non-applicability of the withholding tax is equivalent to an actual withholding tax. This fictional withholding is equal to 10/90 of interest and dividends received by the co-ordination centre. It is chargeable on the tax due by the beneficiary and any eventual overpayments will be reimbursed to him.

The Belgian banks (or the Belgian companies of the group) which lend to a co-ordination centre also receive a reimbursable credit of fictional tax of 25/75 on the interest. The resulting advantage is shared between the borrower and the bank via a reduction in the rate, which the co-ordination centre then passes on to the company to be financed. The advantage thus profits the group in the form of reduction of its financing costs.

Finally, for land and fixed equipment which are used for the professional activity of the centre, a total exemption on withholding tax on real estate is provided for; and the 0.5% tax on contribution and capital to a Belgium company is not chargeable on the capital contribution to a certified centre.

One must pay careful attention to the fact that a possible change in the fiscal treatment of co-ordination centres is sometimes discussed. Recently, a series of proposals were made by the Ministry of Finances, including a lowering of the

ictional withholding tax rate and also a new charge on any interest received by
he centres.

## Notes

1	M. Coipel, 'Evolution du paysage des personnes morales de droit privé', *Chroniques de droit à l'usage du Palais*, T. VII, Story-Scientia, Brussels, 1989.
2	'Loi sur les pratiques de commerce', *Moniteur Belge*, 30 July 1971.
3	Brussels, 7 October 1982, *J. T.*, 1984, p. 7.
4	'Loi sur la protection contre l'abus de puissance économique', *Moniteur Belge*, 22 June 1960.
5	'Loi sur les concessions de vente exclusives', *Moniteur Belge*, 5 October 1961.
6	'Loi sur la réglementation économique et les prix', *Moniteur Belge*, 24 January 1945.
7	While the present overview was in the press, Parliament unexpectedly passed two Acts which, when they come into force, will profoundly modify competition law in Belgium. The Business Practices Act of 14 July 1991 abrogates the Act of 14 July 1971, though the main principles set out in the abrogated Act remain. It will come into force early in 1992. Secondly, the Protection of Competition Act of 5 August 1991, which comes into force in April 1993, abrogates the Protection against Abuse of Economic Power Act of 27 May 1960. It sets out a system which, very much like the system defined by the Treaty of Rome, prevents the concentration of business and restrictive trade practices. In this Act too, the main principles defined in the abrogated regulation remain.
8	P. Quertainmont, *Droit administratif de l'économie*, Story-Scientia, Brussels, 1987, no. 150 et seq.
9	'Projet de loi sur la concurrence', Doc. Sénat, 360/1 (85–86).

# CHAPTER 6
# DENMARK

*Peter Arendorff*

## AN OVERVIEW OF FRANCHISING IN DENMARK

Franchising is a comparative newcomer to the Danish distribution and marketing scene. Although a number of businesses have been operated since the beginning of this century in a manner that resembles franchising, e.g. sales and distribution of beer and soft drinks, and distribution of sewing machines, franchising did not really start to catch on until the beginning of the early 1960s, and until the beginning of the 1980s the development was comparatively slow. In the beginning of the 1980s only about 25 franchisors were in operation as against more than 100 in 1990.

This comparatively slow development is probably due to the fact that Denmark as a small country has never had any big problems with the distribution of products to consumers, and also a number of businesses have been run as co-operatives, which in many ways have the same advantages as franchising although, of course, the ownership structure is completely different.

The current growth in the franchising industry is very encouraging indeed, as, particularly, a number of Scandinavian-based systems in the late 1980s have been able to establish themselves as a true force within their respective sectors. This is particularly true within the kitchen sector, which is dominated by a few franchisors. Also, many international franchisors have established themselves in the late 1980s, and this trend will undoubtedly continue.

The overall economic climate in Denmark is very beneficial to franchising, and as most areas of business life are clearly and well regulated, it is not difficult for the international franchisor to do business in Denmark. The civil service is extremely efficient and especially the patent and trade mark authorities are extremely service-orientated, ensuring speedy and correct protection of essential industrial and intellectual property rights. There is a growing trend, encouraged by the government's restraint on wages and social benefits, towards self-employment.

As Denmark is a small country with a population of around 5 000 000 people, many international franchisors will find that there is not the scope for opening a large number of units. On the other hand, personal income is amongst the highest in Europe and consumers are affluent and quality-orientated.

The business environment in Denmark has also been helpful to franchising in other ways. Because of the regulations of the Unfair Marketing Practices Act there have been virtually no 'fly by night' cases, and on the whole the existing legal regulations have been sufficient to regulate the franchise industry in a way acceptable to both franchisors and franchisees. Similarly there have been no real problems in connection with pyramid selling schemes which the existing legal system has not been able to cope with. The favourable climate is also encouraged by the activities of the Danish Franchisors' Association.

The Danish Franchisors' Association was formed in 1984 by a number of the most important Danish franchisors. After a slow growth, the Association in the beginning of 1990 has a membership of some 40 companies. The Association has recently altered its membership criteria to allow for a slow introduction of new franchise systems. There are currently about 20 active franchisor members, and a similar number are going through the vetting procedures set out by the Association, and will eventually become full, active members as well. The Association found that it was necessary to develop a Code of Ethics early on.

The financial institutions have been slow to catch on to franchising, and this has in turn led to a controlled, but too slow, growth in the number of franchisees. Most international franchisors should therefore be prepared to adopt their existing financing packages to Denmark.

The Danish Franchisors' Association is an active lobby organization whose opinion is quite often sought and heard by the legislature when preparing new legislation. There are no current plans for general regulation of the franchise industry in Denmark. It is expected that future regulations of franchising will only be implemented based on EC initiatives.

In conclusion, a number of factors should make it easy for an international franchisor to operate in Denmark. First of all, the workforce is very well educated, the standard of living is high, and the transport and communication systems are highly efficient and extensive. Being the only Scandinavian member of the EC, Denmark serves as a gateway to the other Nordic countries. The service industry is a very important element of the Danish economy, and is currently growing both in absolute and relative terms. The service sector is widespread and broadly based.

The framework of industry consists of a majority of small family-owned entities. Larger companies are generally publicly held corporations with a wide spread of shareholders, and very few corporations are held by the state, except for public utilities such as mail, railways and telecommunication, although there are planned privatization activities within these fields.

## STRUCTURE OF DANISH BUSINESS VENTURES: BUSINESS ENTITIES

Foreign ownership of Danish companies is common and welcomed. There are no special regulations or legal measures to control or prevent foreign ownership. The

typical form of foreign participation in Denmark is through wholly owned sub
sidiaries, but joint ventures and minority participation schemes are becoming
increasingly popular.

The international franchisor has a free choice to operate through whatever
entity he prefers. However, permission is required for non-EC residents to set up
a branch operation. The most usual form used by foreign investors is a subsidiary
or a branch. A subsidiary may be wholly owned by the foreign company. No
investment permit is required. There are no restrictions on the repatriation of
earnings, except that a limited liability company can only distribute free reserves
as dividend.

There are two main types of limited companies in Danish legislation
namely the Aktieselskab and the Anpartsselskab, which correspond to a public
limited company and a private company respectively. These two kinds of entity
have full legal rights in their own names with limited liability for the shareholders
and are subject to taxation as separate entities.

Other business entities in Denmark are governed by common law.

### The public limited company

The public limited company (Aktieselskab, A/S) is the most advanced form of
business entity in Denmark, and the only one whose shares may be offered to the
public or can be traded on the stock exchange.

The public limited company is defined and regulated by the Act on Public
Limited Companies of 13 June 1973, with subsequent amendments.

In order to form a public limited company (A/S), the following procedures
are necessary:

1  The promoters must prepare and sign a formation agreement.

2  The articles of association must be drawn up.

3  The share capital must be subscribed for.

4  A statutory meeting must be held with the purpose of passing a resolution to
   form the public limited company and to elect the board of directors, management and auditors.

5  The board of directors must apply for registration of the public limited company at the Register of Companies (Erhvervs- og Selskabsstyrelsen) not later
   than six months after the date of the formation agreement.

6  The number of promoters must be at least three, and out of these two must
   be resident in Denmark, unless EC provisions stipulate otherwise or exemption is granted by the Minister of Industry. Such exemption is nearly always
   granted.

7   Promoters are not required to subscribe for any shares, and the entire share
    capital can be subscribed by one shareholder only.

8   The shares of the subscribers must be stated in the formation agreement or
    in a subscription list containing a copy of the formation agreement.

9   It is possible to subscribe for shares against payment in kind or other special
    arrangements. If shares are subscribed for against payment in kind, the
    formation agreement must be accompanied by a valuation report made by a
    public accountant or other authorized person. The valuation report must
    include an audited opening balance sheet prepared in accordance with the
    Danish accounting regulations.

It does not take long to form a company but, unfortunately, the registration
period can be as long as six months with the Register of Companies. Most law
firms with an international clientele therefore hold a stock of already-formed
companies with no business activity. It is quite common for foreign investors to
acquire an already existing company with no activity and use this as a basis for
investment as, otherwise, they, as promoters or members of the board of directors
or management, can be made personally liable, should the company for some
reason not be registered with the Register of Companies or fail for other reasons
at some later date.

The fee payable on formation and increases in share capital is 0.4% as a
registration fee of the nominal value of the shares issued plus a small fixed
amount, and capital investment tax of 1% of the value of contribution to the
capital, including any share premium.

The share capital must have a par value of at least DKK 300 000 and shares
may be issued at a premium but not at a discount.

At least one half and in total at least DKK 300 000 of its nominal value of the
initial share capital and 25% of any subsequent increases in the share capital
must be paid in before registration can take place at the Register of Companies.
The balance must be paid within one year of registration. The minimum number
of shareholders is one, and there is no maximum. There are no requirements in
the Danish legislation that some part of the share capital must be held by Danish
nationals rather than foreigners.

Share certificates may be registered or issued to bearer, but may not be
issued to bearer if there are limitations on the transferability or if the shares may
be redeemed. Share certificates must be issued within one year of registration of
the share or subscription. All shares have equal rights in the public limited company, unless the by-laws stipulate that there may be different classes of shares,
either common or preferred. All shares must have voting rights, but the articles of
association may stipulate that certain shares have a higher voting power which,
however, may not be more than ten times the voting power of any other share of
the same denomination.

The liability of each shareholder is limited to the amount of subscribed shares. The promoters, however, are personally liable until the company has been registered.

Each public limited company must keep a register of all the shares and the holders of the shares. This register is open to inspection by public authorities and an employee representative when the employees are not represented on the board of directors.

Individual shareholders must notify the company within one month after acquisition, if their holding is at least 5% of the voting power or at least 5% of the total share capital with a minimum par value of DKK 100 000. A special register must include the name, occupation and address of such shareholders as well as the number of shares, their par value and the class of shares. The special register is open for public inspection, and the company's annual report must include a list of shareholders contained in the special register.

The management of the public limited company consists of the board of directors, the board of management, and shareholders in general assemblies. To some extent the relationship between these three bodies is determined internally by the articles of association, but the Public Limited Companies Act lays out the general rules.

The board of directors conducts the business of a public limited company. The responsibilities for the day-to-day operations are normally delegated to a managing director (or a board of management). The board of directors must have at least three members.

The majority of the board members are appointed by the shareholders at a general assembly. Under certain conditions, the employees may appoint members to the board. The employee members are appointed for four-year periods, and other members are appointed for periods not exceeding four years. The board members may be re-elected for an indefinite number of periods. The articles of association must contain provisions dealing with the power and the duties of the board members.

Except for the period before registration of the private limited company, the directors are not personally liable towards the company or third parties for their actions, unless it can be proved that they have been guilty of misconduct in the discharge of their duties.

The board of directors must appoint at least one managing director. A managing director can be a member of the board; however, together they may not constitute a majority. A managing director may not be appointed chairman. The managing director and at least 50% of the board of directors must be resident in Denmark or be citizens of an EC country, but exemptions can be granted by the Ministry of Industry.

A public limited company may not grant private loans, pledge securities or issue guaranties to shareholders and members of the board of directors of the company or its parent entity or their relatives or close friends. These restrictions do not apply to loans etc. to parent companies.

A public limited company must not grant or warrant loans that are used to purchase shares in the company itself or its parent company, but can purchase its own shares if the purchase does not exceed more than 10% of the share capital.

A public limited company must hold an annual general meeting within the time limit contained in the articles of association and not more than six months after the end of the financial year. The agenda for the annual general assembly must be laid down in the articles of association. Minutes must be made of all general assemblies and must be signed by the presiding chairman.

The books and records of a public limited company must be made in accordance with the regulations of the Accounting Act of 10 June 1981, which is in accordance with the fourth EC Directive.

## The private limited company

The private limited company (Anpartsselskab, ApS) is the other form of business entity with limited liability used in Denmark. Traditionally it is the form adopted by most foreign investors and for small Danish family businesses with a limited number of shareholders. It is favoured because of the more simple legal formalities, lower minimum capital requirements, etc.

The Anpartsselskab is regulated by the Private Companies' Act (Anpartsselskabsloven) of 13 June 1973, with subsequent amendments. Most of the more important provisions regarding the operation of an Anpartsselskab are similar to those of an Aktieselskab.

The formation formalities of an Anpartsselskab are somewhat simpler than those of an Aktieselskab; however, the following minimum requirements must be fulfilled:

1    The promoters must draw up and sign a formation agreement.

2    The articles of association must be drawn up.

3    There must be subscription for the share capital, which currently is a minimum of DKK 80 000.

Application for registration at the Register of Companies must be made not later than two months after the date of the formation agreement.

The number of promoters need not be more than one, but at least one must be resident in Denmark, unless EC provisions stipulate otherwise or exemption is granted by the Minister of Industry. Such exemption is normally granted.

The formation agreement must contain the same information as mentioned above in connection with the Aktieselskab (public limited company).

The articles of association must include information similar to the requirements for a public limited company. Shares are in principle freely transferable, but the articles of association may restrict the transferability in some way. It is not necessary to issue share certificates.

The formation costs of an Anpartsselskab are generally less than those of a public limited company; however, the capital investment tax of 1 % and the registration fee of 0.4% of the nominal value of the shares issued is also payable for a private limited company.

The share capital must have a minimum par value of at least DKK 80 000.

The entire capital may be held by one shareholder. A foreign investor from a non-EC country who wishes to be the only shareholder should be promoted together with the Danish resident, and the foreign promoter may then subscribe for the entire capital. As mentioned above, it is also possible to acquire the shares in an already registered Anpartsselskab, which has not yet carried out any business.

All shares have equal rights, unless the articles of association stipulate that there shall be different classes of shares.

Convertible loans and debentures may be issued without any limitations in respect to the registered capital.

Companies with a registered capital of less than DKK 300 00 are not obliged to maintain a register of larger shareholders.

A private limited company must have a management consisting of one or more members. If the registered capital is at least DKK 300 000 or the private company meets the conditions to have employee representation on the board of directors, there must be a board of at least three members. In other private companies it may be stipulated in the articles of association that there are less than three members or no board at all.

When a private company has lost 50% of its share capital, the board of directors must further present a detailed action plan to re-establish the share capital or propose a liquidation. The share capital may be written down to cover the deficit but not below the minimum capital requirement of DKK 80 000.

There is no distinction between the public limited company and the private limited company in respect of accounting and auditing requirements.

## Other forms of business entities

*The general partnership*  The general partnership ('Interessentskab', I/S) is a business association of two or more partners, individuals or corporate bodies with joint and several liability. The name of the firm must indicate that it is a partnership (I/S). Foreign persons or companies, other than those resident in EC countries, must apply to the Minister of Industry for permission to participate in a general partnership. Relationships between partners are determined by the partnership agreement. If the partnership is involved in trading or industry, the partnership must have its own name, and all partners must register in the local business register. The local business register will often demand to have a copy of the partnership agreement.

The expenses for founding a partnership are minimal, as no capital investment tax is applicable.

The management of a partnership is usually determined in the partnership agreement. There are no legal formalities governing the management, including maintaining a board of directors' or partners' meeting. Accordingly no employee representation in the management organs is required although most large partnerships have their own internal guidelines for consultations with the employees, following the relevant labour law provisions. Partnerships must maintain adequate books and records, but are not subject to any publication requirements in respect of their financial statement. Partnerships are not subject to audit requirements, but the partnership agreement normally requires an audit in the case of large partnerships. Also, partnerships are not subject to the same liquidation rules as limited companies. They can only be dissolved following the formalities set forth in the partnership agreement.

*The limited partnership* The limited partnership ('Kommanditselskab', K/S) is similar to an Interessentskab except that some partners may limit their liability for the partnership's debts to the amounts of their capital contributions as specified in the partnership agreement.

At least one of the partners must carry unlimited liability – the general partner. If the general partner is a limited liability company, this fact should be listed in the name of the partnership as f.inst. A/S & Co. K/S.

*The co-operative society* The co-operative society ('Andelsforening' or 'Brugsforening') is a corporate body formed for the purpose of processing and selling members' products (Andelsforening) or for the purpose of purchasing goods for sale to members (Brugsforening). There is a large number of both types in Denmark. The former are mainly engaged in marketing and purchasing agricultural products, residential building, and distribution of electricity, while the latter have shops in every city, town and village in Denmark. The co-operatives involved in retail business are, in the public eye, similar to franchised businesses, as there is a strong emphasis on corporate identity, product control, etc.

There is no specific legislation governing co-operative societies in Denmark. The relations between members and toward third parties are stated in the societies' articles of association. Liability of members is normally limited. The structure of a co-operative society is normally very simple, i.e. the annual general assembly appoints a board of administrators that in turn appoints local managers and statutory auditors.

*Branch of foreign company* A foreign limited company registered in its home country according to provisions corresponding to those applying to Danish public companies or private companies may establish a branch, if provided by international treaties or permissions granted by the Ministry of Industry. Legal entities resident in non-EC countries require permission, which generally can be obtained if Danish entities are permitted to establish a branch in the corresponding foreign country. The name of the branch must include the word 'filial' (branch) together with the foreign company's name and country of origin.

The branch must be registered with the Register of Companies and the application for registration must include the following:

1    The certificate of the foreign entity's incorporation

2    A statement in which the foreign entity agrees in all legal matters to submit to Danish law and to decisions of the Danish courts

3    A certified power of attorney to a branch manager together with a copy of his certificate and documentation that the branch manager meets the requirements as to residence in Denmark or an EC country, unless the Minister of Industry has granted dispensation from this rule

4    A copy of the foreign company's by-laws

At the request of the Registrar the entity must provide authorized translations of the above documents.

A branch can be formed within a few weeks. Registration time may be up to six months. The name of the branch frequently causes delay when it differs from the name of the foreign entity. A branch may commence operations on the responsibility of the branch manager from the date the application for registration was filed.

There are no requirements with respect to the registered capital of a Danish branch of a foreign entity.

The branch must be managed by one or more managers. The branch manager is personally liable for any outstanding balances on income tax, customs duty and other liabilities to public bodies.

Within one month after the annual accounts of the foreign entity have been approved, but not later than seven months after the closure of the financial year, the branch manager must submit to the Register of Companies a certified copy of the foreign entity's annual report and auditor's opinion, together with a report on the branch activities.

**Non-registered sales promotion office** A foreign company may set up a non-registered sales promotion office (Salgskontor) or similar office without permission. A sales promotion office is not considered a separate legal entity, and any business carried out is done entirely on behalf of the foreign entity which is fully liable for the debts and obligations of the representative office.

**Joint venture** Joint ventures do not have the status of a legal entity unless registered as a public limited company or a private limited company. Otherwise, the status of a joint venture is determined by the contract between the members and would normally be determined as a general partnership.

*Sole proprietorship* The characteristic of a sole proprietorship (Enkeltmandsvirksomhed) is that the sole proprietor has unlimited liability for the debts of his business.

An EC citizen may establish a sole proprietorship in Denmark without prior permission except that a residence permit must be obtained. Non-EC citizens need to obtain both a residence and a work permit and the business may be registered in the trade register with the local authorities.

*Corporate funds* The Act on Corporate Funds took effect on 1 January 1985 and was amended on 6 June 1991. A corporate fund is a body which can transfer goods or immaterial rights, perform services, carry on the business of selling or leasing real property, etc.

An instrument of foundation must be set up for all corporate funds. This instrument must contain the following information:

1   The fund's name, which must incorporate the word 'fond'

2   The founders of the fund

3   The domicile of the fund

4   The objects of the fund

5   The size of the basic capital at the foundation and how it was paid up – whether in cash or in assets

6   Whether the fund is to take over other assets than cash on its establishment

7   Special rights or advantages given to the founder or to others

8   Number of committee members

9   The preparation of accounts

10   Application of profits

It can be quite difficult to change the articles of association of the fund, as a change always needs to be cleared by the Minister of Justice or Minister of Industry.

A corporate fund must be registered in the Fund Register with the Danish Register of Companies.

A corporate fund must be managed by a committee which, in addition to any representatives elected by the employees, consists of at least three members.

For each accounting year annual accounts consisting of a balance sheet and a profit and loss account must be prepared. The annual accounts must be certified by auditors and filed with the Danish Register of Companies.

## LEGAL CONSIDERATIONS

### Introduction
With the exception of the EC Block Exemption for categorized franchise agreements no laws, acts, rules or regulations in Danish law make any general reference to franchising. The word 'franchise' does not exist in the Danish vocabulary, and there is no appropriate translation of the word to Danish. Franchising has in latter years been described and treated a number of times in the legal literature. The latest edition of the Danish Legal Dictionary defines franchising in the following way: 'An agreement according to which an independent company is authorized to market the goods or services of another company using the trademark or logo of this company.' The Danish courts have made no relevant decisions regarding franchise matters. On the other hand, there is, of course, a lot of Danish legislation which affects franchise activities. The following acts, rules and regulations thus affect franchising directly or indirectly:

1    The Fair Marketing Practices Act 1974

2    The Competition Act 1989

3    The Rental Act 1979

4    Copyright Act 1961

5    The Trademark Act 1959

6    The Industrial Design Act 1970

7    The Patent Act 1967

8    The Petrol Distribution Contracts Act 1985 (by analogy).

### Pyramid selling – the Fair Marketing Practices Act
The main provision of the Fair Marketing Practices Act is the general clause of Section 1 which very briefly lays down that business activities may not involve 'Acts which are contrary to good marketing practices'. The courts may issue injunctions prohibiting acts violating this provision, but violations are not criminally sanctioned. The general clause is supplemented by a number of special

provisions. Violations of these are in most cases criminally sanctioned. The special provisions elaborate the principle of the general clause mentioned above in relation to a number of issues, such as special rules on misleading advertising, collateral gifts, discount stamps and price competition. The Fair Marketing Practices Act is not limited to a regulation of the relation between business and the consumers, but also contains special rules on unfair competition law, such as the protection of trade marks, business secrets and goodwill. Accordingly the Act also regulates the relationship between businesses. In this aspect it differs from the other Scandinavian Fair Marketing Practices Acts. In order to make the administration of the Fair Marketing Practices Act as efficient as possible, a special system of control, enforcement and sanctioning is contained in the Act. A main feature of the system is the introduction of the Institution of the Consumer Ombudsman. The task of judging has been placed with a special section of the Copenhagen Maritime and Commercial Court, namely the Marketing Practices Division.

The Consumer Ombudsman is not a parliamentary ombudsman independent of the government, but a high-ranking civil servant in charge of his own department. His decisions cannot be appealed against to any other administrative or governmental authority. The Institution of the Consumer Ombudsman constitutes a body of supervision and control in accordance with Section 15 of the Fair Marketing Practices Act; the Consumer Ombudsman 'ensures that violations of good marketing practices or any other provisions of this Act do not occur'. The Ombudsman is required in particular to supervise marketing practices areas in which it may be envisaged that violations of the Fair Marketing Practices Act will occur frequently, or areas in which violations will be particularly harmful to consumers, as well as marketing activities of considerable practical significance.

The Institution of the Consumer Ombudsman is also a general regulatory body, as the Ombudsman on his own initiative or in consequence of complaints or applications made by others shall, through negotiation, try to induce businesses to carry on a trade or business in accordance with the regulations of the Act. The Consumer Ombudsman has issued numerous guidelines on what he considers fair marketing practices, and these guidelines are generally voluntarily adhered to by the business community. The Ombudsman in his guidelines generally makes references to established codes of ethics like the Codes of Ethics prepared and published by the International Chamber of Commerce and other representative bodies, e.g. the European Franchise Federation.

In a set of guidelines issued in 1984 the Consumer Ombudsman has dealt with the practice of pyramid selling, and it follows from these guidelines that it is against fair marketing practices to market or sell business systems which mainly consist of the right to sell sub-agencies or smaller territories, if the products or services sold through the business system are secondary to the selling of the distribution rights. After the implementation of these guidelines there have been no serious problems with pyramid selling systems in Denmark, although it was necessary for the Consumer Ombudsman to try a number of such cases at the Copenhagen Maritime and Commercial Court.

A number of the special marketing practices provisions of the Act should also be mentioned here. Sections 2 and 3 of the Act prohibit the use of any 'false, misleading or unreasonably incomplete indication or statement likely to affect the demand for or supply of goods, real or personal property and work of services' when marketing a product. An offence is only constituted, however, where the statement in question 'is capable of affecting demand or supply'.

Other special provisions of the Act deal with unsolicited goods, doorstep selling and telephone advertising.

Discount stamps may only be offered when each stamp is provided with a clear indication of the identity of the issuer and of its value in Danish currency. Discount stamps are hardly used in the Danish retail trade.

Another special provision of the Act provides that 'no person carrying on a trade or business shall distribute prices by the drawing of lots, by price competitions or other arrangements where the results are wholly or partly dependent on chance'. The interpretation of this provision has given rise to a substantial body of case law.

Sections 5 and 9 of the Fair Marketing Practices Act provide for the protection of trade marks, technical drawings, know-how, etc. Furthermore, a general clause of the Act provides a supplementary protection against imitation, passing off, sponging or other improper use or exploitation of the achievements of other business enterprises.

Under s. 5 of the Fair Marketing Practices Act 'no person carrying on a trade or business shall make use of any trade mark to which he is not legally entitled or make use of his own distinctive business marks in a manner likely to cause such trade marks to be confused with those of other traders'. The protection thus includes anything which can reasonably be construed as a business mark (logo) of a particular enterprise. Protection, however, presupposes a certain distinction which may be acquired through use.

Under s. 9 of the Marketing Practices Act 'no person employed by cooperating with or performing work or providing services for a commercial enterprise shall in an improper manner acquire or attempt to acquire knowledge or possession of the trade secrets of such enterprise'. Where knowledge or possession of the trade secrets of an enterprise has been acquired lawfully, no such person may disclose or make use of such secrets without proper authority. This provision applies for a period of three years after the termination of the employment or the period of co-operation. Where a person for the purpose of performing work or for any other business purpose has been entrusted with 'technical drawings, descriptions, formulas, patterns, models or other information', he may not without proper authority make use of or allow others to make use of such knowledge, information or material regardless of whether they contain trade secrets or not.

As mentioned above, the specific rules of Sections 5 and 9 of the Act are supplemented by the general clause of Section 1, under which any article produced, the value of which might be lost with the producer, should some other party copy it, is protected in principle. Protection presupposes, however, that the article which is being copied has a certain distinct mark and is a result of a certain original achievement. The protection presupposes market identity and risk of confusion.

There are a number of detailed, statutory provisions in Danish law regarding drugs and food, chemical products, motor vehicles and other products, laying down requirements regarding the safety of the product. These statutory provisions are to some extent supplemented by the Fair Marketing Practices Act. Under the general clause of the Act, prohibitions may be introduced against the sale of goods for private consumption, if private consumption should involve a major risk of personal injury or extensive damage to property.

## Competition law

In 1989 the Danish Parliament passed new legislation regarding antitrust and competition which completely alters the previous antitrust and competition legislation with the general aim of loosening the control that the monopoly and competition authorities have so far exercised in this area. The new Competition Act of 1989 is also meant to prepare Danish industry and trade for the EC internal market.

The administration of the Competition Act is placed under a Competition Board consisting of a Chairman appointed by the Queen and 14 members appointed by the Minister of Industry. A secretariat under the management of a Director is attached to the Board.

The purpose of the Act is to increase competition and thereby to strengthen the effectiveness of production and distribution of goods and services. The aim is in connection with the increasing internationalization to support a development of the market structure based on competition and effectiveness. The most important means of attaining the object of the Act is transparency, i.e. establishment of the most easy and equitable access for manufacturers, dealers and consumers to obtain relevant information about prices, business terms, etc.

The Act applies to private enterprises and associations of such enterprises and with some limitations to public and publicly regulated enterprises. Furthermore, the Act applies to banking institutions and insurance companies.

The Competition Act does not apply to wages and working conditions, but the Competition Board can obtain information of that kind from organizations and enterprises. As transparency is the main principle of the Act, the statutes on public access to documents and administrative files apply in full to the administration of the Competition Act.

Agreements and decisions, including tacit agreements and consorted practices which exert or may exert a dominant influence on a market and changes of such agreements, etc., are subject to notification to the Competition Board within 14 days after their conclusion. Lack of notification entails invalidity and the Competition Board can impose daily or weekly fines.

The Competition Board publishes investigations of the market structure and information about prices, discounts, bonuses, etc., in sectors where it is found suitable to increase competition and to strengthen the effectiveness. In cases where competition is not sufficiently effective, or where, for other particular reasons, it is found necessary to follow the market structure or create transparency of price conditions, the Competition Board is entitled to order an enterprise within a specified time limit to report on specified types of information about prices, profits, discounts, bonuses, business terms, financial and organizational relations, etc., implement rules on invoicing and other documentation of the price calculation, or lay down rules on marking and display of price and quantity. The Competition Board is empowered to demand the necessary information and, if a court order is issued, to make the necessary investigations on the spot.

The Act also makes it possible for the Competition Board to take measures against harmful effects of anti-competitive practices and restraints on the freedom of trade exercised by private enterprises and associations of such enterprises.

The Competition Act is based on a control system. The fundamental condition for the Competition Board to intervene is that a restrictive practice is exercised on a certain market which leads to or may imply harmful effects for competition and accordingly for the effectiveness of production and distribution of goods and services. If the Competition Board identifies a restrictive practice, it can order total or partial annulment of agreements, practices, etc., but must first attempt to terminate the harmful effects through negotiations with the offenders.

If an order for total or partial annulment of agreements does not have the desired effect, the Competition Board can issue an order to supply and in this way set aside agreed sole distribution rights, if such a measure is found necessary to create effective competition. A franchisor that does not operate a network covering the entire Danish market may in this way be forced to supply products or services to other types of distributors.

Price fixing is, as a rule, prohibited in accordance with Section 14 of the Competition Act. However, the Competition Board can make exemptions from this prohibition, but this would normally only apply to public services. The prohibition is absolute in the sense that it also has to be respected by companies that do not have a dominating position.

Non-binding price recommendations are allowed for both goods and services. The Competition Board has, however, got powers to adjust not only prices but also profit margins. However, the Board would only take such measures as a last resort, and if all other instruments contained in the Competition Act do not lead to any result. It is, furthermore, a condition that adjustments made to prices or profits by the Competition Board are necessary, because the price or profit is clearly above the price or profit that could have been obtained in a market with active competition. If recommended prices are used and indicated for resale, it must be done in a way which makes it evident to the consumer that the price is only recommended.

Decisions made by the Competition Board can be brought before the Competition Appeals Tribunal within a time limit of four weeks. Decisions of the Appeals Tribunal can be appealed to the Supreme Court within a time limit of eight weeks.

## Liability of franchisor

The franchise agreement will normally attempt to define the extent of the franchisor's liability towards the franchisee and with regard to third parties. The contractual liability can be based on explicit or implicit guarantees regarding products supplied, territorial area, validity of trade marks and other intellectual and industrial property rights, etc. In Danish law the franchisor will become liable to the franchisee on a 'no faults' basis, if such guarantees do not stand up.

The Danish Parliament has recently passed the Danish follow-up legislation to the EC Directive on Product Liability. The Danish Act on Product Liability came into force in June 1989. The Act follows, with some noteworthy exceptions, the EC Directive.

The EC Directive and the Danish follow-up legislation only cover personal injury to consumers or damage to property belonging to consumers. This leaves an extremely big area outside the scope of the Act.

The Danish Act prohibits the use of hold harmless agreements between the producer and the distributor. This makes it impossible for a Danish master franchisor to limit his liability towards the franchisee, whether situated in Denmark or outside, for damage caused by defects in products supplied, if such damage or injury is covered by the definition of consumer damage. The foreign franchisor should thus be aware that all hold harmless regulations – and for that matter any other clauses regarding limitation of product liability – should be carefully vetted against the Danish Products Liability Act 1989. It should be noted that the Danish Act excludes liability for development damage.

## Industrial and intellectual property rights

Danish law on industrial and intellectual property rights is essentially statutory law. The most important Acts have all been adopted fairly recently. Denmark has ratified the more important international conventions in this field and participates in the Berne and Paris unions.

*Copyright* The current Danish Copyright Act was passed in 1961 and a few subsequent amendments have been passed since then.

The Act is based upon the fundamental principle that a person producing a literary or artistic work has a copyright thereto. Danish practice is fairly liberal as far as works of applied art are concerned, as they are normally granted protection under the copyright legislation. In this way a broad area overlapping with legislation of industrial design is created. The Copyright Act solves this problem through an explicit provision to the effect that protection under the industrial design legislation does not exclude copyright. It should be noted that photographs are protected not under the Copyright Act, but under the Photograph Act 1975.

The Copyright Act contains few provisions on assignment or licensing of copyright to others. The rules regulating such activities are essentially found in the general law of contract.

Copyright protection has in Danish case law been extended to advertising slogans and the like.

The Copyright Act was recently amended (1989) to include protection of certain computer software programs and printed circuits.

*Industrial design* Since the beginning of the twentieth century Denmark has legislated in the field of industrial design. The current Industrial Design Act was passed in 1970.

The legislation exclusively protects designs for the appearance of goods or purely ornamental goods.

Protection of industrial design is obtained by submitting a written application to the patent authorities in Denmark. A copy of the design must be submitted along with the application. The application is examined with a view to establishing whether the conditions of registration are fulfilled. Among these conditions are that the design must be novel; in other words, it should deviate considerably from anything known prior to the day of submitting the application. The administrative examination is much less deep than in relation to patterns, and registration consequently does not imply any major guarantee that the right has been validly established.

The registration of a design is valid five years from the day on which the application was submitted, and upon application it may be extended for two further five-year periods, yielding a maximum period of protection of 15 years.

It is not permitted to exploit the design commercially by producing, importing, offering, transferring, or leasing goods which are not substantially different from the design, without having obtained the permission of the designer. Combined with the general rules contained in the Danish Fair Marketing Practices Act – see above – the franchisor's possibility of protecting his intellectual property rights are good under Danish legislation.

*The law of trade marks* The Danish Trademark Act 1959 deals with registered as well as unregistered trade marks and provides essentially identical protection for both groups. The scope of the Act is not limited to the classical trade marks, but also includes distinctive signs regarding services (service marks) as well as get-up and the like. Trade marks may consist of figures, words, or combinations of words, including slogans, letters or numbers, or of the get-up or packing of goods.

Trade mark rights are established first of all through registration with the Danish Trademark Register. The procedures of the Trademark Register provide a good certainty that the mark is legal and at the same time provide evidence of its priority. A trade mark right may, however, also be established without any registration, namely through use.

It should be noted that the Act permits references to the trade mark of another party when selling spare parts and accessories, provided reference is made in a way which does not convey the incorrect impression that the spare parts originate from the holder of the trade mark. Current practice also permits a reference to trade marks belonging to other parties as a part of comparative advertising.

Contrary to what has become common in most countries, Danish law has no user requirements for registered trade marks. In other words, the right exists so long as the registration is maintained. Nor is there any prohibition against a defensive registration of trade marks or other types of registration not made with a view to a current or envisaged use.

Registered trade marks are valid for ten years from the day on which the application was submitted. Registration may be renewed for ten years at a time. Trade mark rights may, however, lapse through so-called degeneration. Unregistered trade marks are valid as long as they are in actual use.

The foreign franchisor should note that the trade mark licensee is entitled to have the franchise agreement recorded in the Registry of Trademarks. In order to avoid unwanted publication of the franchise agreement a franchisor should always make sure that any recording of licence rights is made in accordance with the franchisor's instructions.

It should be noted that the Registration of Business Names Act 1989 supplements the Trademark Act and provides a related protection for the trade name used by a franchisor.

## Real estate and leasing

The Danish market for real property is quite elaborately regulated. However, recent changes in the legislation have loosened the regulations regarding business properties. A business property is one or more separately registered properties in respect of which the public authorities have granted permission for commercial use. The individual properties may be purchased and sold freely and mortgaged separately.

The Rental Act 1979 embodies the main part of the legislation regarding letting of real property. A number of amendments have been made recently, and promulgation order No. 129 of 21 December 1988 regarding the adjustment of rent should especially be noted.

The fixing of rent is in principle governed by the market and therefore free except that the rent may be adjusted every four years only. If the landlord demands an increase of the rent with reference to the fact that the rent is lower than the market rent, then such part of the increase as exceeds 20% of the rent applying at the time of the notice must be distributed evenly over four years.

The mentioned promulgation order also provides for a number of formal requirements which must be closely observed when notifying rent increases, and the landlord has the onus of proof that the rent demand is consistent with the market rent, i.e. the rent for a typical number of comparable leaseholds existing in the neighbourhood or area.

In connection with the lease of commercial premises it is customary to incorporate an automatic rent adjustment clause into the lease, either at a predetermined percentage rate (typically 3–4%) or directly linked to the development in the Danish wage regulating index. Such clauses do not rule out any notification of rent increases in step with the development of the market.

The increased cost of land taxes, water, electricity, sewage, etc. automatically releases a corresponding rent increase.

It should be noted that a commercial tenant is entitled to demand a reduction of the rent, if he can show that the rent for the premises is significantly higher than the market rent.

On and off there has been legislation calling for a temporary freezing of rents for commercial leaseholds. The most recent legislation to that effect expired in 1988.

The Rental Act allows the landlord to terminate a leasehold with one year's notice, if the landlord intends to use the premises for his own purposes. In case of commercial leaseholds it is therefore customary for the tenant to reserve the right to a period of non-terminability, typically ten years. If the franchisor is also landlord, note should be made of section 84 C of the Rental Act, which expressly forbids a landlord to terminate a rental agreement when the premises are used for a specific business, and the landlord wishes to use the premises for the same type of business. It has been argued that this restriction does not apply to franchise arrangements, but there is no solution to this conflict in existing case law.

Under the rental legislation the commercial tenant is not entitled to substitute another tenant in his place, except as specifically agreed between the parties. It is therefore customary for the parties to stipulate a right of assignment on the part of the tenant. In the Copenhagen Metropolitan Area and other urban areas in particular the rights to commercial leaseholds are often bought and sold for substantial amounts. If the tenant has been granted a right of assignment, such amount will accrue to him entirely.

Stamp duty and the traditional registration fee payable upon the registration when purchasing real estate currently amounts to 1.2% of the nominal amount of the purchase price, subject to a minimum corresponding to the rateable value of the property. If the property is to be mortgaged as well, the stamp duty amounts to 1.5% of the nominal amount of the mortgage. The costs incidental to the purchase of real property as well as any mortgaging desired by the purchaser are normally for the purchaser's account. The costs of a change of tenant, including stamp duty on the lease and the fee payable for the drawing up of the new lease, are normally for the new tenant's account.

The international franchisor should be aware that the Danish regulations regarding the use of signs on house facades are tightening considerably. Furthermore, many buildings in the city centres are listed, which can make it very difficult for the franchisor to adapt the facade and the premises to suit his system. There is a trend towards greater concentration of retail outlets in big shopping centres outside the cities.

## Foreigners working or establishing a business in Denmark

Citizens of EC countries who want to work in Denmark do not require a work permit. Within three months after arrival in Denmark, however, they must apply for a residence permit from the Chief of Police in the district where they live. A permit of residence is granted when proof of employment and identification is given.

Citizens of the Nordic countries do not require work or residence permits.

Citizens of countries outside the EC and the Nordic countries must apply at a Danish consulate for work and residence permits prior to employment in Denmark. It is quite difficult to obtain permits in this instance, and the applicant must be able to prove that he possesses special skills that are not available locally. Foreign franchisors should note that permit of stay in work is normally, with reference to this rule, granted to staff seconded for training purposes. A permit is very often limited to the period of time needed for the training of local franchisees.

There are no special arrangements or concessions for foreign nationals apart from the tax concession mentioned in the chapter on tax and financial matters. Foreign citizens contribute to and are entitled to social benefits and health care on the same basis as Danish citizens.

There are no restrictions on the number of foreign employees of a Danish company.

## Foreign investments

Denmark encourages foreign investments, and no permission is necessary to invest in practically any field of commerce and industry. Denmark offers free access to virtually the entire Western European market and has strong ties with Eastern Europe.

There are no special opportunities for foreign franchisors in the way of special incentives, etc., but, on the other hand, a foreign franchisor has exactly the same rights and obligations as a Danish company. Repatriation of profits and capital is easy. Foreign exchange control has been abolished, which makes the movement of capital entirely free, except that all transfers from Denmark of more than DKK 60 000 must be reported to the National Bank of Denmark.

The foreign franchisor should be aware that the Danish government puts high emphasis on environmental protection, both internally regarding safety and other matters and externally regarding pollution control, the use of signs in the open landscape, etc.

## Termination

There are no specific regulations in Danish legislation dealing with termination of franchise agreements. Furthermore, there is no case law relating to termination of franchise agreements. To determine whether a termination of a franchise arrangement is lawful, one has to examine and compare the individual contract with the regulations of Danish general contract law.

In dealing with agency and distribution agreements the courts have established as a firm practice that the termination notice should be fair – in many cases from three to six months – and that the agent or distributor is entitled to compensation, if he in good faith has invested in equipment, business premises or the like in order to carry on the business. At present there are no clear indications in existing case law that agents or distributors are entitled to compensation for goodwill, even in cases where it is evident that the producer after the termination obtains direct access to the customers of the agent or distributor. It is likely, however, that Danish law will soon contain rules on goodwill compensation for agents, when the EC Directive on Agents is incorporated in Danish law.

The international franchisor should also carefully vet any clauses in the franchise agreement regarding termination for cause.

Danish law in principle accepts free choice of law, but in determining which law should apply to the contract, the international franchisor should carefully examine the possibilities of enforcing a foreign judgment against a Danish master franchisor or franchisee. There are currently a number of cases pending in the Danish courts where franchisors are trying to recover up-front fees. It is, however, likely that the majority of these cases will be settled out of court.

## Employment laws

Salary relationships between employer and employee are governed by the Employees Act of 30 August 1971, and by the so-called Main Agreement of 31 October 1973, between the Danish Employers' Confederation and the Danish Federation of Trade Unions.

The Salaried Employees' Act concerns more or less all employers. The Act gives the employee a certain minimum protection which cannot be altered by agreement between the employee and the employer to the detriment of the employee. A salaried employee's employment cannot be terminated without observing the minimum notice periods laid down in the Act. Furthermore, salaried employees must receive full salary if absent due to illness. The Employers' and Salaried Employees' Act deals only with some of the obligations of the employees. Questions regarding salary, working conditions, etc. are not governed by the Act but will for most employers and employees be regulated through the relevant collective agreement on pay, if both the employer and employee are members of respectively an employers' association and a labour organization.

The Employers' and Salaried Employees' Act defines a salaried employee as an employee who is employed for a minimum period of 15 hours per week, has to obey the employer's instructions, and is occupied within one of the following functions:

1    Retail or office work, including sales personnel

2    Technical assistance (not factory work)

It is common in employment contracts to agree that the rules of the Act shall apply to the employer–employee relationship, even in cases where it is not evident that the regulations of the Act would apply, if not agreed between the parties.

The main collective agreements are negotiated every fourth year between the Danish Employers' Confederation and the Danish Federation of Trade Unions, if necessary with the assistance of the official mediator. The two federations negotiate wages, working conditions and other matters. Every second year negotiations take place between the two parties on wages.

Labour disputes that cannot be solved by preliminary negotiation meetings and that result in a strike or lock-out are referred to a labour relations court whose decisions are final. Punitive fines are imposed for breach of contract. The collective bargaining system has a long and strong tradition, and labour unrest is virtually non-existent when the employer and employees are members of their respective federations.

All companies with more than 35 employees must have a council through which the co-operation between employers and employees should be maintained and improved through information and discussion.

## TAX AND FINANCIAL CONSIDERATIONS

### The corporate tax system

Corporate income, including capital gains, is subject to corporate income tax. Dividends are, in principle, subject to income tax charged on the shareholders.

However, the Danish taxation system contains a number of extremely advantageous regulations regarding double tax relief and tax relief for foreign trading. These regulations mean in practice that a Danish holding company can obtain tax relief in respect of income from foreign business operations, including those of jointly taxed subsidiaries. The relief is commonly referred to as 'relief for foreign trading' and amounts to 50% of the Danish corporation tax levied on the net taxable income of foreign branches and jointly taxed foreign subsidiaries.

The corporate tax system applies to public limited companies (Aktieselskaber), private limited companies (Anpartsselskaber), other entities with limited liability, co-operative societies, funds, and associations.

A Danish resident company registered in Denmark is subject to company tax on its worldwide profits, including capital gains.

A non-resident company which carries on trade in Denmark through a permanent establishment, or is entitled to a share of the profits of a permanent establishment, is subject to tax on all income arising through or received from the permanent establishment. Non-resident companies are furthermore subject to tax on income from real estate in Denmark owned by the non-resident.

A company's taxable income is determined on the accounts prepared on a historical cost basis and in accordance with internationally acceptable accounting principles. Tax accounting generally determines costs and income when legally incurred, but with few exceptions the accrual principle is acceptable. Adjustments to book accounting profits frequently include non-allowable expenses, depreciation, reserve for bad debts, warranty claims, etc. The Danish tax laws and the provisions of the double-taxation treaties assume that sales and purchases between affiliated companies in Denmark and between Danish and foreign affiliates are carried out on an arm's length basis.

In determining the taxable income the company is permitted to allow for depreciation on buildings and land, and machinery and equipment.

All profits on the sale of goodwill are tax free. Goodwill cannot be amortized for tax purposes and a loss on the sale of goodwill is not tax-deductible.

Profits and losses arising from the sale of know-how and rights such as patents and trade marks are computed as the difference between the sales proceeds and the written-down value for tax purposes and generally included in special income.

Interest income receivable is considered taxable income.

Dividends received from companies in which the recipient holds less than 25% are subject to company tax. A special tax credit applies.

There are special rules regarding intercompany dividends which effectively mean that dividends received from Danish companies, in which a company holds a 25% or more interest, are exempt from company tax.

Other forms of income, such as stock dividends, royalties, and service fees, are all treated as taxable income.

Generally, all expenses are deductible if they are incurred in order to 'obtain, secure and maintain' the income of the company.

## Taxation of foreign companies

The extent of the Danish tax liability of a non-resident company is determined by any existing double-taxation treaty or, if no treaty exists, by provisions similar to the ones in the OECD Model Treaty. In general, the treaties limit the taxation of industrial and commercial activities in Denmark to the profits attributable to a permanent establishment in the country. Where a non-resident company is taxable, the computation of taxes on the profit of the permanent establishment corresponds in general to the computation for a Danish resident company.

Importing goods to a Danish customer without an agent does not create a permanent establishment and profit is not subject to Danish income tax.

The business carried out by an unrelated agent or a sole agent does not generally constitute a permanent establishment of the foreign company.

Employees of foreign corporations carrying out sales activities in Denmark may constitute a permanent establishment if they have the power to conclude contracts on behalf of the employer. If the approval of the foreign employer is a formality only, the sales activities may constitute a permanent establishment.

A branch operation of a foreign company is subject to Danish company tax on any trading income arising directly or indirectly from the branch.

An administrative office or the maintenance of a fixed place of business solely for the purpose of purchasing goods, advertising and similar auxiliary services would not generally result in any tax liability in Denmark.

## Dividends, royalties, and interest payments

Dividends are subject to a 30% withholding tax or a lower tax treaty rate.

Payments of royalties from Danish sources to a recipient abroad are subject to a withholding tax. It should be noted that this tax applies to industrial royalties, licences and use of know-how, but not to certain types of royalty income from copyrights.

The royalty tax is 30%. However, in many double-taxation treaties Denmark has wholly or partly waived taxation of royalties from sources in Denmark. A lower tax treaty withholding tax rate can be used, if certain reporting formalities are observed. This eliminates the need for a refund claim.

There is no withholding tax on interest and pure service fees. Payments for royalties, interest, management services, technical assistance, use of know-how, etc. are tax-deductible provided they are commercially justifiable. With regard to royalties, and possibly also service fees, the tax authorities may well contend that such payments to a foreign parent corporation represent hidden dividends, unless it can be shown that the payments have been made on an arm's length basis.

## Value added tax

The system of value added tax (Mervædiafgift, Moms) used in Denmark is virtually identical to the systems used in the rest of the EC. Denmark has harmonized its VAT legislation to agreed EC standards, but certain differences still exist. The current Danish VAT standard rate is 22% and there are no reduced or luxury rates.

Business entities selling taxable goods or services (including branches or agencies of non-Danish companies) must register for VAT if they have an annual taxable turnover of more than DKK 10 000.

A representative office of a foreign company may apply for voluntary registration in order to obtain a refund of VAT on local purchases of goods or services. Groups of companies may register as one entity even if they are not owned by the same owner.

The VAT Act lists a number of business activities which are exempted from VAT and therefore do not require registration. The most important are hospital, medical and dental care, education, insurance, banking and other financial activities and travel agency services. Certain other goods and services are also exempt from VAT.

For certain items recovery of VAT is not allowed. The main categories are: purchase, lease and running costs of passenger cars; hotel expenses, meals and entertainment; and gifts and prices given for advertising purposes.

Non-residents are liable to register as VAT taxpayers if they sell taxable goods or services within Denmark to a value of more than DKK 10 000 per annum. The foreign company must appoint a local representative who becomes liable for payment of the VAT. A non-resident who exports goods to Denmark from abroad will not be required to register if the sale is made directly to a Danish importer, as in this case the VAT will be paid by the importer. A foreign franchisor who enters into a direct lease with a Danish franchisee for equipment should be aware of this situation. Royalties paid from a Danish franchisee to a foreign franchisor are exempt from VAT, whereas service fees in some instances are subject to VAT.

## Other indirect taxes

The foreign franchisor should be aware of the existence of a number of other indirect taxes such as stamp duties, capital investment tax, employers' tax, excises, etc.

Stamp duties are payable on many types of commercial and legal documents whose 'leading and principal object' determines type and amount of charge. The rate is either a fixed rate or an *ad valorem* rate. Deeds are stamped based on the nominal purchase price of the property, but the stamp tax on real estate cannot be based on an amount lower than the latest available public assessment. Generally, it should be noted that documents must be stamped if they are executed in Denmark or if they relate to property in Denmark. The international franchisor should be aware that signing of legal documents outside Denmark does not automatically exempt the transaction from Danish stamp duty.

There are two main forms of transfer tax. The first is the capital investment tax, which is described above in the section about various business forms. In conformity with an EC directive on capital investment tax, capital investment tax of 1% must be paid on capital raised by Danish companies in a number of cases such as on formation of the company, increase of net equity, etc.

The second kind of transfer tax is the share transfer tax, which determines that a tax of 1% of the market value is payable on the sale or exchange of Danish or foreign shares. Certain securities fall outside the scope of the share transfer tax, especially convertible bonds and parts certificates in private limited companies.

If one party or both parties are resident in Denmark, the tax is payable even though the agreement has been made abroad. If the seller is resident abroad, the Danish purchaser is liable for the tax.

A special employers' tax – the labour market contribution tax – at a rate of 2.5% is levied on the basis of turnover less export sales and Danish purchases. All businesses must be registered for this tax with the customs authorities. Certain businesses, however, are not subject to the tax.

## Excise duties

Excise duties, which in most cases are extremely high, are levied on a variety of commodities, including beer, wines and spirits, mineral waters, tobacco, chocolate, tea and coffee, records, electric light bulbs, matches, cigarette lighters, playing cards, motor fuels, etc. Excise duties are levied on the producer or importer and become due when the commodity is sold to the retailer. Furthermore, there are taxes on heating oil, gas, coal, and electric power. Real estate is also taxed, and the rates vary considerably from one municipality to another.

## Taxation of individuals

Danish tax legislation distinguishes between full tax liability for residents and limited tax liability for non-resident individuals. An individual subject to full tax liability in Denmark is subject to tax on income and capital gains on his world-wide income. Furthermore, residents are liable to wealth tax and other taxes. An individual subject to limited tax liability is only taxed on income and capital gains derived from sources in Denmark and wealth tax is only imposed on net assets effectively connected with a Danish activity. The main criteria for full and limited tax liability are residence, length of stay, place of work, employer's residence, and type of income. Citizenship does not affect Danish tax liability.

As salary income is subject to a tax rate of up to 68%, this distinction could become very important for the franchisor who plans to second employees, e.g. in connection with a joint venture operation.

Interest income is subject to a tax rate of 50–56%, and deductions generally have a tax value of approximately 50%. All interest paid on mortgages, loans, etc. is deductible against ordinary taxable income.

If an international franchisor assigns an individual to work in Denmark, it may be possible to avoid Danish income tax in the year of arrival and the year of departure according to a special 183-day rule in the relevant double-taxation treaty. However, it is necessary that the employee is considered resident abroad.

For a short-term secondment of an employee it may be possible to avoid Danish taxation of passive income if the seconded person is considered as residing abroad in accordance with the provisions in the double-taxation treaty.

The employee's investments in shares, bonds and real estate should be reviewed before the arrival in Denmark, as disposal of shares and real estate may be taxable if it takes place during the secondment period in Denmark.

Great care should be taken when structuring the remuneration package for the employee, as some fringe benefits are heavily taxed and others not at all.

## Social security obligations

Denmark has an extremely comprehensive social security system which includes old age pensions, health care and allowances for children, unemployment and disability financed out of public funds. Further, there are supplementary old age pension and employees' guarantee funds, the former financed by contributions from employees mainly out of public funds. The social security system covers all employers and employees, including foreigners working in Denmark.

Social security contributions are, as mentioned, mainly publicly funded. None of the social security costs are directly financed by the employer. However, as mentioned under indirect taxation, a new tax was introduced with effect from 1 January 1988, namely the labour market contribution tax, calculated as 2.5% of Danish sales less Danish purchases.

According to statistics from the Danish Employers' Confederation, the total labour cost for salaried employees in the first quarter of 1989 was 117.2%, with annual working income equalling 100% salary during holiday and public holidays, and special holiday allowance equalling 15.9%, and various indirect labour costs, such as industrial accident insurance, approximately 0.2%.

All employers are required by law to take out legal accident insurance with a recognized insurance company, a number of which are owned by the employers' federations.

### Investment incentives

Denmark offers no special tax incentives to attract foreign investors. Furthermore, the present government's incentive policy is very limited and is mainly based on the wish to encourage investment in specific regions, but not within specific industry sectors or activities. General investment incentives are limited to research and development projects aimed at new products, production methods or services.

From a financial point of view it is extremely beneficial for a foreign franchisor to establish a holding company in Denmark. The main benefit is that it is possible for a Danish holding company to have joint taxation with Danish as well as foreign subsidiaries. The dividend from a wholly owned subsidiary is normally tax free for the holding company. Furthermore, a special foreign release can be obtained by a Danish company doing business abroad. The relief reduces the normal company tax rate from 40% to 25% on income subject to this rule.

Denmark is also in the unique position of having entered into double-taxation agreements with a number of Eastern European countries and the Soviet Union, which makes Denmark an ideal base for joint ventures with the Eastern European countries.

For franchisors within the food sector Denmark offers a unique opportunity as a supply source, as all agricultural products produced in Denmark are cleared for import to traditionally difficult markets, like Japan and the USA.

# CHAPTER 7
# FRANCE

*Gérard Sautereau*

## AN OVERVIEW OF FRANCHISING IN FRANCE

The word 'franchise' was first used in France in the Middle Ages. At that time, a 'franchise' was the name given to the agreement between the king and the town council under which the town council was granted certain rights in the management of its activities and in its relations with the town and the state. Such franchised towns were called 'Ville Franche'.

Franchising started in 1929 as a legal vehicle for distribution with the Pingouin Company, and the market is shared today by 600 franchisors and 33 000 franchisees, most of them being in the service and fashion sectors.

Government attitudes towards franchising have always been very positive. Franchising is viewed as a way of expansion for small and medium-sized businesses and, as a consequence, a benefit for the economy in general.

The banking system has the same positive view on franchising. Although some banks (i.e. Crédit Lyonnais) are more specialized in the distribution of loans to the franchise business, the banks in general are giving franchisees short- and medium-term loans, with or without personal or secured guarantees.

The most active franchise federation is the French Franchise Federation (FFF), established in 1971 as a federation of franchise networks represented by franchisors. The FFF claims to have more than 100 members representing 70% of the franchise networks doing business in France and 80% of the networks exporting abroad. The FFF was very active in the adoption by Parliament of the new pre-sales disclosure law of 31 December 1989, which imposes new obligations on franchisors at a precontractual level. It was actively involved in the adoption of its new 'Code of Ethics' and of the new 'Code of Ethics' of the European Franchise Federation (of which it is an active member) applicable from 1 January 1991.

The FFF helped establish ten years ago the Salon International de la Franchise (International Franchise Trade Show), which takes place every year at the end of March in Paris and which is the largest of its kind in Europe.

## STRUCTURE OF FRENCH VENTURE – BUSINESS ENTITIES

### Types and formation of business entities

*Commerçant*  A person may do business under his or her own name after being registered at the Registrar of Companies as a merchant (*commerçant*) (Article 1 of the Commercial Code); the personal liabilities incurred and the fiscal and social costs are so high that this is not advisable.

*Groupement d'Intérêt Economique*  There is no such thing under French law as a 'joint venture agreement' within the Anglo-Saxon meaning of the word. The closest would be the *Groupement d'Intérêt Economique* (GIE or Economic Interest Grouping) or the *Groupement d'Intérêt Economique Européen* (GIEE or European Economic Interest Grouping), which France introduced on 13 June 1989.

Neither the GIE nor the GIEE type of organization is consistent with the management of business activities as, although they may be incorporated with no minimum share capital, their activity must have a direct link with the activity of their members. The disadvantage lies with the unlimited joint and several liability of the partners.

*Corporation*  The preferred course will be the establishment of either a corporation or of a branch office.

French law distinguishes between companies with civil objects – essentially in the agricultural and building sectors which are not vehicles for business activities – and companies with commercial objects, all governed by Law no. 66–537 of 24 July 1966 and Decree no. 67–236 of 23 March 1967:

1    'Société en nom collectif' (SNC)

2    'Société en commandite simple' (SCS)

3    'Société en commandite par actions' (SCA)

4    'Société à responsabilité limitée' (SàRL)

5    'Société anonyme' (SA)

which all have full legal status. Other specialized company forms do exist but are not widely used by business persons.

### The 'société en nom collectif' (SNC) or general partnership

This type of company is formed by two or more persons who wish to have the legal capacity to act as merchants, with no minimum or maximum amount of share capital and no minimum or maximum par value of shares. The shares are not negotiable to third parties without the consent of all shareholders. The shareholders are jointly and severally liable for all losses without limitation of time. One or more of the shareholders is or are appointed managing director (*gérant*) for an indefinite period of time.

An SNC form is usually adopted by small family businesses as it is rather easy to manage, or by large companies which do not want their activities to be known to competitors (no publication of accounts, no appointment of auditors). The shares in an SNC are rarely transferred. The difficulty, of course, lies with the joint and several liability of the shareholders without limitation of time.

An SNC is not subject to corporation tax, unless it elects to be. In the absence of such election, profits are subjected to income tax on the share of each shareholder in such profits.

### The 'société en commandite simple' (SCS) or limited partnership

This form of company is a form of partnership with two categories: one or more general partners who actually run the business and are jointly and severally liable for the losses without limitation of time, and one or more limited partners who are only liable for the losses up to the amount of their share in the capital. The rules of the share capital and par value of shares are identical to those of the 'société en nom collectif'.

This form of company is not widely used due to the extreme complexity of its management. The partners are taxed on their share of the profits.

### The 'société en commandite par actions' (SCA) or partnership limited by shares

This form of company, which is not widely used, is very similar to the SCS with the difference that:

1    Its shares are negotiable.

2    The company may be quoted on the stock exchange without the share-holders losing control of the company.

### The 'société à responsabilité limitée' (SàRL) or limited liability company

This form of company is widely used. It is incorporated with a minimum of two shareholders. There is a minimum fully paid-up share capital of FF 50 000 with a minimum share par value of FF 100. The shares may not be sold to third parties without the shareholders' prior consent. They may not be quoted on the stock exchange.

The SàRL is more appropriate for small businesses because decisions are made by the legal representative ('gérant') of the company, who is elected by a 51% majority at a shareholders' general meeting. There is only one compulsory general meeting per year of the shareholders to approve the financial accounts and decide on distribution of the profits. It is possible to restrain the powers of the 'gérant' but such restraint does not affect third parties dealing with the company. The 'gérant' is usually not entitled to sell or mortgage the properties of the company without the unanimous consent of the shareholders. He may be discharged at any time by a majority vote of the shareholders.

Most decisions are taken in general meetings by a majority of 51% of the shareholders. Some decisions relating to changes in the by-laws require a majority of 75% of the shareholders.

The sale of the shares attracts a tax on the value of the purchase price of 4.8% payable by the purchaser, and a copy of the transfer of shares has to be filed with the Registrar of Companies. Third parties are then aware of changes in the control of the company.

The shareholders' liability is limited to the nominal amount of the shares held.

The appointment of an auditor is mandatory when two of the following three thresholds are achieved:

1    Total of gross assets exceeds FF 10 million.

2    Turnover (excluding taxes) exceeds FF 20 million.

3    Average number of employees in any accounting period is 50.

*The 'société anonyme' (SA) or joint stock company*
This form of company is also widely used. It requires a minimum of seven shareholders. Sufficient shares must be issued to equal a nominal share capital of FF 250 000, of which only 25% of the nominal capital needs to be paid up at the time of the incorporation provided that the balance of 75% is paid within five years of the date of incorporation.

The SA is governed by a board comprising a minimum of three and a maximum of 12 directors appointed for three- or six-year terms by the shareholders in general meetings. The board then appoints the 'Président du Conseil d'Administration' (CEO) who is usually also the 'Directeur Général' (general manager). He is then usually known as the 'Président Directeur Général' (PDG), and acts in the name of the company. The PDG is deemed to have full powers to bind the company in dealing with third parties, although the by-laws may limit most of his powers *vis-à-vis* the shareholders.

Most decisions are taken by the board. The shareholders meet annually in general meetings to approve the fiscal year accounts and the distribution of profits. The meeting, to be effective, requires not less than 51% of the issued shares to be represented in a quorum, and decisions are made by a majority vote of those present unless they involve a change in the by-laws, when a two-thirds majority is required.

The transfer of the shares of an SA is free of taxes on the sale price and is not published. A transfer of shares to third parties may or may not be subject to the shareholders' prior approval, depending upon its by-laws.

The appointment of an auditor is mandatory for a six-year term which may be extended.

The SA may be governed by a directorate and supervised by a council of supervision.

*Branch operation*
It is possible for a foreign franchisor to operate through a branch ('succursale') in France subject to compliance with registration requirements which are similar to those which apply to the incorporation of a new company.

A branch is not a legal entity by itself and the foreign company will remain responsible under French law for any problem which might occur (labour contracts, damages, etc.). The branch will pay corporate taxes on its profits in France, exactly like a French company. The sale of the branch is treated as sale of assets ('fonds de commerce') and is subject to taxation on the sale price at the rate of 0% under FF 100 000, 7% between FF 100 000 and 300 000, and 14.2% over FF 300 000.

If it is decided to incorporate a company to take over business of the branch at a later stage, a tax of 1.5% or 11.4% of the net value of the branch assets at the time of incorporation will be payable.

**Statutory requirements**
Incorporating a company in France requires:

1    The signature by the shareholders or the partners of 'statuts', a written document which contains both the by-laws and the articles of incorporation. This document stipulates the rights and obligations of the shareholders or partners, and the purpose of the company, and acknowledges the previously made payment of the capital and the issue of shares.

2    These documents together with the address of its registered office and the appointment of a legal representative are filed with the Registrar of Companies, who in due course will issue a certificate of incorporation. The corporation will only exist as a legal entity upon the issue of the certificate of incorporation.

3    The maximum term of a company is 99 years, which may be renewed for further similar terms.

## LEGAL CONSIDERATIONS

### General legislation applying to franchising
Until 1988, there was no domestic or EC legislation on franchising. Franchising agreements and litigation on franchising were dealt with according to the provisions of the Civil Code and the law of contract.

However, France was the first country in Europe to adopt on 31 December 1989 a law on pre-sales disclosure (at the active request of the French Franchise

Federation), which seems to have been well accepted by the franchising community in France.

The French Franchise Federation has adopted its 'Code of Ethics', which is not binding on parties to an agreement unless they elect for it to be so. It is binding for franchisors who are members of the FFF.

The European Franchise Federation (of which the French Franchise Federation is a member) has adopted a new 'Code of Ethics', which is applicable from 1 January 1991. Although this Code is not legally binding (except for franchisor members of the local franchise federations), its recommendations – which are not applicable between a franchisor and his master franchisee – should be taken into account. The main point of interest is the necessity to have a copy of the franchise agreement executed in the language of the country where the franchisee is doing business.

Franchise agreements have become more and more complex and special care should, of course, be taken *vis-à-vis* other aspects of law related to franchising, namely:

1    Law no. 57–298 of 11 March 1957 on intellectual property

2    Law no. 64–1360 of 31 December 1964 and Law no. 91–7 of 4 January 1991 on trade marks

3    Law no. 68–1 of 2 January 1968 on patents as amended by Law no. 90–1062 of 26 November 1990

4    Law-decree no. 86–1283 of 1 December 1986 and Decree no. 86–1309 of 29 December 1986 on fair competition and price regulation

5    Regulation 4087/88/EC of 30 November 1988 on the applicability of Article 85.3 of the Treaty to certain categories of franchising agreements, applicable from 1 February 1989 until 31 December 1999

6    Article 1 of Law no. 89–1008 of 31 December 1989 on pre-sales disclosure and Decree no. 91–337 of 4 April 1991.

Reference should also be made to all multi- and bilateral agreements and conventions (tax and social security treaties and treaties on establishment) to which France is a party. It should be taken into account that all EC legislation is directly applicable in France at the same time and under the same conditions as in any other EC member state.

The franchise agreement need not be in writing, although then there may be problems of proof. Invariably a written agreement will be entered into, and will be subject to all the provisions of the Civil Code relating to agreements.

The only specific law applicable to franchising is a precontract disclosure requirement contained in Article 1 of the Law of 31 December 1989, nicknamed the 'loi Doubin' (from the name of the Minister of Commerce who introduced it to Parliament), implemented by the Decree of 4 April 1991 and applicable to all new agreements entered into since 8 April 1991. The text reads as follows:

> 'Any person who grants to another person the license to use a trade name, a trade mark or a logo, subject to the commitment of exclusivity or quasi exclusivity for the exercise of the latter's activities shall, prior to the execution of any agreement negotiated in the two parties' mutual interest, furnish to the other party a document giving honest information permitting the other party to make an informed decision.
>
> This document, the contents of which shall be provided for by a decree shall contain, among other things, information on the age and the experience of the Licensor's business, the status and the possibilities of growth of the Market, the importance of the retail network, the term, renewal, termination and conditions of transfer of the agreement and the scope of any exclusivities granted.
>
> When payment of any monies shall be demanded prior to the execution of the agreement hereabove mentioned, especially in order to be granted the rights of exclusivity of a Territory, the undertakings made in consideration of such payment shall be described in writing as well as the reciprocal obligations of the parties in case of forfeiture.
>
> The document provided for under paragraph 1 as well as the proposed agreement shall be delivered at least twenty days before the execution of the agreement or, if the case arises, before payment of the monies described at the paragraph hereabove.'

No case law has been rendered yet, but the following comments may be made:

1   The Law is applicable to the precontractual period of all forms of distribution and licensing agreements (distributorship, agency, etc.) and not only to franchise agreements, when exclusive rights are granted.

2   This Law does not supersede the Regulation 4087/88/EC of 30 November 1988 on the applicability of Article 85.1 of the Treaty to categories of franchising agreements.

3   The Law is applicable whenever the use of a trade mark, a trade name or a logo is granted. It then calls for the prior application in France by the licensor for the trade mark which will be used.

4   It is applicable to all franchisors, whether individuals, corporations or branches, whatever their country of origin and whatever legal vehicle is

used to enter the French market (joint venture, wholly owned subsidiary, master franchise agreement) as long as they are establishing a network of franchisees.

5    There is no requirement for any proof of disclosure to any third party and no agency has been established for that purpose. If a franchisee complains it will be for the franchisor to demonstrate that all documents, the required information and drafts of agreement were furnished 20 days prior to the execution of the agreement. Letters, faxes, telexes, etc. are viewed as evidence under French law. According to the general principles of French contract law, a court could enter judgment calling for early termination of the agreement if the law is not complied with and the franchisee can claim damages.

6    There is no model for the 'document' providing the 'information'. However, the Law lists the information to be given in writing by the franchisor as set out above.

It is advisable to include a clause in the franchise agreement containing an acknowledgement by the franchisee that all the requirements of the Law have been met and to attach copies of the information disclosed to the agreement itself.

## Competition law

Law-decree of 1 December 1986 and Decree no. 86–1309 of 29 December 1986 contain the provisions of French antitrust law.

In principle, all agreements which may prohibit, restrict or restrain free competition in one sector or any market, and any abusive exploitation of a dominant position by an enterprise or group of enterprises in the French market, are prohibited. The exploitation of a position of economic dependence is prohibited.

The Council on Competition and the Court of Appeals of Paris enforce such laws by injunctions, fines and/or other penalties.

Article 7 of the Law Decree prohibits any concerted actions, agreements or tacit or expressed alliances which could restrain competition in a market by:

1    Restricting access to the market

2    Price fixing

3    Restriction or control of production, investment or technological progress

4    Division of sources of supplies

Price fixing is prohibited, but court cases have decided, especially in the ranchising field, that a franchisor could recommend prices so as to protect his network's image and its customers.

Selective distribution is not prohibited by Article 7 of the Law-decree when:

1    It is required by the supplier's choice of strategy.

2    It meets objective criteria.

The Council on Competition has decided, for instance, that cosmetics manufacturers were able to impose certain obligations on their retailers for the purpose of storage of goods, sales personnel and the keeping of a minimum inventory and could then refuse to enter into agreements with, or could terminate agreements with, retailers who did not want to comply with such obligations.

Abuse of a dominant position in the French market or a substantial part of it or abuse of a situation of economic dependence on such a market by another enterprise for which there is no equivalent alternative is prohibited by Article 8.

The Minister of Economy may give negative clearance to certain categories of agreement by decree.

Although the case has not been raised yet, a franchise agreement falling either under the general exemption of EC Regulation of 30 November 1988 or under the individual exemption provided for by such Regulation would be legally binding in France even if some of its clauses were deemed to be illegal by French law. EC law supersedes all domestic laws passed by Parliament.

## Liability of franchisor

The basic principles of the Civil Code allow a claim for damages on the basis of either:

1    Contractual liability against the supplier of services, or goods with latent defects (Article 1146).

2    Tortious liability, when a contract does not exist between the parties (Article 1382). Fault will be presumed by the courts.

The Consumers Protection Law no. 78-23 of 10 January 1978 allows the government to prohibit or control the manufacture, importation, offer, sale, distribution, possession, labelling, packaging and use of products which are dangerous to the public under normal use. The same procedures and prohibitions are applicable to services.

Legal and regulatory measures are taken to prevent consumer accidents. Consumer organizations may act as parties in civil or criminal cases against manufacturers or distributors.

Criminal fraud and falsification legislation allows seizure by the authorities of products which present a serious and imminent danger to consumers, or danger of unfair trade or damage to the interests of consumers, if an order is obtained from the President of the First Instance Civil Court.

Specific legislation deals with the labelling and or importation of goods, agricultural or industrial products, or in order to prohibit pre-established contracts and abusive credit clauses.

The French government has filed on 23 April 1990 with Parliament a bill to implement in French law the EC product liability directive no. 85/374 of 25 July 1985.

As far as franchising is concerned, the liability of the franchisor may be sought either:

1    By the franchisee acting on the breach of any of the franchisor's obligations under the franchise agreement, or

2    By the franchisee as a party to a commercial agreement (sale of products by the franchisor)

According to the French Civil Code rules, any action brought by the client of a franchisee directly against the franchisor would be dismissed on the grounds that there never was any oral or written contract between the franchisor and the plaintiff unless such plaintiff may prove direct 'management' of the franchisee's operation by the franchisor.

## Industrial and intellectual property

*Trade mark law* There are no differences between a trade mark and a service mark, which are both protected by law. French Law no. 64–1360 of 31 December 1964 will not be applicable after 28 December 1991, when Law no. 91–7 of 4 January 1991 on trade marks (implementing EC Directive 89/104 of 21 December 1988) will come into force. All applications filed before 28 December 1991 will be reviewed and granted according to the rules of the Law of 31 December 1964 as amended.

French Law no. 64–1360 of 31 December 1964 makes it mandatory for the franchisor to have a registered trade mark, or to have applied to register a trade mark before doing any business. The trade mark, the use of which is granted by the franchisor to the franchisee, has to be registered in France either under the franchisor's name or, if there is a trade mark licence agreement, under the owner's name with a copy of the licence agreement registered with the Institut National de la Propriété Industrielle (INPI) – a government agency – prior to the execution of any franchise agreement.

French law does not recognize the concept of a trade name which may differ from the corporate name.

A copy of the registration certificate or of the application should be annexed to the franchise agreement, which should include a provision calling for the registration renewal by the franchisor of the trade mark during the course of the agreement.

Trade mark registration may be obtained without showing either previous use of the mark by the applicant or the existence of an established business. A trade mark search is conducted with INPI's data bank, with or without INPI's advice.

The Director of the INPI has the right to refuse an application on technical and/or legal grounds and his decision may, of course, be challenged in court. The Law of 31 December 1964 does provide for forfeiture of all rights in a trade mark which is not publicly and unequivocally exploited without valid excuse for five years preceding challenge in court.

Groups of manufacturers, associations, etc. may register 'collective marks' which may be used by their members to indicate origin, quality or composition of their goods or services.

Under the Law of 31 December 1964, registrations may be obtained by any person or company of any nationality. Registration is valid for ten years and may be renewed indefinitely for any or all of the 42 international classes of 'services' and 'goods' providing that the renewal fees are paid.

According to Article 13 of the Law of 1964, all agreements related to the transfer or the licence of trade marks have to be registered in writing with the Institut National de la Propriété Industrielle, in order to be enforceable against third parties.

The main changes introduced by the Law of 4 January 1991 after 28 December 1991 are as follows:

1    During a two-month period after publication of the application for registration:

   (a)   any person may send written observations to the Director of INPI

   (b)   the applicant for registration of a trade mark previously filed or the owner of a registered trade mark, or the owner of a mark which has a notorious reputation, or the beneficiary of an exclusive right of use, may object to the application in writing to the Director of INPI.

2    Article 11 of the Law provides that the applicant may still ask for the registration of the trade mark if he proves that such registration is necessary for the protection of the mark abroad. If the objection is accepted, the application will then be refused totally or partially and the registration will be cancelled totally or partially.

3    An action for the recovery of property of the trade mark may be commenced by a party who thinks it has rights on such trade mark when such trade mark was registered fraudulently or in breach of a legal or contractual obligation. The statute of limitations is three years from such publication of the application for registration, or 30 years if the applicant is acting in bad faith.

4    Registration renewal may be done only if there are no changes in the sign or logo and no extension of the list of products or services covered by the initial registration of the mark.

5    The owner of a previously registered trade mark may commence an action for infringement of trade mark. Such an action has no legal basis if the use of an infringing mark has been tolerated for five years prior to bringing such action. Upon demand of the owner of the trade mark or the licensee of a trade mark, the customs authorities may stop goods with infringing marks at the border.

6    The invalidity of a trade mark may be requested either by the Public Prosecutor's Office, if the registration has been granted in violation of the law, or by the owner of a previously registered mark, or by the licensee of a trade mark. There are no legal grounds if the mark was registered in good faith and if the use of the mark was permitted without challenge for five years.

Any and all agreements made by a person or a company having its office or place of residence in France whose objects include the sale or the acquisition by a person or a company having its offices or place of residence in another country of rights of industrial property (patents, trade marks, know-how, etc.) have to be filed with the Ministry of Industry within one month after the execution of such agreement by the French party. Such party has to provide once a year before 31 March to the Ministry a list of all financial and intellectual transfers to and from abroad (Decree no. 70–441 of 26 May 1970).

*Trade names* There is no specific legislation calling for the registration or the protection of trade names. A register of all company names is kept by the INPI and a private search should be conducted prior to the incorporation of a company to see whether the proposed name of the company is in use.

Trade mark and trade name infringement includes unlawful copying ('contrefaçon') or imitation ('imitation frauduleuse') of somebody else's registered trade mark or trade name under use in connection with the same or similar goods or services so as to create confusion in the minds of customers or clients. It may be prosecuted in criminal or civil actions and seizure of goods may be ordered ('saisie contrefaçon').

*Copyright law* The Law of 11 March 1957 gives an excellent protection to the author(s) of all written (books) or oral works (video movies, movies, tapes, etc.) as long as they are 'original' works (Articles 1 and 2). This includes the original texts in operational manuals. The title of the work is protected as is the work itself. The author has the exclusive and sole right to exploit his work under whatever form he wishes and to make a profit. This right includes the right of duplication, the right of performance and any other right of reproduction of such work and, of course, the right to oppose any copying, translation or reproduction made without the author's authority.

Protection is granted for the lifetime of the author plus 50 years after the year of his death (or after the year of the death of the last co-author). For works prepared by joint authors, protection is granted for 50 years starting on 1 January of the year following the publication of such work.

It is important to appreciate that any copying or reproduction made without the author's authority is illegal and constitutes by itself the criminal offence of infringement (Article 426 of the Criminal Code) punishable by imprisonment for three months to two years and a fine of FF 6000 to FF 120 000 plus the seizure of the profits made by the infringer and, of course, seizure and destruction of the infringing copies of the work. The copyright owner may elect to take criminal or civil action, to ask for damages against the counterfeiter, with publication of the court decision in the press. Prior to such proceedings, the author may be authorized by the President of the First Instance Civil Court to seize and attach all illicit works and profits.

Some franchise systems include the use of software as part of the know-how licensed to the franchisee. Protection is granted to the author of software under the Law of 3 July 1985 for a 25-year term from the date of creation of such software, with the same being available to a copyright owner of a written work. Any copy of the software other than for back-up purposes is deemed to be counterfeiting (Article 47 of the Law). Further protection is given to the author of semiconductor chips by the Law of 4 November 1987. Registration of the semiconductor may be made with the INPI within two years from the date of its first sale to the public. The ten years' protection commences from the date of such first sale.

Some franchise systems use patents which are the franchisor's property or which he may use under a licence. Inventors who wish to file a patent in France may elect to ask either for:

1    A French patent, valid for 20 years in French territory only (Law no. 68–1 of 2 January 1968 and Law no. 78–742 of 13 July 1978)

2    A European patent, valid for 20 years in the territory of every member state of the Convention of Munich of 5 October 1973

3    An international patent valid for the territory of every member state of the Patent Cooperation Treaty of Washington of 19 June 1970

**Real estate and leasing**
There are two ways to acquire real property in France. Price and scarcity of land makes co-ownership of buildings a very widely used form of acquiring or leasing premises.

*Real estate* The sale of real estate is done through a purchase–sales agreement which must be executed in front of a notary, who has a monopoly from the state on

real estate transactions. Costs of the sale are usually borne by the buyer. Three o
four more certificates must be obtained for the conclusion of the sale. Two of thei
are important:

1    Land tax. This is an annual tax which is payable by the proprietor at the end c
     October and is to be divided pro rata in relation to the period of occupation c
     each of the proprietors.

2    Occupation law. This tax is always due from whoever is occupying the build
     ing on 1 January of the year of the sale. It does not therefore have to be paid b
     the purchaser.

The notary has to carry out all financial formalities after the transfer of the prop
erty. He has two months in which to send a copy of the deed to the Mortgage Regis
try, which will register the property in the name of the purchaser. The transfer wil
be registered at the same time at the Land Registry. Until the change has been reg
istered it is the vendor who will receive notification of land tax which is passed to the
purchaser who is liable for its payment. Of all the formalities to be carried out after
the sale, that of land tax publication at the Mortgage Office is the most important.

The deed of sale will then be returned to the notary with a seal of registration
and a list of mortgages (if any). If this reveals mortgage entries, these will have to be
removed by a deed of discharge. The notary will send the purchaser a certified copy
of the deed received by the Mortgage Registry as well as a copy of the mortgage lis
and a statement regarding taxes and fees paid.

The notary will always keep in his office the original of the deed which was
executed, and a copy of the deed may be ordered either from the notary or the Mortgage Registry for a nominal price by any third party.

**Leases**  It is much more common for people doing business in France to have a lease
of their premises. Leases of premises used for business, industry and trade are
called 'commercial leases' ('baux commerciaux') and are governed by the Decree
of 30 September 1953 which gives a very high level of protection to the tenant, and,
consequently, a financial value to his lease.

The term of a commercial lease has to be for a minimum of nine years with a
right of termination by the tenant only at the end of each three-year period. The
tenant has the right to have a renewed lease upon expiry for the same period of time
and under the same terms as the expired lease. The landlord may refuse renewal
provided that he pays an indemnity for loss of leasehold rights which takes into
account, among other things, the value of the goodwill ('fonds de commerce') and
all costs incurred in connection with removal. The rent is index-linked and may be
adjusted either up or down every three years. If no agreement is reached, the new
price is decided upon by the court with the advice of a court-appointed expert.

The price of leasehold rights ('droit au bail') is usually high in France and the
cost of such rights, paid for by the franchisee, or by the franchisor incorporating a

company in France, should be taken into account. The tenant has the right to sell his title to the premises to the buyer of his business and, in some instances, such a title is almost as expensive as the property itself. This has to be taken into account when preparing a business plan.

## Foreigners working or establishing a business in France

For employment purposes, foreigners are divided into two categories:

1  Ordinary residents qualifying for and holding a residence permit allowing them to live in France for ten years and to work with the same rights as a French national with no formalities.

2  Temporary residents, being admitted to live in France for one year, renewable, and having to apply for a special business permit.

EC nationals do not need any authorization as they are deemed to have rights equal to those of French citizens. They do need to apply for a residence permit which will be granted for five years and is renewable for subsequent ten-year periods.

Non-EC nationals must apply for a residence permit through their proposed employer who must file with the local administration, among other documents, a draft of the proposed employment contract. Proper authorization will allow the non-EC national to receive a visa and other relevant administrative documents for his entry and stay in France. Such requests are refused unless the worker fits into one of the following categories:

1  Highly qualified individuals (e.g. professors)

2  Scientific researchers at specific research institutes

3  Highly paid executives

4  Spouses of persons working legally in France

The foreign employee and his family have to be registered under the French social security system (unless he is a citizen from a country which has entered into a separate social security agreement with France) and enjoy similar treatment to a French worker.

## Employment laws

All employment relations are governed by the Labour Code, which sets out all basic requirements, and no written employment agreement is necessary. In many branches of commerce and industry, collective bargaining agreements entered into between the trade union(s) and the employers association(s) who have been approved by the government are applicable on a nation-wide basis to such types of business regardless of any other agreement.

Specific obligations may be imposed on the worker (secrecy requirements, non-competition clause, etc.). Employment agreements may be entered into for a specific period of time, or for an indefinite period of time.

Dismissal of an employee with an indeterminate-period contract requires compliance with complex rules which are designed to protect the employee. The rules vary according to the size of the employer's business, the seniority of the employee, the nature of dismissal and the protective status of the employee (trade union representative, for instance). Employees may be dismissed on an individual basis for 'personal reasons', though the employer must have a real and serious reason for dismissal. An employee may be dismissed for economic reasons either on an individual basis or on a group basis. Other good causes for termination may be *force majeure*, prolonged sick leave, work-related sickness or accident, retirement or receivership or liquidation of the employer.

All employees must be affiliated with French social security. Provisions include social revenue, unemployment pay and retirement pensions, whose costs are shared between the employer and the employee.

## Foreign investment and foreign exchange controls

Freedom of investment and freedom of repatriation of profits are some of the main concerns of investors and franchisors in a foreign country.

The rules of foreign exchange control have recently been relaxed by the French government, after more than 50 years of uninterrupted controls. Although Law no. 66–108 of 28 December 1966 has worked on the assumption that there were no controls, government had been given total freedom to establish controls when necessary without having to refer to Parliament. Two years prior to achievement of the unified Common Market on 1 January 1993, the decrees of 29 December 1989 and the circular of 15 January 1990 have dramatically changed the rules as far as foreign investment and exchange control are concerned:

1    Transfers between France and abroad are totally free of control and may be made by any means (bank transfers, cash, credit cards, etc.), although French residents must declare any transfer of funds over FF 50 000 per transfer. French companies whose transfers to and from abroad are in excess of FF 5 000 000 000 have to be declared direct to the Bank of France.

2    Total freedom is given to direct investments (incorporation of a company in France, buying of an existing company's assets, loans to a French company) made in France by investors from EC member states. Such investors have to prove that they have their main place of business in a member state and that they are directly or indirectly controlled by person(s) from an EC member state having a minimum of 50% of the shares and the majority of the votes.

Such investment has to be declared only for statistical purposes to the Ministry of Finance.

3  Direct investments made in France by investors from outside the EC have to be declared to the Ministry of Finances prior to their implementation. The authorization is deemed to have been granted after the expiry of a one-month delay. There may be further delay if the Ministry so requires, and a special declaration must be filed with the Ministry by at the latest 20 days after the completion of the investment.

4  The following investments, whatever the country of origin of the investor, have to be approved by the government prior to their execution – investments made in activities which could deal, even partially, with functions reserved to the state (e.g. prison system), and investments in the fields of public health and in the sale and production of armaments.

All violations of these rules are punished according to Article 459 of the Customs Code by imprisonment for one to five years and by a fine equal to, or up to twice the amount, involved.

## Other significant issues specific to French law

*Goodwill or assets ('Fonds de commerce')* All companies or sole proprietors operating a business have what is called a 'fonds de commerce'. No French law defines this term, which does not have any good translation in English. (It is the equivalent of the sale by a business of all its assets.) The 'fonds de commerce' may be sold apart from the shares of the company which owns it. It is one of the most important assets of creditors, who may attach it and have it sold.

*Judicial receivership and liquidation* A company or merchant ('commerçant') has to file for receivership within 15 days from the date when he is unable to meet his payments when they fall due, even though his assets may exceed his liabilities.

Proceedings for the appointment of a receiver may be commenced by any creditor, by the Public Prosecutor's Office or by the First Instance Commercial Court. Under Law no. 85–98 of 25 January 1985 and Decree no. 85–1388 of 27 December 1985, a receiver is appointed by the local Court of Commerce. The receiver may sell the business on a going concern basis with full or part payment of the debts. If no such solution is achieved, the company will be put into liquidation and all assets auctioned off by a trustee appointed by the same court.

All creditors must lodge their claims with the receiver or the trustee within two months from publication of the court order. The creditors have no right to continue with any proceedings from the date of the court decision due to the new 'status' of their debtor. If the business of the company is continued in receivership, the receiver becomes personally liable for all payments to the company's creditors for liabilities incurred by him.

Needless to say, a franchisee in receivership or liquidation may be a problem for a franchisor. It is, of course, possible for the franchisor to negotiate with the receiver or the trustee to buy some of the franchisee's assets and to prohibit the future use of its logos and trade marks.

**Territory** France is divided into 95 Metropolitan Departments, Five Overseas Departments (Martinique, Guadeloupe, French Guyana, St Pierre and Miquelon and La Réunion) and Five Overseas Territories (New Caledonia, French Polynesia, Wallis and Futuna, Mayotte, and the Austral and Antarctic Lands). Some provisions of French law are still not applicable in the French province of Alsace-Lorraine, which was part of the German Empire from 1870 to 1918. French (and EC) law is applicable to French territory, with some exceptions in the Overseas Territories.

Classical definitions of France include: 'Continental France', i.e. the French territory in the EC excluding Corsica; 'Metropolitan France', including 'Continental France' plus the island of Corsica. Overseas Departments and Territories are usually excluded. They should be listed and dealt with specifically.

**Computers and freedom** France adopted on 6 February 1974 a law called 'Informatique et Libertés' (Computer Science and Freedom) with a view to protecting the right to privacy of individuals against the state and other individuals or groups. The law is administered by a national commission, the Commission Nationale Informatique et Libertés. Its 17 members are appointed for five-year terms by the government.

All processed or manual files having information on individuals must be declared to, and authorized by, the Commission, whether they are run by the state or by private companies. The following information may not be collected or kept:

1    Information on crimes or criminal sentences

2    Information on a person's racial origins, political, philosophical or religious opinions, or trade union membership

3    Information taken by the police if no charges are made against the person

4    Information on banks' credit lists

Any person may have free, direct or indirect access to such information about him. All information must be kept confidential and must be suppressed upon demand by the individual concerned.

The Commission has the broadest powers of inquiry. The penalties incurred for the violations of the provisions of the law are a fine of FF 2000 to 200 000 and/or imprisonment from six months to three years, with a maximum of one to five years and a fine of FF 20 000 to 2 000 000 if the offence is repeated.

*Use of the French language*  Law no. 75–1349 of 31 December 1975 makes the use of the French language mandatory for all business related to the sale of goods and services (including advertisements, drafts of agreements, etc.) and *inter alia* certificates of quality and employment agreements. A list of mandatory French words in technical fields is published from time to time and has to be used.

Penalties are a fine from FF 600 to 1300. Although this law has been implemented more with the view to protecting the French language in the modern world, court cases indicate that it is viewed as part of consumer protection. All labelling and advertising literature which will be offered by franchisors and franchisees in French territory have therefore to be written in the French language.

## Terminations

French law envisions unilateral breach of contract, termination of contract and cancellation of contract.

The word 'termination' is translated in French by two words: 'résolution' or 'résiliation'. The consequences of each are quite different.

The consequence of 'résolution' is to release the parties from their commitments with the obligation for them to give back what has been received during the term of the agreement (i.e. to restore the position to what it would have been had there not been any contract). 'Résolution' may only be asked for when it is possible to achieve this outcome. It may be provided for by a clause of the agreement ('résolution conventionnelle') or be ordered by the judge ('résolution judiciaire).

The consequence of 'résiliation' is to release the parties from their commitments for the future without any obligation to give back what has been received during the term of the agreement.

*Unilateral termination of contract*  One of the parties to an agreement may terminate such agreement at will without notice when no fixed term of agreement has been agreed upon or if the agreement so provides, without having to go to court (Article 1183 of the Civil Code). Such a clause should include the grounds for such termination, the necessity of a prior formal notice, the time when such termination may be done and the termination consequences.

A good cause for termination may be non-compliance by the other party of his undertakings under the agreement, his acting in bad faith or the violation of public order. The agreement will terminate at the date set forth by the party in its notice and the consequences of such termination may be provided for in the agreement. The parties have the right to sue for damages.

*Termination of agreement*  The conventional termination clause is totally acceptable (Article 1656 of the Civil Code) and may be included in the agreement (termination notice or not, right of the parties to renounce such a clause, recourse to court or not, etc.). The existence of a termination clause does not prevent the party from asking for specific performance of the agreement. The scope of the termination should be provided for in the details. Recourse to the judge may, of course, be provided for either for a money order or for the enforcement of post-termination clauses.

Judicial termination may only be requested in the case of bilateral agreements where so provided for in the agreement (Article 1184 of the Civil Code). The judge is totally free to decide whether termination should be ordered and if so will enforce the post-termination clauses.

*Cancellation of agreement*  The agreement is cancelled when it is deemed not to have come into existence because a condition precedent has not been satisfied. This principle is not derived from the Civil Code but from jurisprudence.

The most important consequence of such cancellation is that the agreement is void from the date of the court order.

### *Frustration of agreement*

1    Agreement becomes frustrated when its performance becomes impossible without any fault from any of the parties (death of one of the parties, exceeding of the maximum term provided for by law, etc.). The agreement is then deemed to be extinct or 'caducq'. Each party is then released from performing the agreement and no damage may be sought.

2    Agreement may be terminated as its normal term has elapsed. Parties may either decide to renew this agreement or tacitly continue its execution (Article 1738 of the Civil Code).

*Consequences of termination*  All post-termination clauses provided for in agreements have to be executed and may be enforced.

## TAX AND FINANCIAL CONSIDERATIONS

Every year, parliament passes a financial law which defines the budget for the year to come, sets the rates for the existing taxes, imposes new taxes and changes existing tax provisions. Taxes are levied on a national, regional and local level. They do not include social security taxes. Taxes are:

1    Direct taxes, on a taxpayer's earnings, income or value of his property owned or used ('Impôt sur les Sociétés', IS, 'Impôt sur le Revenu des Personnes Physiques'), IRPP

2    Turnover taxes such as VAT

3     Registration duties

4     Capital taxes on property owners

5     Tax on wealth ('Impôt de Solidarité sur la Fortune', ISF) imposed on
      certain possessions of the taxpayer, adding to his personal IRPP. A progres-
      sive rate from 0% to 1.5% is levied on the net value of the assets, after deduc-
      tion of debts

## Corporation tax

Adjustments are made from the company's audited results according to fiscal and
accounting rules in order to come to the net revised earnings of the company for
tax purposes. Corporation tax is then assessed at the rate of 34% on retained
profits. The rate is at 42% on distributed profits.

French corporation tax is limited to 'French activities' performed on
'French territory', which for tax purposes includes Metropolitan France and the
Overseas Departments, with some exceptions in order to allow French companies
to create new foreign establishments.

Corporation tax is imposed on net profits based on the profits and losses
from industrial or commercial operations carried out by the company, including
all sources of profits.

Since Law no. 87–1060 of 30 December 1987, a special corporation tax
regime for groups of companies has been established. According to the law, a
parent company may be solely liable for payment of corporation tax on the net
earnings for tax purposes of the group comprising companies which the parent
company has, directly or indirectly, 95% of the issued shares during the whole of
the relevant accounting period.

## Personal income tax

Personal income tax is assessed and paid by every fiscal household liable for the
income of all its members. A single person represents a fiscal household. A
married couple (with or without children) represents a fiscal household.

The gross taxable income includes both national and international income
(salaries, profits from self-employment, etc.) and is adjusted: deductions or tax
credits may be applied. The net taxable income is then subject to a progressive tax
rate (e.g. see below).

There is no withholding tax on sales or wages. Annual declarations are filed
by the end of February of the year in respect of the tax year ending on the previous
31 December. Two partial payments are made in February and May and the tax
is usually settled by the end of that year.

Non-resident individuals liable to French income tax are subject to withholding tax on remittances.

Dividends paid to shareholders are subject to either personal income tax or

**Table 7.1 Examples of tax rate for a married couple for fiscal year 1991**

| Income bracket | Portion of taxable income | Tax rate |
|---|---|---|
| 1st | under 36 280 francs | 0.0% |
| 2nd | from   36 280 to   37 920 francs | 5.0% |
| 3rd | from   37 920 to   44 940 francs | 9.6% |
| 4th | from   44 940 to   71 040 francs | 14.4% |
| 5th | from   71 040 to   91 320 francs | 19.2% |
| 6th | from   91 320 to 114 640 francs | 24.0% |
| 7th | from 114 640 to 138 740 francs | 28.8% |
| 8th | from 138 740 to 160 060 francs | 33.6% |
| 9th | from 161 060 to 266 680 francs | 38.4% |
| 10th | from 266 680 to 366 800 francs | 43.2% |
| 11th | from 266 800 to 433 880 francs | 49.0% |
| 12th | from 433 880 to 493 540 francs | 53.9% |
| 13th | in excess of 493 540 francs | 56.8% |

corporation tax. If the shareholder is a French tax resident, he is granted a tax credit ('avoir fiscal') equal to 50% of the dividend paid which may be offset against his personal income tax.

### Value added tax ('Taxe à la Valeur Ajoutée', TVA)

VAT was introduced in France in 1955. VAT is only applicable to taxable transactions taking place in France. There are three rates:

1    The standard rate of 18.6%

2    The reduced rate of 5.5% applicable to food, social services and books

3    The higher rate of 22% applicable to luxury items (cars, video equipment, perfumes and 'X'-rated movies)

Certain transactions are specifically exempt from VAT:

1    Exports and international transport

2    Medical, paramedical and related services, writers and composers, painters, sculptors, artists

3    Some financial services

4    Insurance and reinsurance

5    Non-profit charitable associations

## Local direct taxes
There include:

1   Real property, tax on developed land ('taxe foncière sur la propriété bâtie')

2   Real property tax on undeveloped land ('taxe foncière sur la propriété non bâtie')

3   Residence tax ('taxe d'habitation')

4   Business licence tax ('taxe professionnelle')

These taxes are deductible for income or company tax purposes when they are business expenses, with the exception of the residence tax which is never tax-deductible.

The business licence tax is levied on any taxable person having a non-salaried professional activity on a habitual basis as at 1 January of the year for which the tax is due.

## Real estate taxes and expenses
Costs include land registry fees, stamp duty, costs and disbursements, notary's fees and negotiation fees.

Land registry fees vary according to the regions (roughly 9.5% of the value of the transaction).

Stamp duty is charged at the rate of FF 32 for each page of the deed, including schedules.

Fees and expenses include the local search certificate (FF 1000), administrative enquiries, notifications, the fees of the Registrar of Mortgages (0.1%) and fixed fees. Fees of the notary for the preparation of the deed, including VAT at the rate of 18.6% are based as follows:

1   5% from FF 0 to 20 000

2   3.30% from FF 20 000 to 40 000

3   1.65% from FF 40 001 to 110 000

4   0.825% above FF 110 001

Fees for negotiating the sale payable by the purchaser when the transaction is concluded by the notary who has offered the property to the purchaser are:

1   5% from FF 0 to 175 000

2       2.50% above FF 175 000, with VAT added at the rate of 18.6%

**Employee-related taxes and social security obligations**
Social security in France is compulsory and all employees (French and foreign nationals working in France) must be registered under the general social security regime. The general social security system includes three programmes:

1       Social insurance, providing medical, maternity, disability, old age, retirement and death benefits, funded by employer and employees. The employer's contribution is paid directly to the social security administration and the employee's contribution is deducted by the employer from his salary and paid to the social security administration.

2       Family allowance, financed by employer contributions.

3       Work persons' compensation system and work-related accidents financed by employer contributions.

A decree is published twice a year which establishes for calculation purposes a minimum salary and social security ceiling with special ceiling calculations.
       Complementary plans have been devised since 1945 to benefit high-wage employees, who are called 'cadres'.
       All contributions are allowable expenses for tax purposes both by the employer and the employee.
       Self-employed persons and merchants ('commerçants') have their own social security schemes which are tax-deductible.
       Unemployment insurance, managed by two institutions, UNEDIC and ASSEDIC, and financed by the employer and the employee, pays initial benefits to persons out of work and subsidies to persons who are no longer eligible for such schemes. The minimum benefit is 57.4%, the maximum 75% of reference salary with a maximum coverage of 15 to 21 months. Partial unemployment benefits are granted to a person who is wholly or partially laid off.

**Investment incentives**
Many incentives exist in France either at the national, regional or local level, either for new or for existing enterprises.

*New enterprises*
1       Reduction of personal income tax for the shareholders of a new incorporated company for a maximum of 25% of their application to the shares on the sum of FF 80 000 for a married couple, or FF 40 000 for a single person for a period of three years after the incorporation of such company

2       Exemption from annual minimum corporation tax for the first five fiscal years from the incorporation of the company

3     Exemption from payment of corporation tax instalments for such period of time

4     Deduction from corporate tax of dividends paid to the shareholders up to a maximum of 53.4% of payment during the six first fiscal years from the incorporation of the company

5     Deduction of costs of foreign establishment with a tax-free reserve

6     No tax for investment in unemployment zones.

### Existing enterprises
1     Business licence tax exemption

2     Depreciation of some investments in research, conservation of energy and control of pollution

3     Tax credit for investment in research equipment

4     Deductible dividends for capital increases

5     Special loss carry-over rules for acquisitions of failing companies

6     Good merger or dissolution rules

7     Reduction in transfer duties

# CHAPTER 8
# GERMANY

*Albrecht Schulz*

## AN OVERVIEW OF FRANCHISING IN GERMANY

### General

In recent years franchising has become a well-accepted form of business, both in the retail and service industries. Its economic importance, however, stems from the growth of existing networks rather than from the introduction of new systems. In 1990, over 250 franchisors with approximately 13 000 franchisees were operating in Germany, some 150 of which were members of the German Franchise Association (Deutscher Franchiseverband, DFV). These numbers do not include car dealers, petrol stations and beverage bottling companies, which are not really considered as 'franchise' operations by German standards. The total turnover of all franchise operations in 1990 can be estimated at DM 13 billion. The annual growth rate of turnover in the last few years was always in the range of 5–10% higher than the general growth rate of the national economy – and is expected to remain there in the next few years.

Such development may benefit from a tendency among younger, gifted businessmen and -women which runs counter to the general trend towards concentration in national and international big industry and commerce. This tendency is leading not only to an increasing number of management buy-outs, but also to an increasing number of well-trained young employees with entrepreneurial skills who want to own their own business and who seize the chances offered by – more or less – well-established franchise networks. The establishment of such new businesses is encouraged by numerous national or regional business incentive schemes, which do not, however, always help to overcome three serious, often underestimated obstacles: the lack of sufficient financial resources, the lack of affordable locations, and the lack of a qualified workforce.

The whole scenario may change now that the unification of Germany is a reality. The emphasis of developing the franchise industry has shifted to the five new eastern states of Germany (the territory of the former GDR). The figures indicated above for 1990 already include operations in this area. Since no official statistics exist on franchising, figures in this field always were rough estimates, and now, estimates including eastern Germany will, of course, have to be looked at with even more caution. But all indications are that of all new franchise outlets more than half are in the East.

The German Franchise Association has been actively involved in preparing the terrain and the people for franchising since the opening of the border between the two Germanys. In view of the development during the first year of unification, the author is convinced that, in the long run, franchising will be a very successful business method in eastern Germany. But in the light of the total lack of business skills, franchisors must modify their normal approach. They will have to adapt their standard systems by seriously increasing their educational efforts, and by introducing complete financial packages.

The government of the Federal Republic of Germany has expressed its favourable attitude towards franchising on several occasions, but never as clearly as in an answer to a parliamentary question in 1986 where no discernible differentiation is made with respect to foreign franchising:

> 'The Federal Government considers that franchise-systems with independent partners are positive, since they are able to animate the market. Frequently, only such systems give small and medium-sized enterprises the chance to face competition with big companies and, thus, build up resistance against the general concentration process.'

The government underlined that franchise systems must respect the antitrust laws which give, however, 'sufficient opportunities to use and to develop franchise-systems, particularly to small and medium-sized enterprises'. The government's favourable attitude now extends to the positive role which franchising is supposed to play in the economic recovery of eastern Germany.

### Legislation which concerns franchising

There is no specific legislation on franchising in Germany. The relationship between a franchisor and its franchisees is, in principle, ruled by the freedom of contract. This relationship, as well as the position of franchising in general is, however, influenced by a large number of statutory laws and regulations of which quite a few, being enacted for the protection of the economically weaker members of society, are mandatory. Not very many, but some, court rulings have been based on such general legislation and have shaped and established in the last ten years 'franchise agreements' as a distinct legal form of distribution, as they had, in applying by analogy the provisions concerning commercial agents of the Commercial Code (Handelsgesetzbuch, HGB), shaped 'dealership agreements' in the two preceding decades.

Since in both fields quite a number of legal issues remain open, one legal principle which governs all contractual relationships in Germany should be stressed, i.e. the principle of 'good faith' stipulated in s. 242 of the Civil Code (Bürgerliches Gesetzbuch, BGB). This basic rule has been interpreted by countless court rulings, but the issue is always determined objectively: the search for an interpretation which reflects the justified concerns of the parties and which is in accordance with honest business practice. Since franchise relationships are invariably of medium or long duration, during which legislation or case law may change, it must be emphasized that one should not use contractual clauses or techniques infringing the basic rule of good faith. They will not only harm the contractual relationship and business development in the long term, but they will sooner or later run into trouble with the German courts, which like to establish 'justice' in applying this basic rule.

## BUSINESS ENTITIES FOR USE IN FRANCHISE OPERATIONS IN GERMANY

### General
Theoretical discussions on the nature of franchising are still going on, despite the definitions given by the EC Block Exemption Regulation No. 4087/88. It is, however, generally understood that a franchise agreement is (or should be) concluded between autonomous business entities.

### Advantages and disadvantages
*Introduction* Besides carrying on business as an individual, the most common business entities in Germany are:

1    Various forms of partnership

2    GmbH (Gesellschaft mit beschränkter Haftung or limited liability company)

3    AG (Aktiengesellschaft or stock corporation)

4    Branches

*Individuals* Many small franchises in Germany are operated by individuals. For the franchisor this has the advantage of being able to develop a close and personal relationship with the franchisee, something which might not always be the case with the changing personnel of a company. It would be unusual, although possible, for the franchisor to be an individual.

An individual businessperson is personally liable and stands behind his obligations with all of his present and future assets. Depending on one's perspective, this is either an advantage or a disadvantage.

Each business entity, including individuals, must obtain a trade permit, which is in general granted without difficulty (see p. 154). An individual is not obliged to register with a commercial register; if he does, he becomes a 'registered merchant' (eingetragener Kaufmann) in the sense of s. 5 of the HGB.

An individual can always do business under his personal name unless he does so in order to confuse the public about the nature or origin of his business. He can also add a fictitious trade name, which must not, however, suggest any corporate structure.

***Partnerships*** German law offers a large number of different types of partnership.

### oHG

An oHG (offene Handelsgesellschaft or commercial partnership) is, according to s. 105 of the HGB, formed when two or more natural or legal persons join to conduct a business under a common name. A franchise will nearly always involve such a business. Where two people (for example, husband and wife) sign a contract as joint franchisees they will form an oHG even if they have not specifically thought about forming a partnership. Even where no business is involved, a civil partnership can be formed. In both oHG and civil partnerships the partners have unlimited liability.

An oHG can be formed with an oral agreement (see the above example of husband and wife). But since it is not at all unusual to conduct business in this form and even for longer periods, it is always wise to fix the basic rules in writing. The oHG must be carried on under the name of at least one of the partners and with a designation which shows its character as a commercial partnership. It must be registered with the commercial register.

### KG

The KG (Kommanditgesellschaft or limited partnership) is, according to s. 161 of the HGB, a form of partnership in which at least one partner (the general partner) has unlimited liability while other partners (Kommanditisten or limited partners) have their liability limited to the amount of an agreed contribution. Normally it is the general partner who manages the partnership.

To develop its legal effects a limited partnership, which can theoretically also be formed by an oral agreement, has to be registered with the commercial register. In its classical form the KG has become rare.

### GmbH & Co. KG

A particular form of KG has been developed which effectively limits the liability of all partners. This is the GmbH & Co. KG. Under this form of KG the general partner – the one with unlimited liability – is a GmbH which itself has limited liability (it could also be a different form of or even a foreign incorporated company). Thus, if someone sues the general partner he will come up against the limited liability of the GmbH. The other partners of the GmbH & Co. KG have limited liability anyway.

**GmbH** The GmbH is the simplest and most common German corporate entity. It is the form most commonly chosen by non-residents wishing to set up a subsidiary in Germany. It is regulated by the Law on Limited Liability Companies (Gesetz betreffend die Gesellschaft mit beschränkter Haftung, GmbHG).

Limited liability is one of the main advantages of forming a German corporate subsidiary. By interposing a subsidiary, liability is limited to the assets of the subsidiary rather than the total (maybe worldwide) assets of the parent. The

German courts only very rarely pierce the corporate veil and hold the owners of a corporate subsidiary liable for its actions and obligations. However, it is not possible to escape all liability by interposing a subsidiary. In product liability claims, for example, consumers can claim against manufacturers and suppliers whatever the relationship is with them.

Of the German corporate entities offering limited liability, the GmbH is the easiest to form and the simplest and cheapest to run. This explains much of its popularity.

**AG**  The AG is the standard form used for a public company. The main advantage of an AG over a GmbH is that an AG's shares are easily transferable and so can, for example, be used for raising money from the public. However, AGs are more complex to set up, more expensive to run and more heavily regulated by the Law on Stock Corporations (Aktiengesetz, AktG). It is relatively unusual for any but very large franchisors to be AGs. If ever an existing German AG decides to enter into a master franchise agreement with a foreign franchisor, it would probably set up for that purpose a subsidiary in the form of a GmbH.

**Branches**  A non-resident can also set up a branch in Germany to carry on his business there. To form a branch it is necessary to lodge specified details about the branch and the company itself with the local court (Amtsgericht) for entry in the commercial register. Generally, all documents must be provided in German and this adds to the cost and time involved in establishing a branch. It is normally quicker and probably cheaper to form a subsidiary. Forming a corporate subsidiary (or a GmbH & Co. KG) also has the advantage of offering limited liability.

For these reasons it is rather uncommon for non-resident franchisors to open branches in Germany.

**Conclusion**  Residents and non-residents, both franchisors and franchisees, can opt for the forms described above. The choice will depend on the individual, commercial and financial circumstances.

By far the most common corporate entity used to set up a new business in Germany, but also selected by non-resident franchisors, is the GmbH. The following sections will therefore focus on the GmbH. In certain circumstances, it might be advantageous from a tax perspective to conduct business as an individual, through a branch or as a partnership. In the latter case one should consider a GmbH & Co. KG, as it also offers limited liability.

### Most common legal entity: GmbH

**Formation**  The formation of a GmbH starts with a legal act of the founders, who can be just one natural or legal person only. This act must be executed in the German language before a public notary (who can simultaneously be an attorney in some German states) and must contain the articles of association (Satzung or Gesellschaftsvertrag). Such articles of association can be very simple and their drafting very inexpensive as long as there is only one shareholder. More sophisticated drafting is required as soon as there are several shareholders, especially if they are of different national and legal background.

A GmbH is formed when it is entered in the commercial register of the local court. The one or several Geschäftsführer (approximately equivalent to managing directors), in general appointed in the notarial act mentioned above, must sign an application for registration containing specified details. The signature of this application must also be certified by the public notary. As discussed below, a specified amount of capital must be paid up before the GmbH will be registered.

Shelf companies are rare in Germany. Thus, one has in general to form one's own custom-made GmbH, which takes at least two to three months.

### Statutory requirements

#### Identification

The articles of association must identify the company by a name, the objectives and a registered office. The name must contain the full name of at least one of its founding shareholders or a fictional name derived from its objectives. Both name and objectives (and the articles of association in general) are carefully screened by the civil servants of the competent commercial register, who can create unexpected and, to foreigners, often incomprehensible difficulties.

#### Share capital

The minimum capital of a GmbH is DM 50 000. This is divided into shares (Anteile, of at least DM 500). Each share must be a multiple of DM 100.

Contributions to capital may be in cash or in kind. Special legislative provisions apply to contributions in kind to ensure that what is contributed is worth at least as much as the cash value it represents.

Twenty-five per cent (or DM 25 000, whichever is the higher amount) of the share capital must be paid up at the time of registration of the GmbH unless a contribution is made in kind, in which case the share capital must be paid up in full. If a GmbH has just one shareholder, the latter must provide security (e.g. a bank guarantee) for all the unpaid capital of the GmbH. The GmbH can make calls on unpaid share capital. If a shareholder cannot pay up the call, then the other shareholders are required to pay it.

A notarized deed is necessary to transfer a share in a GmbH. In addition, the articles of association can impose additional requirements, such as the consent of the other shareholders and/or of the company.

#### Voting

At shareholders' meetings, each shareholder has one vote per DM 100 share capital unless the articles of association provide otherwise. Normally resolutions require a 50% majority, although some (e.g. amending the articles of association or increasing share capital) require a 75% majority. In addition, the obligations attached to a share cannot be increased without the consent of all affected shareholders.

A shareholder cannot vote on certain issues involving a conflict of interest unless the articles of association provide otherwise. The articles of association of a 100% owned subsidiary would normally provide otherwise.

*Other formalities*

Once a year a GmbH must file a list of its shareholders with the commercial register. A GmbH must also file its annual financial statements with the commercial register. Large GmbHs must even publish them. Small GmbHs (under at least two of the following criteria: annual sales of DM 8 million, balance sheet of DM 3.9 million, 50 employees) have only to file a simplified balance sheet together with a simplified annex.

**Directors** Generally, a GmbH is only required to have one 'Geschäftsführer' (approximately equivalent to a managing director) although more than one can be appointed. A Geschäftsführer need not be a shareholder, a German citizen or a German resident. However, only a natural person can be a Geschäftsführer.

The Geschäftsführer is appointed by and can be dismissed by a simple majority of the shareholders unless the articles of association provide otherwise.

As against third parties, the Geschäftsführer can exercise all the powers of the GmbH. Any restrictions (in the articles, the Geschäftsführer's employment contract or elsewhere) do not bind any third parties without notice but, if breached, can give rise to a claim for damages by the company against the Geschäftsführer.

If one Geschäftsführer is appointed, he represents the GmbH alone. If more than one is appointed, they jointly represent the GmbH unless the shareholders grant a Geschäftsführer the right to act alone or to act together with only one other Geschäftsführer (as opposed to having to act jointly with all of them). The names of the Geschäftsführers and the extent of their right of representation (that is, whether they can act alone, etc.) are noted in the commercial register, which can be relied on by third parties.

The Geschäftsführer can be dismissed at any moment from his function as legal representative of the company. In general, he is, however, also an employee with an employment contract which ought to be in writing. As an employee he can be dismissed with immediate effect only with cause; otherwise according to the terms of the contract.

In addition to a large variety of duties to the GmbH itself, a Geschäftsführer has other duties imposed by law. He must mainly ensure a diligent management, promote the purpose of the company, keep proper books and records and ensure the contribution and preservation of the share capital. He must ensure that the company pays taxes and social security contributions. He can be personally liable if such payments are not made. He must promptly file for bankruptcy if the company is overindebted or becomes insolvent. He risks personal liability and severe criminal punishment if he does not.

*Supervisory board* A GmbH can, and in some circumstances must (see below), have a supervisory board (Aufsichtsrat). If the supervisory board is optional, its members are appointed by the shareholders. The main purpose of the supervisory board is to oversee the directors of the company, and involves examining both the legal and commercial aspects of their acts. The supervisory board does not itself manage the GmbH, but the shareholders can provide it with far-reaching instruction rights. An optional board can also be called a 'Beirat' or 'Verwaltungsrat'.

*Co-determination* Co-determination is the right of employees of a company (or in some cases even a partnership) to participate in the company's management. Co-determination is regulated by four different laws: Law on Coal and Steel Co-Determination, Supplementary Law on Coal and Steel Co-Determination, Enterprise Constitution Law of 1952, Law Concerning the Co-Determination of Employees of 1976.

When one of these laws requires a supervisory board for a GmbH, it also gives the rules governing such supervisory board, sometimes by referring to the Stock Corporation Law. Provisions of the co-determination laws concerning supervisory boards are mandatory and supersede any conflicting provisions of the law on GmbHs, the articles of association of the company and shareholder resolutions. Since no supervisory board is required for companies with less than 500 employees, it is not necessary to provide any further details.

## LEGAL ASPECTS OF FRANCHISING

### General

The possible methods of doing business in Germany are the same as in most other countries, as discussed in Chapter 3 of this book. Whatever method is chosen, one has to know and carefully respect the laws of Germany, many of which are similar to those of other statutory-law countries, but some of which are, however, special and not easy to perceive.

As mentioned above, there are no federal or regional statutory laws or regulations concerning franchising in Germany, either concerning the private, i.e. contractual, side or the public, i.e. registration, side. They are not considered necessary, and no legislation is pending. But there are more and more court rulings on franchising, generally with respect to the protection of the franchisee and often concerning his status as independent merchant, unfair contractual clauses or insufficient precontractual disclosure of relevant information.

Although theoretical discussions on the nature and definition of franchising are still going on, it nevertheless common ground that franchise agreements are hybrid contracts which contain numerous elements of legally related contracts.

Thus, in respect of each of these elements the laws and rulings (clearly) appropriate are to be applied. The laws which influence the different elements, but also the whole substance of franchise agreements, are presented in the following sections.

### Rules concerning dealerships and sales agents

Since franchising is mainly considered as a new form of distribution, it is largely the rules concerning dealerships that are applied. In the absence of any legal provisions for dealerships, the courts have developed extensive legal standards for this kind of contract, applying by analogy the provisions concerning commercial agents in the German Commercial Code (HGB). Thus, courts are likely to refer to these latter provisions if no other rules more appropriate for franchise agreements exist. A few elements of this legal field will be mentioned:

*Length of the contract term*  No rule exists about the length of the contract term. With regard to the importance of investment, it should never be too short. Three to five years seems to be appropriate for standard agreements; in the case of substantial investments, ten or even more years may be better. However, courts rarely admit more than 20 years.

*Non-competition clauses*  Non-competition for the duration of a contract is, according to German understanding, an inherent element of the franchisee's loyalty to his system and its obligations, and therefore admissible. The effectiveness of such a clause may now be limited by the EC Block Exemption Regulation No. 4087/88.

Non-competition clauses for the time after termination of contracts are only admissible if they do not hinder excessively the former franchisee in the local, temporary and material performance of his profession and if they do not exceed the legitimate interests of the franchisor. With regard to the rulings of the Federal Court, a subsequent non-competition clause must not be imposed for more than two years and be accompanied by the payment of appropriate compensation (one cannot say in general terms what 'appropriate' compensation is). In a recent case the Federal Court has ruled that a post-term non-competition clause is not void if such compensation is not provided for, but that the compensation has to be paid anyhow.

*Termination, notice, requirements*  An agreement with a fixed duration simply expires at the end of its fixed duration if no renewal is foreseen. Normally there is no obligation to renew.

For an 'ordinary termination' of a franchise agreement of indefinite duration no reason or 'good cause' has to be given. The termination has only to be served with an appropriate notice. In the absence of rules for the reasonable period of notice (the Commercial Code only mentions minimum periods for agents), it should be fixed in the contract. Three to six months to the end of a calendar quarter are in general appropriate. For a contract with a long duration, a notice period of one year may be more appropriate. In a recent case, the Federal Court considered a notice period of two years as appropriate for a distribution agreement which had lasted 36 years.

In another case, the Federal Court ruled that a manufacturer could not unilaterally reduce the contractual territory of a distributor, even if so provided in a contractual clause. The clause was considered void, as being an infringement of the Law on General Terms of Trade.

A termination without notice for an 'important reason' or 'cause' is recognized for all permanent contractual relationships, including, according to s. 89a of the HGB, those for agency agreements. According to this rule, which is applied by analogy to franchise agreements, termination with immediate effect is justified if the reason is of such importance that the other partner cannot be expected to pursue the relationship until its expiry or until the expiry of an ordinary notice period. This is the case when a breach of duty is damaging to such a degree that it puts in jeopardy the entrepreneurial aims of the system.

But, even in the case of a justified 'important reason', notice has to be given promptly, i.e. within a reasonably short period and not months after the event (two to six weeks after having learnt of the event should be prompt enough).

*Compensation upon termination* After termination of his contract, a commercial agent is, according to the mandatory s. 89b of the HGB, entitled to a compensation claim (for his loss of 'goodwill' for his newly recruited clients). A contractual exclusion of this legal claim (which corresponds to Article 17 paragraph 2 of the EC Directive on Commercial Agents) is not valid and has no effect.

For many years, the courts have – by analogy – applied this stipulation on dealership agreements on condition that:

1   The dealer is fully integrated in the distribution system of the manufacturer or supplier.

2   The dealer is bound by contract to make available to the manufacturer or supplier the names and addresses of his clients, which can be done at the termination of contract, but also by ongoing instruction during the contractual period and which must enable the manufacturer to use the customer's data after the termination of contract.

It is therefore advisable – if appropriate in the respective case – to abstain from the contractual obligation to transmit the clients' addresses.

In the absence of a court ruling concerning the compensation of a franchisee, it is to be presumed that the courts will come to similar conclusions as in the dealership cases, if similar conditions are found.

The maximum compensation amount to be paid according to s. 89b of the

HGB is the average annual 'commission' for the last five years. In the case of a franchisee it might be his gross margin or part of it.

No compensation has to be paid for the fact that the franchisee has to cease, upon termination of contract, the use of trade marks, know-how, name or any other sign of the system.

It is also to be noted that there is no compensation according to s. 89b of the HGB, if it was the commercial agent who terminated the contract or if it was by his fault that the contract was terminated for an 'important reason'.

## German competition law

*Distinction of German from European competition law*  The German Law against Restraints of Competition (Gesetz gegen Wettbewerbsbeschränkungen, GWB) distinguishes between horizontal and vertical agreements restricting trade, whereas Article 85 of the Treaty of Rome makes no distinction between horizontal and vertical restrictions (concerning EC competition law see Chapter 2 of this book).

According to s. 1 of the GWB horizontal restrictive agreements are considered as – in principle – prohibited cartels unless expressly admitted by law. Such cartels must be registered with the Federal Cartel Office and become effective only if the latter does not oppose them.

On the contrary, vertical restrictive agreements are not basically prohibited by German competition law. According to s. 15 of the GWB, there is a general ban only of contracts which limit the freedom of one partner with regard to the content of deals to be made with third parties, e.g. concerning prices, terms of trade. Otherwise, vertical agreements containing restrictions are only subject to a control of abuse according to s. 18 of the GWB; registration or authorization are not required.

*Franchise contracts as contracts of vertical co-operation*  In principle, a franchise contract is to be considered as a contract of vertical co-operation and, consequently, according to s. 18 of the GWB, is subject only to control of abuse by the Cartel Office.

Franchise agreements may, however, contain 'horizontal elements' or they can be integrated in other organizational structures, such as co-operative associations. Both situations may end up by being considered to be in contradiction to s. 1 of the GWB. In creating such formulas, the whole contract and the underlying basis have to be examined very carefully for competition law implications.

Even if the attitude of the Cartel Office towards co-operative associations and franchise systems is basically favourable, it might be wise for advisers to contact the Cartel Office at an early stage and discuss the critical points with them. The Cartel Office provides a telephone service (number 030/6901200 or 6901206) through which it is possible to obtain advice from highly competent civil servants on German and European competition laws.

### Individual clauses
*Written form*
If the franchise agreement contains exclusive, even mutually exclusive, commit-

ments and thus falls within the scope of s. 18 para. 1 of the GWB, it has to be made in writing according to s. 34 of the GWB. This form requirement is fulfilled only if the agreement is personally signed by the contracting parties and if it contains all reciprocal rights and obligations in clear and unambiguous form. In a recent decision the Court of Appeals of Düsseldorf (in the 'Eismann-Partner' case) confirmed these principles, but considered the franchise agreement only as the legal framework for the subsequent purchase contracts, so they did not share the fate of the franchise agreement, which was void for lack of form. It has to be stressed that this opinion might not be shared by other courts in other cases. The effects of s. 34 of the GWB may, even after many years of implementation of an agreement, lead to its nullity because one party rightly invokes the issue of the lack of due form.

*Clauses of special interest for control of abuse*
None of the following clauses is prohibited *per se*. Whether any of the clauses or a combination of them constitutes an infringement of the competition rules of s. 18 of the GWB depends on the individual circumstances:

1    Exclusive dealing

2    Territorial restrictions

3    Restricting sources of supply

4    Tie-in sales

5    Non-competition clauses

It is very rare that action is taken by the Cartel Office on the basis of s. 18 of the GWB, but, whenever using such restrictive clauses, one should respect the basic rule: as much freedom as possible for the franchisee and the imposition of restrictions only for good reasons.

*Non-admissible clauses*
According to s. 15 of the GWB, the fixing of resale prices or the prescription of terms of trade to be used by the retailer is prohibited. This rule also strictly applies to franchise systems.

For goods bearing a sign of origin (manufacturer or dealer), so-called brand name goods ('Markenwaren'), however, the manufacturer or the importer can make 'non-compulsory' price recommendations under certain conditions detailed in s. 38a of the GWB.

In principle no price recommendations can be made for services or for non-brand name goods. The Cartel Office maintains this legal position despite the Pronuptia judgment of the European Court and Block Exemption Regulation

No. 4087/88, both of which stated that price recommendations which are not enforced do not infringe Article 85 of the Treaty of Rome. The Cartel Office has, however, announced that it would take into account the attitude of the Court of Justice and of the EC Commission and intervene in the case of price recommendations within franchise networks only if serious abuses are established. This would certainly be the case if a price recommendation is, by complementary measures, turned in fact into a compulsory mechanism.

*Other critical points* Franchise systems are subject to control of s. 26 para. 2 of the GWB, which prohibits dominant enterprises or groups of enterprises from unfairly obstructing, directly or indirectly, other enterprises in the general course of business or from treating single enterprises differently from similar enterprises without a reason justifying such different treatment. Thus, within a franchise network, the franchisor cannot discriminate between individual franchisees concerning prices or other conditions; even the termination of arbitrarily chosen single franchise contracts can be prohibited.

The same prohibition applies to enterprises or groups of enterprises if small or medium-sized suppliers or buyers depend on them for certain goods or services. Any identified abuse of a dominant position (imposition of unusual commercial conditions or unfair obstruction) can be forbidden by the cartel authorities.

Abuse of a 'dominant position' of one or several enterprises is also forbidden in general according to s. 22 of the GWB. Such a position may exist not only at the national level, but also in a regional market or even in a specific branch.

*Special rules for licence agreements* For franchise agreements which contain licences on patents, utility models, know-how, or other technical knowledge, attention has to be drawn to ss. 20 and 21 of the GWB. They allow restrictions which go beyond the nature of the protected right only for a certain number of cases specified in s. 20 para. 2 of the GWB. Such cases are, for example,

> '(1) restrictions imposed upon the acquirer or licensee insofar and so long as they are justified by the seller's or licensor's interest in a technically faultless exploitation of the protected matter,
> (2) obligations of the acquirer or licensee with respect to the price to be fixed for the protected article,
> (3) obligations of the acquirer or licensee not to challenge the protected right,
> (4) obligations of the acquirer or licensee relating to the regulation of competition in markets outside the area of application of this Act,
> insofar as such restrictions do not remain in force beyond the expiration of the acquired or licensed right.'

One must stress that restrictions allowed according to these provisions of German aw may enter into conflict with EC competition law. Other restrictions are void, but can be authorized by the Cartel Office.

In examining a franchise agreement under these provisions, the Cartel Office separates in its judgment the licence part which is subject to ss. 20 and 21 of the GWB and the general part which is subject to ss. 15 and 18 of the GWB; but, of course, no agreement escapes the criteria of s. 1 of the GWB.

*Enforcement of competition law*  It is impossible to make a general statement that the antitrust law is enforced 'more or less vigorously'. The (mainly responsible) Federal Cartel Office is a highly regarded and competent authority which super- vises seriously – and without discrimination towards foreign-based companies – the market in Germany. Of course, it intervenes only when it learns of or receives a complaint on abuse, discrimination, or other illegal acts. Progress is not always made very quickly upon the opening of an investigation, but in general the Office succeeds in prohibiting what it can prove are illegal activities.

In any civil action a party can claim that an agreement is null and void by being contrary to ss. 1, 15 or similar provisions of the GWB. Any private party who has suffered damages can base a compensation claim on s. 35 GWB if that party is a victim of any infringement of a provision of the GWB intended for the protection of private parties.

### Franchisor's liability
#### Contractual liability
*Implied warranties for defective goods*
If a franchisor or some other enterprise – manufacturer or otherwise – supplies goods to the franchisee, it is in the first instance the contractual liability according to the Civil Code which applies, if the contractual relationship is subject to German law.

In this case, the supplier can be held liable for defective goods and be obliged to take them back or to reduce the price. If the product lacks a quality which was assured by the contract, or in the case of malicious non-disclosure of a defect, the supplier is liable for all damages occurring. If a defective product does harm to other property or to a person, the supplier is liable if he had a special obligation to advise or to instruct the client or to control the quality of the product. Contractual liability, if it applies, always exists parallel to product liability.

*Prescription*
Any liability claim for defective moveable goods, except in the case of malicious non-disclosure, becomes statute-barred six months after delivery.

*Other contractual liabilities*
Beyond this implied warranty for proper quality, any contractual party is fully responsible for breach of contract, which includes delayed delivery and faulty action or omission of all persons employed in performing the contract, e.g.

employees, sales agents, sub-contractors. The same principles apply to the rendering of services. Misleading actions performed during the contract negotiation – *culpa in contrahendo* – may also give a claim to the other party.

### Limitation of liability

All these contractual liabilities may be greatly reduced in individually concluded contracts. If general terms of trade are used, the possibilities of limiting contractual liabilities are, even for contracts with merchants, considerably narrowed down. If goods are supplied from abroad by a foreign supplier, the application of a foreign law and a non-German forum can be agreed upon. Thus, a limitation of contractual liability might be achieved more easily.

## Product liability

### Principles

In the last 15 years, German courts have developed a system of product liability of the manufacturer – whether he is the contractual party or not – which is based on the law of tort, but with a reversal of the burden of proof: if injury to a person or damage to property results from the normally intended use of a defective product, the manufacturer has to prove that he is not responsible for the fault (of construction, fabrication, control or instruction). If he cannot provide such proof, he is liable for all damages, including pecuniary losses and compensation for pain and suffering.

Product liability can also be based on the violation of a protective law, e.g. the Law on the Safety of Technical Equipment or the Law on Medical Preparations which institutes strict liability, and similar safety laws.

Germany has with effect from 1 January 1990 implemented the EC Directive on Product Liability of 25 July 1985, thus introducing strict liability for all products, which does not, however, include compensation for pain and suffering. 'Producers' are considered to be not only the manufacturers, but also persons fixing their names or trade marks on a product or persons importing goods into the EC. This new legislation did not have a major impact on product liability in Germany as it was already established by decisions of the courts.

### Prescription

Product liability claims become statute-barred three years after knowledge of the damage and of the identity of the manufacturer. According to the new Product Liability Law all claims become void ten years after the defective product was put into circulation by the manufacturer. The absolute statutory limitation of 30 years laid down in the Civil Code remains valid for claims which can also in the future be based on the traditional civil law rules.

### Exemption from liability

There is no way for a franchisor who is also the manufacturer to exclude his product liability *vis-à-vis* the clients of the franchisee.

The franchisor can try to limit – with very clearly written terms – his product ability *vis-à-vis* the franchisees, but concerning construction, instruction, and control faults, exemption clauses run the risk of being held to be void by the courts.

A 'hold harmless' clause in a standard form contract, according to which the franchisee has to indemnify the franchisor from consumers' product liability claims, has little chance of being effectively enforced.

### Punitive damages

There is no such remedy in the German legal system.

## Trade marks and other intellectual property aspects

*Trade mark by registration* Trade mark protection is available at law for products as well as services (Warenzeichengesetz, WZG). A franchisor who was not able or has not even tried to register a trade mark for his trade name has not done his homework. A franchise network lives on its 'image', of which the trade mark is a key value. If it is not protected, it can be put in jeopardy permanently, or at least for a long time after the start.

### Registration

Trade marks are primarily protected by being entered into the Register of the Patent Office with whom an application has to be filed. The trade mark has to be connected with an enterprise engaged in producing or trading in goods or supplying services.

Foreign enterprises can, according to s. 35 of the WZG, file an application if they have established a branch in Germany or if they operate in a country which grants reciprocity to German enterprises. For most countries the requirement that a foreign enterprise has to file evidence with the application for the protection of the trade mark abroad has also been done away with.

Foreign enterprises which do not have a permanent establishment in Germany have to appoint a resident attorney or patent attorney as representative.

### Eligibility for registration

To be registered, a trade mark must be distinctive. It must not be mistakeable. Mere letters, numbers or words of common language can only become distinctive by extensive use and general acceptance in trade. For common words in one of the main business languages (English, French, Spanish, Italian) more or less the same rules are applied. The German Patent Office is much stricter than most other European offices concerning the 'distinctiveness' of a trade mark.

If the Patent Office considers a sign or words as registrable, it will publish the application. Any objection can be filed during three months after publication.

The grant of the trade mark is published. A normal registration procedure takes at least six months. Under certain circumstances an accelerated procedure is possible.

*Use of the trade mark*

No use of a trade mark is required prior to filing an application or a registration. A registered trade mark does not lose its validity simply by not being used. A third party may, however, ask for the cancellation of a trade mark if the enterprise which is the owner of the trade mark has ceased its business or if the trade mark has been registered for at least five years but has not been used in the last five years prior to the demand for cancellation. It is not sufficient that a 'licensee' uses a registered mark if the owner does not have a business where the mark is used.

*Protection*

The registration of a trade mark is valid for ten years, effective from the date of application. It may be renewed for multiple subsequent ten-year periods. No use has to be proved to the Patent Office to renew the mark.

Actions based upon alleged trade mark infringements have to be brought before the civil courts. Legal action can be started by the trade mark owner or by the German representative of a non-resident trade mark owner, without joining any licensee as a party.

A licensee can, however, be entitled or even obliged by the licence agreement to take action against any infringement in his own name. Clear rules on this subject should be established in a franchise agreement.

*'Licences'*

The trade mark can only be transferred together with the enterprise or with the part of the enterprise in which the mark is used.

Licensing of trade marks is not provided for by law. In fact, agreements for the use of trade marks are common and recognized as restrictive covenants. Such a 'licence' agreement has to respect the limits imposed by German or European competition law.

Neither the 'licence' agreement nor the 'licensee' can be or has to be registered in its trade mark register.

The licensee cannot 'sub-license' the use of the registered mark. But with the owner's consent he can attribute to third parties the right to use the mark.

### Non-registered 'trade marks'
*Protection of the 'famous mark'*

Beyond the trade mark law there exists, developed and recognized by the courts, the protection for the 'famous mark'. Such a mark must enjoy an extraordinary acceptance in trade and a very high reputation; it must also have a very outstanding position and great originality.

Such a mark can be protected not only against the use on similar products, but also against the 'danger of being diluted' by the use on goods of other categories. It must be stressed that it takes a long time and a very strong commercial performance before the status of a 'famous mark' is achieved.

*Protection of appearance and presentation*
Section 25 WZG grants an exclusive protection to the way in which an enterprise presents its goods in trade if it has gained, within the concerned trade circles, general acceptance as identification for the origin of the goods. This protection can be granted to all elements of presentation – wrapping material, advertising material, writing paper, price lists, etc. – which are used to distinguish one's goods from identical or similar goods of a different origin. This protection also applies to the presentation of services. In case of infringements, action by way of injunction as well as a claim for damages can be based on s. 25 of the WZG.

***Protection of trade secrets*** 'Know-how' is a key element of franchising, but it is neither defined nor protected by German law. As far as it can be considered a 'trade secret', it is protected by s. 1 of the UWG, provided the violation is made for the purpose of competition.

Protection of trade secrets is also granted by s. 17 UWG, which is mainly applicable to employees and former employees. Section 17 para. 2 UWG may, however, apply, under certain circumstances, to the special situation of a franchise agreement. Section 90 of the Commercial Code protects trade secrets to which (former) commercial agents had access; it is not yet established by court judgments if this provision can be applied by analogy to (former) franchisees.

Since the legal situation is not fully satisfactory for a franchisor, it is advisable to mention confidentiality obligations very clearly in franchise agreements, also for the time after termination of a contract. The easiest way to enforce the respect of such obligations is to support them with appropriate penalty clauses. If the franchisee is not a registered merchant, the penalty can be reduced by the court, but even if the franchisee is a merchant, a penalty clause can be considered void if it is completely disproportionate to the infringement.

An infringement of a secrecy clause during the term of a contract can justify termination without notice. Damage claims can be based on s. 823 of the Civil Code in combination with s. 1 of the UWG. One should, however, have no illusions on the difficulties in proving infringement of a secrecy clause, or on basing a damages claim on such an infringement.

## Leasing and real estate
*Lease agreements* Although the tenant of residential space has much protection under the law there is very little protection for tenants under commercial lease agreements. The basic rule of freedom of contract can still largely be applied. The only problem a franchisor may face is how to construct a three-party agreement with landlord and franchisee in order to ensure that the lease agreement can be transferred to the franchisor, should the franchise agreement be terminated. But this is just a general problem of contractual law, not of a special tenancy law.

***Real estate*** The acquisition of real estate is achieved by a purchase agreement in form of a notarial deed, but in the original states of the Federal Republic there are no practical restrictions concerning the acquisition of real estate by foreigners. The same rules will apply after a transitional period in the new five eastern states of Germany.

## Employment laws

*General rules* There are no specific employment laws or rules concerning the franchise business. It has to be underlined that employees are strongly protected by the labour laws – even more than in many other EC countries – and that the social costs are high.

### Contract of employment

A contract of employment follows the general rules of the Civil Code for contracts, but numerous mandatory rules, which cannot be waived in advance, protect employees. There exist no minimum salaries or wages, but statutory regulations on maximum working hours, work on Sundays and legal holidays, minimum vacation, working conditions, special protection for expectant mothers, youth, disabled persons, safety regulations, medical care, etc.

Termination of employment is strictly regulated, but varied – until recently – for salaried employees and wage earners, according to age, seniority and other special circumstances (e.g. pregnancy). For salaried employees the minimum notice was and still is six weeks to the end of a calendar quarter; for wage earners the minimum notice was normally two weeks. The minimum periods increase with seniority; they are often extended by collective agreements. This difference to the disadvantage of wage earners has recently been declared unconstitutional by the Federal Constitutional Court. Parliament now has to establish new rules.

An even stronger protection is granted by the Dismissals Protection Law (Kündigungsschutzgesetz) to any salaried person who has been employed for more than six months by an enterprise which employs permanently more than five persons: he or she can only be dismissed for a 'socially justified' reason. The practical consequence is that it is very difficult to get rid of an employee; this is the case even when an employer thinks that an 'important reason' justifies a dismissal without notice. Most litigation concerning dismissal ends with the payment of a more or less substantial compensation by the employer.

A 'non-competition clause' is inherent to any employment contract for its duration, but can also be expressly agreed for a maximum of two years after termination of employment, under a certain number of conditions (e.g. payment of compensation of at least 50% of the salary at the end of employment for the relevant period).

Employment contracts can be and are normally made with the legal representatives (managing directors) of corporations without turning them, however, into 'employees' and thus beneficiaries of the protection of the labour laws.

*Jurisdiction of labour courts*
Litigation in the labour field is handled by special labour courts according to their
own procedural rules. Employers and employees are equally represented in this
judicial system as non-professional judges, but one cannot say that under their
influence the dispensation of justice of labour courts is equally balanced in favour
of both sides.

*Social insurance*
Social insurance schemes cover sickness, pensions, unemployment and workmen's compensation. The latter scheme is entirely financed by the employers;
employers and employees pay 50% each to the other schemes.

***Employees' council*** The Enterprise Constitution Law (Betriebsverfassungs-
gesetz) provides for the institution of a works council for enterprises with at least
five permanent employees entitled to vote (which is not the case for executives) This council represents the employees *vis-à-vis* the management and
enjoys a wide range of rights of co-operation and co-determination concerning
social, personnel and security matters, but in principle not entrepreneurial
matters.

***Collective agreements*** Collective bargaining is handled as a rule by employers'
associations and trade unions, in general on a regional level and by categories
of trade. The resulting agreements only apply to members of the negotiating
parties. But in fact, the same conditions are usually applied to all members of an
enterprise, whether they are members of a union or not; there are not too many
enterprises outside an association which do not apply the wage and other conditions of the collective agreement of their trade.

***Qualification of a franchisee as employee*** There have been a few lower court decisions and some opinions in the judicial literature which have qualified an individual franchisee as an employee of the franchisor. General opinion, however,
including the Federal Court, the Federal Labour Court and several Courts of
Appeal, has considered the typical franchisee who bears the entrepreneurial risks
as an independent merchant, even if he is fully integrated into the franchise
system and if certain rights of control, instruction and direction of the franchisor
restrict his independence.
    To avoid any unnecessary risk in this field, franchisors should not restrict the
independence and liberty of franchisees any more than is really necessary for the
good functioning of the system.
    This has been underlined by a decision of the Labour Court of Appeal of
Düsseldorf in the 'Jacques' Wein-Depot' case. The fact that the franchisees had
to transmit the clients' addresses every week to the franchisor, had to deliver
regularly complete returns of the net turnover and had to allow the franchisor
permanent access to the books did not turn them into employees. However, the

court considered the combination of the following stipulations as characteristic for a salaried person rather than a franchisee:

1   Working hours fixed by the franchisor

2   Period of the annual main vacation unilaterally fixed by the franchisor

3   Almost total dependence on the franchisor's 'apparatus', including book-keeping

4   No freedom for the choice of services or goods to be sold in the franchisees' outlets

5   Personal submission of the main shareholder of a franchisee to the obligations of the franchise contract with his legal entity

6   Right of the franchisor to name a replacement (under certain conditions)

7   Prescription of the (re)sale prices (a clause which is an infringement of German competition law and which would have been void in a real franchise agreement)

For some specific procedural reasons, the Federal Labour Court did not uphold this judgment. A multitude of the elements mentioned above will, however, always be of crucial importance for the distinction of a salaried, and thus dependent, person from a real franchisee, who is an independent business person.

### Foreign investment

*Foreign Trade Law*   The general attitude of the Federal Republic of Germany to foreign trade is expressed in the Foreign Trade Law (Außenwirtschaftsgesetz, AWG). This Law of 1961 establishes in s. 1 the principle of freedom of foreign trade, giving, however, to the government a number of mechanisms for the regulation of foreign trade by imposing restrictions and introducing reporting requirements. Theoretically, there are many possibilities for the government to impose restrictions on transactions in general as well as in the case of specific transactions; the first has rarely been invoked, the second only with very limited or temporary effects.

*Effects of Foreign Trade Law*   Imports do not need any licence if they are included in the so-called 'import list'. At present, practically all imports from free-market countries are included in that list. Extended delivery terms for generally licensed imports are, however, submitted to prior approval (with the exception of agreements within the EC).

The import of capital by non-residents (not only foreigners!) may be estricted if it relates to the purchase of certain goods or rights or to certain other ransactions (e.g. real estate, ships, enterprises or interests in enterprises, bills of xchange, loans or other credits to residents) and if this is necessary to counteract decrease in the purchasing power of the Deutschmark or to safeguard Germany's balance of payments. Restrictions were based on this authorization on everal occasions; none of them is in force anymore, as, for example, the much-iscussed Cash Deposit Ordinance of the 1970s.

The Deutschmark has been freely convertible into other currencies since 958. The export of capital may, if it is necessary for the safeguard of the balance f payments, be restricted by the government for certain kinds of transactions; one of these possibilities has been used so far.

The repatriation of money invested in Germany and the payment of dividends to non-resident recipients or the participation in foreign enterprises is not ven subject to potential restrictions.

In spite of these very liberal principles, which require no approval of foreign nvestment, very extensive reporting requirements have to be met for numerous ransactions, e.g. the establishment or acquisition of domestic enterprises or ranches or the acquisition of interests in such enterprises by non-residents, the urchase or sale of participation in foreign companies and branches by or to residents, the establishment of loans, any claims, liabilities and payments between esidents and non-residents, etc.

*ree entry of foreign services or goods* Given the liberal principles concerning oreign trade there is no instance in which services or goods within the general cope of franchising are favoured or disfavoured by government or legislation. This great liberty in the movement of goods and services does not extend so far as o exclude:

Restrictions concerning services delivered by the classical 'liberal professions'; even within the EC restrictions still exist

Practical restrictions stemming from all kinds of rules or standards for technical, safety or health reasons, valid for national and foreign products

What the EC declares from time to time – also for purely political reasons – as 'unwanted' goods; such 'political' restrictive measures are practically never developed solely by Germany

The restrictions mentioned under 1 and 2 will be eliminated or at least be reduced within the EC as part of the 1992 liberalization process.

**Foreigners working or establishing a business in Germany**
*Labour laws, work permit, residence permit* Labour laws apply equally to all people employed in Germany, to Germans as well as to aliens. Foreign law can be

applied if so stipulated by an employment contract where there is a justified rela tionship to a foreign country.

Aliens from non-EC countries, employed in Germany with a foreign o national enterprise, need work permits prior to the commencement of their work In recent years work permits, which are issued by the locally competent labou office (Arbeitsamt), are in general only granted for very specific jobs, and with th huge influx of people from Eastern Europe it is becoming increasingly difficult t obtain such permits. Aliens from EC and a few other countries (Austria, Finland Sweden and Switzerland) as well as self-employed aliens do not need a wor permit.

All foreigners intending to work in Germany need a residence permit nationals of EC member states enjoy far-reaching privileges. If one obtains ε work permit, one should in general be able to obtain a residence permit, th granting of which is regulated by the Foreigners Act (Ausländergesetz). Citizen from most non-EC countries must obtain the residence permit in the form of ε visa before entering Germany. Austrians, Australians, Canadians and US citi zens may apply for a residence permit after arrival in Germany. Foreigners whc have legally resided for at least five years in Germany can apply for a permanent residence authorization.

Citizens from most Western countries working for their non-resident employer do not need a work permit or residence permit for temporary missions up to two months.

**Establishing a business** The principle of freedom of enterprise is expressly men tioned in s. 1 of the Business Practice Act (Gewerbeordung, GewO) applying to Germans as well as to foreign nationals. Nevertheless, any business entity, indi vidual, company or corporation must register with the local and tax authorities competent for its domicile. Special requirements are laid down for the exercise of itinerant trades and of businesses where the health, the safety, or the general well being of employees, clients, or the general public are at stake, e.g. for the hotel, restaurant or transport business. This legislation is aimed at the prevention of risks caused by unqualified business operators and dangerous business practices. It does not allow the public authorities to refuse a trade permit (Gewerbe erlaubnis) on the grounds that such trade or business is not needed.

Another special field comprises business activities which are inherently dangerous, polluting, or otherwise damaging to the environment or the public. They need a special trade permit, which is granted in accordance with the Federal Pollution Control Act (Bundesimmissionsschutzgesetz), setting very tough emis sion standards for businesses or plants discharging noise, gas, smoke, or other noxious substances. The licensing procedure for these mandatory permits applies to Germans as well as to foreign nationals, but the latter may have more practical difficulties in complying with the requirements.

Still another field comprises businesses considered as the trade of an artisan, regulated by the Handicrafts Code (Handwerksordnung), where at least one manager or employee has to be a master craftsman enlisted in the respective register of his branch. It is often difficult for foreigners to comply with these rules, but far-reaching alleviations exist for citizens of EC origin.

On the contrary, it is easy for aliens to set up a GmbH, the most common form of a corporation (see p. 136). Being individuals or corporations, the shareholders of a GmbH do not need any authorization for its incorporation. Neither does a foreigner, whether resident in Germany or not, need an authorization or a work permit to be managing director of a GmbH.

*Income tax, investment incentives*  These subjects are dealt with below.

### Other significant issues

*Law on General Terms of Trade*  It has been said already that a franchise agreement must be in accordance with the principle of 'good faith' stipulated in s. 242 of the Civil Code. The more detailed expression of the same principle can be found in the Law to Regulate the General Terms of Trade (Gesetz zur Regelung des Rechts der Allgemeinen Geschäftsbedinungen, AGBG) of 1977. This law applies to 'all contractual clauses, used in standard forms for a large number of contracts, which one party presents to the other for the conclusion of a contract'.

It does not apply to contracts which are individually negotiated (in reality!). As practically all franchise agreements are made on standardized forms established by the franchisor, it is evident that they are subject to control by the AGBG. This has been confirmed by the Federal Court in the McDonald's judgment.

This law was essentially made to protect the individual consumer from the intellectual and economic superiority of the merchant who uses standardized contract forms which can contain all kinds of legal traps. Therefore, the law as a whole – especially the 'blacklist' of its ss. 10 and 11 – only applies to individuals who are not merchants. There is, however, legal uncertainty as to whether the law applies with its full scope to individuals who form into merchants.

As many franchisees will be merchants it is only the general clause, s. 9 of the AGBG, which applies on the standard agreements concluded with them. According to this provision 'stipulations in General Terms are void if they are, against the rule of good faith and disproportionately, disadvantageous to the partner or the user of these General Terms'. A 'disproportionate disadvantage' has in general to be seen 'if a contractual stipulation is contrary to the basic idea of a legal regulation which is modified by the contract'.

Even if these criteria are less stringent in their application to contracts concluded with merchants because – according to s. 24 of the AGBG – the usual customs and practices in trade have to be considered, they nevertheless constitute a serious instrument of control. In recent years the courts have been more and more inclined to use the scope provided by this law to remove 'unfair' clauses in contracts imposed by a partner who is considered 'the more powerful'. This attitude of the courts will surely be reflected by their approach to franchise contracts. Therefore one should take into account at least the points mentioned hereafter (unless to be on the safe side, one does not also want to take into account all the limitations of ss. 10 and 11).

*Some regulations of the AGBG*
Section 3 prohibits so-called 'surprising' contractual stipulations.

Section 4 rules that individual agreements always prevail over standard forms; thus, even a clause saying that 'only written agreements are valid' can be overruled if the franchisee can prove an oral agreement to the contrary.

Section 5 says that ambiguous clauses are interpreted against the user of the General Terms.

The invalidity of General Terms cannot only be claimed at any time by the contractual party, i.e. the franchisee, but, according to s. 13, also by consumer or business associations.

*Careful drafting of standard contracts*
In view of these risks, a franchisor should be very careful in drafting his standard franchise agreements. In particular the following items should be drafted so as to ensure sufficient respect for the interests of the franchisee:

1   Non-competition clauses.

2   Duration, termination clauses.

3   General sales conditions: the franchisor's responsibilities according to his own general sales conditions shall not be more restrictive than the responsibilities which the franchisee has towards his clients according to the law or according to his own general sales conditions, proposed to him by the franchisor.

4   Liability clauses: the position must be clearly stated; liability for damage caused by a deliberate or a grossly negligent act by the franchisor or his employees cannot be excluded towards a non-merchant franchisee; towards merchants, liability for gross negligence of employees can be excluded.

5   Product liability: the franchisor cannot transfer his liability to the franchisee.

6   Insurance clauses: responsibilities for the conclusion of insurance contracts and for the payment of premiums have to be clear.

7   Full enumeration of rights and obligations: to avoid an allegation by the franchisee of 'disproportionate disadvantages', the franchisor should very clearly enumerate all rights and obligations of both parties. Some legal authors even think that the contract should fully disclose the business and financial schemes. In one case, the Federal Labour Court decided that the franchisor has to give full advice to the franchisee and has to protect him

from business mistakes. It would be consistent to say that the franchisor is liable for damages for lack of full advice or information; the Court of Appeals of Munich has done so in a judgment of 1988, because the franchisor could not prove to have given full information.

8 Entrance fee and royalties: they have to be appropriate to the franchisor's services and calculated on a clear basis.

9 Minimum purchase: cautious quantities seem appropriate.

10 Defence of trade marks, patents, etc. – clear division of responsibilities.

11 Penal clauses: they are useful to ensure the respect of non-competition, confidentiality and similar clauses, but penalty amounts have to be appropriate to the infringement.

12 Consequences of the termination of contract: acceptable solutions for all practical problems, i.e. termination of the use of trade marks, patents, documents etc.; transfer of the business premises; transfer of the enterprise; repurchase of equipment and goods; evaluation methods; compensation of the franchisee.

13 Sale or transfer of the franchise or the enterprise must be permitted, but can be bound to the franchisor's permission if he does not prefer a pre-emption right; in this case permission can only be refused for important reasons.

14 Choice of law: for international contracts the choice of law is free (Article 27 paragraph 1 of the Introductory Code to the Civil Code (EGBGB, the German Private International Law); compulsory rules of German law for certain contracts apply anyhow (Article 34 EGBGB); if German law is chosen, German courts would accept this choice even if it excludes a mandatory foreign law (e.g. for an American franchisor).

15 Forum of jurisdiction: it can be freely chosen if at least one party has no place of general jurisdiction in Germany (s. 38 of the Code of Civil Procedure); special rules exist within the EC (Article 5 no. 1 and Article 17 to the Brussels Convention).

16 Language of the contract: it is recommended to write the contract in German in order to avoid the allegation of 'surprising clauses'.

**Instalment Purchase Contracts Act** In order to protect the consumer, there was a law concerning instalment purchase contracts (Abzahlungsgesetz, AbzG), containing safeguard clauses for purchase contracts in which the parties have agreed on a payment in at least two instalments. The law did not apply to buyers who were – at the moment of signature – merchants registered in the Commercial Register (e.g. companies).

The Federal Court and the Court of Appeals of Hamburg had applied this law to certain forms of franchise agreements where the potential buyer 'wishes to conclude a contract containing his obligation to purchase or repeatedly obtain goods'. According to these courts the law applied even if the rhythm of purchases only followed the needs of the franchisee. The consequences of these judgments for the franchise business were as follows.

The franchisor had, at the moment of the signature of a franchise agreement which contained purchase obligations, to inform the franchisee in a clear, written (or separate) statement, also to be signed by the franchisee, about his right to withdraw from his purchase obligation within one week. If this information was not given, the franchisee could withdraw from his purchase obligation even years after the signature of the contract. If the purchase obligation was a *conditio sine qua non* for the conclusion of the franchise agreement, there was the risk that the whole agreement and other closely linked contracts would be considered void according to s. 139 of the Civil Code.

This Law has, however, lost its possible effects on future franchise agreements. The Law has been absorbed by the new Consumer Credit Act which came into force on 1 January 1991 (see below). The Law, as it was interpreted by the courts, will nevertheless remain of importance for franchise agreements concluded before 1 January 1991 which did not respect the formal requirements of the old Law.

**Consumer Credit Act**  The Federal Parliament has, taking also into account EC Directive No. 87/102/EEC of 22 December 1986, but going beyond its scope, adopted this new Consumer Credit Act (Verbraucherkreditgesetz, VerbrKrG) of 17 December 1990, mainly in view of the need to protect the inexperienced citizens of the former GDR.

This Law applies, in the first instance, to all remunerated credits granted or arranged by a commercial or professional institution in the form of a loan, a deferment of payment or any other financing aid to an individual in his private capacity. The burden of proof that the credit was granted for private use has been imposed on the lender.

The new Law also applies, according to s. 2, to contracts with consumers which

1    provide for the successive supply of connected goods which were sold as a single unit, the total price being paid in instalments;

2    provide for the regular supply of goods of similar kind;

3    oblige the periodical purchase of goods.

Thus, no commercial activities are affected by this Law, with the exception of credits granted or purchase contracts entered into for the establishment of a new business or professional practice which had not yet been started at the execution of the credit agreement. But according to s. 3 para. 1 no. 2, the exception is limited to credits up to DM 100 000. It is not significant that the contractual partner is registered as a merchant in the commercial register. It is the actual start of the commercial or professional activity which counts.

The credit or the purchase agreement has to be made in writing in accordance with s. 4. If this form requirement is not respected, the agreement is void.

According to s. 7 of the Law, the borrower or the purchaser can withdraw from the credit agreement within one week after having received a written statement on his right to withdraw. Without such a statement, the right of withdrawal expires one year after the execution of the agreement. In cases where the borrower has received the payment of the loan, the withdrawal loses its effect if the loan is not reimbursed within two weeks after the right of withdrawal was used. Thus, the right to withdraw will often be useless in practice, and it will be interesting to see how the courts will handle cases they consider 'unfair'. It is evident that the new Law will not only affect the financing of new franchise businesses, but will be, in view of the interpretation given by the courts to the old AbzG, of the same importance for all franchise agreements where the regular purchase of goods is involved.

### Fair trade practices
#### General rules
Provisions sometimes astonishing to foreigners relating to fair trade practices are contained in several statutes, mainly in the 'Gesetz gegen unlauteren Wettbewerb', UWG (literally 'Law against Unfair Competition', but better 'Law against Unfair Trading' since it has no antitrust implications – which are regulated by the Law against Restraints of Competition. Some of the more important rules, which are refined by an extensive case law, are as follows:

1   Unfair trade practices which are contrary to public morals are prohibited in general, such as impeding competitors' business and marketing efforts, boycotts, exploitation of inexperience, emotions or gambling instincts, imitations, violation of statutory contractual obligations, etc.

2   Information on goods, and especially advertising, must be true, correct and unambiguous.

3   Comparative advertising is allowed only within certain limits.

4   Trade names are protected; similar names, that might cause confusion, may not be used by other businesses.

5   Discounts to the last consumer for payment upon delivery may not exceed 3%; other rebates are strictly regulated.

These rules can be enforced by any competitor, but often also by business or consumer associations.

*Pyramid selling*

'Pyramid' or 'snowball' selling has generally been considered as a violation of s. 1 of the UWG. Furthermore, s. 6c of the UWG was enacted in 1986, providing punishment by a fine or by imprisonment of up to two years for initiating a snowball system. According to this provision, it is forbidden for any person to 'undertake by himself or through other persons, in the course of business activity, to induce non-merchants to purchase goods, commercial services or rights by promising to grant them special advantages in the event that they induce other persons to enter into similar agreements who, according to this type of sales promotion, shall in turn receive such advantages for the corresponding solicitation of further customers'.

## TAX AND FINANCIAL CONSIDERATIONS

### General

The German tax system is a complicated balance between the interests and needs of the federal government, the individual states and the municipalities. This balance is now put into question by the unification of Germany, and will be newly defined in the months and years following unification on 3 October 1990. Since everybody in both the West and the East underestimated the financial needs of the new five eastern states, the political statements made before the general elections of 2 December 1990, stating that the unification of Germany would not provoke any tax increases, were unrealistic.

All serious observers had agreed that there would be tax increases if the public administration did not make budget cuts (which nobody really expected); it was only a question of when, where and to what extent. Therefore, one or other of the tax rates indicated hereafter will be modified in the future, although the government from time to time announces a reduction of the tax burden for enterprises. The tax system as such is unlikely to change.

A similar situation exists for the social security system. The western system has been introduced in eastern Germany; this has caused enormous starting costs which, again, are financed by the (west) German taxpayer. But, in the long run, it is the contribution to the different social security schemes which will be affected.

However, the orientation of the existing investment incentives will be profoundly modified.

### Tax Code

The different tax categories are regulated by different laws and numerous regulations; the procedure of levying taxes is, however, laid down in one general law, the Tax Code (Abgabenordnung, AO). It contains the rules concerning:

1    General definitions (ss. 3ff.)

2    Competence of tax authorities (ss. 16ff.)

3    Tax liabilities (ss. 33ff.)

4    General duties of any taxpayer (ss. 140ff.)

5    Tax declaration (ss. 149ff.)

6    Tax assessment (ss. 155ff.)

7    Field inspection and investigation (ss. 193ff.)

8    Payment and execution (ss. 218ff.)

9    Appeals against a tax assessment (ss. 347ff.)

10   Punishment of tax infringements (ss. 369ff.)

**Taxation and customs laws**
*Income tax* Income tax is imposed by the Income Tax Law (Einkommensteuer-
gesetz, EStG):

1    On the worldwide income of persons who have their residence or their
     habitual abode in Germany (unlimited tax liability)

2    On non-residents only on their German source income (limited tax liability)

These domestic rules may be modified by double-taxation treaties, at least by
allowing tax credits to eliminate double taxation. Income tax is assessed on the
basis of tax returns to be filed annually by the taxpayer.

Individuals and partners of partnerships (of oHG or KG) pay income tax
(Einkommensteuer) at progressive rates, starting with a rate of 19% for net
income (all deductions made) above DM 5617, up to a maximum rate of 53% for
net income above DM 120 042 (an income of DM 120 042 is taxed at an average
rate of approximately 33.5%; figures of 1990).

*Corporation tax* Business entities in the form of a corporation (AG, GmbH)
and some other forms – but not partnerships – are subject to corporation tax
imposed by the Corporation Tax Law (Körperschaftsteuergesetz, KStG). This
tax is governed by similar rules as the income tax. There are corporations with
'unlimited' and 'limited' tax liability: this roughly corresponds to the distinction
between 'resident' and 'non-resident'. A German corporation is always a tax
resident; a foreign corporation can become a German resident by having a
permanent establishment or management in Germany. Resident corporations
are taxed on their worldwide income (subject to double-taxation treaties).

The tax rate is 50% for undistributed and 36% for distributed profits. Non-resident corporations are taxed on their German income at a flat rate of 46%. Monetary advantages granted to related persons (e.g. shareholders or affiliated companies) are considered to be disguised distribution of profits and are added back to the corporation's profits. They are subject to corporation tax.

**Wage tax** Wage tax (Lohnsteuer) is a form of income tax levied on gross income from dependent labour. It is withheld by the employer on each payment to be made to the salaried person and directly paid to the tax authorities. Very few deductions are allowed from the requirement of withholding. But for the yearly assessment of taxable net income, deductions can be made for a certain number of special personal expenses (e.g. contributions to private pensions and other insurance schemes, home building, tax consulting fees, professional ongoing education, etc.), and also for extraordinary charges. Tax rates and allowed tax credits are the same as for income tax.

**Trade tax** Trade tax is imposed by the Trade Tax Law (Gewerbesteuergesetz, GewStG) on business profit and business capital of any person (not only companies) running a business in Germany. The tax has in general also to be paid by non-residents with a permanent establishment on their German source income.

Trade tax is levied at rates determined by the municipalities, which often try to attract business by offering low rates. The basic rate for business profit is 5% and for business capital 0.2% (both profits and capital especially defined for trade tax purposes). Basic rates are multiplied by factors usually between 240 and 450; for example, the highest multiplication factor of 450 gives tax rates of 22.5% for business income and 0.9% for business capital. It is these multiplication factors which the municipalities 'manipulate'. Smaller towns tend to have lower rates than large cities.

Trade tax is deducted from income before assessing corporation tax and trade tax itself.

**Net worth tax** Net worth tax is imposed by the Net Worth Tax Law (Vermögensteuergesetz, VermStG). It is assessed on the total value of a business's total net assets. For corporations the tax rate is 0.6%; for natural persons (or individual partners of partnerships) it is 0.5%.

Residents pay this tax on worldwide net assets, non-residents only on their net assets situated in Germany. For a corporate business, net worth tax results in a burden of around 1%.

### Withholding taxes
#### Dividends
Distributed income is subject to a withholding tax at a rate of 36%. Resident shareholders (only) receive a tax credit for this 36% tax to be imputed on their own income tax.

Dividend payments to non-residents are subject to a 25% withholding tax (according to s. 43a of the EStG). Under many double-taxation treaties (e.g. the present US–German Treaty) the rate is reduced to 15%.

### Royalties

Royalties paid abroad are subject to a withholding tax of 25%, unless otherwise provided for in double-taxation treaties. Under the US–German and quite a few other tax treaties, licensing income is only taxed in the country of recipient's residence.

Royalty payments by a (master) franchisee are deductible as a business expense under German income (corporation) tax law. Payments to parent companies abroad are thoroughly checked in accordance with the 'arm's length principle', in order to see if they exceed those normally paid to an unrelated foreign licensor.

### Ongoing fees

Insofar as ongoing fees are paid for services rendered by a foreign franchisor (without permanent establishment in Germany) they are not subject to withholding tax. Fees for services rendered by a franchisor with a permanent establishment in Germany are subject to the limited income tax liability.

### Interest

According to most double-taxation treaties (also the US–German Treaty) interest on bonds, securities or any other form of indebtedness (including debts secured by mortgages) received by the resident or corporation of a foreign country is exempt from withholding tax in Germany. There is no German withholding tax on ordinary fixed interest from a loan to a German resident evidenced by a loan agreement or a similar document.

**Value added tax (VAT)** VAT is imposed by the Turnover Tax Law (Umsatzsteuergesetz, UStG) and is payable by businesses on the supply of goods or services in Germany. 'Services' include, for example, licensing of patents or trade marks, delivery of blueprints or know-how. The general VAT rate is presently 14%. A lower rate of 7% applies to:

1    Certain foodstuffs

2    Books, newspapers, magazines, motion picture rentals and royalties

3    Licence fees and royalties with respect to items protected by copyright

VAT is ultimately borne by the end consumer, who pays the 14% added to the last sales price. At the preceding sales levels, each reseller can credit against the VAT he has to pay to the fiscal authorities, the VAT he has paid on purchases.

There is always VAT on the importation of goods or services to Germany, which can also be credited against the VAT the recipient has to pay. In many cases where services are provided, there is no VAT to be paid as the services are zero-rated.

Non-residents are liable to VAT on their taxable transactions in Germany. Since the tax authorities cannot directly levy VAT from them, the resident purchaser of goods or services has to withhold the VAT and pay it to the authorities. In many cases, however, these VAT payments are either deductible or reimbursable.

*Capital transfer tax* Capital transfer tax is imposed by the Capital Transfer Tax Law (Kapitalverkehrsteuergesetz, KVStG) as a special turnover tax on transactions exempted from VAT. It exists in the two following forms:

1    As an incorporation duty on the original acquisition of interest or the later contribution of capital in a corporation (including a GmbH & Co. KG)

2    As transfer tax on the transfer of stock and securities, mainly on a stock exchange

For the incorporation duty the corporation is taxed, but also the persons making the payments are liable. The tax rate is 1%. For the transfer tax both parties to a transfer are liable; if a professional trader is a party, he alone is liable. The regular tax rate is 0.25% of the agreed price.

*Customs duties* Non-EC goods are subject to customs duties which, in general, are *ad valorem*. Customs duties are instituted by the EC authorities. No extraordinary tariffs, restrictions, import quotas or licensing requirements of special concern for franchisors from OECD countries exist in Germany.

### Social security obligations
A complex and comprehensive system of laws and regulations assures each salaried person and his dependants in Germany of a minimum level of existence, which protects them against the adverse consequences of sickness, disability, old age, and unemployment. Self-employed people (artisans, liberal professionals, etc.) do not enjoy the same all-round protection by the state, but they are to a certain extent allowed to join the mandatory schemes. Quite a few professions have created their own self-regulated old age pension schemes. Every resident is, in case of need, entitled to a minimum level of aid from the public welfare. The latter system is entirely financed by general resources, i.e. taxes. The other social security schemes are largely or entirely financed by contributions from employees and/or employers. The total benefits from these schemes are good. They are so good that western Germany has become very attractive to many immigrants purely for social reasons. Nevertheless, the German social security system still

costs less to both employees and employers than its equivalent in most neighbouring countries.

## Social security contributions

The following social security contributions are to be paid by employees and/or employers up to the specified maximum salaries (figures for 1991):

| | | |
|---|---|---|
| Pension | 18.7% | up to a monthly salary of DM 6700 |
| Sickness | 11–12%* | up to a monthly salary of DM 5025 |
| Unemployment | 4.3% | up to a monthly salary of DM 6700 |
| Workmen compensation | 2–5%* | up to a monthly salary of DM 6700 |

*Percentage figures vary for different schemes and professions.

The workmen compensation scheme is entirely financed by the employers; to the other schemes employers and employees each contribute 50% of the charges indicated above. The total charges for an employer thus vary between 19% and 22.5% of the gross salaries (up to the maximum amounts mentioned above) which include bonuses, holiday pay and some other fringe benefits. Employees with monthly salaries above DM 5025 can opt out of the social sickness insurance and join a private health insurance. A salaried managing director (Geschäftsführer) of a GmbH, although not considered an 'employee' in the sense of German labour law, is automatically insured in the mandatory social security schemes.

## Investment incentives

As mentioned before, the orientations of the different investment incentive programmes are expected to undergo profound modifications in the near future. Therefore only a very general outline is provided.

*Incentives to foreigners* In principle, no particular investment incentives (cash subsidies, financing aid, tax incentives, etc.) are granted to foreigners. In exceptional cases – when the investment is supposed to create employment or taxable revenues – local or regional authorities tend to make special arrangements, e.g. sell good real estate below market prices or suspend local taxes for an initial period.

*Incentives in general* A great number of investment incentives exist in the form of federal or state programmes, all of which aim at helping to create permanent self-supporting businesses. With a few limited exceptions, none of these programmes grants cash subsidies, but financing aids or tax incentives.

*Financing aids*

Favourable financing is available for small and medium-sized businesses, especially in so-called development areas, which exist in most of the German states. They also exist for certain qualifying purposes, which change from time to time with the general political or economic climate. The emphasis in the next years will shift to the new five east German states, to be considered as a whole as a 'developing area', especially in the field of environmental protection measures.

One federal programme which helps to increase the capital resources of the founders of enterprises is managed by the Deutsche Ausgleichsbank, a public federal institution. Under this programme, the resources of an entrepreneur of at least 15% of the total investment can be increased to a maximum of 40%. Such a loan can be used as proprietary capital and does not have to be guaranteed. The interest and repayment conditions are very advantageous. The qualifying conditions are, however, not easy to fulfil. Expert opinions must confirm to the Deutsche Ausgleichsbank the professional and personal qualifications of the entrepreneur and the commercial prospects of the planned investment. Under this programme existing enterprises can also receive a loan.

The European Recovery Program (ERP) and numerous programmes by the different states grant loans on similar conditions: up to 50% of an investment of up to DM 300 000, or even more, can be obtained at very favourable interest rates and with deferred amortization. Such loans have to be guaranteed personally by the entrepreneur. Where these personal guarantees do not satisfy the lender, a great number of guarantee institutions, often organized at state level, can intervene. They deliver sureties of up to 80% of the credits at very advantageous costs in circumstances generally not acceptable as risks for banks.

There is one strict rule concerning these privileged loans: there must be no activities establishing the project at the moment of application. In the case of franchising, not even a franchise agreement should be signed by the potential franchisee.

In general, the applicant cannot be a foreign franchisor with its supposedly substantial financial resources, but has to be the resident entrepreneur, but this does not exclude a joint venture.

In the early days of franchising many financing institutions regarded this new method of business with suspicion. Now the Deutsche Ausgleichsbank and most of the other public institutions have acquired solid experience with franchise systems and consider them a good method for creating new businesses (unlike the private banking networks in Germany, which are still not very familiar with franchising and of which, to the author's knowledge, only a few have specialized programmes). Especially in the new five eastern states franchising as a business method is positively viewed by the public financing institutions – if it is thoroughly prepared by a serious franchisor.

The favourable attitude of the public institutions does not mean that the proposed projects are not very carefully screened, especially the conditions of the franchise agreement. The agreement must reflect the applicant's position as an independent entrepreneur who is not subject to unfair and inadequate restrictions. Special attention is paid to the duration of the contract (not less than five, better ten years), exaggerated penalties, easy termination possibilities, minimum turnover or turnover increase conditions, liberty in choosing consultants and insurance firms, etc.

## Tax incentives

Special tax incentives were offered in West Berlin and certain designated development areas bordering the former GDR and Czechoslovakia. These schemes will certainly be modified: they will, on the one hand, after a transitional period be stopped for West Berlin, but, on the other hand, probably be extended to the whole of eastern Germany. Such programmes cannot be autonomously established by the German government, but must comply with the Treaty of Rome and other EC legislation.

# CHAPTER 9
# GREECE

*Yanos Gramatidis*

## AN OVERVIEW OF FRANCHISING IN GREECE

Franchising has not yet developed in Greece to the extent that it has in other EC and non-EC countries. However, a good number of industrial franchise agreements, relating to relationships between foreign and Greek producers and consisting of manufacturing alliances based on patterns and/or technical know-how combined with trade mark licences, have been concluded in the last ten years. At the same time many distribution franchise agreements have been concluded between foreign and Greek companies, either in the form of producers' or in the form of distributors' franchise. On the other hand, a substantial number of franchising agreements for the distribution of goods have been concluded between Greek companies, mainly in the form of distribution agreements between a producer or distributor and other retailers.

Certain franchise agreements, mainly in the service areas, have already been concluded in Greece despite the difficulty that service marks cannot be protected in this country.

The lack of experience in developing a franchise, in adopting an operation manual and in choosing a most suitable way of expansion, even on a national level, makes Greece a particularly interesting target country for any international franchisor. Thorough preparation is essential in taking one's franchise to Greece. A careful selection of the appropriate structure of the Greek venture should be made while other legal considerations as well as tax and financial issues are not of minor importance.

The Greek government recently expressed interest in franchising, mainly in the sense that it could use the concept in the framework of the recent privatization process in the country. More specifically, state-controlled department stores could develop a franchise network, in a way which would increase their overall value and make them an attractive target for any private investor.

No bank in Greece, Greek or foreign, has any departments involved in franchising in Greece and it is doubtful whether a bank in Greece could be of assistance to local or foreign franchisors owing to the lack of experience. There are, however, certain firms of accountants which have developed franchise consultancy departments. For the moment there is no national franchise association for the promotion of the concept and of business opportunities for franchisors.

## STRUCTURE OF GREEK VENTURE: BUSINESS ENTITIES

The two general kinds of corporate entity in Greece are personal companies and capital companies. Personal companies may be unlimited, limited or civil partnerships. Capital companies are either limited liability companies or corporations (sociétés anonymes). There are also branches of foreign corporations, offshore branches of foreign corporations established under Law 89/1967, joint ventures and sole trader.

Local franchisors are organized in the form of capital companies, usually in the form of corporations, and the same applies to joint ventures with foreign franchisors. The main advantage in choosing corporations instead of limited liability companies is flexibility in the passing of resolutions and common policies of the partners, since for the formation of a resolution in the case of a limited liability company the majority both of capital and partners are required, while in the case of a corporation only the majority of capital is required. More specifically, it is quite possible in the case of a limited liability company that a partner having a 70% stake is not in a position to pass a resolution at the general meeting of partners if the remaining 30% of the capital votes against him. The only disadvantage of corporations is that they are more expensive than any other company to form and run.

### General rules on personal companies

There are no minimum capital requirements or requirements for publication of accounts for personal companies. They are established through a private agreement (the partnership contract) between two or more persons, such contracts being their articles of association. Once the partnership contract has been executed, various publication procedures must be followed. Initially this includes registration of a summary of the partnership contract with the Registry of the appropriate Court of First Instance, the so-called Book of Partnerships. A copy of such a summary is presented to the public for a three-month period in the main courtroom of the Court of Registration.

One of the main obligations of the partners is the contribution to the partnership of such funds as are necessary from time to time on the basis of the ratio of their capital shares. Such contribution could also consist of non-cash considerations (moveable and immoveable property) which the partnership could either own or simply use. In the case of contributions consisting of such consideration, its transfer into the partnership should be effected through a private agreement (in the case of the transfer of moveables) or through a notarial deed (in the case of the transfer of any right over real estate).

The duties of partners include the duty to effect their contribution, to manage and represent the partnership if they have so agreed, to see that the operation of the partnership complies with the fundamental objects agreed, not to do anything damaging to the interests of the partnership, not to disclose confidential information of the partnership and not to compete with the partnership. If any of the partners breaches his duties, there is an *actio pro socio* whereby each of the other partners has the right, on behalf of the partnership, to demand immediate remedy of such breach.

As already mentioned, the partners have a duty to manage and represent the partnership. Such a duty is also a right of the partners (the rights to participate in administration and representation are forbidden in the case of a limited partner in a limited partnership). They also have the right to participate in the operation of the partnership and to vote on any issue concerning the partnership, and to examine the documents and all official books of the same. They also have direct rights over the assets of the partnership and the right to participate in the collection of the net proceeds remaining after liquidation of the partnership.

All unlimited partners have the power to act for the partnership or administer the same unless such an administration has already been transferred to administrators through the partnership contract or through a resolution made by the majority of the partners.

For the protection of the partners, the law provides that the death or bankruptcy of a partner shall constitute a reason for the dissolution of the partnership. This rule, however, is of a voluntary character and is not used where other arrangements have been specifically provided for within the partnership contract (for example, rules relating to the continuation of the partnership between the remaining partners or between the heirs or the legal representatives of the deceased partner). Partnership rights cannot be transferred unless it is specifically provided for in the partnership contract or unless all the partners give their approval. The new partner assumes the rights, obligations and duties of his predecessor and is liable for the past debts of the partnership.

The entrance of new partners into a partnership is possible only after a unanimous resolution of the partners. Creditors of a partnership have a direct claim against the individual partners and any and all judgments against a partnership can be executed against its individual partners.

A partnership shall be dissolved when its duration has expired, its objects have been realized or it has become impossible for the same to be realized, when only one partner remains in the partnership or when any of the partners have served upon the partnership a notice of termination based on serious grounds. The partnership can also be dissolved by a unanimous resolution of the partners or by a majority resolution should the partnership contract so provide.

For a resolution to be passed in general meeting a simple majority of partners is required.

On dissolution of the partnership the net proceeds of the liquidation, if any, are distributed to the partners.

## General rules on capital companies

There are different minimum capital requirements for capital companies according to the nature of their commercial operations. For a corporation the minimum capital is Drs 5 million, or more in special cases. For example, for the establishment of a bank corporation the minimum capital must be Drs 2 billion, for a capital investment corporation Drs 30 million and for an insurance corporation Drs 25 million. To qualify for quotation on the Greek stock exchange the corporation should present between three and five profitable annual accounts to obtain the necessary permits.

The following should be published in the form of the publication procedures provided by law in the Bulletin of Corporations and Limited Liability Companies of the Greek Government Gazette for both corporations and limited liability companies: (a) the articles of incorporation and any modifications thereto; (b) the balance sheets and any modifications thereto; (c) all notices to shareholders of general meetings of the shareholders; and (d) all resolutions of the general meeting of partners of limited liability companies and of the board of directors of corporations which relate to: (i) the election of administrators of limited liability companies or of the members of the board of directors of corporations; (ii) the transfer of the registered offices of limited liability companies or the new address of corporations; and (iii) any increases of the share capital of both limited liability companies and corporations. The state, therefore, supervises not only the establishment but also the operation of capital companies.

Shareholders of corporations have numerous rights, including: (a) the right to vote at a general meeting, (b) the right to the profits and (c) the right to the proceeds of liquidation in proportion to their contributions to such corporations. The minority shareholders also have the right to question the administration of a corporation, the right to request a postponement of a resolution of the general meeting, the *actio pro socio* and other special rights described by the law and requiring various capital proportions.

The partners of a limited liability company also have the right to administer the company (including the right to manage, vote and control the company) and the right to the profits or the proceeds of the liquidation of the company. The partners also have special rights, including the right to convene a general meeting of the partners or to ask for the dissolution of the company. A majority of the partners of a limited liability company is required for the passing of many resolutions of shareholders in general meeting.

The directors of corporations are appointed at a general meeting of the shareholders while the members of the initial board of directors of corporations are appointed through the memorandum and articles of incorporation. Such a text may also very well provide that a specific shareholder(s) may appoint directors of his or her own choice, but not in any event more than one-third of the total number of directors.

The directors exercise the management of the corporation and represent it in dealings with any third party transactions and also before courts and other public authorities.

The directors of corporations are liable *vis-à-vis* the corporation for any offence committed in the exercise of their management duties, namely for any false statement related to the financial situation of the corporation and for any omission in the balance sheet of the corporation. Any action by a corporation against its directors has to be sanctioned by an absolute majority vote of the shareholders in general meeting. The directors of corporations are also liable *vis-à-vis* third parties for any offence or damage. Such liability may be of a civil or criminal nature or both.

Since 1986 Greece has adopted the Directives of the Council of the European Communities No. 68/151 of 9 March 1968, and No. 77/91 of 13 July 1983 for the harmonization of the rules related to establishment and operation of corporations and limited liability companies in the member states of the EC.

## Special rules concerning corporate activities

Corporations can be converted under special laws to limited liability companies or to personal companies and vice versa. In the case of such a conversion, the whole procedure required for the establishment of a new company has to be followed. Personal companies can also be converted into limited liability companies and vice versa. A merger between capital companies can be realized either through the establishment of another company or the acquisition of the issued shares of one company by another.

## Reporting and disclosure requirements

The annual financial statements comprise a balance sheet, a profit and loss account (income statement), a distribution of profit table, and an appendix (notes). The balance sheet, income statement and distribution of profit table must be prepared in accordance with models provided by corporate legislation. Subject to certain conditions and exemptions, the parent company and its subsidiaries must prepare consolidated financial statements. The most important matters to be included in the appendix are: accounting methods for valuation of assets, depreciation and provisions, changes in accounting principles or valuation methods, including their effects on the financial statements insofar as these can be quantified, and the basis for conversion of foreign currency balances.

## Statutory audit requirements

Certain categories of business which are obliged to be incorporated such as banks, insurance companies, investment companies, mutual funds, petroleum companies, and, generally, all corporations (AEs) and limited liability companies (EPEs) which fulfil certain criteria must appoint a qualified accountant as statutory auditor. Companies quoted on the stock exchange must appoint two qualified accountants as statutory auditors. All other corporations appoint two persons who must have a university degree in business management or economics (alternatively, one qualified accountant) as statutory auditors.

## Accounting principles and practices

Accounting principles and practices are governed primarily by tax legislation; however, corporate law includes certain principles. Because there is no standard setting body or enforcement rules, caution is needed when reviewing financial statements.

# LEGAL CONSIDERATIONS

## Introduction

A foreign franchisor who targets Greece as the territory for the establishment of a franchise arrangement should consider various legal issues including local competition laws, industrial and intellectual property, real estate and leasing laws, employment laws, protection of foreign investments etc.

## Pyramid selling

There are no laws in Greece relating to pyramid selling schemes.

## Competition law

Until 1977 the Greek antitrust legislation was mainly regulated by Law 146/1914 which related to unfair competition. The provisions of this Law had been used very frequently in the past for the protection of individual enterprises. However, it did not serve as an institution for the systematic protection of the competitive structure of the economy and its mechanisms through the responsible intervention of the state. This need was covered by Law 703/1977 relating to the control of monopolies and oligopolies and to the protection of free competition. Since 1 January 1981 the Greek antitrust legislation has been fully harmonized with the rules of the Treaty of Rome governing competition.

Law 703/1977 prohibits all agreements between undertakings, all decisions of associations of undertakings and any form of concerted practice of undertakings which have as their object or effect the prevention, restriction or distortion of competition, particularly those consisting in (a) the direct or indirect fixing of purchase or selling prices and any other trading condition, (b) limiting or controlling production, distribution, technical developments or investments, (c) the sharing of markets or the sources of supply, (d) the application in commerce of unequal conditions for equivalent supplies in a manner preventing the operation of competition and in particular the unjustified refusal to sell, purchase or enter into any other transaction, and (e) making the conclusion of contracts subject to acceptance by the other contracting party of supplementing grants which by their nature or according to commercial usages have no connection with the subject of such contracts.

Law 703/1979 also provides the possibility for an undertaking or an association of undertakings to file a notification or request a negative clearance in relation to a specific agreement.

Article 1 of Law 146/1914 provides that in commercial, industrial and agri cultural transactions, any act which is opposed to morality is prohibited. The transgressor may be restrained from continuing such acts and liable for damages Such acts include (a) any misrepresentation concerning transactions under Arti cle 1 made in public, communications or announcements addressed to a larger circle of persons and in particular misstatements concerning the quality, the source of origin, the process of manufacturing or the pricing of goods or of indus trial activities, the manner or the source of procurement, the possession of awards or other honourable distinctions, the cause or the aim of the sale, or the size of the applicable stock, if such statements are apt to give the impression of a particularly favourable offer; (b) public announcements of sales of goods for the purpose of liquidation of a business or a branch of a business, including clearance sale; (c) the use of a trade name, a trade mark, an emblem or a distinctive sign of which a third party is the legitimate holder; and (d) the disclosure of business secrets by an employee of such business for competition purposes or by any third party who obtained knowledge of such secrets through an employee of the business and by anyone who discloses to third parties or makes an unauthorized use of technical data or of particular drawings, patterns, samples or instructions which were entrusted to him in the course of business. All valid claims also justify injunctive relief. Transgressors may be prohibited from making such misrepresentations and sued for damages and in the case that such misrepresentations were made fraudulently he would be subject also to criminal prosecution. Transgressors may be restrained from conducting any such activity in the future.

## Industrial and intellectual property

*Trade marks and trade names* Law 1998/1939 relating to trade marks as amended by Law 3905/1955 provides that a trade mark is any sign used to designate the origin of a product from a certain industrial, agricultural or stock breeding business as well as of the trade objects of a certain commercial business. The mere registration of a trade mark enables the proprietor to enjoy the exclusive use of the registered trade mark. Whoever imitates a trade mark belonging to another may be sued before the appropriate courts in respect of such infringement and/or for damages. Insofar as the claim for damages is concerned, there is a three-year statute of limitation commencing from the end of the year in which such violation occurred.

A trade name is the name a merchant uses in his everyday commercial activities, while a distinctive title or emblem is a name or a sign used by a merchant or a business to distinguish such business. Trade names, distinctive titles and distinctive shapes of goods are protected by Article 13 of Law 146/ 1914, provided that whoever in commercial transactions uses a name, a trade name or a distinctive sign for a shop or for an industrial business or for printed matter in such a way that it may create confusion with the name, the trade name or the distinctive sign which another lawfully uses may be compelled by the latter to refrain from such use and that he is also held liable to indemnify the latter for the damage sustained by the same if he knew or ought to have known that damage could occur from such use. Trade marks are also covered by the same provision.

Further, Article 14 of the same law provides that the intentional use of such a trade name or distinctive sign belonging to another is punishable by up to six months' imprisonment and/or a fine. There is a six-month statute of limitation commencing from the date that the owner of a trade mark or trade name was informed of the infringement.

Trade marks, trade names and distinctive signs and titles may also be protected by the provisions of the Greek Civil Code relating to unlawful acts. More specifically, Articles 914 and 919 of the Code provide that whoever illegally and intentionally or in a manner violating morality causes a damage to another shall be liable to compensation. Such compensation covers not only damages for pecuniary injury but also for moral harm. The illegality of the action would be based on Article 281 of the Civil Code providing that the abuse of a right in a manner obviously exceeding the limits imposed by good faith or morality or finally by the social and/or financial purpose of a right, is prohibited. There is a five-year statute of limitation commencing from the date when the legitimate owner was informed of the offence.

The general provisions on unfair competition also protect utility models and industrial designs in the absence of specific legislation. On the other hand, Law 2527/1920 provides full protection to patents. Pursuant to such law patent is a right of exclusive exploitation of inventions which are susceptible of industrial use. Whoever intentionally or by gross negligence uses an invention in violation of the provisions of the law, is subject to damages and in case of fraudulent use, to criminal prosecution. There is a three-year statute of limitation in relation to such a protection.

*Copyright* Copyright is covered by Law 2387/1920 as subsequently amended. Such law provides that authors, musical composers, painters, designers, sculptors, turners and carvers of originals or adapted and arranged, copied or translated works, enjoy for a lifetime the exclusive right of publication or reproduction of their works under any manner and form, of the performance of musical compositions, theatrical plays, fragments and extracts thereof and of their assignments to third parties. The same Law provides full protection of the above persons against anybody who knowingly or fraudulently violates these provisions.

Greece is also a signatory to the Berne Convention of 1886 relating to the protection of literary and artistic works as amended by the Brussels Act of 1948.

## Real estate and leasing

In Greece a person or a corporate entity may have the following rights in relation to real estate:

1    Ownership

2    Rights *in personam* and rights *in rem*

3    Mortgage

The above rights of ownership and rights *in personam* and *in rem* may be acquired by a deed executed by the parties involved before a public notary and recorded with the land registry of the district where the real estate is located. A mortgage may be perfected either by a deed executed by the parties involved before a public notary, or by a court judgment or finally directly by the law.

Under Article 17 paragraph 2 of the Greek Constitution, ownership of real estate in Greece by foreign nationals is protected, despite the fact that such protection is not specifically mentioned. This interpretation of the law derives from the statement 'nobody shall be deprived of his property . . .', as well as from the fact that had the draftsman intended to exclude foreign nationals from this protection he would have done so expressly.

The above provision is read in conjunction with the provisions of Article 4 of the Greek Civil Code which states that 'A foreign national shall enjoy the same civil rights as a national', this being a broader rule under the area of private international law. Through the above rule, the principle of equality between foreign nationals and nationals is established from the private international law standpoint without establishing actual uniformity in the treatment of foreign nationals and nationals by the state. Based on this principle, differences in the treatment of foreign nationals and nationals are not prohibited by the law; however, *in dubio*, a presumption of equality exists between both pursuant to the rules of private international law and the enjoyment of rights.

The Greek Constitution implicitly prescribes the deprivation of real estate lawfully acquired by foreign nationals subject, of course, to expropriation proceedings, as they affect Greek nationals. A foreign national is equal to a national from the standpoint of legal protection from the moment that he has actually acquired real estate in Greece. Moreover, expropriation can only be exercised by the state to satisfy a public necessity, with compensation always granted to the property owner, so entitled, prior to any such acquisition.

It must be noted, however, that the state does have the power to impose stricter conditions on the acquisition of residential or commercial estate in border areas by foreign nationals as well as nationals, even to the point of absolute prohibition. By the term 'border areas' we mean those areas near Greek borders, including the islands closest to the borders with other countries.

The islands of Rhodes, Chios, Samos, Lesbos, Cos, Skiros, Santorini, together with Florina, Thesprotia, Kastonia, Xanthi, Rodopi, Kilkis, Evros, Pogoni, Konitsa, Almopia, Edessa, Sintiki and Nevrokopi on the mainland, have already been identified as border areas. All foreign nationals and nationals or corporate entities are even prohibited from leasing or being granted the use of civil real estate located in border areas for periods which exceed six years.

The transfer of real estate by means of a parental gift, the arrangement of boundaries, the distribution of a joint property and all transactions related to the transfer of a non-definable percentage in a joint property between co-owners have been provided as the sole exceptions to the prohibition rule mentioned above.

The above prohibitions may be lifted only in the case of individuals or legal entities of Greek or Cypriot nationality and in the case of EC nationals or legal entities applying to that effect before a special committee based at the prefecture of the place where the relevant real estate is located. Such a committee consists of the prefect and one representative from each of the following Ministries: Defence, National Economy, Public Order and Agriculture. In the application those interested in buying real estate in border areas should state the reasons dictating each particular purchase or the future use of the property for sale from the point of view of the prospective purchaser.

Such a possibility provided by the law only covers certain categories of transactions defined by their legal form, and the value and location of the properties involved. The relevant Committee's decision must be ratified by the Minister of National Defence, who retains the right to revoke the same in the future.

Individuals or foreign entities originating from foreign countries can also make use of the above possibility by applying to the Minister of National Defence who will decide on the lifting or not of the existing prohibition.

In the case of a lease a lessee acquires from the owner of the real estate the right to use the same during the term of the lease and is bound to pay the owner of such real estate a rent agreed upon. A lessee does not acquire any property rights through the lease agreement.

Lease agreements are generally valid regardless of form. Lease agreements related to both residential and commercial property may very well take the form of a private agreement between the owner of the real estate and the lessee, while in the cases of lease of a duration longer than nine years such an agreement will usually take the form of a deed executed before a public notary.

A lease terminates on the expiry of the term granted. In the case of leases of an indefinite duration either party may give notice of termination.

In the absence of agreement to the contrary the lessee is entitled to transfer the use of the leased property to any third party, particularly to sub-let the property, in which case the lessee remains liable to the owner of the property for any default or act of the sub-tenant. In the case of commercial leases a sub-lease usually bears the form of a sub-lease agreement, the text of which is similar to a head lease.

Law 813/1978 provides that the duration of any commercial lease should be at least six years, even in cases where a shorter or indefinite term has been agreed. As mentioned above, a commercial lease terminates on the expiration of the agreed time. However, the lessor of a property may at any time terminate a commercial lease giving three months' notice to the lessee in the case that such a property has been characterized as dangerous. The lessor may terminate a lease agreement after the expiration of the contractual duration of the lease and in any case not before the lapse of three years from the commencement of such a lease on the grounds that he wishes to use the relevant premises. Finally the lessor may terminate the lease agreement on the grounds that he intends to build on such a property, in which case such termination may be effected only after the lapse of three years from the commencement date of the lease if the same is shorter than three years or for an indefinite term.

A lease agreement may also be terminated by the lessee following the expiration of the contractual duration of the lease and in any case not before the lapse of three years from the commencement date of the lease. In this case the lessee is liable for the payment to the lessor of compensation equal to four months rent.

A commercial lease may be extended for such a further period which would make the total duration of the lease ten years from the commencement day of the same.

## Foreigners working or establishing a business in Greece

There are no particular requirements for an EC national to reside, work or establish a business in Greece. There is a very simple announcement procedure before the appropriate authorities. Non-EC nationals, however, should apply to the Greek police authorities for the issue of a residence and a work permit prior to engaging in any private or commercial activity.

## Employment laws

Greece has ratified the following international conventions: the ILO Conventions 87 (freedom of association), 98 (organization and collective bargaining), 100 (equal pay for both sexes), the European Social Charter of 1961, the UNO Convention of 1966, the EC legislation and others. Such conventions prevail over any different arrangement provided by national laws.

Employers and employees are concluding private employment agreements including the terms of employment under the condition of equal treatment of men and women. Such contracts may be of definite or indefinite duration and such a distinction has a particular importance in cases of termination of employment. More specifically, a contract of definite duration could be terminated by either party only for important reasons. In the case of a breach of the agreement full compensation may be claimed. If the contract is terminated by the employer in the case of a change of his personal or economic conditions, the court may impose upon him the payment of a reasonable severance pay. In the case of a contract for an indefinite term either party may terminate the same at any time and without reason. The law provides, however, that dismissal should be given in writing, that there should be an offer of compensation and that there should be always a fair use of such a right.

The National General Collective Agreement of 1984 provides for 40 working hours a week while recent collective agreements and arbitration decisions have introduced a compulsory five-day week. Employees are mainly insured with

KA, which is the largest social insurance organization in the country, and both employers and employees pay monthly social security contributions to such organizations. Finally, employees with a minimum employment of 12 months by the same employer are entitled to paid annual leave which is in the region of approximately 23 days.

## Foreign investments

Foreign investments are regulated by LD 2687/1953 relating to investment and protection of foreign capital. Such law has been given full constitutional powers.

Foreign capital can benefit from the provisions of the above law when it is used for the creation of productive investments. Once those investments qualify for the application of the above law, they benefit from a number of tax exemptions and facilities such as a frozen income tax rate for ten years, adjustable only if the tax rates in force are reduced, a reduction or exemption of income duties or other taxes for the import of machinery or of duties imposed by local government as well as exemptions from stamp duties and turnover tax in connection with certain transactions. Company assets are exempt from expropriation and requisition and are guaranteed not to be subject to retroactive taxation.

Further, Presidential Decree 207/1987 provides for the complete deregulation of funds for all permanent residents of EC member states (except Greeks). Such deregulation of funds covers almost all possible business activities, namely direct investments, listing of securities, transactions involving securities, long-term credits and guarantees, thus enabling the EC investor to engage in virtually any business activity in Greece. The capital movements relating to investors residing outside the EC are regulated by Decision 825/1986 of the Bank of Greece providing that an application and other relevant documents (articles of association, feasibility study, balance sheets, etc.) must be submitted to the Bank of Greece for approval. Only direct investments originating from non-EC countries benefit from the same terms as those applied to the investments of residents of EC member states for matters relating to the export of capital, profits, dividends, interest and repayment of loan principal. All other types of investment are excluded and are subject to different treatment.

In relation to repatriation of funds there is also a clear distinction between non-EC investors and investors from EC member states. In relation to non-EC investors the export of foreign currency may not exceed 10% of the profits of the investment in any one year and no export can take place until one year after the commencement of the productive operation or three years after the import of the funds in Greece, whichever is the earlier. The Bank of Greece is required to verify the authenticity and legality of the investment and to provide the foreign exchange necessary for the company to meet its obligations. For investors from EC member states, on the other hand, PD207/1987 liberates all capital movements relating to the repatriation of funds. While for transfers of know-how or transactions incorporating foreign technology to be used in Greece the control of legality and authenticity of all capital movements necessary for effecting payments in foreign currency is exercised by the Bank of Greece, for royalties arising in connection with direct investments these controls are exercised by the Ministry of National Economy.

Restrictions in relation to the free flow of capital out of Greece are expected to be removed in 1992 or soon thereafter but only in relation to member states of the EC. The equalization of treatment of inward investment opportunities from third country investors to EC investors was decided upon the strength of its contribution to the national economy. Therefore, it is unlikely that equal treatment would be afforded to outward flows of capital to third countries and EC countries after 1992.

### Terminations
The franchise relationship is contractual and the provisions of the Civil Code related to contract apply. There are no special considerations.

## TAX AND FINANCIAL CONSIDERATIONS

### Income taxation
Legal entities which are subject to income tax include the following:

1    Greek corporations

2    Co-operatives

3    Public and municipal enterprises

4    Branches of foreign companies

5    Foreign enterprises operating in any form

Partnerships, limited liability companies and joint ventures are not taxed as legal entities.

Greek corporations are those which have been incorporated in accordance with the laws of Greece and which have their domicile in Greece and are taxed on their worldwide income. Foreign corporations with a permanent establishment in Greece are taxed only on profits generated in Greece and on income derived from a permanent establishment in Greece.

*Permanent establishments* A company is considered to have a permanent establishment in Greece under any of the following circumstances:

1    If an agency, branch, office, warehouse, plant, laboratory or other processing facility is maintained in Greece.

2    If business transactions or services rendered are entered into or provided in
     Greece through a representative.

3    If services of a technical or scientific nature are rendered in Greece, even
     without a representative.

4    When stocks of goods are held in Greece from which orders are filled.

5    When machinery and equipment are leased in Greece to third parties.

6    When the right to exploit patents, know-how, manufacturing methods, etc.
     is granted to third parties resident in Greece.

7    If a foreign enterprise participates in an EPE or a partnership in Greece.

In cases where treaties for the avoidance of double taxation between Greece and
certain countries exist, a different definition of a permanent establishment may
be provided.

*Corporate income tax rate*  The tax rates applied on undistributed profits of Greek
corporations and foreign companies operating in Greece are set out below.

Quoted:
| | |
|---|---|
| Manufacturing | 35% |
| Handicraft | 35% |
| Mining and quarrying | 35% |
| Other | 40% |

Unquoted:
| | |
|---|---|
| Manufacturing | 40% |
| Handicraft | 40% |
| Mining and quarrying | 40% |
| Any of the above which have made productive investments under the terms of L. 1262/82 and have opted for the related cash grants | 35% |
| Other | 46% |

*Branches*  Branches of foreign corporations or the equivalent of a limited liability
company are taxed on their total annual profit in Greece at the rate of 46%.

*Partnerships, limited liability companies and joint ventures*  Greek partnerships,
limited liability companies and joint ventures are not taxed as legal entities.

Revenues generated are taxed in the hands of the partners, irrespective of whether or not they are distributed. Non-Greek partnerships, limited liability companies or other non-corporate forms are taxed as non-resident corporations.

*Local construction companies* The taxable income of local construction companies is determined by applying deemed profit percentages to gross revenues as follows:

1    Companies engaged in constructing projects for resale must use a profit percentage of 10%.

2    For non-governmental contracts, the profit percentage is 12%.

3    If the company only provides services and not materials, the percentage is 25%.

*Foreign construction companies* Foreign construction companies (contractors) which undertake public or private works in Greece are taxed at the following rates, applied to their total gross revenues:

1    Government projects, 5%

2    Private projects, 6%

3    Government and non-government projects for which the contractor does not use its own materials, 12%

*Determination of taxable income* Taxable income, for all legal entities, for income tax purposes consists of annual gross income less allowable expenses. The following expenses may be deducted:

1    'Business' expenses which are incurred for necessary business purposes, as well as 'productive' expenses which are intended to generate revenues or profit.

2    Bad debts, provided that tax authorities recognize the insolvency of customers in debt.

3    Rates of depreciation as specified in taxation law, ranging according to the type of asset.

4    Administrative and other expenses allocated to branches by the head office of foreign companies, operating overseas, not exceeding 2% of gross revenues earned in Greece.

*reatment of tax losses*  Losses can be carried forward for three years, except for
Janufacturing companies and enterprises in the mining and hotel industry,
-hich are allowed a five-year carried-forward period. Losses cannot be related
ack. It should be noted that tax losses cannot be transferred within a group of
ompanies.

*ccounting year*  In general the accounting year coincides with the calendar year.
Iowever, companies are allowed to choose 30 June or 31 December as the end of
Jeir accounting period. An exception to this rule is the case where a foreign
arent company has a different accounting year.

*iling of income tax returns*  Income tax returns must be filed annually:

Corporations must file tax returns within four months from the end of the
accounting year.

Limited liability companies must file tax returns within one month from the
date of approval of the financial statements by the partners and within three
months from the end of the accounting period.

Partnerships and joint ventures must file tax returns as follows: for either up
to 25 February of each year or within three months from the end of the
accounting period.

'or all of the above cases, except for partnerships and joint ventures which keep
:ategory A and B books of account, the companies may apply to the tax authori-
ies for an extension of the filing date by ten days.

*Payment of income tax*  Income tax on profits generated by partnerships, limited
iability companies and joint ventures is not paid by the legal entities but by the
Jartners.
      Corporate income tax is paid by seven equal monthly instalments, the first
nstalment being due upon filing of the tax return. If the entire tax is paid in one
nstalment then a 10% discount is given. In addition to the income tax the com-
Jany must also pay 50% of the current year's income tax as an advance of next
years income tax.

**Indirect taxation/VAT**
Value added tax (VAT) was introduced in Greece effective 1 January 1987 and
replaced a number of indirect taxes, the most important of which were turnover
tax and most of the stamp tax. The general principles of the tax are governed by
EC Directives, and more specifically by the Sixth Directive.

*Taxable transactions*  VAT is a tax on consumption, which is charged at each
stage in the chain from raw material to final product. Therefore VAT is a tax on

most business transactions taking place in Greece where the cumulative VAT paid by the final consumer. Imported goods and some imported services are als subject to VAT.

The following are examples of business transactions subject to VAT:

1    Supply of goods

2    Supply of services

3    Transfer of immoveable properties

4    Importation of goods

*Exemption without credit (exemption from tax)* A number of exemptions ar granted from VAT, including:

1    Services supplied by lawyers, doctors, dentists, veterinarians, nurses an physiotherapists

2    The supply of educational services by public or private education institution

3    Tuition given privately by teachers covering all levels of education

4    The income (rent) from buildings excluding the exploitation of hotels, fur nished rooms, parking places, etc.

5    Hospital and medical care and the supply of goods incidental thereof pro vided by bodies governed by public law or by other institutions which operate under conditions comparable to those applicable to bodies being governed by public law

*Exemption with credit (zero-rate)* The following are examples of zero-rated sup plies (exemption with credit):

1    Export of goods from Greece

2    Insurance and reinsurance services rendered to non-EC residents including related services performed by insurance brokers and insurance agents

3    Air, sea and rail transport of passengers from within the country to a destina tion outside Greece and vice versa, and services closely connected with such transport

4    Delivery of gold to the Bank of Greece

both cases (zero-rated or exempt supplies) the taxable person does not charge
AT on his supplies. However, the person who makes only zero-rated supplies
ormally recovers all of his input tax, whilst the person making only exempt
upplies does not recover any input tax.

*ternational supply of services* The VAT law describes a number of services
hich when supplied to a taxable person established in another member state of
ie EC or to any recipient established outside the EC are zero-rated for VAT
urposes, as the place of supply of services is considered not to be in Greece.
hese services include amongst others:

Transfers and assignments of copyrights, patents, licences, trade marks and
similar rights

Advertising

Services of consultants, engineers, consulting firms, lawyers, accountants
and other similar services as well as data processing and any other supply of
information

Supply of staff

*AT rates* The local VAT rates are:

Zero rate (exporters, etc.)

3% (newspapers, books, magazines)

6% (necessities of life products)

16% (standard rate)

36% (luxury products such as television sets, videos, etc.)

*iling tax returns and payment of taxes* The VAT tax return is filed on a monthly
r bimonthly basis, with the taxes being due when the return is filed.
    An annual VAT return should also be filed within two months following the
nd of the financial year, summarizing the contents of the monthly returns.

**Vithholding of taxes**
*ividends* Dividends which are paid to Greek companies, foreign companies or
ndividuals are subject to the following withholding taxes:

Shares listed on the Athens stock exchange:

   (a)  Registered          42%
   (b)  Bearer              45%

2    Shares not listed on the Athens stock exchange:

   (a)  Registered          47%
   (b)  Bearer              50%

The tax is withheld by the paying company and is paid to the tax authoritie
within the following month. The foreign company's or individual's tax liability i
Greece ceases at this point.

***Royalties***  Royalty payments either of a fixed amount, or a percentage of receipt
to foreign companies not operating in Greece through a permanent establish
ment, are subject to tax withholding as follows:

1    Film rentals                        10%

2    All other payments of royalties     25%

The tax is withheld by the paying company and paid to the tax authorities withi
the following month. The foreign company's tax liability on the above incom
ceases at this point.

   For royalties which are paid to persons or corporations which are residents o
countries with which there is a treaty for the avoidance of double taxation, th
provisions of the treaties apply.

***Interest***  Interest arising from bank deposits, government bonds and certain othe
securities is exempt from income tax, and therefore is not subject to withholdin
taxes. Interest paid to resident corporations or foreign enterprises having a per
manent establishment in Greece, such as loan interest paid to a bank, or interes
paid to a supplier, is considered part of the recipient's trading income and is
therefore, not subject to any withholding tax. In all other cases the amount of ta
to be withheld on interest paid depends on the status of the recipient as explainec
below:

1    If the recipient is an individual, the tax withheld is computed using the per-
     sonal tax scale on the assumption that the interest paid is the recipient's only
     source of income for the year.

2    If the recipient is a resident corporation or partnership (EPE, OE, etc.), the
     tax withholding rate is 25%.

3    If the recipient is a foreign corporation with no permanent establishment in
     Greece, the tax withholding rate is 46%.

Where interest is paid to persons or corporations resident in countries with which there is a treaty for the avoidance of double taxation the specific provisions of the treaties apply.

The withholding and payment of taxes on interest is made by the person or corporation paying the interest.

## Other taxes

*Stamp taxes* The most important transactions which continue to be subject to stamp taxes are:

| | |
|---|---|
| Salaries | 1.2% |
| Profits (either distributed or retained) of partnership and limited liability companies | 1.2% |
| Private loan agreements | 2.4% or 3.6% |
| Property rentals | 3.6% |

*Levy on company capital* The following transactions are subject to a 1% levy:

1. Any increase in the capital of business entities from establishments, conversions and mergers

2. Increases in assets or equity capital

3. Loans intended to increase participation

4. Loans of foreign companies to branches operating in Greece, except for companies resident in EC countries

Exemptions apply to shipping companies, co-operatives, and welfare organizations providing social, philanthropic or communal services. Furthermore, increases of capital by capitalization of profits, retained earnings or reserves are not subject to the levy.

*Property tax* Property tax is imposed annually on the value of real estate. All individuals and legal entities owning real estate within Greece, regardless of whether they are residents or non-residents, are subject to this tax.

1. For individuals, the tax is calculated on the value of the taxpayer's real estate in excess of Drs 35 000 000 as follows:

| | |
|---|---|
| Up to Drs 35 000 000 | Nil |
| Additional Drs 10 000 000 | 0.5% |
| Additional Drs 10 000 001 to Drs 20 000 000 | 1.0% |

> Additional Drs 20 000 001 to Drs 30 000 000     1.5%
> Additional Drs 30 000 001 plus     2.0%

In cases where both spouses own real estate then the spouse with the largest real estate holding will be exempt from property tax up to Drs 35 million and the other spouse up to Drs 15 million.

2 For companies and other legal entities the tax rate is 1.5% on the value of real estate in excess of Drs 40 000 000.

A separate annual return must be filed by 25 February each year by individuals and legal entities, who are liable to property tax. All individuals and legal entities who file an income tax return, or who own real estate the value of which exceeds Drs 15 million in the case of legal entities, or Drs 30 million in the case of individuals, must also file a property tax return.

### Investment incentives

*General notes* Development Law 1892 was introduced in 1990, superseding and improving Law 1262/83. Since then, however, this Law has been amended on certain points to improve the incentives for the establishment and growth of productive units in the country.

*Definition of 'productive investment'* The Law defines as productive investments the following:

1 The construction, extension and modernization of industrial premises, buildings, hotel facilities and also of related auxiliary facilities.

2 The purchase of completed or semi-completed industrial or handicraft building, installations which are located in and belong to Hellenic Bank of Industrial Development (ETVA) industrial estates. This also applies to the purchase of other used completed or semi-completed industrial or handicraft buildings provided they fulfil certain conditions which are specified in the law.

3 The purchase of new machinery and other mechanical or technical production equipment. The purchase and installation of new automation and computerization equipment as well as the costs of the necessary software and staff training costs.

4 The cost of investments designed to import, develop and apply modern technology, such as information technology, telematics and the cost of ergonomic studies and studies for the protection of employees' health.

5  Moving expenses for the relocation of existing manufacturing in small craft industry and units in all sectors as well as costs of erecting the necessary building installation in the new locations.

6  The construction of new warehouse space, cold storage space or space for drying or preserving products. The purchase of new refrigerator trucks or refrigerator ships.

7  The purchase of new means of transportation for materials, personnel and equipment and installations for the movement of goods.

8  The building of nursery schools, new workers' homes to accommodate the firm's personnel or of premises for their recreation, provided they are built in the same area in which the business has been established.

9  The building, expansion and modernization of hotel units, tourist apartments, hostels, camping sites, facilities of winter tourism, mineral spa facilities and the purchase of equipment for the above.

10 Expenses for the repair, restoration and conversion of designated traditional houses and buildings for their use as tourist accommodation (hostels/hotels) as well as the renovation of hotel units of a traditional style.

11 The purchase of reproductive material in farming, livestock or fish farming enterprises.

12 The cost of investments involving the construction, expansion, modernization and equipment of central markets, slaughterhouses, premises for social, cultural and other functions.

13 The purchase of small craft industry premises in industrial estates or centres constructed by ETVA or with ETVA funding, irrespective of their time of construction and use.

14 The building, expansion and modernization of facilities and the purchase of equipment for enterprises supplying support services for tourist hotels.

15 The construction, extension and modernization of marinas, provided they comply with certain specifications set by the Greek Tourism Organization.

16 The construction, extension and modernization of conference centres, provided they comply with certain specifications set by the Greek Tourism Organization.

17   The construction, extension and modernization of golf courses as well as the cost of necessary installation and the purchase of equipment, provided they comply with certain specifications set by the Greek Tourism Organization.

The following are not regarded as productive investments and consequently are not eligible for the Law's benefits:

1    The purchase of a passenger car with up to six seats.

2    The purchase of office furniture and fixtures.

3    The purchase of land, sites and agricultural plots.

4    The construction or extension of building installations on land which is not owned by the investor (with certain exceptions).

5    The construction, extension and modernization of unserviced accommodation and hotel accommodation of all types lower than class C.

6    The modernization of all types of hotel units less than ten years from the time in which they commenced operating or the date in which the investment for their modernization was completed if such investment was carried out under the provisions of Law 1892/90 or 1262/82 or 1116/81.

*Minimum limits of productive investment*  Minimum limits are specified for investments that are entitled to fall under the provisions of the Law. These are amended from time to time by decisions of the Minister of National Economy.

For most types of investment, this minimum is Drs 60 million, although lower minima are permitted for certain categories specified in the law while some special types of investment are without restriction as to the minimum amount. Investors are advised to check carefully the classification of their business in case there is a possibility that their investment falls below the specified minimum.

*Development areas*  Law 1892/90 divides the country into four areas – A, B, C and D – on the basis of their economic and regional development. In addition, the law provides for special incentives applicable to Thrace. The incentives are provided on a rising scale from area A to area D and Thrace.

By decision of the relevant governmental authorities, certain prefectures and communities are entitled to the incentives applicable to more favoured areas.

*Special zones*  In addition to the areas that are specified by Law 1892/90, the government may define zones within each subsidized area which is confronting an acute development problem and provide increased incentives. It may also define special zones for the implementation of special plans of regional development and/or utilization of agricultural products.

Government may also specify areas with congested tourist activity in which the incentives, grants and interest subsidies available under the Law do not apply or in which the percentage grant and interest subsidy or other less favourable incentives are applied, depending on the degree of concentration of tourist activity and the type of investment.

Units established within ETVA industrial estates or zones, handicraft centres of EOMMEH and other similar centres, are eligible for the additional incentives provided for special zones. The incentives which are available for the special zones are those for the next less developed area.

Businesses of all categories which invest in the special zones or the ETVA industrial estates of area D are entitled to grants, equal to five additional points or, in the case of Thrace, seven additional points.

## Forms of incentive
### General notes
The Law provides five basic types of aid for productive investments: investment grants, reduced tax rates on profit, interest subsidies, tax allowances and increase of depreciation rates. The prospective investor has the option to select either of the following (mutually exclusive) combinations:

1    Grant, reduced tax rate, interest subsidy and increased depreciation rates

2    Tax allowances and increased depreciation rates

For the selection of the best combination, what is taken into account are the nature of the investment, the area where it takes place, the size of the investment, the requirements of the investor, etc.

### Investment grants
Subsidies in the form of equity participation by the state in productive investments are available for investments of up to Drs 2.5 billion. This limit can be amended by the Minister of National Economy.

In calculating the amount of Drs 2.5 billion the total amount of the investment programme must be taken into account. Specifically, the total amount of the investment programmes is calculated as the sum of all investment programmes relating to the same production procedure submitted by the same investor for approval in terms of the provisions of the Law, within five years of the completion of the first investment that was approved under the Law.

The grants provided for the various areas may be up to 45% of the value of the whole investment and the investor's own minimum participation varies between 15% and 40%.

The investment appraisal is based on the criteria which are described briefly below. The first three criteria relate to the investment's viability and, if they are satisfied, the remaining criteria are then evaluated.

1    The experience and activities of the investor, his creditworthiness and finan-
     cial standing. For existing businesses the financial results of the latest years
     are taken into account.

2    The sector in which the investment will take place and the investment's con-
     tribution to the profits of the business.

3    The organization of the business.

4    Conditions and prospects of the sector and its importance for the economic
     development of the country.

5    The investors' equity participation.

6    Export prospects so as to evaluate the project's competitiveness not only in
     the local market but also internationally.

7    The investment's contribution to employment, energy conservation, reduc-
     tion of environmental pollution, improvement in the quality of life, etc.

8    An assessment of the technology involved and of the investment's produc-
     tivity, especially with respect to investments of the same sectors and the level
     of organization of the business.

9    The extent to which international, commercial or technical collaboration has
     occurred.

Applications submitted for the eligibility of an investment under the law and requests for amendments to such applications which have been rejected cannot be re-examined.

*Interest subsidy*
The investments that have been included in the law's system of grants are also awarded a percentage subsidy of the interest rates applicable from time to time for bank loans, debenture loans, publicity issues, or loans received from other institutions, if such have been received in order to finance the invest-ment. The percentage subsidy is equal to the percentage grant. The interest subsidy is provided for the first three years of a loan's service except for invest-ments of area D which take place in special zones and investments for the protec-tion of the environment and pollution control in areas A, B, C and D for which the interest subsidy is available for six years. In calculating the amount of the bank loan eligible for the subsidy, the value of the land is not taken into account.

For investments in the prefectures of Evros, Rodopi and Xanthi, the interest subsidy is available for the whole period of the loan repayment for a maximum period of ten years.

The amount of the subsidy is deducted from the gross income of the firm, thus reducing the taxable profits. The interest subsidy is not given in cases where the investment has qualified for the system of tax allowances.

## Increased depreciation rates

The increased rates of depreciation (in addition to those laid down by law) which are given to investments that will be affected up to 31 December 1994 and are subject to the system of Law 1892/90 depend on the location of the unit and the number of shifts worked.

Increased depreciation rates only apply if the company works a second shift during which the average number of persons employed is at least 50% of those employed in the first shift. If the company works a third shift, the average number of persons employed in the first and second shifts combined must be equal to at least 80% of the persons employed in the first shift.

Normal and accelerated depreciation rates are calculated by reference to the cost of fixed assets after deducting grants received from the state.

The additional depreciation rates may also be granted in the case where the investment has been included in the system of tax allowances.

## Tax allowances

Businesses eligible for the provisions of the Law which are already established, relocated or being established in areas B, C, and D are eligible for tax allowances provided that they undertake productive investments as provided by the Law up to 31 December 1994.

Investments which have received grants are not eligible for tax allowances.

A further incentive, which is subject to certain conditions, is available under the law; this is a reduction by 5% of applicable appropriate income tax. Industrial, handicraft, mining and quarrying businesses are eligible for this incentive.

## Special investments

Certain special investments are entitled to increased grants of up to 55%. These are investments relating to:

1    Environmental protection, soil, subsoil, water and atmospheric pollution, rehabilitation of the natural environment and recycling of water

2    Energy and specifically (i) development of replenishable energy sources, (ii) substitution of liquid fuel or electrical energy, and (iii) energy conservation

3    Establishment or extension of laboratories of applied industrial energy or metallurgical research undertaken by productive units eligible under the law

4    Businesses involved with the manufacture of goods and the supply of services
     of exceptionally advanced technology

5    Special institutions and workshops for the rapid retraining for employment
     of persons with special needs

*Incentives provided to commercial businesses*
The new Law also provides tax incentives for trading companies which build up
tax-free reserves in order to undertake investments which fall under the provisions of the Law.

# CHAPTER 10
# IRELAND

*Michael Fitzsimons and Francis Fitzpatrick*

## OVERVIEW OF FRANCHISING IN IRELAND

Franchising has become a readily recognized concept in Irish commercial life. The origins of franchising can be traced to the necessity of selling and distributing goods under which the relationships of agency and distribution were most prevalent. This new concept of franchising has its roots firmly fixed in commercial-type relationships which are more extensive and complex than traditional agency and distribution.

Franchising in Ireland is continuing to expand, growing from 1988 when there were approximately 35 franchises to 50 in 1989. The number of indigenous franchisors in Ireland is small; however, growth in this area is also envisaged. Government policy has always encouraged investment in Ireland and franchisors will be welcomed in the same way as any potential employer in this jurisdiction.

There is a distinct lack of legislation governing franchising in Ireland. The major portion of legislation affecting franchise agreements comprises restrictive pricing orders and these are of little significance for prospective franchisors/ franchisees. The only intervention by legislation into the franchise area came in 1980 with the Pyramid Selling Act. Pyramid selling schemes, although not specifically prohibited under Irish law, are regulated by this Act.

1984 saw the formal establishment in Ireland of the Irish Franchise Association, which has adopted a code of ethics similar to the then version of the code adopted by the British Franchise Association. The Irish Franchise Association, like its British counterpart, favours self-regulation. No government intervention in franchising is predicted at present.

Typical franchises which can be seen in Ireland are those in the fast food area such as McDonald's, Burger King and Kentucky Fried Chicken. Examples of retail franchises are international convenience store chains such as 7-Eleven, Tie Rack, The Body Shop and, in the motor trade area, Fast Fit Exhausts. These examples indicate that the majority of franchises in Ireland have emanated directly from the United States and the United Kingdom. There are some indigenous Irish franchises and a particularly successful one has been Nectar, which markets products similar to those marketed by The Body Shop.

The MTS (Management Training Services) survey on 'Franchising in

Ireland' 1988/1989 revealed that the franchise industry in Ireland then employec 1945 people and forecast that in 1991 employment would increase to approxi- mately 3300. On average each franchised unit employs approximately ten people The franchise industry in Ireland averages a current growth rate of 39% in the entire industry and an annual projected growth rate of 29% is forecast over the next two years. The majority of expected new franchisors will come from the UK and up to 50 new outlets could be created in Ireland by 1991 with the consequen creation of 350 new jobs.

An analysis of the Irish franchise market reveals that franchises at presen can be categorized into three different main areas: (a) fast food – 18% of fran- chises; (b) home improvements and fittings – 16% of franchises; and (c) home cleaning and repair – 11% of franchises. Other notable categories are business/ professional – 9% of franchises. Health, beauty, clothes and accessories are also categories actively being franchised.

A review of the ages of persons currently in the franchising industry reveals that franchising is attractive to young business persons with only 21% over the age of 50. The number of women in franchising has increased and they now account for 16% of all franchisees.

Ireland is an excellent country for the potential franchisor wishing to expand or initiate a franchise network. The population of the Republic of Ireland is approximately 3.5 million and 60% of the population is between the ages of 15 and 64, 29% being under 14 years old. Ireland's young, well-educated popula- tion is available to both work in, and particularly become consumers of, service- orientated franchises. Income in Ireland measured by gross national product (GNP) per capita was IR£5032 in 1987, and Ireland ranks as the third lowest of the 12 members of the EC in terms of private consumption per capita using purchasing power priorities.

Financial support for prospective franchisors/franchisees in Ireland is avail- able through the local banks. As with any financial package for business, a combination of own funds and borrowed funds is evident. The banks estimate that younger franchisors, namely those under 40, provide on average 5% of equity, whereas those over 40 tend to provide a larger amount of their own equity, i.e. 40%.

## STRUCTURE OF IRISH VENTURE: THE BUSINESS ENTITIES

The usual legal entities, such as limited companies, unlimited companies and partnerships, are available in Ireland as in most other jurisdictions. The advan- tages of limited liability still persist in that the company is a separate entity; however, banking practice requiring security has translated itself into all types of commercial arrangements and personal guarantees are now sought in that a guarantee is required from a franchisee should the franchisee be a limited liability company.

There are two types of limited liability company in Ireland – the public limited company and private limited company. The two types of company are full legal entities and ensure limited liability for their shareholders; they have full legal rights and can own property and are subject to taxation as an entity. A private company has a share capital which restricts the right to transfer its shares, limits the number of its members to 50, and prohibits itself from making any invitation to the public to subscribe for its shares or debentures. The Companies Act 1983 provides that a public limited company is one which:

1  Indicates its status by the use of the words public limited company or the abbreviation plc.

2  Is limited by shares.

3  Has an allotted share capital of a nominal amount of not less than the authorized minimum IR£30 000; at least one-quarter of this nominal amount must be paid up together with any premium on its shares. The 1983 Act also contains provisions for the maintenance of the share capital of plc's which do not apply to private companies. Companies can convert themselves from being unlimited (another style of corporate structure defined below) into limited and public limited into private limited. Each conversion requires the approval of the shareholders by special resolution. In the case of a public limited company which resolves to convert into a private company, an application to cancel the resolution may be made to the High Court by dissenting shareholders.

### Incorporation of a private company limited by shares

Registration usually takes approximately six weeks from the date that all necessary incorporation forms are lodged in the Companies Registration Office. However, 'off the shelf companies', namely companies already incorporated, are available to persons requiring immediate corporate status. The cost of company formation is approximately IR£299 for a new 'off the shelf' company and stamp duty of 1% is payable on the capital which is issued. The private limited company is the form of business entity most favoured by business people. The advantages over public limited companies include the simpler legal formalities, the small minimum capital requirement and easier formation procedures. The shares in private companies are of the same class, ensuring equal rights in the absence of a provision in the articles of association defining the rights of different classes of shares. The private limited company must have a minimum of two directors and two shareholders and normally the same persons operate as both.

The following documents are required and must be filed in the Companies Registration Office:

1  Memorandum and articles of association – these are the rules of the company regulating its external affairs, and detail the objects for which the

company was formed. The form of the memorandum is set out in table A of the Act, and it must be divided into paragraphs and numbered consecutively. The memorandum must contain the following particulars:

(a) The name of the company with limited or Teoranta (Gaelic translation) as the last word of the name.

(b) The objects of the company must be stated (the company cannot do anything unless it is expressed as such an object) as must the fact that the liability of the members is limited, the amount of share capital with which the company proposes to be registered and the division thereof into shares of a fixed amount. No subscriber of the memorandum may take less than one share. The memorandum must be signed by at least two subscribers. Their addresses and descriptions must be stated and their signatures must be witnessed and dated.

2   A form No. A 1 containing a declaration of compliance, i.e. that the incorporation is in compliance with the Companies Act, must be signed by a solicitor engaged in the formation of the company or by a person named as a director or secretary of the company.

3   Companies capital duty statement must be completed and signed.

4   Particulars of directors and secretary – all names must be set out in full with home addresses and details of nationality if not Irish.

The articles of association is the document which regulates the internal affairs of the company and details such matters as the issue and transfer of shares, the rights attaching to the shares, meetings of the company and power and duties as directors. The articles are subordinate to the memorandum and if there is any conflict between the two, the memorandum will prevail. The articles and the memorandum are in effect a contract between the members *inter se* and between the members and the company. A standard form of articles is set out in table A of the 1963 Act and will apply to a company limited by shares unless excluded or modified by articles actually adopted by the company. The articles can be amended by special resolution.

**Incorporation of a public limited company**
The following documents are required to form a public limited company:

1   Memorandum and articles of association.

2   Form No. A 1, detailing names and addresses of directors and secretary (see above in relation to private company). The company must not commence

any business or exercise any borrowing powers until a certificate authorizing the company to commence business has been issued by the registrar. This is different from the case of a private company, which can immediately begin business, borrow money and enter into contracts once its certificate of incorporation has been issued.

The regulations for management of a public limited company are set out in table A, part 1, of the 1963 Act. This is a standard set of articles which can be varied if required provided the Companies Act is complied with. The memorandum and articles must be typed or printed and must be signed by at least seven members. The memorandum must contain the following particulars:

1 Name of company with public limited company or Cuideachta Phoibli Theoranta (Gaelic translation) as the last words of the name, and that the company is to be a public limited company.
2 The objects of the company must be stated and it must state that the liability of the members is limited.

The amount of share capital with which the company proposes to be registered must be stated and also the division thereof into shares of a fixed amount. No subscriber of the memorandum may take less than one share, the memorandum must be signed by the subscribers, their addresses and subscriptions must be stated and their signatures must be witnessed and dated.

A limited company, whether private or public, is controlled and administered by one of two organs of the company, namely its shareholders or directors.

The Companies Acts reserve certain powers and functions of a company to the shareholders, which can only be exercised by them by resolution passed in general meetings. All other powers of the company are usually exercisable by the directors. In short, the business of the company is managed by the directors, who exercise all powers except those which can only be exercised by the company in general meeting.

The directors can, and often do, delegate some or all of their powers to one in particular and the office of managing director is typical of this form of delegation. There are two types of resolution which can be passed by shareholders: the ordinary resolution requires a simple majority, while a special resolution requires 75% of the shareholders to vote in favour thereof. A special resolution is, for example, necessary to effect any alteration of the memorandum and articles of association.

*Capital* Capital is created in a company either through contributions received from shareholders or by way of loans which can be secured or unsecured. Issued capital is the aggregate value of the shares which have been issued to subscribers to the extent of amounts paid up in respect thereof. Normally, companies will not issue all their authorized capital. The nominal capital of the company is the amount of capital that is or was available to be issued. The company can issue shares up to the amount of its maximum authorized nominal capital. The nominal capital may be increased from time to time by shareholders' resolution.

*Dividends* The major legal principle relating to dividends is that dividends cannot be paid out of the capital of the company since this would effectively constitute an unauthorized reduction of the company's capital. The payment of dividends and the procedure relating to the declaration of dividends is normally set out in the company's articles. The Companies (Amendment) Act 1983, which implemented the second European Directive on Company Law, details specific regulations regarding the distribution of profits. Section 45(ii) of the 1983 Act defines 'profits available for distribution' by reference to the excess of realized profits over realized losses as shown in the accounts.

Pursuant to Section 46(i) of the 1983 Act, a public limited company is subject to an additional restriction in that it may not allow a distribution to reduce its net assets to below the amount of its called up share capital and undistributable reserves.

## Business entities other than public or private limited companies

*Partnerships* A partnership is deemed to be 'the relationship which subsists between persons carrying on business in common with a view to profit'. In Irish law partners are jointly liable for the debts and obligations of the partnership and may be jointly and severally liable for its torts. If a foreign national wishes to become a partner with an Irish citizen, exchange control consent is required. It is arguable that after 1992 exchange controls between EC member states will be abolished. A partnership must state the name of its partners on its stationery. A partner is deemed to be the agent of his fellow partners and any act conducted by him within the scope of his ostensible authority is binding on all other partners. Section 24 of the Partnership Act 1890 lays down certain ground rules, but the partners themselves can regulate their dealings by way of internal agreement. If they do not, the Act implies certain terms. The major terms are as follows:

1    Every partner may participate in the management of the business.

2    Consent of each partner is required to vary the partnership agreement.

3    Profits and losses are shared equally.

The partner's duties to his other partners include a duty of utmost good faith, and he must therefore render true accounts and full information on all partnership matters.

*Limited partnerships* This form of relationship is governed by the Limited Partnerships Act 1907. The difference between a limited partnership and a partnership is, briefly, that a limited partnership has general partners and limited partners. The limited partner's liability is limited and he is excluded from the management of the business and has no authority to bind his fellow partners.

*Unlimited companies* An unlimited company can be formed in substantially the same way as a limited company as described above. The main feature of an unlimited company is that on winding up its members have unlimited liability for its debts and liabilities. A major advantage attaching to the status of an unlimited company is the ability of the members to alter the share capital of the company, such alteration not being subject to the strict legal formalities which relate to a limited company. A further advantage is that an unlimited company is not subject to the financial disclosures required by the 1986 Companies (Amendment) Act.

*Branches of foreign corporations* The most common business entity through which foreign companies operate in Ireland is the wholly owned subsidiary (private limited company). Another option is the establishment of a place of business in Ireland. There are certain exchange control requirements in relation to remission of funds in and out of Ireland and these are dealt with below. A corporation incorporated outside Ireland wishing to establish a place of business within Ireland must within one month provide the following documentation to the Companies Registration Office:

1   A copy of its charter, statutes, memorandum and articles certified to be correct either by the government official who has custody of the original or by a public notary.

2   A list of the secretaries and directors with their addresses, occupations and nationalities and the name and address of at least one person resident in Ireland authorized to accept service of documents on its behalf. Furthermore, the address of the principal place of business of the company within Ireland must be stated.

The foreign corporation is required to print on its stationery the following information:

(a)   The names of its directors,

(b)   their nationality (if not Irish),

(c)   the country of incorporation,

(d)   the fact that the liability of its members is limited (if this is the case).

A foreign corporation having a branch in Ireland is required to file in the Companies Office an annual return showing a balance sheet and profit and loss account, and these documents together with copies of the associated directors' and auditors' report must be filed. The accounts are required to be filed in the same format as if the company was incorporated in Ireland; however, concessions to the rule are available if this would cause undue hardship.

The foreign branch is obviously subject to the Irish courts; however, in dealing with matters relating to the foreign branch's internal constitutional arrangements,the law of the country of incorporation will be applied and notIrish law. A branch of a foreign corporation which has ceased to trade or exist under or by virtue of the law of its country of incorporation can be wound up by the courts in Ireland.

The Irish branch of the foreign corporation is deemed for exchange control purposes resident in Ireland; therefore, central bank consent is required for the making or receipt of loans to or from the foreign corporation's head office. Consent is required to remit profits, dividends, sale or liquidation proceeds to non-residents.

*Joint ventures* A joint venture entered into between the parties does not create a separate legal entity unless the parties themselves create a new entity, for example a limited liability company, private or public. Where no such company has been created the legal status of the joint venture must be assessed by the agreement entered into between the parties. The general view taken is that a joint venture constitutes some form of general or limited partnership between the parties involved.

## LEGAL CONSIDERATIONS

### Introduction
The EC block exemption for franchise agreements is the only legislation directly governing franchising in Ireland. The Irish judiciary has, in the few cases in which franchising has been considered, treated it as if it were synonymous with commercial contractual relationships, such as agency or distributorship, and has applied general principles governing commercial contracts to franchise relationships.

### Pyramid selling
The major piece of national legislation in the franchise area is the Pyramid Selling Act 1980, which regulates pyramid selling schemes which are not specifically prohibited under Irish law. These, of course, are separate and distinct from the true franchise relationship; however, the Act might have implications for a franchisor seeking to establish a series of sub-franchisors which might conceivably be deemed to be prohibited by the Act.

### Competition law
Articles 85 and 86 of the European competition provisions are dealt with elsewhere in the book; however, it should be pointed out that these competition articles are directly effective in Ireland and may be pleaded in Irish courts.

The Competition Act 1991 came into operation on 1 October 1991. The Act repeals in total the Restrictive Practices Act 1972 and those sections of the Restrictive Practices (Amendment) Act 1987 which relate to restrictive practices and fair trade. The previous provisions are replaced by a system with a provision for direct recourse to the courts for anyone adversely affected by anti-competitive activity prohibited under the Act. The Act, which is based on Articles 85 and 86 of the Treaty of Rome, replaces the old system of restrictive practices orders. This system of orders had become cumbersome and was ineffective to deal with the increasing complexity and sophistication of business. The other major statutes which are relevant to trade in Ireland are the Takeovers and Monopolies (Control) Acts 1978 and 1987. Other than these two statutes, the Competition Act 1991 and of course European law, trade in Ireland is largely unregulated.

Pursuant to the new Competition Act, the former Fair Trade Commission is replaced by the Competition Authority. The Authority will have power to grant licences to companies that apply for the continuation of certain restricted arrangements with other companies. The Authority has also been given wide-ranging investigatory powers under the Act and can arguably pursue the 'dawn raids' of the European Commission by entering premises and inspecting documents.

The monopolies provisions of the Mergers, Takeovers and Monopolies (Control) Act are linked in the Act, with the new concept of 'abuse of a dominant position', and this means that the definition of a monopoly is now more flexible, permitting a case-by-case study of market positions. In addition, Part IV of the Act, s. 19, accommodates Council regulation (EEC no. 4064/89) on the control of concentrations between undertakings. It is worth quoting the long title of the Act in its entirety as this explains the purpose of the Act: 'an act to prohibit by analogy with Articles 85 and 86 of the Treaty establishing the European Economic Community and in the interests of the common good the prevention, restriction or distortion of competition and the abuse of dominant positions in trade in the State, to establish a Competition Authority to amend the Mergers, Takeovers and Monopolies (Control) Act 1978 and to provide for other matters connected with the matters aforesaid'.

The effect of the Act is to provide consumers and suppliers with the entitlement to obtain damages if they can prove loss caused by anti-competitive action by an 'undertaking'. An undertaking is defined in the Act as a person being an individual, body corporate or non-incorporated body of persons engaged for gain in the production, supply or distribution of goods or the provision of a service. The inclusion of the words 'engaged for gain' in the definition means that the definition probably does not include bodies such as trade unions. Examples of anti-competitive behaviour include agreements to fix prices or charges, setting of terms for the supply of goods or services and, arguably, informal conversations between competitors that include a discussion of prices, pricing practices or factors affecting them as prohibited by the legislation. The Mergers Act is amended by the Competition Act in that an enterprise acquiring 25% or more of another should notify the Minister of Industry and Commerce; this trigger mechanism for notification of acquisitions is reduced from 30% to 25%. The fines for failing to notify the Minister of such acquisitions have also been increased up to a maximum of £200 000 with a daily notification default fine of up to £20 000 per day.

The Mergers Act comes into play where there is a proposed merger between an acquiring and target company both of whose gross assets exceed £5 million or where aggregate sales of each exceed £10 million. It should be noted that s. 5 of the Competition Act prohibiting 'abuses of dominant positions' is important in the context of the small nature of the Irish economy in that many enterprises could arguably be dominant within their own spheres. The dominant under-taking must obviously ensure compliance with the new rules of competition.

Under common law, commercial agreements can be deemed to be void and unenforceable in instances where there is economic duress, unreasonable restraint of trade, or the inducing of breach of contract.

### Liability of franchisor

The precise relationship between franchisor and franchisee has not yet been determined definitively by the courts in Ireland. The relationship contains elements of: (i) master–servant; (ii) partnership; (iii) agency; and (iv) contractual licence arrangement.

The parties to a franchise agreement may agree that the agreement itself is a franchise; however, a court may interpret the agreement as being one of distribu-torship or partnership. In short, the true nature of the relationship will always be examined by a court.

*Tort* Since there are no laws dealing specifically with franchising, one must apply general legal principles to any franchise relationship. The franchisor must be aware that tortious liability could arise in the following areas:

1    Negligent advice given to the franchisee

2    Misrepresentations made when introducing or selling the franchise package to the franchisee

3    Vicarious liability, which includes claims by franchisees and third parties against franchisors

The well-established rule that advice negligently given can manifest itself in legal action is applicable in Irish law. The franchisor must take cognizance of this rule in dealing with his franchisee.

In relation to misrepresentation, a prospective franchisee is entitled to rely on statements/representations made in relation to the product/service, the subject matter of the franchise relationship. The courts, in determining the franchise relationship, can reasonably be expected to consider that a franchisor is a person

olding himself out to be a specialist/professional, and therefore owing a special
uty of care to the franchisee.

*ontract* The Sale of Goods and Supply of Services Act 1980 provides the con-
umer with certain protection in relation to the supply of goods and services. In
hort, the retailer has responsibilities to the purchaser, even for defects which may
e the fault of the manufacturer. The consumer is entitled to rely on the fact that
he goods are of merchantable property, fit for their purpose, and they 'must be as
escribed'. In relation to the area of services, consumers are entitled to expect
hat the supplier of the service has the necessary skill, that the service will be
rovided with due skill and diligence, and that any goods supplied will be of
nerchantable quality. The Consumers Information Act 1978 aims to protect the
onsumer against false or misleading claims about goods, services and prices. An
ffence is committed if false claims are made about goods, services and prices in
he course of a business, trade or profession.

The Sale of Goods and Supply of Services Act 1980 provides that a supplier is
leemed to carry out the service with reasonable skill and care. This term is
pplicable to any franchise and can be relied on by the franchisee.

*roduct liability* The EC Product Liability Directive which is intended to make
nanufacturers liable for defective products without proof of negligence has not
et been implemented in Ireland (however, its implementation is expected in the
ery near future). The Directive seeks to impose liability on producers and manu-
acturers of goods. The definition of producer includes anyone who holds himself
ut as being the producer by putting his name or mark on the product, anyone
vho imports a product into the EC, and the supplier of a product if he is unable to
dentify the producer, importer or supplier of the product.

Under the Directive a franchisor is arguably liable if he puts his mark on the
roduct, or holds himself out to be the producer of the product.

## ndustrial and intellectual property

The core of any franchise operation is the bundle of intellectual property rights
vhich the franchisor owns. Trade marks in Ireland are protected in two ways by
tatute and the common law of passing off. The legislation governing trade marks
s the Trade Marks Act 1963, which has been supplemented by practice rules
nade under the Act by the Minister for Industry, Trade, Commerce and
Tourism, namely the Trade Mark Rules 1963 (S.I. No. 268 of 1963).

An important distinction should be made between Irish and UK law. In the
JK service marks can be registered, but in Ireland this is not possible; however, it
s expected that it will be possible in the future. The statutory protection for trade
narks is founded on a system of registration and in practice the common law
emedy of passing off is rarely invoked once there is a registered trade mark in
peration.

Under Irish law a trade mark must be used in relation to goods. At present service businesses must seek protection of their names under the common law and the difficulty with passing off is that there is a need to establish an exclusive reputation and the existence of damage.

The register of trade marks in Ireland is divided into two parts, Part A and B, and from a commercial point of view there is little difference between the two. Registration in Part B is necessitated chiefly because of a lack of distinctiveness and therefore protection rights under registration in Part B are less than those associated with Part A registration. There is no necessity to publicly describe whether a mark is a Part A or Part B mark, the chief difference being that a mark registered in Part A which has been on the register for seven years cannot be attacked on any grounds save those where the registration was obtained by fraud. On the other hand a Part B mark is less secure and open to attack on a number of grounds.

There is no requirement that the mark must have been used prior to registration; however, an intention to use the mark must be apparent. The most important right granted by registration as a trade mark is 'the exclusive right to use of the trade mark in relation to those goods'. Registration in Part B is limited in that it is a defence to an action by a Part B proprietor if the defendant can show that the use to which the mark is put is not in fact likely to deceive or cause confusion.

Registered trade marks are valid for an initial period of seven years renewable upon payment of a specified fee for successive periods of 14 years at a time.

The Patent Act 1964 is the principal Act dealing with grants of patents. The law of copyright is governed in Ireland by the Copyright Act 1963. Irish copyright, although similar to that of the UK, is not identical.

## Real estate and leasing

The Land Act 1965 controls ownership of non-urban land in Ireland; however, nationals of and corporations incorporated in EC member states are deemed to be qualified persons and therefore no restrictions on ownership of land in Ireland apply to such qualified persons. The most common form of property ownership by persons wishing to do business in Ireland is business tenancies. These are regulated by the Landlord and Tenant (Amendment) Act 1980, which gives the business tenant an absolute right to renewal of a lease, after satisfying a number of criteria, the most important being that the tenant must have been in occupation for the purposes of his trade, business or profession for the previous three years. In effect, the business tenant acquires an equity in the premises and can only be refused a new tenancy if the landlord has obtained planning permission to demolish and reconstruct the premises or proves that he needs the premises for a scheme of development involving it and other property. The business tenant is entitled to a renewed lease for a term of 35 years, unless he accepts a lesser period. A tenant's entitlement to a new lease is also necessarily predicated on observance of covenants and conditions in the lease; fundamental breaches of same might lead to forfeiture.

The tenant has certain duties and obligations which must be complied with, such as the regular payment of rent and observation of covenants, i.e. keep prem-ses in state of repair, not cause a nuisance. The landlord can in certain instances erminate the tenancy for breach of covenant by the tenant.

These business tenancies normally include a rent review clause whereby the ent can be increased or decreased according to market conditions. The rent review eriod is normally five years, with a provision for arbitration if the landlord and enant cannot agree.

## Foreigners working or establishing a business in Ireland

reland has an unfortunate history of high emigration, and this underlies government policy to actively encourage foreign investment. As a result there are no pecific restrictions placed on foreigners wishing to carry on business in Ireland and no requirement that shares in Irish companies must be held by Irish citizens.

A foreign national other than a national of another EC member state must make application through his employer to the Minister of Labour, requesting a work permit. The Department of Labour will normally seek a reason for the employment of the person concerned. However, where an overseas firm is commencing business, it is accepted that persons with prior knowledge of the business may be required. Work permits only last for one year and can be renewed.

The Aliens Act 1935 specifies that an alien needs business permission in order to engage in business in Ireland. The permission is sought by way of application to the Department of Justice. The Department requires that a minimum of £150 000 be available for the establishment of the business, and certain criteria, such as the number of persons employed and their nationality, are applied. The permission is only required by citizens from countries other than EC member states who wish to work or establish a business in Ireland.

A foreigner taking up employment or establishing a business must within seven days of his entry into Ireland for this purpose make application to the registration office of the district in which he intends to reside and give details such as identity and other information which may be required. The Irish police (Garda Siochana) handle the registration of aliens, and their registered head office is in Dublin Castle. A foreigner is not permitted to remain in Ireland for a period exceeding one month without receiving a registration certificate. In the case of a foreigner visiting Ireland other than for employment or business, a registration certificate is only required if he intends to stay for longer than three months. Registration certificates are issued within two weeks of application.

Foreign nationals in employment are entitled to the same rights and have the same obligations as Irish citizens in relation to social security. Under EC Regulations 1408/71 and 547/72 nationals of an EC member state working in another may transfer both social security contribution records and benefits from their own country to their host country.

## Employment laws

Ireland has developed a comprehensive body of employment/labour law in recent times. Previously, aspects of employment law were dealt with under contract law and trade disputes fell under the law of torts. There is a large body of legislation dealing with employment law and some of the principal Acts are the Unfair Dismissals Act 1977, Minimum Notice and Terms of Employment Act 1973 and the Safety in Industry Acts 1955 and 1980.

The total workforce in the Republic of Ireland is approximately 1 312 000 and approximately 230 000 are registered as unemployed. The normal weekly hours of the labour force are between 37 to 42 hours, and overtime work can be agreed between the parties.

Ireland is, in European terms, a highly unionized country, with the Irish Congress of Trade Unions being the major trade union body in the country. In 1979 it was estimated that 499 000 members were affiliated to 85 trade unions representing about 65% of all employees. The Irish Congress of Trade Unions advises that at the end of 1974 there were 74 trade unions in Ireland with affiliated membership of 474 000. The 15 biggest unions represent about 80% of total trade union membership and the remaining 59 unions represent only 20%.

The employer–employee relationship in Ireland is based on a contract of employment which has been influenced by statute law.

There is a fine distinction between an employee–employer relationship and that of a contract for services. If the relationship is deemed to be one of a contract for services then employment law as set out herein may not apply. The normal franchisor–franchisee relationship/agreement would not appear to create a relationship of employee–employer and therefore is deemed to be outside the scope of employment law. Various tests have been used by the courts to determine whether the intention was to create an employment relationship or a contract for services. The idea of control is the regulating factor in deciding whether a relationship is one of employment or a contract of services. An employee as defined by Section 1 of the Unfair Dismissals Act 1977 is 'an individual who has entered into or works under a contract of employment'.

The Unfair Dismissals Act 1977 recognizes that an employee has certain rights to continue in employment unless, having regard to all the circumstances, there were substantial grounds for justifying his dismissal. The Act provides protection against arbitrary or unjustified dismissal, providing the dismissed employee with the option of re-instatement or re-engagement unless the dismissal was fair.

Minimum Notice and Terms of Employment Act 1973 – the contract of employment cannot be terminated without the employee receiving his minimum period of notice. The notice period is dependent on the period of service, with a minimum notice of one week. The employer is also entitled to a maximum one week's notice from his employees. The employee is also entitled to be provided with a written statement of his conditions of employment.

The rights and obligations in the contract of employment arise from three sources: (a) the contract itself, (b) the constitution and (c) the obligations imposed by statute. Since many contracts are not in writing, except that a written statement of terms and conditions pursuant to the Act can be requested, sources such

as collective agreements, employment regulation orders and registered employment agreements detail the contract. Another source is the custom and practice in
the trade. Since 1970 a series of national pay agreements have been negotiated.
Certain minimum terms and conditions of employment and remuneration for
some industries are fixed from time to time by joint committees. The joint labour
committee consists of equal numbers of representatives of employers and
employees appointed by the labour court, and the chairman, who is an independent member, is appointed by the Minister for Labour. The Holidays
(Employees Act) 1973 provides that paid vacations (three weeks per annum) plus
payment for the statutory public holidays must be given to full-time employees.
The termination of employment is also affected by the Redundancy Payments
Act 1967 to 1979 and the Unfair Dismissals Act 1977. An employee is entitled to
redundancy payments if he has been continuously employed by the same
employer for two years or more. An employee can lose his right to a redundancy
payment if he is dismissed fairly and with due notice for any reason other than
redundancy (e.g. misconduct or inefficiency). Two other Acts should be noted,
namely the Employment Equality Act 1977 based on EC Directive No. 77/207,
which prevents discrimination in employment on grounds of sex or marital status,
and the Maternity Protection of Employees Act 1981, which provides legal rights
to female employees during pregnancy.

The Labour Services Acts 1987 created the Training and Development
Authority, which is given responsibility to ensure that a well-trained workforce is
available to meet labour requirements of new and existing industries. Training
courses are provided and trainee employees subsidized to work in industry. The
body is funded by the industrial training levy, which is a levy imposed on
employers amounting to between 1% and 1.25% of total payroll.

## Foreign investment

The general policy pursued by the government through its agent the central bank
is to welcome investment in Irish industry. The principal regulations relating to
establishing a new business in Ireland by a non-resident deal with the following
issues:

1   Permission for initial direct investment

2   Loan financing required for project

3   Right to repatriate profits and capital

4   Operation of inter-company accounts

The aim of exchange control is necessarily to safeguard the national reserves and
regulate the effect of capital movements on the exchange rate of the Irish pound.
In practice, exchange control consent for the establishment of businesses in

Ireland is normally a procedural matter, and furthermore EC residents investing in Ireland are entitled as of right to such consent.

The central bank of Ireland is responsible for the administration of exchange control. The principal Acts are the Exchange Control Acts 1954 to date, and the Exchange Control Regulations 1959 to date. The aim of the legislation is to impose certain duties on Irish residents regarding their financial dealings with non-residents. Exchange control permission is required by private Irish companies to issue shares to non-residents. The permission is normally a formality on receipt of details of the share issue and certificate of an Irish bank confirming that the full purchase price has been paid. Direct investment by non-residents may be undertaken either through a new company incorporated in Ireland or by the establishment of a branch or partnership or other entity. Exchange control permission is normally a formality once full details of the investment are forwarded. Irish companies and Irish branches of foreign companies require exchange control permission for borrowing outside Ireland and this permission is a formality if the bank is satisfied that the interest payable will not exceed the normal commercial rate and that the loan is for productive purposes.

### Terminations

The franchise agreement, like any other commercial agreement, will invariably contain an express provision for its termination in the event of a default by the franchisee. The franchisee should have the opportunity of remedying any breach within a certain specified time, failing which notice of termination can be served. The agreement might terminate through the effluxion of time or alternatively through the conclusion of a further agreement between the parties. Furthermore, the termination might be brought about as a result of a subsequent event resulting in the discharge of existing obligations. An example of such a subsequent event would be the bankruptcy of the individual franchisee or, in the case of the franchisee being a company, the presentation of a winding-up order against the said company.

The franchise agreement can be terminated by an express provision in the event of a default by the franchisee as outlined above. On termination the franchisor will ensure that the franchisee ceases to be associated with the franchisor and desists from the use of the trade mark/trade name and other proprietary rights of the franchisor. Furthermore, the franchisee will probably be restrained from competing with the franchisor or other franchisees for a specified period.

## TAX AND FINANCIAL CONSIDERATIONS

### Principal taxes

The following are the principal taxes exigible in Ireland: income tax, corporation tax and capital gains/capital acquisitions tax. The principal statute dealing with income tax is the Income Tax Act 1967, which has been amended by subsequent Finance Acts. The tax is payable on the annual gains made by individuals

d certain non-resident corporations; the tax rates are set out below under
mployee-related taxes.

Irish resident individuals, partnerships and trusts are subject to income tax
1d capital gains tax on their worldwide income and capital gains. Non-resident
dividuals, partnerships and trusts are subject to income tax only on income
om sources in the Republic. A non-resident company is liable to capital gains
x other than gains on development land, if such arise from assets used in
mnection with a trade carried on in Ireland through a branch or agency. The
rst £2000 of an individual's taxable gains is exempt in any tax year and for
arried couples the first £4000 of taxable gains is exempt.

Corporation tax is the method of charging to tax the profits of a company
1d is chargeable at a rate of 43% (except for manufacturing; see below).

The tax is chargeable in respect of the taxable profits of a company for an
:counting period and is payable in one instalment six months after the end of an
:counting period. Profits of a company are deemed to have two constituents,
amely income and chargeable gains. Gains from the disposal of development
nd are treated as capital gains and assessed under capital gains tax. Corpora-
ons resident in Ireland are subject to corporation tax on profits from every
urce. The place of management and control and not the place of incorporation
etermines residence for the purpose of corporation tax. In computing corporaon tax the accounts of the company form the basis of assessment. Expenditures
tay be deducted if these are incurred wholly and exclusively in the course of trade
r business and special capital allowances apply to capital expenditures.

Companies resident in Ireland are subject to payment of corporation tax on
teir worldwide income. Non-resident companies which have a branch or agency
t Ireland are subject to payment of corporation tax on the income of such branch
r agency. The non-resident company may also be subject to paying income tax
n any income arising in Ireland from sources not connected with the branch.
he company is deemed to be resident in Ireland if its central management and
mtrol is located here. In general, any income which arises in Ireland is subject to
ther corporation tax or income tax; however, there is relief available to non-
ationals and foreign corporations under the tax treaties to which Ireland is a
arty.

Profits subject to corporation tax are computed by totalling the income and
ten deducting charges on income. Categories of income include the profits of the
orporation, public revenue dividends, investment income, rental income, and
come from pensions. Charges on income deducted from a company's total
rofits include annual interest, patent royalties, annuities, certain covenanted
ayments and trading expenses.

The Revenue Commissioners are a separate division of the Department of
inance and are charged with the responsibility of operating the taxation system.
urrently, tax returns are assessed by the taxation authorities on the basis of
iformation filed with them. However, a change to a self-assessment system is in
rogress. Overdue tax is subject to a penalty interest rate of 1.25% per month.

Where a double-taxation treaty is in place with another country, the treat will determine whether and to what amount a non-resident company is liable t Irish tax. Treaties normally exist with countries that trade with Ireland and it important to note that there is a distinction between trading in Ireland and merel trading with Ireland. The factors which indicate whether or not there is trading i Ireland include the making of contracts in Ireland, delivery of goods and paymer for same in Ireland.

A non-resident company which does not trade in Ireland through a branch c agency but has income arising in Ireland is not subject to corporation tax, bu rather to income tax at 35% on income received from an Irish source. The nor resident company is also liable to capital gains on disposal of lands and buildings i Ireland. Where the goods are manufactured outside Ireland but sold in Irelan through a branch or permanent establishment in Ireland, liability to corporatio tax can be confined to the sales (merchanting) element of the overall profit of th entity concerned.

In order to encourage manufacturing industry in Ireland, a 10% corporatio. tax rate applies to companies deemed to manufacture. 'Deemed to manufacture includes any process whereby the final product is inherently different from the rav material input. Certain services also qualify for the 10% tax rate and these includ computer, engineering, research and development services.

The Capital Gains Tax Act 1975 is a tax on individuals in respect of realize( capital profits and on corporations in relation to capital profits gained from sale of development land. Value added tax is a tax on the supply of goods and service and this is dealt with below, as are customs duties. Capital acquisitions tax is tax on gifts and inheritance and is regulated by the Capitals Acquisitions Tax Ac 1976.

### Tax implications of setting up franchises in Ireland

A foreign franchisor outside Ireland who receives franchise fees from a franchise conducted in Ireland (initial franchise and periodic payments, i.e. royalty o management fee) will not, unless the franchisor is operating through a per manent establishment in Ireland, be liable to Irish tax, the argument being tha the franchisor is a person who is trading with, as distinct from within, Ireland Apart from patent royalties, no other royalties received by a franchisor outside the jurisdiction from franchise operations conducted in Ireland are subject to Irish tax.

### Indirect taxation

Value added tax is a tax on the supply of goods and services which was introduce( by the Value Added Tax Act 1972, which has been amended by subsequen Finance Acts and by the Value Added Tax (Amendment) Act 1978. Taxes at the upper rate of 21% are exigible on goods and services. Customs duties are irrelevan since Ireland now operates according to the Common Customs Tariff of the EC. Excise duties are taxes which are levied on specific products such as alcohol.

obacco and vehicles. These latter taxes are imposed by a number of Customs and Finance Acts and the Minister for Finance has the power to amend same by statutory instrument. Currently a person supplying taxable goods or services in Ireland whose annual turnover exceeds IR£15 000 from services or IR£32 000 from goods must register for VAT. Goods imported into Ireland are subject to VAT at the same rate as applies to the sale of similar goods within Ireland.

### Employee-related taxes/social security obligations

Pay-related social insurance is deducted at the rate of 12.20% from the employer, and the employee must contribute 7.75%. An employee who pays PRSI is entitled to certain medical and dental benefits. The employee's contribution of 7.75% is broken down as follows: (a) social insurance 5.50%; (b) health contribution 1.25%; and (c) youth employment levy 1.0%. Taxation of the employee is deducted at source from wages under a Pay as You Earn system. The employee receives a net salary after deductions have been made.

### Investment incentives

The Industrial Development Authority (IDA) is a semi-state body charged with responsibility for the development and expansion of industry. Investment incentives, namely cash grants and tax reliefs, are available to foreigners wishing to establish industry in Ireland. The range of financial and fiscal incentives offered to prospective investors include capital grants, training grants and various forms of tax reliefs. Typical incentives include grant aid for buildings and equipment, grants for research and development, a special development programme for small industries (those employing fewer than 50 people with fixed assets of less than £400 000), loans for fixed assets and working capital, fixed asset grants and training grants.

Ireland has actively encouraged foreign investment for more than 30 years. The primary objective is to increase employment opportunities. In the early stages investment incentives were focused on traditional labour-intensive industries; however, in the 1970s the emphasis changed to more technically advanced projects including electronics and pharmaceutical and chemical companies. There has been in the 1980s a greater emphasis on service activities such as software development, the design and planning of international construction projects and financial services. The USA is the largest investor in Ireland; however, new sources of investment are being encouraged from the Far East and in 1986 nearly 20% of total IDA foreign investment approvals came from the Far East. The development agencies offer a number of incentives, both financial and fiscal; the financial incentives include grants and subsidies, i.e. project-related grants to help reduce the costs of fixed assets to new industry and grants for the training of staff, and research and development.

Where inward investment has been undertaken and granted, permission is readily given for the transfer of dividends and profits outside Ireland. Permission can be obtained at any time for the repatriation or for the sale or liquidation proceeds of the investment and permission for borrowing outside Ireland allows the repayment of loan capital in addition to the payment of interest. The central bank will authorize payment for royalty and service fees provided they are on a commercial basis and that relevant agreements have been submitted to and approved by the central bank.

Exchange control permission is normally granted for companies to offset proceeds due for exports against liabilities for imports.

The active encouragement of foreign investment by the government is also evident in the tax incentives available. The principal ones are as follows:

1   Corporate tax rate of 10%; all manufacturing operations in Ireland qualify for a reduced corporation tax rate of 10% on manufacturing profits, and this is guaranteed until 31 December 2000. Certain services can also qualify for this reduced rate, such as those involved in the computer and engineering service areas.

2   Accelerated tax depreciation; up to 50% of the cost of new plant and industrial buildings can be claimed against tax in the first year.

3   Tax-based financing; there are two types of tax-based financing, namely leasing and Section 84 financing, which both provide reduced rates of interest on loans to businesses establishing in Ireland.

4   Remittance of profits; there are no withholding taxes in Ireland on dividends paid to non-residents.

5   Expatriate taxation; certain income tax relief is available to non-Irish executives sent to Ireland to establish a business. The executive is only taxed on income brought into the country and not on total earnings, providing these are paid outside the country.

# CHAPTER 11
# ITALY

*Aldo Frignani*

## AN OVERVIEW OF FRANCHISING IN ITALY

There are grounds for substantial optimism regarding the prospects for the continuing growth of franchising in Italy.

As citizens of an advanced consumer society, Italians share the habits and tastes of consumers in other developed countries in clothing, sports and entertainment, household appliances, cars and services. Rising affluence is creating new demand for goods and services for a people eager to catch up with the more advanced countries of the EC. Suitable foreign franchisors will find that this country traditionally welcomes novelty from abroad.

Italians are an energetic and dynamic people who look upon an integrated Europe as the best, and perhaps only, hope for introducing a degree of order and efficiency into Italy's stifling and costly public administration. The perennial inefficiencies of the postal service, trains, telephones and other services in the public sector are legendary. These, plus the huge public deficit, are also the source of growing anxiety for Italy's place in a unified European market.

The country is not lacking in problems, which may explain in part the reason why Italy recently installed government No. 49 in the 46 years since the end of World War II.

But with it all, the Italian economy grew by a robust 3.9% in 1988 and was expected to post growth in excess of 3% in 1989. There is, in short, an enormous resilience at work here, a capacity to overcome self-inflicted wounds and muddle through. Perhaps symbolic of Italy is the Tower of Pisa, which leans a trifle more each year and is constantly worrisome to the engineers, but which continues as a rich source of tourist revenues.

There is still an excess of regulation in the field of retail sales, the social security costs of labour are high, rentals of commercial property are exorbitant and the general level of professionalism in retail sales leaves much to be desired. And there are far too many small shop owners, many of whom cling tenaciously to their entrepreneurial independence.

At the same time, there is a growing sensation that as the 1 January 1993 deadline approaches, it will become increasingly necessary for many small merchants to join some form of associated sales network in order to survive the more competitive conditions of the 1990s.

As an historical phenomenon, franchising first made its entry on the Italian scene in 1970 and has enjoyed steady, if not spectacular, growth ever since.

If franchising was originally conceived abroad as a means of competing with the large retail chains, in Italy it was the well-known chains which gave franchising its initial impulse. As will be explained in more detail below, the franchising formula enabled them to circumvent bureaucratic difficulties in connection with the procurement of operating permits essential for opening new points of sale. Small, independent merchants, already in possession of the required permits and operating in communities in which the chain store operators preferred not to open company-owned outlets, were attractive targets for conversion franchising.

In the absence of registration requirements, it is difficult to know with any degree of precision how many franchises are presently operating in Italy. The most reliable private census available dates back to 1 January 1989. At that time, there were 210 franchises identified, of which 161 were in the distribution of goods and the remaining in various services: car rentals, fast food, real estate, hotels, etc.

Given the substantial expansion of franchising in the past two years, the above figures no longer offer a remotely reliable reading of the current status of franchising in Italy. The Italian Association of Franchising (AIF) estimates that there are no less than 250 franchise systems currently operating in Italy (January 1991), with no less than 12 000 franchisees, and the number is growing.

The general business climate for franchising is positive. Foreign franchisors with products or services favourably received in other EC countries should find the Italian economy, with its population of over 57 million (second only to Germany), an equally rewarding market, without prejudice or legal restrictions directed against foreign business ventures. Finally, in the almost 20 years of franchising in Italy, there has been remarkably little litigation involving parties to a franchise.

It is encouraging that a greater public awareness of the meaning of franchising has begun to develop in Italy in the past five years. The literature in Italian on franchising is growing and the number of seminars and round tables dedicated to examining the various aspects of the franchising formula is increasing annually. The annual Franchise Show held in Milan each year in early November offers the opportunity for prospective franchisees to meet with franchisors/exhibitors, an important contribution to a more sophisticated knowledge of the workings of the franchising formula.

While there is still a considerable educational process to perform in order for franchising to achieve maturity, there can be no doubt that franchising has established a solid beachhead in Italy.

# STRUCTURE OF A FRANCHISE VENTURE IN ITALY:
## BUSINESS ENTITIES

The principal methods of structuring a business venture in Italy are the following:

Joint stock company or corporation (Società per Azioni, S.p.A.)

Limited liability company (Società a responsabilità limitata, S.r.l.)

General partnership (Società in nome collettivo, S.n.c.)

Limited partnership (Società in accomandita semplice, S.a.s)

Limited partnership with shares (Società in accomandita per azioni, S.a.a.)

Sole proprietorship (Impresa individuale)

Branch office (Sede secondaria)

Business participation venture (Associazione in partecipazione)

## Joint stock company (S.p.A.)

This is a company which has the same features as the joint stock company or corporation in other countries. Shareholders are issued stock certificates and their liability is limited to corporate assets. It is the most common venture for large undertakings.

The minimum capital required to form the S.p.A. is L. 200 million (ECU 130 300) (1 ECU = approximately L. 1535) of which not less than 30% must be deposited with an Italian bank at the time of formation of the corporation, funds which are then transferred to the corporation's account once formation has been effected. The remaining 70% of capital is subject to call by the board of directors as and when it is needed to carry out company business.

Special authorization is required for companies formed to conduct banking or insurance or for any company whose capital exceeds L. 10 billion (ECU 6.5 million).

The S.p.A. must be formed by at least two promoters, who may be Italian or foreign citizens, corporations or individuals. While the number of shareholders may subsequently be reduced to a single shareholder, in such event the Italian corporation will lose its limited liability and the sole shareholder will be subject to unlimited liability for company obligations.

Formation of the S.p.A. is carried out by a notary and does not require the physical presence of the founding shareholders. Foreign corporations or individuals may grant a power of attorney to persons living in Italy for the purpose of incorporating the S.p.A.

Management of the S.p.A. is entrusted to a board of directors or sole director, all of whom may be foreign citizens and residing abroad. They need not be shareholders. Directors of the S.p.A. have the usual responsibility to promote the best interests of the corporation and are liable to the corporation or its creditor for negligence or fraud. Management by a legal entity is not admitted.

The S.p.A. must have a board of statutory auditors (Collegio Sindacale) which is composed generally of three members, plus two alternates. The board of auditors is not to be confused with an auditing firm engaged by management to certify the financial statements. The auditors are required by law to conduct quarterly reviews of the corporate accounts; they must approve the annual balance sheet and generally ensure that the accounting records are properly kept and recorded. The board of auditors is invited to take part in all meetings of the board of directors as well as meetings of shareholders.

Members of the board of directors and board of statutory auditors are elected for a term up to three years and are eligible for re-election.

Meetings of shareholders of the S.p.A., as well as board meetings, generally take place at the company's registered office, but may take place elsewhere within or without Italy, if the articles of incorporation so permit. A meeting of shareholders must be held once a year to approve the company's financial statements.

The S.p.A. must maintain the customary corporate books: minute books of shareholders' meetings and directors' meetings, shareholders book, journal, inventory book, VAT records, etc.

## Limited liability company (S.r.l.)
The S.r.l. has most, but not all, of the same attributes as the joint stock company, except that there are no shares of stock. Equity is represented by quotas as recorded in the required company book, but transfer of quotas may be restricted.

The S.r.l. is generally used for small or medium-sized ventures and provides the benefit of liability limited to company assets. The minimum capital requirement is L. 20 million (ECU 13 030), of which 30% must be deposited with a bank as in the case of the joint stock company. The company may be managed by a board of directors or a sole director. The board of statutory auditors is not required if the capital of the S.r.l. is less than L. 200 million (ECU 130 300).

The S.r.l. may not, as distinct from the joint stock company, issue bonds or debentures.

By virtue of a 1988 Law imposing a government concession tax on company capital, the S.r.l. has acquired enhanced popularity and many joint stock companies were, as a result, converted to the S.r.l. The difference in the annual concession tax burden between the S.p.A. and S.r.l. was very substantial and the S.p.A. suddenly became an unattractive format for doing business for companies of relatively modest dimensions. After widespread protest, the tax was revised, but the difference still exists.

## General partnership (S.n.c.)

The S.n.c. does not enjoy limited liability, but may assume obligations in its own name. The partnership agreement must be filed with the Registry of Enterprises by the notary engaged to form the partnership. All the partners are jointly and severally liable for the obligations of the partnership. No minimum capital is required. There are no restrictions on foreigners forming a partnership, but a foreign partnership is treated as a corporate entity for tax purposes (in the absence of a tax treaty provision to the contrary).

## Limited partnership (S.a.s.)

With the S.a.s., the general partners are jointly and severally liable without limit, while the limited partners are liable only to the extent of their capital contribution to the partnership. Only the general partners may manage the partnership. The rules applicable to the general partnership apply to the S.a.s. unless the partnership agreement provides differently.

## Limited partnership with shares (S.a.a.)

The S.a.a. is distinguished from the limited partnership (S.a.s.) by virtue of the issuance of shares. The general partners are jointly and severally liable without limit for partnership obligations, while the limited partners are liable to the extent of the subscribed shares.

If not for the purpose of keeping closed assets among family members, the S.a.a. is infrequently used.

## Sole proprietorship

A sole proprietorship must register with the Chamber of Commerce in the city in which the proprietor conducts his business. The proprietor is liable without limit for the obligations of his business.

## Branch office

In lieu of establishing a business entity in Italy in one of the forms indicated above, a foreign company may open a branch office. While the branch has some attributes of an independent business, the foreign parent company is liable without limit for the obligations of the branch.

The branch must be registered with the Registry of Enterprises and the Chamber of Commerce. No minimum capital requirement exists. The branch must file its own financial statements on an annual basis, as well as those of the parent company, the latter obligation being frequently ignored in practice. The tax authorities, however, have the right to demand from the parent company financial statements, an obligation which frequently discourages foreign companies from opening a branch in Italy.

## Business participation venture

A contractual relationship to create a special business participation venture (Associazione in partecipazione) is contemplated by the Italian Civil Code, generally for relatively short duration. Under this formula, party A grants associate B the right to participate in the profits of a business venture organized by A in return for a specified capital contribution by B. Third parties have rights only against party A. The venture terminates upon completion of the project for which it was intended, a factor tending to distinguish this formula from a limited partnership, which is usually formed with the intention of operating on a more or less long-term basis.

Associate B has a right to an annual accounting. Unless the business venture agreement provides for the contrary, associate B shares in the losses of the venture to the same extent to which he participates in the profits.

From a review of the various ways of organizing a business venture in Italy, it would appear that the franchisor or sub-franchisor would be well advised to operate under the format of a joint stock company (S.p.A.) or limited liability company (S.r.l.), both of which provide for limited liability. The corporate law and income tax requirements applicable to the two formats are substantially alike. The other business structures briefly reviewed above are ill-suited to the needs of the foreign franchisor and should, in the opinion of the author, be disregarded.

We have seen that the S.p.A. requires a substantially higher minimum capital commitment (L. 200 million, ECU 130 300) than the S.r.l. (L. 20 million, ECU 13 030), but confers upon the shareholders a considerably higher degree of prestige than the more modest S.r.l.

The S.r.l., however, offers cost savings related to its exemption from the requirement of appointing a board of statutory auditors if the capital of the S.r.l. is less than L. 100 million (ECU 67 150).

With respect to the franchisee or sub-franchisee, the most effective format would be dictated by the nature of the business and its financial dimensions. The franchisee, for example, who opens a motel will make a substantial investment of capital and the benefits of limited liability would dictate the formation of either the S.p.A. or S.r.l. On the other hand, a franchisee opening a small photocopy shop might find a general partnership (S.n.c.) or the sole proprietorship sufficient for his needs.

## LEGAL CONSIDERATIONS

There is no legislation in Italy directly related to franchising, nor are there requirements for the registration by the franchisor with a governmental agency of his franchise programme or contract. The franchisor has no obligation to make disclosure of information to potential franchisees, as is the rule in the USA or France.

The foreign franchisor will find no restrictions to doing business in Italy. The payment abroad of franchise fees, initial and continuing, and indeed the repatriation of earnings generally from Italy have not been a problem for foreign business enterprises.

There are only a few industries in which restrictive legislation of some kind applies to foreign interests, all of which are of generally marginal interest to franchising: aviation, banking, communications, government procurement, insurance, newspapers and shipping.

## Pyramid selling

The term 'pyramid selling' is used here to mean a chain-letter mechanism whereby party A (passing himself off as a 'franchisor') enters into a so-called franchise agreement with B (styled 'franchisee') who pays A an initial franchise fee to cover in part the purchase of goods for resale and in part the benefits of entering into the network; but B undertakes, as his principal contractual obligation, to effect the recruitment into the network of other so-called 'franchisees', C, D, E, etc. Once recruited, the latter assume all the same obligations as B, including the payment to A of the initial franchise fee; their earnings result from the recruitment of F, G, H, etc.

While there is no legislation prohibiting the use of such pyramid schemes, they will be found null and void and quite probably result in criminal charges against the perpetrators for fraud.

In the one important case of a pyramid scheme in Italy under the guise of franchising, the contract was found to have violated basic principles of contract law, as well as the law regulating the sale of merchandise, and tax law (VAT), and was held to have induced the so-called 'franchisees' to have entered into the contract and paid the initial franchise fee under false representations.[1]

The pyramid selling mechanism should, of course, be clearly distinguished from the relationship established between a bona fide franchisor and a sub-franchisor who takes upon himself the obligation to sell franchises to a certain number of sub-franchisees and, most importantly, to administer the network once organized. There is nothing of the chain-letter scheme in this relationship. The sub-franchisees are engaged to sell the goods or services inherent in the franchise and are not expected to recruit into the network other sub-franchisees. So, too, the sub-franchisor has a very clear management function to perform on behalf of the franchisor, the most important phase of which begins after the sub-franchisees have been brought into the network.

## Competition law

Until mid-October 1990 Italian domestic competition law was very limited. The three main provisions in the Civil Code can be summarized as follows:

1    Article 2595: Competition must be carried out in a manner which does not damage the national economy (almost never applied by the courts).

2    Article 2596: Agreements limiting competition must be in writing, limited to a specified geographic area or specified business activity, and may not exceed five years. (Upon expiration of the agreement, the parties may enter

into a new agreement on the same terms as the prior one, including the five
year limitation.)

3    Article 2598: Unfair competition means

    (a)  the use of names or distinguishing marks legitimately used by others or
        the servile imitation of the goods of a competitor or the use of any means
        intended to create confusion with the goods or business of a competitor

    (b)  the attempt to discredit the goods or business of a competitor or the
        attempt to appropriate as one's own the benefits of the goods of a
        competitor

    (c)  the use of any other means in contrast with the principles of professional
        ethics and capable of damaging a competitor's company

These were the provisions of interest under Italian competition law. But the
picture has changed radically since 14 October 1990, when the Italian antitrust
law no. 287 came into force. The statute contains provisions which are almost
identical to Articles 85 and 86 of the Treaty of Rome, besides rules on public
undertakings and mergers control. In particular, Article 2.2 prohibits the agreements between undertakings which have as their object or effect the prevention,
restriction or distortion of competition, unless they are authorized by the
Autorità. Worthy of note is Article 1.4, which states that in construing the
statute reference should be made to the principles laid down in the EC antitrust
law.

In view of the foregoing, franchisors are strongly advised to structure their
franchise agreement for use in Italy to comply as far as possible with the EC regulation providing a block exemption for categories of franchise agreements, as discussed elsewhere in this book.

**Liability of franchisor**

The franchisor is advised to insert in his franchise contract in Italy a hold harmless clause relieving him of liability in the event of injury to a third party doing
business with one of his franchisees. It should be noted, however, that such a
clause will not absolve the franchisor of liability in the event of malice, gross negligence or violation of public policy, nor under the 1988 products liability law (see
below).

In addition to the foregoing, the franchisor should take due care to distinguish a franchised outlet from one owned by the franchisor himself, one of the
principal reasons being to discourage attempts by parties injured in a franchisee's
outlet to make a claim against the franchisor on the grounds that he was misled by
the appearances of the outlet into thinking that he entered a shop owned and
managed by the franchisor. In passing, Article 4, paragraph (c) of the EC Block

Exemption Regulation requires the franchisee to indicate his status as an independent undertaking, but without interfering with the common identity of the franchised network.

As required by EC Directive No. 85/374 regarding products liability, Italy in 1988 passed legislation providing for strict liability for injury resulting from defective products (DPR 24 May 1988, No. 224). The EC Directive left each of the member states to decide the following issues:

1   The Italian law in question provides for the so-called 'state of the art' defence being available to exonerate the manufacturer who has placed in circulation a product which, while it may have caused injury, represents the latest in technological development, so at the time of manufacture, it was not possible to consider the product defective.

2   Italy did not take up the EC option to place a financial ceiling on the amount of recovery permitted as a result of a single defect.

Interpreting the Italian products liability law, it would appear that the franchisor who puts his distinguishing mark (name, trade mark, logo, etc.) on a product manufactured by a third party will be deemed under the law to be a manufacturer of the goods and, thus, subject to the same strict liability as would be applicable to the actual manufacturer. It need hardly be added that, under the circumstances, the franchise contract should require the Italian franchisees to stipulate an insurance policy with a reputable insurer against the risk of products liability, with extension of coverage to the franchisor.

## Industrial and intellectual property
The reader need hardly be reminded of the importance for a franchise operation of adequate protection of the franchisor's industrial and intellectual property. At the same time, it is settled law within the EC that trade marks and other intellectual property rights may not be used in a manner to preclude otherwise legitimate competition.

While Italian law in the field of industrial and intellectual property is generally in line with that of other industrialized countries, it offers some peculiarities which merit the reader's attention.

***Patents***   There is no examination for novelty in Italy. Patents are granted for 20 years from the date of filing the application. The law provides for compulsory licensing for patents unused within a period of three years from the date of issuance of the patent.

Italy is a party to the European Patent Convention signed in October 1973 which provides for centralized filing of patent applications. In addition, Italy is a signatory to the EC Community Patent Convention which is expected to enter into effect during 1991. Application for a European-wide patent must be submitted to the European Patent Office (Munich) for an examination of novelty. The grant of the European Patent will be valid in all the member states.

Italy is a signatory to the Paris Convention for the protection of industrial property of 1883. As in other Convention states, an application for a patent in one country provides for automatic priority of filing in Italy for a 12-month period.

*Copyright* In Italy, copyright provides for protection for the lifetime of the author plus 50 years with respect to literary works and their translations, music, art, etc.

Italy is a party to the Berne Convention of 1886 and the Universal Copyright Convention of 1952, as amended. A reform of copyright law is currently under consideration.

The operations manual of a franchisor which is protected by copyright in the Convention country will automatically benefit from the same protection in Italy. Software has found protection in case law as literary work.

*Trade marks* Italian trade mark law offers some peculiarities and grey areas which merit the attention of franchise operators.

The foreign franchisor may register his trade mark in Italy on the same terms and conditions as an Italian citizen or company. Registration is effected at the Central Patent Office in Rome or with the Chamber of Commerce in the province in which the applicant resides. If the applicant is a non-resident, he must appoint a representative in Italy to file the application.

To remain in effect, a trade mark must be used within three years of issuance. Trade mark protection will also be lost in the event of interruption in its use for a period of three years.

Italy is a signatory to the Paris Union of 1883, as amended, and the Madrid Arrangement for the International Registration of Trademarks of 1891, as amended.

Registration of a trade mark in Italy is for 20 years and is renewable any number of times. The user of a trade mark which has not been registered may continue to use it notwithstanding later registration of the same mark by another party, such use to be limited to the geographical area in which the user has already used the mark.

Italian law provides for individual, collective and service marks. With respect to service marks, registration applies to the fields of transportation, communications, advertising, construction, insurance, credit and banking, entertainment, radio, television, the processing of materials and the like. A service trade mark for a retailing network in franchising has been held to be valid in the Computerland case.[2]

One of the requirements for the transfer or license of a trademark in Italy is contained in Article 15 of the special law on trade marks of 1942, which reads as follows:

> A trademark may not be transferred unless in relation to the transfer of the business or a particular branch thereof, provided further that the transfer is for the exclusive use of such mark.

In any event, the transfer of the trademark must not result in misleading the public as to the essential qualities of the products or goods.

The above language speaks in terms of (a) transfer of the business or a
particular branch of the business and (b) how such transfer must be for the exclusive use of the mark. These requirements raise at least three questions of interest
to the franchising community:

1    Does the requirement of the '*transfer* of the business or a particular branch
     thereof' preclude the granting of a *licence* of a trade mark?

2    What is meant by the expression 'transfer of the business or a particular
     branch thereof?'

3    Does the requirement that the transfer be for 'the exclusive use' of the trade
     mark mean that there can be only one licensee of the trade mark?

Both the Italian Supreme Court and leading trade mark experts have given
the following interpretation to these questions:

1    No. The requirement of 'transfer' of the business does not preclude the
     granting of one or more licences of a trade mark provided certain conditions
     are met.

2    The requirement of 'transfer of the business or a particular branch thereof'
     will be satisfied if the licensor grants the licensee all the know-how, designs,
     secret processes or formulae, etc. in sufficient detail to permit him to effect a
     faithful reproduction of the original product.

3    No. There may be a number of licensees, but each of them should be
     granted an exclusive territory for the production and sale of the trade
     marked goods.

The problem for the establishment of a franchising network in Italy has been
solved in two ways: on the one hand, the 'licence of use' (i.e. to show the goods
sold in a given shop) is different either from the transfer (or assignment) of a trade
mark or from a licence of manufacturing the goods bearing such trade mark, and
thus no reason exists to require the exclusivity.
On the other hand, when the trade mark is used simply as a shop sign we are
outside the realm of trade mark law, since the shop signs or insignia differ from
a trade mark (this view has been expressed in the *Benetton* case[3] and implicitly
upheld in the *Standa I* case[4] and the *Standa II* case.[5]
Italian law does not require the recording of a separate registered user
agreement, the licence need not be in writing and may also be implied. The

licence agreement may be deposited with the Central Patent Office, but this is not compulsory. If deposited, the trademark licence is enforceable against third parties.

The relationship between a trade mark and a trade name was clarified by decision of the Supreme Court in late 1987, which is not without relevance for franchisors.[6] In this case, the court reviewed the use of the same name, 'Peter Pan', by two retailers of children's clothing, one of them having adopted 'Peter Pan' as his registered trade mark, and the other as his trade name and shop sign. The court handed down the following ruling:

1    A party who first uses a name as his trade name has exclusive right to use such name as a trade mark.

2    A party who first uses or registers a name as his trade mark, however, does not have the exclusive right to use such name as his trade name.

3    It is legitimate for a party to use the name 'Peter Pan' as his trade name and shop sign even if the same name was previously registered by another merchant as his trade mark, provided such trade name is used only to identify the company and not to identify or advertise its products.

4    With respect to the question of unfair competition resulting from the alleged confusion in the public eye between the two companies, the court ruled that there was no effective risk of competition between the parties to this action, inasmuch as there was very considerable distance between the cities (800 km) in which the parties carried on their respective businesses.

The Peter Pan decision points up the distinction in Italian intellectual property law between trade marks and trade names:

1    A trade mark in Italy serves to distinguish the product or service of the owner from the product or service offered by other merchants.

2    A trade name serves to distinguish one business venture from another. There is no registration of trade names in Italy except for companies or partnerships. (A shop sign has the purpose of identifying the place where a merchant conducts his business.)

What is the significance for franchisors of these fine distinctions in intellectual property rights?

Many franchises require the franchisee to resell products manufactured, labelled and packaged by the franchisor. The franchisee, in purchasing and reselling such products, does not manipulate or otherwise affect the quality of the products.

The granting of a licence of the franchisor's trade mark is, in the case of the mere distribution of already trade marked goods, a particular type of licence (one might say, only for promotional purposes).

As far as the trade name is concerned, the franchisee must always use his own trade name, to which he may add – insofar as explicitly specified in the franchise agreement – the trade mark or the trade name of the franchisor, accompanied by the word 'affiliato' (franchisee).

A final word of caution – given the complexities involved in industrial and intellectual property law and the concurrent requirement of complying with EC and domestic antitrust law, the foreign franchisor is strongly advised to consult trade mark counsel before launching his franchise in Italy.

## Real estate and leasing

Given the historical tendency to concentrate much of Italian urban life within the centre of cities and towns, it should come as no surprise that finding suitable site locations for purchase or leasing for franchise outlets is difficult and expensive.

As a result of such overcrowding and the consequent closing of the downtown areas to vehicular traffic, a slow, but steady, trend towards decentralization to the periphery is developing. Shopping centres and malls are beginning to appear, a phenomenon which in time should offer very interesting prospects for franchising.

There are no restrictions imposed on individual foreigners or foreign companies in connection with the purchase or leasing of real property.

Some franchisors may be tempted to think in terms of purchasing space in prime locations in major cities for the purpose of leasing the premises out to their franchisees. If the relationship with a franchisee should then be terminated for any reason, the franchisor would take repossession of his valuable property and lease it out to a new franchisee. There are, unfortunately, two substantial drawbacks to this strategy:

1   The Italian rent control law of 1978 provides, with certain exceptions, that the tenant of commercial property has the right to occupy the premises for a period of six years, plus a lease renewal for an additional six years, even if the lease agreement should provide for a shorter term. Thus, the owner/franchisor of the premises used by the franchisee could terminate the franchise agreement after, let us say, five years, but will not be able forcibly to evict a franchisee who regularly pays the rental and otherwise carries out the lease agreement until 12 years have elapsed.

2   But there is another provision of the rent control law which would discourage all but the most persistent franchisor from leasing commercial space to his franchisees. If the rental agreement is not renewed by the franchisor/lessor or is terminated for reason other than breach of the rental agreement by the franchisee/tenant and provided the premises are used for direct contact with the public, the franchisee has the right to receive from the franchisor an

indemnity equal to 18 months' rent (21 months' if a hotel) for the loss of goodwill.

If the franchisor/lessor then leases the same premises to another party to carry on the same business within one year of the termination of the lease with the first franchisee, the latter has the right to the payment of a second 18-month (or 21-month if a hotel) indemnity from the franchisor, equal in amount to the first one. A franchisor/lessor would, then, find himself in the position of being required to pay an ex-franchisee to whom he had leased the premises a sum equal to 36 months' rent.

It is the view of the author that the leasing by the franchisor of commercial premises to his franchisees would, for the two reasons explained above, appear to pose unacceptable risks for most franchisors. Attempts to circumvent the rent control law – for example, by not charging the franchisee rent for use of the premises, but increasing the franchise fees to serve to 'cover' the loss of rent – will in all likelihood be quickly unmasked by the courts.

A viable, although expensive, alternative for the franchisor would be for him to lease to his franchisee not the bare premises, but a fully functional turnkey business. The rental of a business, as opposed to the rental of business premises, is not subject to the rent control law and, thus, does not call into play the problems we have discussed above (for this reason, some franchisors choose this route; see 14 February 1987, *Bratti* case).

Because of the problems connected with the location of suitable sites for franchises, there is a strong tendency to seek out potential franchisee candidates from among businessmen who already conduct a business more or less similar to that of the franchisor, who already have the precious operating permit and who have premises in a desired location (see also p. 230).

### Foreigners working or establishing a business in Italy

As a member state of the EC, Italy makes a clear distinction with respect to work permits between citizens of EC countries and non-EC workers.

Workers from other EC countries are treated for work purposes like any Italian citizen and are not required to obtain a special work permit before coming in Italy (see below). Workers from EC countries must, of course, obtain a permit issued by the police granting them a right to reside in Italy ('Permesso di Soggiorno'). The formalities are relatively simple and can be completed within 30 days.

For non-EC nationals, the requirements are more restrictive and consider-ably more time-consuming. The foreign worker must make an application at an Italian consulate in his country of origin requesting permission to work in Italy. The processing of the application can be painfully slow, inasmuch as three ministries are involved in processing the application (the Ministries of Foreign Affairs, Labour and the Interior). The applicant cannot begin to work in Italy until the work permit has been issued to him. A wait of some 12–18 months is not unusual. The permits, issued by the police to the applicant, usually have a duration of not more than one year and are generally renewable.

The whole application process for the non-EC national is less cumbersome when the foreign worker will enter Italy in a role other than as an employee, such as a fiduciary, corporate director or professional person, capacities which do not involve competing with Italian citizens for employment.

There are no visa requirements for citizens coming from OECD countries.

With respect to establishing a business in Italy, there is no discrimination or other form of restriction applicable to foreigners whether coming from EC or non-EC countries. Foreign investment is welcome and treated in the same fashion as domestic investment.

Investment in the Mezzogiorno, the Italian South, is always particularly welcome, especially if it is labour-intensive. Special investment incentives in the Mezzogiorno are available (see p. 235).

## Employment laws

Employment laws and collective bargaining agreements are complex and all-encompassing. They govern all aspects of the employment relationship: hiring, trial period, minimum wage, sick leave, maternity leave, military service leave, vacation rights, seniority rights, resignation, dismissal for cause and leaving indemnities.

Employees are paid on a 13- or 14-month basis. The employer is required to set aside as leaving indemnity for each employee approximately one month's gross salary for each year of service.

Most companies are completely unionized by the three major unions (CGIL, CISL and UIL). Though the unions have been weakened in recent years in their control over employees and bargaining power with management, they still wield considerable power and are a force to be reckoned with at the political level.

Companies with at least 15 employees are subject to the so-called 'Workers' Statute', a 1970 law which offers workers substantial protection against employer surveillance and inspection of the person and strict requirements for dismissal of employees for cause. Law No. 108 of 1990 has extended this protection also to employees of undertakings with less than 15 employees and of professionals.

In labour law cases, the courts were for many years strongly orientated in favour of the workers in disputes with employers, but this has changed in recent years to a more balanced treatment of labour disputes.

Foreign franchisors are strongly advised to move with particular caution in hiring and dismissing employees in Italy, preferably only after obtaining professional advice.

## Foreign investments

As has already been pointed out above, foreign investments are welcome and treated no more restrictively than domestic investments.

The 1956 foreign investment law No. 46 guaranteeing the right to repatriate profits and disinvestment of funds previously invested in Italy has been repealed. At no time since passage of this law have there been restrictions placed on the repatriation of dividends or profits.

In compliance with the EC Directive regarding the free movement of capital, Italy has substantially reduced its earlier restrictions on the import and especially export of capital. A 1987 law changed the previous negative approach to permit transactions to take place unless specifically disallowed.

Since regulations issued by the Italian Exchange Office (UIC) are complex and subject to change on short notice, foreign franchisors are advised to check with their local bank prior to effecting transactions with Italy to assure that they are in compliance with the latest regulations.

Foreign franchisors will have no difficulty in repatriating franchising fees or royalties. They should, on the other hand, be especially careful, for both tax and currency control purposes, when charging an Italian company for management fees, technical assistance or service fees. The charges must be related to the rendering of bona fide services, be documented and calculated on an arm's length basis, as well as be reasonable for the nature of the services. These rules are of even greater importance in intercompany transactions between the foreign franchisor and an affiliated or related company in Italy.

Continuing franchise fees for vague grants of unspecified know-how could be disallowed as a taxable deduction to the Italian taxpayer recipient of the know-how. In this connection, it is most important that the know-how be in documented form (as required by EC Regulation no. 4087 and, probably, by the interpretation of the Italian antitrust law).

### Legislation affecting retail sales
Italian law regulates to a significant extent the wholesale and retail sale of goods, with obvious relevance for the franchising community.

A 1971 law establishes the basic rules regarding professional qualifications for the opening and administration of wholesale or retail sales outlets, and establishes the basis for city zoning plans in relation to the obtaining of operating permits for the opening, expanding or moving of sales outlets. The delay encountered in obtaining permits for the opening of new points of sale is a sore point for businessmen and franchise operations.

Ironically, the difficulties in obtaining operating permits have been to no small degree instrumental in promoting franchising in Italy, especially by the large department stores. Franchising serves as a legitimate means of circumventing the permit problem: by approaching small retailers who already possess the permit with a proposal to enter into a franchise relationship, the large chains have found in conversion franchising a valuable tool for expanding their business activities without excessive bureaucratic delays.

Given the lack of suitable locations and the concurrent difficulty in obtaining operating permits, merchants who have premises and the all-important permits are being offered substantial payments of key money to induce them to abandon the premises and the accompanying permit, in order that franchisors may establish pilot operations or for the opening of a point of sale by a franchisee.

Another law regulates store hours, allowing some degree of autonomy to regional governments. As a general rule, retail shops are required to close on Sundays and holidays and, in addition, one half day during the week, usually Monday morning. There are several exceptions to this rule regarding tourist areas, toll roads, petrol stations, airports and train stations.

The regional government of Lombardy, for example, has authorized city councils to experiment with allowing retail shops to remain open two days a week in the evening for a maximum of 110 days per year. It is probable that other regions will follow suit and sooner or later the facility for families to shop in the evening will become an accepted national practice.

The proliferation of fast-food outlets in recent years has led environmentalist groups to seek remedies against the alleged degradation of central-city areas. In February 1987, following the loudly protested opening of the first McDonald's outlet in the heart of Rome, a provision was inserted in legislation primarily directed to revision of the rent control law to give city governments substantially more discretionary power to deny operating permits in cases where the activities in question were deemed to be 'incompatible with local traditions and areas of particular interest within their boundaries'. This provision was immediately (and correctly) dubbed by the press 'anti-fast food'.

The Rome City Council's recent recourse to the provision in question to deny a permit to a new fast-food opening in Rome has been upheld by an administrative court as a legitimate use of the city's discretionary authority under the aforesaid 1987 law.

While fast-food establishments will continue to open, it is increasingly evident that the new entries will have greater difficulty in finding choice locations.

## Contract draftsmanship requirement

The franchise agreement presented for signature to the franchisee candidate has in most cases been drafted by the franchisor for use with a number of franchisees and, as such, is intended as a final text ready for signature. Under Italian law, certain provisions of such an agreement must be specifically accepted by the offeree/franchisee by way of a second signature which follows a listing of those provisions in the agreement for which the law required the specific acceptance.

The contractual provisions in question are the following:

1    Limitations on the liability of the offerer

2    The offerer's right to withdraw from the agreement or to suspend execution of the agreement

3    Provisions imposing time limitations on the offeree

4    Limitations on the offeree's right to raise defences

5    Restrictions on the offeree's contractual freedom to deal with third parties

6    Tacit extension or renewal of the agreement

7    An arbitration clause or other derogation from the competence of the law courts.

Failure on the part of the offerer to call the offeree's attention to the foregoing provisions in the agreement with the requirement of a second signature attesting to his specific acceptance of these clauses will result in the non-enforceability of the provisions by the offerer (Article 1341, Civil Code).

### Termination of a franchise agreement

There is no requirement under Italian law to show cause for the non-renewal of a franchise agreement.

With respect to termination for a breach of agreement, the Civil Code provides that an agreement may not be terminated if the default or breach is of minor importance (Article 1455, Civil Code). For this reason, it is advisable that the franchisor specify in the agreement those clauses which he deems of major importance, the violation of which by the franchisee will result in termination of the agreement (arbitral award Rome, 31 October 1989, *MIDAL* v. *Toson*).

There is no provision in Italian law for a right to compensation for loss of goodwill in the event of non-renewal or termination of a distribution or franchising agreement. As a matter of prudent draftsmanship, however, the franchise agreement should specify that the non-renewal of the agreement will confer no rights upon the franchisee to claim any form of indemnity or payment for loss of goodwill.

It is also advisable for the franchisor to specify the duration of the franchise agreement. An agreement entered into on an indefinite basis requires the party seeking to terminate the agreement to give the other party 'adequate' advance notice. The concept of 'adequacy' leaves a certain amount of room for interpretation, a risk which the franchisor would surely prefer not to run (see Pretore Rome, 14 June 1989, *Schweppes* case where the judge – mistakenly in the author's opinion – ordered the continuation of a franchise agreement for a further 13 months after notice was given).

## TAX AND FINANCIAL CONSIDERATIONS

As in other highly industrialized societies, the Italian tax system is complex. Tax collection continues to be an apparently insoluble problem. Italy has yet to establish an efficient system to limit tax evasion and, thus, tends to favour indirect taxes, which are more difficult to escape; tax rates may vary from one year to another.

## Corporate tax

Direct taxes applicable to the joint stock company (S.p.A.), the limited liability company (S.r.l.), the partnership limited by shares (S.a.a.) and foreign partnerships are subject to the corporate income tax known as 'IRPEG' and the local income tax known as 'ILOR'.

A company with a registered office in Italy or its administrative headquarters or principal business activity in Italy is taxable on its worldwide income.

Corporate tax rates are: IRPEG, 36%; ILOR, 16.2%.

Since ILOR is an expense deductible for calculating taxable income subject to IRPEG, the effective overall tax rate is 46.37%.

Capital gains applicable to a company are treated as ordinary business income. With respect to the tax on the gain from the sale of a fixed asset used in the company's business, the company may include the gain in income in the year in which it was received or in fixed instalments in the year earned and in the following four years.

A 1990 law introduced a tax on capital gains on the stock market.

A non-resident company is liable for IRPEG and ILOR on income produced in Italy, unless modified by a tax treaty.

## Dividends

Dividends received by domestic shareholders from an Italian company are subject to withholding of 10% as an advance on their annual tax obligation. Dividends paid to a non-resident are subject to 32.4% withholding as a final tax on the foreign shareholder, unless modified by a tax treaty.

## Interest

On ordinary loans the tax is 12.5%. If paid to a resident, withholding is an advance on the recipient's annual tax obligation. If paid to a non-resident, the above amount is withheld as a final tax, unless modified by a tax treaty. On bank deposits the tax is 30%, on government securities 12.5%, and on other private bonds 10.8%.

## Royalties

Royalties paid to a resident company are not subject to withholding. Royalties paid to non-resident companies or physical persons are subject to final withholding of 21%, which is a tax of 30% calculated on 70% of the royalty amount.

Royalties are a fully deductible expense to the paying company. They should, as stated elsewhere, be computed on an arm's length basis and are reasonable for the benefits received.

## Indirect taxes

*Value added tax (VAT)* The standard rate at present is 19%. Other VAT rates are:

1    4% (many foodstuffs, etc.)

2    9% (hotel services, restaurant meals, beer, etc.)

3    38% (luxury items, furs, precious metals, etc.)

**Registration tax**  Registration tax at variable rates is due on the required registration of written contracts or deeds. Some examples of registration tax rates are:

1    Issuance of shares of a company: 1% tax on the value of the shares

2    Transfer of real estate: 8% of the sales price

3    Merger of companies: 1% of the value

Where a transaction requires the payment of VAT, registration of the contract is presently at the fixed rate of L. 100 000 (ECU 65).

Voluntary registration of a contract is permitted and serves to establish legal proof of the date of the contract in the event of later controversy.

**Property appreciation tax (INVIM)**  INVIM is payable on the increase in value of real property whenever transferred. In addition, all land and buildings owned by businesses must be revalued every ten years and the INVIM tax paid on the appreciated amount.

The tax is a graduated tax, ranging from a minimum of 5% to a maximum of 30% computed on the property appreciation.

**Government concession tax**  This tax is assessed on companies as follows:

1    Joint stock companies (S.p.A.)      L. 12 million (ECU 7820) per annum

2    Limited liability company (S.r.l.)  L. 3.5 million (ECU 2280) per annum

3    Other forms of companies            L. 0.5 million (ECU 325) per annum

**Excise taxes**  There are various minor taxes on alcohol, petroleum products and mineral oils.

**Stamp duties**  Stamp duties are minor and levied on documents filed with any government or official agency, as well as on contracts, promissory notes, bills of exchange, etc. circulating in Italy.

### Employee-related taxes

A employee of an Italian company is subject to graduated personal income tax known as 'IRPEF' on his employment income produced in Italy.

If the employee is a resident of Italy or has the principal centre of his affairs in

Italy or merely lives in Italy for more than six months during the tax year, in any of such instances he will be subject to tax on his worldwide income.

Gross income is reduced by social security contributions and personal allowances (for example, dependent spouse and children, low income allowance, etc.) to arrive at taxable income. Tax is effected by withholding at the source by the employer.

In the absence of any special tax treaty provisions, there is no special tax treatment of foreigners who come to work in Italy on a short-term basis.

## Social security obligations

Social security charges in Italy are very high and assessed against both the employer and employee, amounting to a cost equal to 53–54% of gross income. (Slightly different rates apply to different sectors of the economy: manufacturing, sales, agricultural, housing, etc.) The cost to the employer is approximately 45% and to the employee 8.5%.

These substantial social security charges tend to discourage companies from employing high-income personnel to open branch offices, an additional factor in favour of recourse to franchising to achieve expansion.

The social security payments cover principally pension, disability and health insurance benefits. Lower rates apply in southern Italy as an inducement to investment.

## The tax problem created by a 'permanent establishment'

The foreign franchisor should be particularly alert to the tax implications resulting from the creation in Italy, at times unwittingly, of a so-called 'permanent establishment' which creates a tax liability on its profits or presumed profits. The most obvious example of a permanent establishment is the setting up of a branch, but numerous other situations can be found which result in Italian taxation.

A foreign franchisor who hires or enters into an agency relationship with a person in Italy to recruit and supervise his franchise network, for example, might discover that the Italian tax authorities deem such a person to be a 'permanent establishment' and, thus, subject the foreign franchisor to Italian taxation on his income, or presumed income, produced in Italy thanks to the services performed by his employee or agent in Italy.

## Investment incentives

There is a variety of investment incentives available to business, with particular reference to scientific and technological innovation, creation of research centres and the development and modernization of the industrial base in the South. Labour-intensive businesses established in the South would be viewed as good candidates for incentive benefits under the programmes offering cash grants and subsidized loans.

While franchise businesses in general – unless labour-intensive – would not be especially favourable targets for benefits under the various incentive pro-grammes, a 1986 law (Law no. 44 of 28 February 1986) may hold some interest for unit franchisees. This law provides for cash grants (up to 60% of the initial investment) and subsidized loans for businesses set up by young businessmen in the 18–29 age bracket in the South. Contributions to business operating expenses are also contemplated by Law 44.

Tax incentives, labour cost incentives, and export incentives are available to investments which meet the basic criteria underlying the incentive programmes, as briefly mentioned above.

While the incentive programmes sound attractive, many foreign companies have found that there are frequently other drawbacks to setting up in a depressed area of the South which offset the benefits offered. The foreign franchisor would be well advised to obtain qualified bank or other advice before leaping into an investment incentive programme in Italy.

## CONCLUSION

As a major consumer society with the second highest population in Europe, Italy offers significant room for growth in the field of franchising. As the target date of 1 January 1993 for the single European market approaches, this growth is expected to accelerate.

The foreign franchisor should keep in mind that Italy is not a single market. Over the above regional differences such as exist in other European nations, in Italy there are substantial social and economic differences between the North and South which affect consumption patterns, educational and income levels, busi-ness experience and sophistication.

The most suitable operating format for the foreign franchisor, in the opinion of the author, is the master franchise relationship. The choice of the sub-franchisor is critical and should be orientated towards a party qualified to build a solid, long-term relationship. The search for a sub-franchisor who will pay sub-stantial upfront fees will, in most instances, be difficult; it may also attract the wrong kind of partner.

The areas of law which require special attention for franchisors are those related to trade marks, real estate, city operating permits and antitrust law.

*Notes*
1   *Trib. Firenze*, 30 May 1985, Gem Collection.
2   *Trib. Manta*, 19 October 1988.
3   *Trib. Lecce*, 9 February 1990.
4   *Trib. Milano*, 30 April 1982.
5   *Trib. Milano*, 16 December 1986.
6   *Cassazione*, 28 October 1987, No. 7958, in Foro It. 1988, II, 405.

# CHAPTER 12
# LUXEMBOURG

*Charles Duro*

## AN OVERVIEW OF FRANCHISING IN LUXEMBOURG

The concept of franchising has recently become extremely popular in Luxembourg. The exceptional development of the franchising sector is linked to the fact that Luxembourg is situated at the centre of Europe, at the intersection of several countries, which facilitates the ability of franchisors to extend their operations into the surrounding countries.

There are approximately one hundred franchise operations in existence in the Grand Duchy of Luxembourg, either in clothing, food, industrial or service sectors.

Franchising already represents a large percentage of the business turnover in Luxembourg commerce. To this percentage, there should be added an incalculable amount of commercial activity which resembles franchising, but which does not amount to business franchising.

The current popularity of franchising is encouraged by the fact that there are no specific laws which regulate it. This lack of legal regulation, which in one sense seems to be limiting, can actually be regarded as a positive factor. Indeed, the setting up of a franchise in the Grand Duchy (taking into account the lack of regulation) allows the interested franchisor/franchisee to explore his options and activities, without being over-regulated by the maze of legal provisions which are normally inherent in so many other areas of commerce. However, it is inaccurate to say that there are no regulations whatsoever in Luxembourg which may be generally applicable to a franchise operation. Luxembourg law includes a number of provisions which have an effect upon and are applicable to trade in general, and may thus influence a franchise operation having a connection with the Grand Duchy of Luxembourg. Several of these provisions will be more fully considered below.

Furthermore, the Association of Merchants of Luxembourg, the Belgian Association of Franchising and the Ministry of the 'Classes Moyennes' all recognize the fact that the franchising sector is fast gaining importance in the commercial sector, and accordingly they have set up a non-profit organization called the Association Luxembourgeoise de la Franchise, with the following stated purpose:

1    To contribute in both a judicial and economic fashion to the development and implementation of franchising, acting as a networking system, to facilitate the collaboration of distinct commercial enterprises. Those enterprises will, however, remain linked by a contract by virtue of which one concedes to the other (through the payment of royalties) the right to exploit a trade mark or a commercial formula represented by a distinctive mark, and by economic conditions determined with reference to regular assistance, the purpose of which is the facilitation of this exploitation.

2    To defend the interests of the professionals, as well as the adherents or future adherents of a franchising operation.

3    To participate in the associations or similar organizations in foreign countries and in the international context.

4    To place at the disposition of its members the information and contacts which may be necessary to facilitate a franchise operation.

5    To defend the interests of any eventual association, including the professionals who may become dependent upon a franchising system, before the public and administrative authorities, both in Luxembourg and elsewhere.

The Association Luxembourgeoise de la Franchise, through its articles of incorporation, envisions the elaboration of a Luxembourg Ethics Code for franchising, which will probably follow the model that has just been adopted by the European Franchise Federation. This Code of Ethics, although having no obligatory force of law, could invite a judge, in the absence of any formal law existing on the matter, to base any eventual decision on equity, and to follow custom in the concerned profession. The principle of equity provides for reference to the law of custom, in the absence of any other expressed norms, provided in Articles 1135, 1159 and 1160 of the Luxembourg Civil Code.

## STRUCTURE OF LUXEMBOURG BUSINESS ENTITIES

In Luxembourg, a business enterprise may be established in either one of two forms: as a sole proprietorship or as a commercial corporation.

### Sole proprietorships
Persons who engage in commerce as their primary profession are considered as merchants. In order to become a sole proprietor, an authorization (permit) of 'establishment' must first be obtained from the Ministry of the 'Classes Moyennes' (see p. 248). The status of 'commerçant' requires that merchants place an entry in the Commercial Register, acquire a registered number, keep financial records, and publish their marriage contract deed (if one exists between

he merchant and his/her spouse). All commercial disputes are resolved by the
Commercial Court.

## Commercial corporations

Luxembourg law provides for six different corporate entities:

1  La société en nom collectif (general partnership)

2  La société en commandite simple (limited partnership)

3  La société anonyme (public limited corporation)

4  La société en commandite par action (partnership limited by shares)

5  La société à responsabilité limitée (private limited liability corporation)

6  La société coopérative (co-operative corporation)

In addition to these forms of corporate entities, Articles 1832 to 1873 of the
Luxembourg Civil Code also recognize civil corporations in the form of temporary organizations and non-profit organizations (see Law of 21 April 1928).

### Advantages and disadvantages of the two forms

Luxembourg law attributes a legal personality to a corporation, authorizing the
corporation to act as a person in relation to its objects. In its capacity, it is able to
exercise rights and obligations.

The corporation may own assets which are different from the capital owned
by each of the persons who constitute it and may act for itself in the same way as
a physical person may act.

The most important advantage of a corporation is that, unlike a sole
proprietorship, which is characterized by the unlimited personal liability of the
merchant for all acts that he carries out in such capacity, the partners in a corporation generally enjoy a liability limited to the amount of their investment.

Legal and fiscal considerations allow us to distinguish between commercial
corporations with a personal character or partnerships (private corporation) on
the one hand, and commercial corporations with a public character or capital
corporation (public stock corporation) on the other.

Aside from the civil corporation, the basic forms of the private corporation
are the general partnership, the limited partnership, and the 'société en participation'. The basic forms of public stock corporations are the public limited corporation, and the partnership limited by shares.

The private limited liability corporation (société à responsabilité limitée)
and the co-operative corporation (société coopérative), although they are essentially stock corporations, represent a compromise between the two types of

enterprises. Related to partnerships, the Sàrl is *intuitu personae*, as its partners are limited in number and may all effectively participate in the management of the corporation. The shares are not freely transferable. Also related to the 'société de capitaux' (public limited corporations), the Sàrl has a fixed working capital. The partners of a Sàrl enjoy a liability limited to the amount of their investment. From a fiscal point of view, the Sàrl is considered as a public limited corporation.

The basic differences between private corporations and public limited corporations, including their essential characteristics, can be summarized as follows:

1   Unlike a public stock corporation, which is characterized by its institutional nature, a private corporation is characterized by its contractual nature, more precisely, a contract *intuitu personae*.

2   Absence of assent or incapacity of one of the partners in a private corporation will result in the nullity of the corporation, whereas in a public stock corporation, absence of assent or incapacity of a shareholder only results in the annulment of that shareholder's rights and liabilities.

3   The death or change of status (interdiction, bankruptcy, etc.) of one of the partners in a private corporation will result in the dissolution of the corporation, unless otherwise provided in the articles of incorporation, whereas a public stock corporation is not affected by the death of a shareholder.

4   The articles of incorporation of a private corporation may only be modified by unanimous agreement of all the partners, whereas in a public stock corporation, the articles of incorporation may be modified by a special majority vote.

5   Transfer of shares in a private corporation to a third party requires unanimous agreement of all of the partners, unless otherwise provided in the articles of incorporation. Shares in a public corporation may be in bearer form and are freely transferable, subject to any restrictive provision which may be in the articles of incorporation.

6   The management of a private corporation, unless provided otherwise in the articles of incorporation, belongs to each of the partners subject to the veto of any one of the partners. Public stock corporations are not managed by the shareholders, but by a board of directors.

7   From a fiscal point of view, income derived from a private corporation is taxable for each partner in his private capacity. The public stock corporation is considered as a different person from its shareholders and its profits are taxable. However, shareholders are also taxable on dividends earned from

the corporation. As a result there may be double taxation on the same income.

In addition to these differences, private corporations are characterized by the unlimited personal liability of each of the partners, for all commitments of the corporation, as opposed to the public corporation, whose shareholders enjoy a liability limited to the amount of their investment.

The principal differences between, and advantages and disadvantages of the 'société anonyme' (the most widely used public corporate form) and the 'société à responsabilité limitée' (the most widely used mixed corporate form) may be summarized as follows.

Advantages of a public limited corporation:

1    Liability of shareholders limited to the amount of their investment

2    Legal personality distinct from the shareholders

3    Negotiability of shares

4    Shares may be in bearer form if fully paid up

5    Management body separated from shareholders

6    Directors may be removed *ad nutum*

7    May be constituted for unlimited duration

8    The constitution of the corporation requires a minimum capital of Flux 1 250 000, which must only be 25% paid up

Disadvantages of a public limited corporation:

1    Publication of accounting and balance sheets of the corporation

2    Articles of incorporation require an authentic act

3    Liability of the corporate founders

Advantages of a private limited corporation:

1    Liability of partners is limited to their contribution.

2    Possibility of creating a partnership with one person is not authorized yet, but there is a project which will be enacted in the near future.

3    May be managed by one person.

Disadvantages of a private limited liability corporation:

1    Limited transferability of shares.

2    The constitution of the corporation requires a minimum fully paid up capital of Flux 500 000.

3    Management cannot be removed without legitimate reason.

4    Publication of the corporate accounting.

5    Fiscally, the corporation follows the same tax treatment as a public limited corporation.

6    No more than 40 associates.

7    Prohibition of public issuance of shares or bonds.

The choice between a public limited corporation and a private limited liability corporation will depend on the advantages and disadvantages mentioned above as they relate to the particular aims of an enterprise. The public limited corporation appears to be the most effective for enterprises with international objectives. Generally, the private limited corporation is established for small to medium-sized firms as well as enterprises of a family character. Taking into account the above considerations, all following developments in this chapter will, more particularly, concern the public limited corporation.

### Formation of a corporation
For all Luxembourg corporations, the articles of incorporation are subject to the following regulations of form.

General partnerships, limited partnerships, co-operative corporations and civil companies are established by means of special notarial instruments or unattested instruments (in the latter case conforming to Article 1325 of the Civil Code), failing which their constitution shall be void. Two originals are sufficient for civil companies and co-operative corporations. Public limited companies, partnerships limited by shares, and private limited companies are incorporated by means of special notarial instruments, failing which their constitution shall be void.

There are no legal requirements concerning the language of the articles of incorporation. However, a decision of the Luxembourg Conseil d'Etat has limited this choice to French, German or English. In practice, if the articles of incorporation are drafted in English, a French translation is required.

The capital of a corporation may be denominated in any currency which is gal in Luxembourg.

An extract of the instruments establishing general partnerships and limited artnerships must be published. The instruments of constitution of public limited ompanies, partnerships limited by shares, private limited companies, cooperative corporations and civil companies must be published in their entirety. 'hese instruments, or extracts from instruments, for which publication is :quired by law must, within one month of the conclusion of the definitive instruaents, be filed with the appropriate officials. The publication must take place 'ithin one month of filing. The publication takes place in the Memorial Special upplement for Companies and Associations; the documents published are sent ) the Registry of the Court and Tribunals where they may be examined by any erson free of charge, and must be filed in a special register.

The documents and extracts of documents may normally not be relied upon gainst third parties until the day of their publication in the Memorial.

## tatutory requirements

'he articles of incorporation must conform to certain legal requirements.

In the formation of a corporation, drafting must conform to the requireaents of general contract law, subject to special exceptions.

For the public limited corporation, Article 26 of the Commercial Corporaon Law of 10 August 1915, as modified, provides for the following requirements:

There must be at least two shareholders.

The capital must be at least Flux 1 250 000.

The capital must be subscribed in its entirety.

Each share must be paid up at least one quarter in cash or by means of noncash contributions.

'he notary who draws up the instruments must verify that all of these conditions ave been met and swear to their accomplishment.

Moreover, in compliance with Article 27 of the Commercial Corporation ,aw, articles of incorporation must contain certain fundamental information bout the corporation, more particularly:

1   Identity of the legal or natural persons by or on behalf of whom the act has been signed

2   The form of the corporation and its name

3   The registered office

4    The corporate object

5    The amount of the subscribed capital, and, where applicable, the authorize
     capital, and the amount initially paid up in respect of the subscribed capita

6    The classes of shares, where several classes exist, the rights attached to eac
     class, the number of shares subscribed for and also, in the case of authorize
     capital, the shares to be issued in each class and the rights attached to eac
     class, and the nominal value of the shares or the number of shares for whic
     no nominal value is specified

7    Any special condition restricting the transfer of shares

8    Whether the shares are registered or bearer

9    The details of each contribution made other than in cash, in respect c
     Article 26–1 of the Commercial Corporation Law

10   The duration of the corporation

Article 27 of the Commercial Corporation Law also requires description of th
governing bodies, control of the corporation, and description of the function c
the governing bodies to the extent that they may derogate from civil law.

Finally, the articles of incorporation must indicate the approximate sum c
all expenses, fees, and remunerations incurred by the corporation in respect of it
incorporation.

## Appointment of directors, duties and responsibilities
*Appointment*  In principle, the directors are freely elected by the general meetin
of shareholders. However, the first appointment may be made in the instrumen
constituting the corporation by extraordinary general meeting (Article 51 of th
Commercial Corporation Law).

Directors are not required to be shareholders of the corporation, and the
may receive a salary or not. They are elected for a term which may not exceed si
years, and they may be re-elected, subject to any contrary provision of the instru
ment of constitution.

In case of a vacancy of a director's position before expiry of a director's term
of office, subject to any provision to the contrary in the articles of incorporation
the remaining members of the board of directors may co-opt another director
who will serve until the time of the next general shareholders' meeting. Such
annual general meeting of shareholders shall decide upon the definitive appoint
ment.

The number of directors is determined by the by-laws. However, the law
prescribes a minimum of three directors for a public limited corporation. The

number of directors is increased to nine for companies which regularly employ more than 1000 employees over a period of three consecutive years (Law of 6 May 1974).

Generally, there are no residence or nationality requirements for corporate directors. However, before the authorization is given to conduct certain businesses, the law requires from the person entrusted with the effective management of the corporation, certain conditions of residency, professional qualification, honourability and competence (see p. 248).

Legal capacity of corporate directors is governed by the general principles governing the agency contract.

*Conflict of interest* When a director has an interest opposed to those of the corporation, he is obliged, under Article 57 of the Commercial Corporation Law, to:

1   Inform the board of directors

2   Mention the conflict in the minutes of the meeting

3   Abstain from taking part in the resolution relative to the question

If the conditions of Article 57 are not observed, it will not result in a nullity of the resolution, but may result in the liability of the director concerned.

*Termination of term* The term of a director will expire upon his death; he may also be removed *ad nutum*, and without indemnity. This principle is based on public order and any attempt to limit this right of revocation will be null and void. The removal may be made at any time by a general meeting of shareholders.

Further, according to Article 2007 of the Civil Code, all directors are free to resign. However, they are still obliged to conduct the daily business until their successors are elected.

*Duties* In a corporation, the board of directors, which serves as the collective corporate managing body of the corporation, may only exercise the powers granted to it by the by-laws of the corporation. In the case where the by-laws do not regulate it, the powers of administration and accomplishment of corporate objectives belong to the board of directors, except those expressly reserved to the general meeting of shareholders by the Commercial Corporate Law.

The board must, in the absence of a contrary provision in the by-laws which may particularly empower one or more directors, represent the corporation with respect to third parties and in legal proceedings, either as plaintiff or as defendant. Judicial documents served on behalf of, or upon, the corporation must be validly served in the name of the corporation alone.

In respect of the above, the directors must not incur any personal obligations by reason of the commitments entered into by the corporation.

The corporation shall be bound by measures adopted in its name by the directors, even if such measures fall outside the corporate object, unless it is proven that the third party knew that the measure fell outside the corporate object or could not have been unaware of that fact, taking into account all circumstances; mere publication of the by-laws shall not constitute such proof.

*Liability* Luxembourg law distinguishes between (a) liability of directors *vis-à vis* the corporation for acts committed while carrying out management functions, (b) liability for acts and faults which violate the law on commercial companies or the by-laws of the corporation and (c) common civil liability.

Any right to maintain a suit against corporate directors concerning liability for acts performed while carrying out management functions (*actio mandati*) belongs exclusively to the corporation. If the corporation is in bankruptcy, liquidation, or under management control, suit may be brought or pursued by the curator, liquidator, or auditor against the management (this latter with the authorization of the court).

Determination of any question of fault shall be left to the court.

Liability of a corporate director may arise as a result of lack of action, negligent action or careless action. It does not matter whether or not the director was remunerated.

Liability of a director for acts performed while carrying out management functions is of a contractual nature and, in principle, will only result in damages (and interest) which were sustained and foreseeable, but not for unforeseeable damages.

Article 59–2 of the law of 10 August 1915 provides that directors are jointly and severally liable, whether towards the corporation or towards third parties, for damages arising from violation of the provisions of the corporate law (see Law of 10 August 1915 as modified) and/or the by-laws of the corporation.

Suits concerning liability of directors may be instituted by either the corporation or by a third party, but may not be brought by shareholders acting in their individual capacity. Receiving a discharge at the annual general meeting of shareholders does not protect a director from liability based under Article 59–2 for suits instituted by third parties. These suits may only be instituted in cases of violation of the corporation law or by-laws of the corporation. If the action is instituted by the corporation, it is based on contractual liability; if it is instituted by a third party, it is based on tort liability.

Actions against a corporate director based on Article 59 (1) involve the joint liability of all the corporate directors.

In addition to the two cases of liability mentioned above, the directors may also, according to Articles 1382 and 1383 of the Civil Code, be liable under the general principles of tort liability in circumstances other than those provided for in Articles 59 (1) or (2). (For example, in the case of antitrust, liability is based on general Civil Code articles.)

## stablishing a business in Luxembourg

he Constitution of 1948, as amended, guarantees freedom of commerce and .dustry as well as freedom of establishment for every Luxembourg citizen. This ght is also recognized for citizens of EC member states by virtue of the Treaty of ome of 25 March 1957, as well as for citizens of other nations that grant recip- )cal rights to Luxembourg citizens. However, all physical persons, legal per- )ns, and branch offices that undertake commercial or industrial activity must )mply with certain formalities.

The Law of 28 December 1988 requires that all industrial or commercial :tivity be subject to written governmental approval from the Ministry of :lasses Moyennes'. This request may be written in French or German. The )llowing documents must accompany the request:

A written request either on regular paper or on a form affixed with a stamp of Flux 1000.

A document proving honourability. This generally consists of a police record for the Luxembourg resident and a certificate of solvency or non-bankruptcy for the non-resident. If the request is made in the name of a corporation, the certificate must be drawn up in the name of both the corporation and the name of the corporate manager.

A certified copy of the diplomas proving professional qualification.

Registration in the Commercial Register of Firms, kept by the 'Tribunaux d'Arrondissement' of Luxembourg and Diekirch, in the month of the begin- ning of activity. A registration number is issued to the enterprise which henceforth must accompany all of its official documents.

Generally, the administrative procedure will not take longer than two months rom the date of submission of the request.

Authorization is strictly individual and may be revoked for serious infrac- ions. Further, the certificate will become invalid if it is not used for more than wo years from the date it was granted, or in the case of voluntary discontinuance, t will become invalid if not used for more than one year.

In addition to these requirements, the legislature requires certain special .uthorizations as well as certain declarations for dangerous or unhealthy enter- )rises, for imports, sale of foodstuffs, sales of alcoholic beverages, and other :nterprises.

In order to enforce fiscal obligations, enterprises are also required to register vith the direct and excise tax administration, as well as the registration tax .dministration.

Finally, legislation concerning social security requires membership in differ- :nt branches of social security and medical and pension programmes.

## Branch offices

*Establishing a branch in Luxembourg* A company incorporated outside of th
Grand Duchy of Luxembourg which intends to establish a place of business i
the Grand Duchy of Luxembourg must·first file its articles of incorporation wit
the officer of the Luxembourg District Court, for the purpose of control an
subsequent publishing in the Luxembourg Memorial, Special Supplement fo
Companies and Associations. At the same time, the company must apply fo
registration in the Commercial Register of Companies.

A list of the directors of the company, as well as a list of those Luxembour
representatives of the company who are authorized to act on behalf of the com
pany, must be deposited with the Commercial Register and Court Officer.

The branch office will need to apply for authorization to do business i
Luxembourg with the Ministry of 'Classes Moyennes', according to the terms o
the law dated 28 December 1988 (see below). This authorization must be issue
in the name of one physical person who is able to demonstrate adequate busines
experience, acumen and professional respectability in the area of business to b
engaged in.

*Law of 28 December 1988 relating to the authorization to open branches* Article
of the law of 28 December 1988 provides that a legal establishment may b
authorized to open a maximum of five branches. This limitation of five doe
not apply to the following undertakings: travel agencies, accommodation an
restaurant establishments, sale of beverages, supply stores for cars, newspape
stores, film and photograph development stores and whitewash and dry cleanin
stores.

No authorization will be delivered to non-profit organizations, for exampl
consumers' mutual associations.

## LEGAL CONSIDERATIONS

Franchising is not addressed by any specific legislative or regulatory provisions o
Luxembourg law. Further, there is no case law in Luxembourg that might add to
the legal framework.

Taking into account this legislative and jurisprudential gap, franchise agree
ments are therefore subject to the same general rules applicable to all contracts
and reciprocal obligations between parties. These agreements are governed by
the terms of the contract, the principle of autonomy, and the will of the partie
(Article 1134 of the Civil Code). It is by these principles and those established by
the EC regulation of 30 November 1988, which are made directly applicable to
Luxembourg, that franchise agreements are defined and governed.

It should be noted that the similarities between certain franchise clauses and
those found in distribution agreements should result in similar determinations in
the event of litigation.

## Pyramid selling
There are no laws in Luxembourg concerning pyramid selling schemes.

## Antitrust considerations
The Grand Ducal Regulation of 9 December 1965 prohibits fixing of a minimum price for goods and services in the following ways:

1    Imposing a fixed minimum price at the suggested or recommended price

2    Prohibiting a fixed minimum price which corresponds to the maximum price established by the Office of Prices

3    Prohibiting a minimum price which is the maximum retail price indicated on the product packaging.

This regulation is not applicable for the sale of books, newspapers, or similar published materials. However, an exemption can be granted by the Ministry of Economic Affairs, based on the newness of the product or service and the exclusivity of the patent. This exemption is usually limited in time.

On the contrary, the Law of 30 June 1961 and the Grand Ducal Regulation of 15 February 1964 regulate the fixing of a maximum price. Indeed, these regulations prohibit requiring a price in excess of the normal price. Normal prices may be fixed by the Ministry of Economic Affairs, and are the maximum price allowed for a product. All disputes in cases of this type of price fixing may be deferred to the court.

Aside from these minimum and maximum price guidelines, there are certain products for which the prices are fixed by the Office of Prices, and are invariable (e.g. cigarettes). In these cases, no recommendations or price fixing are allowed at all.

It appears from the above that if the fixing of prices is expressly regulated, the recommendation of price is not specifically prohibited. As long as the recommendations are not intended to violate the above regulations, recommended prices may be suggested to the franchisee by the franchisor.

Also important are the Laws of 5 July 1929 and of 27 November 1986 relating to illegal competition, as well as the Law of 7 October 1970 concerning the restriction of commercial practice.

The latter provides in Article 1 that all enterprise agreements, all decisions of business associations, and all concerted practices which have as their object the limitation, the restraining, or the falsifying of free competition in the marketplace, and which by their nature may restrict or have negative effects on general interests, are prohibited.

Article 2 provides for an exemption for business agreements, business decisions and concerted practices, resulting from the application of a legislative or regulatory text, or when the concerting parties can show that they are contributing to better the production or distribution, or improving technical or economic progress, at all times respecting the interest of the user.

It appears from the project of Law no. 1236, concerning restrictive commercial practices, that the form and the basis of Articles 85 and 86 are, to a large extent, incorporated into Luxembourg law.

Moreover, according to the commentary of Article 1 and the text of Article 85 of the Treaty of Rome, the Luxembourg legislation is primarily concerned with practices that affect trade exclusively within Luxembourg, and the European law is concerned with transnational practices.

However, it appears that, given the size of Luxembourg, there is difficulty in determining the exact limits of application of national and European law, and most of the questions concerning antitrust law either in franchising or in any other matter become immediately transnational in character, and require the application of the EC regulations, and not solely internal domestic law.

## Intellectual property

Intellectual property provides, in one part, a legal protection for products, processes, technical measures or technical devices through patents or trade marks, and, in the other part, protection of designs, denominations, prints, forms of products or services or products of a national or foreign enterprise in Luxembourg.

The copyright law protects authors of artistic or literary productions against any unauthorized public dissemination or reproduction.

The Luxembourg Service of Intellectual Property is the competent office to receive the request for all registration of Luxembourg, European or international patents, and all applications for Benelux trade marks and Benelux designs and models. It is also in charge of maintaining Luxembourg and European patents for holders who have expressly requested that their rights have effect in Luxembourg.

It must be pointed out that the introduction of an application and request for protection must necessarily be made through the intermediary of a company which is specialized in introducing such request for protection to the appropriate agencies. Indeed, the Law of 2 June 1962, as modified by the Law of 28 December 1988, as well as a Grand Ducal regulation of January 1977 determining the conditions of access and exercise of certain professions, provide that the exercise of this type of intellectual property advice is reserved to certain persons who are authorized by the government to act in this capacity.

*Trade marks*  The Law of 17 May 1985 and the Benelux Convention on Trademarks, signed in Brussels on 19 March 1962, established a joint process for the registration of trade marks for Belgium, the Netherlands and Luxembourg.

Article 1 of the Law provides that all the denominations, designs, prints, impressions, letters, numbers, form of products or services, or any other sort of sign which distinguishes services or products of an enterprise, are considered as trade marks.

In order to be protectable, a name or logo must be particular in nature.

The protection may be acquired by the first registration of a trade mark in the Benelux countries, or may result from an international registration.

Registration of a trade mark is valid for ten years and is renewable. The trade mark rights expire if the trade mark is not used in the Benelux countries within three years of registration or for more than five consecutive years.

**Patents** The inventor's or owner's rights in any new invention likely to have an industrial application may be protected under the Luxembourg law on invention patents. Luxembourg is also a signatory to the various international agreements on patents, including the 1883 Paris Convention on the protection of intellectual property rights and its subsequent amendments, the Washington Patents Cooperation Treaty of 19 June 1970 and the European Patent Convention, signed in Munich on 5 October 1973.

In order to qualify for patent registration and enjoy protection of a patent from any illegal exploitation, an invention must be:

1   New

2   Arising from an inventive activity

3   Likely to receive a business application

The patent ensures the exclusive right to use and otherwise profit from the protection of invention.

Protection from a patent is granted for a period of 20 years.

**Designs and models** According to the Law of 13 July 1973, the exterior aspect of a product which has a utilitary function may be protected as a model or design. Expressly excluded from this protection are all devices which are indispensable for technical purposes. However, these devices may be protected under other patent legislation.

If the model or design has an artistic character, it must be protected by both legislation of the Uniform Benelux Law and laws relating to author's rights (Law of 25 October 1966).

Registration of designs or models is valid for five years and is only renewable twice.

## Real estate and leasing
**Purchase/sale of building located in Luxembourg** Article 3 of the Civil Code subjects all buildings situated within Luxembourg to Luxembourg law, even if the buildings are owned by foreigners.

Sales must be registered at the Bureau of Registration of Mortgages. The costs for acts and other expenses related to the sale are normally the responsibility of the buyer (Article 1593 of the Civil Code). The registration duty is proportional and amounts to 6% (5% + 2/10th) of the actual price of the property.

A transcription duty is additionally levied at the rate of 1% on the real price of the property and an additional surtax of 3% on the real price is additionally levied in respect of transfers of real estate properties located on the territories of Luxembourg city and Esch/Alzette.

Article 17 of the Law of 17 August 1935 organized a derogatory system if the buyer declares in the notarial deed of transfer that the purchase of real estate is made in view of a resale. In such a circumstance, the registration duty initially to be paid by the buyer amounts to 7.2%, of which 5% is reimbursed to the buyer, if the deed of retransfer is registered within the two following years, and of which 4% is reimbursed if the deed of retransfer is registered, at the latest, four years after the initial transfer of property.

The sale of buildings not yet constructed falls within the scope of Articles 1601-1 to 1601-14 of the Civil Code.

The Law of 27 July 1978 governs taxation of capital gains realized on the transfer of real estate held by individuals. Capital gains are to be classified in three categories depending on how long the real estate has been owned by an individual.

1    Short-term capital gains are those in respect of items held for not more than two years. They qualify as speculative capital gains (Article 99 bis LIR).

2    Medium-term capital gains are those in respect of items (building or land) transferred more than two years but less than ten years after their initial acquisition (Article 99 ter LIR).

3    Finally, capital gains are deemed to be long term if the transfer is made after more than ten years from the initial acquisition (Article 99 quater LIR) (the last is applicable for transfer of land without buildings).

Capital gains which are not speculative are deemed to represent extraordinary income (Article 132 LIR) which may be submitted to a reduced income tax rate. These capital gains are taxed only at a rate equal to 50% of the rate corresponding to the total net taxable income of the taxpayer. A non-resident taxpayer may not be granted these favourable tax rates (Article 131 LIR). Nevertheless, these taxpayers are granted a personal allowance of Flux 1 250 000 (Article 130 LIR).

Speculative capital gains are subject to income tax at the ordinary tax rate.

Generally, for the computation of the taxable capital gains, the difference between the transfer price and the acquisition price less the depreciation, plus related costs of purchase, is taken into account.

If the capital gain is related to a business entity, it is deemed to be part of the business profit, which is established by the difference between the net assets invested at the end of the fiscal year and the net assets invested at the beginning of he same fiscal year. A capital gain realized on the real estate forming part of a permanent establishment in Luxembourg is considered to represent ordinary business profit and as such is subject to ordinary corporate tax.

Under certain circumstances, a capital gain realized by a business entity in respect of real estate located in Luxembourg may be exempted from taxation if the transfer price has been used to acquire real estate in replacement, to be invested in Luxembourg in an establishment located in Luxembourg (Articles 53 and 54 LIR).

**Building leases** The legal regulations governing contracts for leasing of buildings are found in the Civil Code, Articles 1713 to 1778.

Further, the Law of 14 February 1955, as modified by the Law of 27 August 1987, has served to complete the legal regime by providing protection to tenants.

Finally, Articles 1762 *et seq.* of the Civil Code as supplemented by the Grand Ducal Decree of 31 October 1936 address the protection of businesses in regard to leases.

Note: The legislation concerning leases has the character of mandatory application. In case of litigation, the competent judge (by definition, the judge of the jurisdiction where the building is situated) is not allowed to apply any laws other than the ones of his own jurisdiction. Further, the lease contract must conform to all legal requirements of Luxembourg regarding tenant protection.

*General law: Civil Code Articles 1713ff.*

A contract of lease may be either in written or oral form. However, for purposes of proof, written contracts are preferable. The principal obligations of the parties are as follows.

Lessor (Article 1719ff.):

1    To deliver to the lessee the estate which is leased.

2    To maintain the premises leased in a condition fit for the purpose for which it was leased.

3    To allow the lessee peaceful enjoyment of the premises leased for the duration of the lease.

Lessee (Article 1728ff.):

1    To use the premises leased as would a reasonable prudent person, and in conformity with the intended purpose as stated in the lease contract, or the presumed purpose in absence of a written contract.

2    To pay the price of the lease according to the terms of the agreement.

*Law of 14 February 1955*

The essential provisions of this text address the ceiling on the price of rentals, the nullity of 'value' clauses, rental price controls, as well as extension of leases in favour of the tenant and expiration of lease periods.

For furnished apartments and rooms, the rental ceiling is doubled. The system of rental price control and lease extension as provided in the Law of 1955 does not apply to residential homes, villas, and modern equipped apartments of at least seven rooms, occupied by one family. This law also does not apply to commercial professional leases.

*Protection of business leases*

When the lease relates to a building which is, by its nature, or by express or tacit agreement between the parties, to be used for commercial purposes, the building may be sold or sub-let with or without the business, on the condition that the same type of business shall be allowed to remain, except in cases where the lessor cancels the lease for just reasons.

Lessees engaged in business for more than three years but less than 15 years are allowed a priority over all other persons to have their lease contract renewed (Article 1762–4). The owner may only evict the lessee if he has in fact received a superior offer, in good faith, from a third party. Where it is established that there was no real offer, or it was not made in good faith, the lessee can claim damages and interest in an amount of three times the difference between the new annual rent actually paid and the offer, or, if the lessee chooses to stay in the building, three times the difference between the actual price paid and the amount before the alleged or bad faith offer.

The owner may oppose the tenant's priority rights only in the following circumstances:

1    In the case of legitimate grievances against the tenant, which will be determined by a competent judge.

2    When the owner or his descendants want to personally occupy the building.

3    In cases where the building will no longer be leased to that type or a similar type of business.

4    In case of construction or transformation.

In instances where the parties do not agree on the lease or other changes which the tenant does not accept, within the renewal period, these disputes will be settled by one or three experts (Article 1762–5).

The commercial or industrial tenant whose lease is about to expire may demand two successive extensions of a maximum term of six months each, on the condition that the demand is made at least two months before the expiration of the lease or the first extension.

## Foreigners working or establishing a business in Luxembourg

In order to hold a salaried position in the Grand Duchy, it is necessary to first satisfy the conditions of entry and residence and, subject to certain exceptions, to have obtained a work permit.

The Law of 28 March 1972 generally regulates entrance, residence, and establishment for foreigners in Luxembourg.

Additionally, treaties regulate the situation of foreigners, as for example the treaty of 19 September 1960 for persons from Benelux.

**EC workers** Nationals of the EC may enter the Grand Duchy on simple presentation of a national identity card or a valid passport (or one which has expired within the last five years).

Foreigners who desire to stay in Luxembourg for more than three months must apply for an identity card from the municipal authority in charge of arrival declarations. In order to receive an identity card in Luxembourg, they must also have the following documents: (1) passport or identity card; (2) an attestation of medical condition; and (3) certain documents relative to their situation in Luxembourg. These cards, once issued, are valid for a period of five years and are automatically renewable. A renewed card will be valid for ten years.

According to Article 2 of the treaty of 19 December 1961, a national of Belgium or the Netherlands who desires to reside in Luxembourg needs only a certificate of good standing and proof of sufficient means of income, but does not need to present an attestation of medical condition.

EC workers do not need to have work permits, according to EC Regulation No. 1612/68, which came into effect on 8 November 1968.

Equality of treatment in the employment domain is guaranteed between Luxembourg and other EC nationals, subject to temporary measures applicable to Spanish and Portuguese nationals, which will apply to 31 December 1995. Spanish and Portuguese nationals may, according to the Grand Ducal regulation of 24 December 1985, have access to salaried positions on the condition that they have been granted special permits (E permits for Spanish and P permits for Portuguese). These permits are of unlimited term and authorize the exercise of all types of professions for all employers. For seasonal workers who are admitted for a period of less than 12 months, the validity of the permit is limited to the length of the contract.

**Non-EC workers** Foreigners who are not nationals of EC member states may not enter Luxembourg without the presentation of a valid passport and, where required, the appropriate visa.

The regulation of 28 March 1972 requires non-EC foreigners to address an 'arrival declaration' to the municipal administration, even when the visit will be for less than three months. For short-term visits, registration in a hotel registry will take the place of an arrival declaration, provided that the foreigner does not undertake any profit-making activity.

Foreigners who wish to stay longer than three months in Luxembourg must, in addition to the arrival declaration, apply for an alien identity card. However, foreign workers who are employed by a foreign firm and detached to Luxembourg for a foreseeable period of less than one year are not required to apply for an alien identity card.

Access to salaried positions for non-EC members is subject to the provisions of the Grand Ducal regulation of 12 May 1972. This regulation requires a work permit from the 'Ministre du Travail' (Labour Minister) or his representative, on the advice of the employment administration. The letter will take into account the work situation, trends, and needs of the employment market.

In Luxembourg, there are four categories of work permits. The period of validity for these permits varies from one year to unlimited. The permit, regardless of category, will become invalid if the worker is absent for a period of more than six consecutive months, unless the employment relationship is maintained during the absence.

Procedurally, before a non-EC foreigner may cross the border and commence work for a Luxembourg employer, and not yet having obtained a work permit, the employer must submit a declaration, in duplicate, in regard to the type of position which is to be filled, to the employment administration. At the time of the declaration, the employment administration will issue a receipt which will serve as a temporary work permit.

## Employment laws

The relationship between employer and employee is, in principle, individual. The reciprocal rights and obligations are generally regulated by the Articles 1779 *et seq.* of the Civil Code, and the general law of obligations.

A written contract is always required. Contracts must stipulate the nature of employment, hours of work, salary, period of employment, and any special conditions.

The legislature has regulated service contracts, by special texts, principally by the Law of 24 May 1989 on employment contracts. As concerns the specific status of employees, some special points continue to be governed by the Law of 7 June 1937, as modified by Laws of 20 April 1960 and 12 November 1971. Status of workers is governed by the Law of 27 June 1970 and by the Law of 24 May 1989. These legislative acts ensure a minimal protection to workers which cannot be departed from by the parties.

Generally, Luxembourg law guarantees a minimum wage to all employees. The rate of pay depends on the age of the employees and whether or not they have a family. Wages are tied to a cost of living index.

The normal work week is 40 hours and overtime work must be compensated by granting extra leave and/or by paying an overtime wage.

*Termination* A contract of service can, generally, be terminated at any time by one of the parties. Unilateral rescission is lawful only if it conforms with the prescribed procedure and time limits.

A worker can terminate the contract after giving notice orally, or in writing. The employer is bound to release the worker from his contract by registered letter. He must, in addition, inform the Department of Employment and, if the worker is dismissed, state the reasons therefor, if the worker so requests.

A contract of employment cannot normally be terminated by an employer during the employee's justified absence or sickness. Neither may the contract of a female worker be terminated immediately following her marriage, during pregnancy or during the 12 weeks following childbirth.

A party revoking the contract without complying with the prescribed time limits must pay compensation to the other party equivalent to the wage payable during the period for which he is in default under the time limits prescriptions.

*Gross misconduct* In the event of gross misconduct by one of the parties, the law recognizes the right of the other party to forthwith terminate the contract. To be valid, the termination must be communicated by registered mail within three days of the misconduct and must state the grounds for termination. Termination of a contract owing to gross misconduct entitles the innocent party to damages.

*Staff representation* Private enterprises employing 15 or more employees must have staff representation. The role of a representative is to defend the interests of employees in matters relating to conditions, job security, and social legislation. They liaise between employees and employers in matters of job protection and submission of any employee demands. There are further provisions for establishments that employ 150 or more employees and also for those with more than 1000 employees.

*Collective bargaining agreements* The Law of 12 July 1965 permits collective bargaining agreements between employee union organizations and employers. A collective bargaining agreement which is reached by a group of enterprises in the same sector of industry will be equally applicable to all labour contracts concluded in that sector. In effect, it is superimposed over the work contract. This generally defines the work contract, in terms of general conditions and employee–employer relations.

## Social security contributions

In Luxembourg, the social security system is built around a series of independent public institutions, each insuring a particular kind of risk, and organized into socio-professional categories.

Sole traders are thus registered with the Caisse de Pension des Artisans, des Commerçants et des Industriels, staff employees with the Caisse de Pension des Employés Privés and manual employees with the Caisse Nationale d'Assurance Maladie des Ouvriers. Businesses employing staff must also register with the Association d'Assurance contre les Accidents.

An administrative centre, the Centre Commun aux Institutions de Sécurité Sociale, is responsible for data processing, membership records and contributions for all the various schemes.

On 1 January 1991 the main social security contribution rates were as follows:

### Sickness insurance

|          | Rate   | Employer's share | Employee's share |
|----------|--------|------------------|------------------|
| Workers  | 8.70%  | 4.350%           | 4.350%           |
| Staff    | 4.85%  | 2.425%           | 2.425%           |

### Pension

|          | Rate    | Employer's share | Employee's share |
|----------|---------|------------------|------------------|
| Workers  | 16.00%  | 8.00%            | 8.00%            |
| Staff    | 16.00%  | 8.00%            | 8.00%            |

These rates are applied both for sickness insurance and for pensions to wages, salaries and professional earnings subject to certain contribution ceilings.

*Family allowances* The employer is wholly responsible for paying this contribution. The rate of 1.70% is applied on wages and salaries.

*Accident insurance* Accident insurance covers industrial accidents, travel accidents and occupational disease and is paid for by contributions from employers and heads of undertakings. The rate is fixed at a rate proportionate to the degree of risk inherent in the various industrial, commercial and agricultural activities involved. Contribution rates range from 0.50% to 6% of wages, salaries and professional earnings.

### Construction licences for large surfaces

According to Article 12 of the Law of 28 December 1988, the local authorities can only deliver a construction licence for a large surface after a specific authorization has been obtained.

The construction licence for large surfaces for retail sale, single or grouped, with a surface of more than 400 square metres, has to be delivered by the minister entitled to deliver the establishment authorization. The offices, outbuildings, shop windows, entrances, exhibition rooms, counters and storage accommodation are not included in the surface. This specific authorization is required in case of establishment, extension, transformation or takeover.

The minister requests a reasoned opinion from a commission, as described in Article 2 of this law; however, this opinion is not needed when the transformation only contains a material arrangement or when the takeover does not entail a change of destination.

The specific authorization may be refused if the project could endanger the global or local balance of distribution. It expires in case of non-performance or in case of default of implementation of the project of establishment, extension, transformation or take over, in a period of two years from the date of its delivery. It may be delivered for large surfaces for retail sale, single or grouped, with a surface smaller than 2000 square metres, in municipalities that hold less than 5000 inhabitants.

For larger surfaces for retail sale, single or grouped, with a surface larger than 2000 square metres, the specific authorization may only be delivered if the request is accompanied by a market survey confirming that the implementation or extension of the project does not endanger the distribution balance of the municipality and the area in which they are situated.

The market survey has to be elaborated by a specialized firm, previously approved for each project by the minister who is entitled to grant the authorization for the establishment.

As opposed to the above, no specific authorization is required in the following situations:

1   Single large surfaces for retail sale, in municipalities with more than 5000 inhabitants, if the required surface is not larger than 1000 square metres.

2   Commercial units grouped in commercial centres or malls, if their total surface does not exceed 2000 square metres and under the condition that the surface for retail sale is situated in a commercial avenue.

The applicant must submit all information that is required to the minister, who verifies the conformity of the information with the present article.

## Liability of the franchisor
*Liability of the franchisor* **vis-à-vis** *the franchisee* In Luxembourg, the liability of the franchisor *vis-à-vis* the franchisee is governed by the general principles of contractual liability. Thus, if the franchisor fails to meet his obligations under the franchise agreement, the franchisee may sue for damages under Article 1142 of the Civil Code. In this case, the franchisee will have to prove that he has suffered damage and that this damage is due to the non-performance by the franchisor of a principal or collateral obligation provided for in the agreement. According to

Article 1146 of the Civil Code, the franchisee will have to send a formal notice to the franchisor before taking legal action against him.

*Liability of the franchisor* vis-à-vis *third parties* The cases in which the franchisor's liability may be involved *vis-à-vis* third parties will be uncommon as the clients will, in principle, be dealing with the franchisee and not with the franchisor. A client may, however, take legal action against the franchisee who is of the opinion that the franchisor is responsible for the damage suffered by the client. In this case the franchisor may incur his liability in interference proceedings.

### Termination of franchise agreements

Franchise agreements are general civil law contracts which may be terminated according to the principles of general civil law applicable to contracts.

These contracts may be of limited term, in which case the term normally determines the method of termination (unless renewable), or they may be of unlimited duration, in which case each party remains free to withdraw from the contract providing certain conditions are fulfilled (example: notice to the other party of the intention to terminate the contract and observation of the formal requirements and delay periods previously established in the contract).

Although a franchisee is free to withdraw from a franchise agreement, he may not sell his franchise without authorization of the franchisor, owing to the *intuitu personae* character of the franchising agreement.

The franchisor is the owner of the trade mark in respect of which he has merely granted rights of use to the franchisee who is not free to transfer them.

Further, according to general contract law, non-performance of contractual obligations by one of the parties gives the other party the right to terminate the contract under Articles 1184 and 1144 of the Civil Code. The termination must be instituted in a court of law and may be accompanied by a demand for damages and compensation for losses suffered by the party arising from the failure of the breaching party.

The franchise agreement establishes a personal legal relationship between the parties. Unilateral cancellation for serious personal reasons such as misunderstanding between the parties or non-performance of one of the parties of his fundamental obligations will permit immediate cancellation by the other party. However, it should be pointed out that the party who cancels the contract should possess proof of the breach in case of subsequent verification by the court.

*Status of licence contracts in case of cancellation* Termination of the franchise agreement results in cancellation of the licence contract. Indeed, licence contracts are accessory to the franchise agreement and confer to the franchisee the rights of usage. According to general civil law, the accessory contract follows the principal contract.

*Unfair competition in case of cancellation*  The Law of 5 July 1929 provides in Article 4 that Article 309 of the Penal Code is applicable in case of any unfair competition. Article 309 of the Penal Code provides that any disclosure of trade secrets during the term of employment or within two years of termination of employment is prohibited. Any attempt to make such disclosure can be punished by imprisonment from two months to three years, and payment of fines up to Flux 150 000.

## TAX AND FINANCIAL CONSIDERATIONS

Luxembourg income tax laws were originally inspired by the German tax system, which was introduced during World War II. Although the actual Luxembourg income tax laws are still influenced by the German tax system, many changes have been made in the meantime, with the introduction, for example, of the duty taxes, which were non-existent in Germany, or of the VAT, according to the EC regulation.

In 1990, a major reform of Luxembourg taxation was voted through the Luxembourg Parliament and became effective from 1 January 1991. This reform is going to have an impact on the situation of every taxpayer, physical person or public corporation. The detailed provisions of a number of items still need, however, to be clarified by Grand Ducal Decree.

### Physical persons

The Luxembourg fiscal legislation has established the principle of subjecting physical persons to taxes by making reference to their actual residence.

Article 2 of the Luxembourg Fiscal Code stipulates that residents of Luxembourg are liable for taxes on Luxembourg income as well as on income from foreign sources (worldwide income). A physical person is considered to be a resident taxpayer of Luxembourg if he has his fiscal domicile or his habitual residence in Luxembourg. Fiscal domicile or habitual residence is defined by making reference to the place where any given person uses, retains and otherwise keeps his primary domicile.

### *Personal income tax*

#### Residents

The personal income tax is fixed by assessment. The basis of assessment is calculated on total net income, less special expenses. Total net income is calculated by taking net income, which is determined separately for each of the eight categories of income, minus losses. Losses made in one category may be set off against net income from other categories.

Certain income, for example payment in cash from legal insurance against sickness, accident and unemployment or interest on certain types of government loans, is exempted from income tax, and certain deductions are also permitted.

Tax is payable annually on the basis of a tax return. Tax is paid in quarterly instalments in advance and/or withheld at source on certain forms of income.

For workers receiving income from employment or former employment, the income tax due on wages, salaries and pensions is withheld at source. The tax is to be deducted by the employer or the pension fund for the account of the worker or the pensioner in accordance with tables of monthly, or daily amounts which are drawn up on the basis of the general scale for personal income tax.

The advance payments and the tax withheld at the source are deductible against final income tax liability.

Any overpayment of tax is refunded. Tax withheld on wages and pensions is adjusted annually when the tax is not calculated by assessment.

Until recently, the taxpayers were divided into three classes (1, single without dependants; 2, married without dependants; 3, married with dependants), and within the last class, according to the number of their dependants.

With effect from 1 January 1991, this classification has been revised. Class 3 has been abolished and a new class 1a introduced. Class 2 is, in principle, reserved only for married couples (with or without children) subject to collective taxation. Single, divorced or separated taxpayers over 65 years of age or with children or descendants are excluded from the splitting system, but included in class 1a. Divorced, separated or widowed taxpayers benefit from a transitory arrangement granting them class 2 for three additional years. Taxpayers with children to support benefit from child allowances, irrespective of their tax class.

The progressive bands of taxation have also been adjusted. Under the new law, individuals are able to earn higher amounts, depending on their tax class, before being taxed. A graduated scale with income brackets is applied to each of which corresponds a rate of tax ranging from 0% to 50% (56% before 1991).

Application of the rates varies according to the class to which the taxpayer belongs. This basic scale is adjusted periodically to variations in the consumer price index.

Furthermore, a tax resident can set aside from his gross salary approximately 2.425% for social security and 8% for retirement pensions.

*Non-residents*

A non-resident person is, generally, liable only for certain income earned in Luxembourg. The tax is directly set aside from his salary by the employer, in respect of applicable rates.

Non-resident married couples, single people or those widowed over 65, and divorced or separated people with children with at least one professional income source in Luxembourg are taxed under the above-mentioned class 1a tariff. If married couples earn more than 50% of their income in Luxembourg and they live together permanently they may opt for taxation under class 2. Collective taxation only occurs if both spouses earn an income in Luxembourg. All other taxpayers with professional income or other income taxable in Luxembourg are taxed under class 1. Non-resident taxpayers with any professional income are allowed to deduct Luxembourg social security charges from their taxable income.

*Special case of splitting between foreign and Luxembourg income*
With reference to the aforementioned principles, in the event of a splitting, where in one party who is a Luxembourg resident receives income from a foreign country, what would be the resulting tax implications?

Application of the above-mentioned Article 2 of the LIR may have as a consequence a double imposition of taxes both in the foreign country and in Luxembourg. In order to avoid this double taxation, Luxembourg has signed several double-taxation treaties which permit a Luxembourg resident to impute the income tax which he has already paid in the foreign country towards his taxable income in Luxembourg.

Where there is no such treaty, the law of 30 November 1978 introduced into Luxembourg national law a general principle of imputation of foreign taxes corresponding to the Luxembourg income tax, in respect of certain conditions. Specifically, the Luxembourg resident must prove to the tax administration that he has already paid the income tax in the foreign country. This proof must be evidenced by the presentation of a receipt for payment of taxes, or any other documentation emanating from the foreign country and attesting to payment of an income tax, to the competent Luxembourg fiscal authorities.

**Withholding tax on income from capital** According to Article 147 of the LIR, dividends were subject to income tax at a rate of 15%, whereas interest was tax-exempt.

On 11 June 1990 an EC Directive was issued requiring member states to enact domestic legislation abolishing withholding tax on dividends distributed by a resident of one EC state to a resident of another member state under certain restrictions before 1 January 1992. Under the new law, which is also transposing this provision into national law, the tax exemption on dividends will apply under two conditions:

1   The corporation has to be a resident of one of the EC member states.

2   The parent company must have a direct participation of 25% during an uninterrupted period of two years at the moment of distribution of the dividends.

This provision will, however, not apply to Luxembourg tax-exempt holding companies. Dividends from holding companies have always been exempted from tax, when paid to a non-resident; interest on bank deposits, loans and bonds is always paid to non-residents without any tax in Luxembourg.

Residents are also liable for tax on property.

## The fiscal treatment of Luxembourg companies
In relation to their fiscal treatment, Luxembourg commercial companies, generally, are liable for contribution duty, income tax, municipal business tax, net

worth tax, and an annual subscription tax (see, however, p. 266), all discussed below.

***The contribution duty*** The incorporation, or 'contribution', duty (i.e. 'droit d'apport'), as provided by the law of 29 December 1971, governing the taxation of capital collections in civil and commercial companies, is levied at a rate of 1% of the total subscribed capital, upon incorporation, and is also due upon any capital increase.

### The income taxation
#### The taxable basis
Following basic rules of assessment, the taxable basis for corporate income tax is determined as follows:

1    All profits, whether distributed or not, are to be included (Article 164, LIR).

2    Losses incurred in accounting periods ending after 31 December 1990 may be carried forward for an unlimited period. Losses incurred prior to that date may only be carried forward for a maximum of five years. However, no provision permits losses to be carried back.

3    Income tax, net worth tax and subscription tax (see, however, p. 266) are not deductible from the taxable basis. However, both contribution duty and municipal business tax are deductible (Article 168, LIR).

4    Allowances to the members of the board of directors are not deductible, except those remunerating those who perform the tasks of the daily management of the company (Article 168, LIR).

5    Capital gains on assets are not to be expressed as profit in the balance sheet as long as they are not realized. Such assets may remain quoted at their acquisition price, and, as such, their increase in value will not affect the taxable basis. When realized, these capital gains may be tax-exempt within the conditions of Article 54 of the LIR. Fixed assets subject to depreciation need only be capitalized if their purchase price exceeds Flux 35 000.

6    Legal possibilities aiming at reducing the taxable basis are provided for in the LIR and its implementation decrees (i.e. depreciation and constitution of provisions rules).

7    Provisions for specific risks (capital losses on securities, doubtful debtors (Article 23, LIR).

8    General, extraordinary and special depreciations (Articles 31, 32 and 32 bis LIR).

*The affiliation privilege*

Under certain limits a company is not liable to corporate income tax on dividends collected from a company of which it is a major shareholder ('Schachtelprivileg'). According to Article 166, paragraph 1, LIR, the participation must exceed 10% or Flux 50 000 000 and must have been held by the company for one accounting year.

This affiliation privilege is now to be extended, by a Grand Ducal Regulation which has not yet been adopted, to exempt from tax any capital gains made on the sale of the shareholding. The participation and retention limits will, only in this case, be increased to 25% or Flux 250 000 000.

*Group taxation*

Under the actual system of group taxation, the parent company must own 99% of the capital of a subsidiary before it is permitted to be taxed on a consolidated basis. As a result of the tax reform, the Ministers of Finance and Economy may exceptionally authorize the taxation on a consolidated basis if the parent company owns at least 75% of the subsidiary's shares and if at least 75% of the minority parties agree to this procedure.

*The income tax rate*

According to the new law, the income tax rates, including a special unemployment contribution of 1%, are as shown in Table 12.1. These are the nominal rates. It should be kept in mind that, due to the liberal attitude of the Luxembourg legislative bodies and the tax authorities relative to risk provisions and depreciation, the taxable basis can be significantly lowered and, hence, the effective rate of taxation minimized.

**The municipal business tax** This tax is assessed on the basis of two elements:

1   Exploitation profit: the tax is assessed on the same basis as the income taxation, subject to some addition and deduction allowances (including a deduction of the municipal business tax itself from its taxable basis). The

Table 12.1

| Income | Rate |
| --- | --- |
| Up to Flux 420 000 | 20% |
| Between Flux 400 000 and Flux 600 001 | Flux 80 000 plus 50% of the income in excess of Flux 400 000 |
| Between Flux 600 000 and Flux 1 000 001 | 30% |
| Between Flux 1 000 000 and Flux 1 313 000 | Flux 300 000 plus 42.6% of the income in excess of Flux 1 000 000 |
| In excess of Flux 1 312 000 | 33% |

municipal business tax will further be deductible from the taxable basis upon which the income tax is assessed. The rate in Luxembourg city is 10%.

2    The exploitation capital: the tax is assessed on the same basis as the net worth tax, subject to some specific additions and deduction allowances. The rate in Luxembourg city is 0.5%.

*Net worth tax*   This tax is assessed at a rate of 0.5% on the aggregate net worth of the corporation.

*Subscription tax*   The Laws dated 23 December 1913 and 13 May 1964, as amended, had introduced a subscription tax, which was levied annually at the rate of 0.36% of the effective value of the shares issued by the commercial company in the form of a public limited corporation or a private limited liability corporation. Under the new law, this tax will only remain applicable for holding companies and investment funds at the rates of 0.2% and 0.06% respectively.

Unlike a holding company, the commercial company may avail itself of treaties promulgated between Luxembourg and other countries for the prevention of double taxation.

*Withholding tax in an international context*   In the case of payment of dividends and royalties to non-residents of the Grand Duchy of Luxembourg, the law provides that there is a non-tax treaty standard rate of 15% for withholding tax (see, generally, Articles 146, 148, 156 and 157 of the LIR).

### Luxembourg holding companies consideration
*Definition*   The basic Commercial Law of 1915, as amended, together with the Law on holding companies dated 31 July 1929, as amended, regulate Luxembourg holding companies. Article 1 of the Law of 1929 defines a holding company as 'any company which has for its sole object the acquisition of any form of participations in other Luxembourg or foreign entities, as well as the management and development of those participations, in such a manner that it shall have no industrial activity of its own and shall keep no commercial establishment open to the public'. The portfolio of holding companies may include Luxembourg or foreign public bonds.

*Legal regulations*   The legal status of a company remains regulated by the general principles of Luxembourg company law of 10 August 1915 as modified. The holding company may take any of the six forms that are provided for by the law of 1915. However, in practical terms, most holding companies adopt the form of a public limited company (société anonyme).

*Activities*   Holding companies have seen their activities limited by the foundation law of 1929. Their activities were later clarified and enlarged by the fiscal administration; for example, a holding company may exercise, particularly, the following activities:

1    Holding of patents: The holding company may hold patents in its portfolio, although any industrial and commercial activity is prohibited; the exploitation of patents may in fact be carried out through the mediation of commercial or industrial companies, using exploitation licences.

2    Holding of trade marks and other intellectual property rights: In certain instances, the fiscal administration permits holding companies to hold trade marks and other intellectual rights which do not include know-how. The exploitation of these rights must be made through the use of a licence agreement; it must be emphasized that the holding of trade marks may only form an accessory or portfolio part of the general investment policy of the company, and the legislation of the involved country should further authorize the transfer of the industrial or commercial activity to which it relates. Also, the trade mark in question may only be placed at the disposition of the company in which the holding company holds a reasonable participation.

*Fiscal treatment of holding companies* The holding company is required neither to pay ordinary corporate income tax nor to pay net worth tax, municipal business tax or tax on income emanating from securities.

Dividends distributed by the holding company are also, to a certain extent, exempt from withholding tax. A fiscal non-resident shareholder of Luxembourg is not subject in Luxembourg to any tax on the amount of dividends received.

The sole taxes for which a holding company is liable are the following:

1    The holding company is subject to a capital duty tax (droit d'apport) of 1% upon the formation of the company, as well as upon any eventual increase in the share capital. The basis of the assessment is the total subscribed capital. In the event that the capital is increased by incorporating reserves, the capital duty tax is not payable.

2    The shares issued by the holding company are subject to an annual subscription tax in the amount of 20 centimes per 100 francs. The basis for the calculation of the subscription tax is the actual value of the shares issued by the company. In conformity with Article 7 of the Law of 19 December 1986, the annual subscription tax is not due on bonds, as of 1 January 1987. The annual subscription tax is calculated and due quarterly, based upon a declaration which must be submitted to the fiscal administration. As a result of the favourable fiscal regulation granted to them, the holding companies are excluded from the advantages of the international conventions which have been concluded between Luxembourg and other countries relating to the prevention of double taxation.

## Value added tax

The value added tax was introduced in Luxembourg by the law dated 5 August 1969 and modified by the introduction of European Regulations in 1979, 1980 and 1981.

All physical and legal persons who carry out, in a habitual and independent manner, operations arising from economic activity, as well as all importers, are subject to a value added tax (VAT).

According to Article 39 of the Luxembourg fiscal law dated 12 February 1979, relative to VAT, the normal rate on the sale of goods, the provision of services, and importation of goods, is 12%. The law provides in Article 40 for a reduced rate of 6% for goods and services which are specifically enumerated in the law. This reduced VAT rate of 6% will from 1991 on be applied to the custody and management of stocks and shares as well as to the management of loans and loan guarantees. Additionally, there is a 3% rate for some food and pharmaceutical products.

VAT is levied on the delivery of goods and furnishing of services for money inside the country; it is also applied to foreign goods needed by enterprises, and to all imports.

The basis of VAT is the price of the goods and services. The normal basis of assessment of VAT for persons or businesses is the sales price or normal value (including all duties, fees, and taxes and all accessory costs, up to the time of the first place of destination of the goods within the interior of the country).

The tax is, in principle, recoverable for persons subject to VAT.

All goods and services for export as well as international transport (crossing the country) are exempt from VAT, and VAT previously added may be deducted. Also exempted, but without a similar deduction for previous VAT additions, are postal operations, delivery and rental of real property, banking operations, insurance operations, and other operations such as sanitary, social, cultural and educational operations.

Rental transactions are normally exempt from VAT (Article 44, law on VAT). However, any individual or legal entity that rents real estate properties can elect to have the rentals subject to VAT. This option is only given if the contract has been made in writing, by mutual agreement, and if the lessee is himself subject to VAT.

Those subject to VAT must file a VAT declaration monthly, trimestrially or annually.

## Fiscal treatment of royalties

According to Article 98 of the fiscal law, the following are considered as income emanating from the rental of goods:

1   The royalties paid for the usage, or the concession of the usage, of a copyright, patent, or trade mark.

The royalties paid for the usage and/or the concession of the usage of industrial, commercial or scientific equipment.

The royalties paid for the information related to a certain experience acquired in the industrial, commercial, or scientific areas.

This above-mentioned income is considered as resident income when the debtor is either a company which has its corporate registered offices or principal business establishment in the Grand Duchy of Luxembourg, or a physical person who has his or her fiscal domicile in Luxembourg.

For the non-resident taxpayers benefiting from the royalties, the withholding tax is set aside from the resident income (Article 152 of the fiscal law), taking into account the treaties for the prevention of double taxation.

The rate of the withholding tax is applicable to the totality of the amount received, and may not be greater than 15%. It is, more precisely, 10% of the gross, or 11.11% of the net, revenues for the revenues emanating from literary or artistic professions, or for the revenues emanating from temporary concessions related to an artistic or literary copyright. The rate is fixed at 12% of the gross or 13.5% of the net revenues for the revenues emanating from income concerning patents. This withholding rate is calculated based upon the global income of the non-resident taxpayer.

The deductions for the right to use the patent, exploitation expenses, or taxes levied on the non-resident taxpayer are not permitted by law. (See paragraph 4 of the Luxembourg Ordinance dated 6 February 1935.)

## Investment incentives for enterprises

In Luxembourg, a whole set of public measures has been adopted in order to stimulate the modernization and diversification of the economy through private investment, especially in the industrial sector. Different forms of public aid are available, as follows.

Building plots provided with all the necessary infrastructure are available to new companies in industrial zones on favourable terms (Law of 14 May 1986). The land is made available under the form of a 30-year renewable superficial right deed.

Investments in infrastructure, buildings and equipment are eligible for financial assistance of up to 25% in the form of cash grants or interest rebates on bank loans (Small and Medium-Sized Firms and Trades Framework Law of 29 July 1968). Financial and technical assistance is also available for personnel training and for research and development. Under the law of 1968, a contribution is made to the cost of studies carried out by recognized experts in connection with projects for extension, rationalization or adaptation of undertakings up to a maximum of 50% of the total cost of the study, subject to a ceiling of Flux 100 000.

During the first financial years, a tax relief is granted to new enterprises or to enterprises manufacturing new products (Law of 14 May 14 1986). 25% of the profits of new businesses or works are exempted from income tax for the first eight fiscal years of operation and a 14% tax credit is granted on investment in equipment. These two measures are cumulative.

In addition, the Société Nationale de Crédit et d'Investissement (SNCI), a public law banking and savings institution established by the law of 2 August 1977, helps to finance industrial investments and exports by means of:

1    Ten years equipment loans at a fixed interest rate of 4.5% p.a. for the full term of the investment loan.

2    Innovation loans at a fixed rate of 5% p.a.
     These loans are generally for 25–50% of the eligible amount of the cost of a specific, clearly defined, research and development project. They are paid in one or more instalments after the recipient has provided evidence that the research and development project is in progress.

3    Medium and long-term loans at an interest rate fixed for a minimum term of five years: the purpose of these loans is to finance equipment used directly in production activity or in the provision of services, including safety and environmental protection equipment or premises or parts of premises used exclusively for professional purposes. The loans are paid in one or more instalments pro rata with the payments which have to be made towards the eligible investment. Invoices and other documents have to be produced for this purpose.

4    Export credit facilities: the action which gives rise to an export credit is a contract between seller and buyer specifying *inter alia* the full financial terms of the transaction. Export credits may be in the form of supplier credits or buyer credits.

# CHAPTER 13
# THE NETHERLANDS

*Patricia B. Hamelberg-Scheephorst*

## AN OVERVIEW OF FRANCHISING IN THE NETHERLANDS

### General

The franchising system has become increasingly popular in the last few years as a method of conducting business in the Dutch business sector, both in the retail and service industries. In 1988, the retail sector in the Netherlands saw approximately 200 franchisors doing business in more than 7000 franchise establishments and employing close to approximately 28 000 people.

The fast food franchising sector is experiencing the greatest amount of annual expansion in the Netherlands. While the number of franchisors has remained constant since 1987, the number of franchisee establishments in this area has increased by 50%, rising to 326 in 1988. The result has been positive, since both the number of people employed and gross income have increased. McDonald's, Febo and Kentucky Fried Chicken are important participants in the field of Dutch fast food franchising. (This information was obtained from the outline in the franchising brochure produced by the Dutch Franchise Association in Hilversum.)

Total gross income of franchise operations in the Netherlands in 1988 was valued at Dfl 12.5 billion. A considerable portion of this figure was generated by franchise organizations such as Mister Minute, Toerkoop and Foto Plus which focus their operations in the service industry in one way or another.

The future of franchising in the Netherlands most likely will result in a sharp increase in the number of franchise establishments, mainly because this business method provides an excellent means of expansion and an efficient system for improving the utilization of the resources of many businesses.

The Dutch Franchise Association (NFV) has established as a primary goal and service the compiling and updating of knowledge and expertise relating to franchising, as well as allowing for the dissemination of same. In addition to the membership offered to parent franchisors, it is also possible for membership to be granted to natural persons or others with interest in this area. Further, legal entities may also become members, even if neither is franchisor or franchisee. The NFV is an active association which assists both the established and entry level franchise owners with financial, legal and fiscal advice, in addition to advice in the area of administration and other problems relating to franchising. The NFV is domiciled in Hilversum.

### Legislation in the area of franchising

While in the Netherlands no specific legislation governs franchise agreements, the following acts, general regulations, and provisions will influence the legal relationship of the parties and will guide their respective business practices.

In addition to these general regulations, which will be dealt with in greater detail in subsequent paragraphs, the franchise agreement is governed, broadly speaking, by principles of freedom of contract. Consequently, the parties are themselves free to determine the content of the franchise agreement. However, their freedom is limited by mandatory legislative provisions which have been enacted to protect the economically weaker parties to an agreement; the parties may not deviate from these provisions. Many of these stipulations are found in the labour and rent acts.

The franchise agreement must also comply with the doctrine of good faith and fair dealing imposed on all parties to a contract. Articles 6.3 and 6.248 of the new Dutch Civil Code provide that the agreement must be carried out in good faith. In the context of the article, the meaning of the term 'good faith' is determined objectively: how a reasonably prudent person should act under the given circumstances.

Jurisprudence has interpreted this provision to mean that where supplementary law does not provide guidance for a solution to a particular case, a solution will be obtained by application of the good faith doctrine. Additionally, the article has been interpreted to allow the doctrine of good faith to overrule a contract provision if that provision cannot be upheld under the particular circumstances of the case.

One can therefore conclude that the following elements are relevant to the formation of franchise agreements:

1    Mandatory legislative stipulations, from which the parties cannot deviate.

2    That which has been explicitly agreed upon by the parties can be supplemented by good faith and, under particular circumstances, can also be deviated from by an appeal to good faith.

3    Prior to making an appeal to good faith, regulations of supplementary law can fill in a gap in the agreement.

4    Good faith.

# THE TYPES OF BUSINESS ENTITY IN THE NETHERLANDS

## Introduction

Franchising can be defined as a type of commercial collaboration between autonomous business entities. The Netherlands recognizes various business entities in which the entrepreneur can operate his business. The legal principles of these various entities are of primary legal importance. Thus, the legal implications arising from the entrepreneur's association with a franchise organization are of secondary importance. The franchising organization will therefore not be considered in the following summary of the type of business entities existing in the Netherlands.

## General

Any Dutch or non-resident individual, partnership or company can operate inside the Netherlands with or without adopting any of the following types of Dutch legal business entities:

Unincorporated:

  (a)  partnership (maatschap)

  (b)  general partnership or firm (vennootschap onder firma)

  (c)  limited partnership (commanditaire vennotschap)

2   Incorporated:

  (a)  public company with limited liability or corporation (naamloze vennootschap, legal abbreviation N.V.)

  (b)  private company with limited liability or closed corporation (besloten vennootschap, legal abbreviation B.V.)

In addition to these business entities, there exists a type of enterprise entitled the 'one-man business' (eenmanszaak). Such a designation is informally adopted by an entrepreneur who fails to adopt any of the formal legal business entities. An entrepreneur who runs his enterprise as an one-man business is ultimately legally responsible for all agreements and legal relationships.

The choice of one of the above-mentioned types of business entities will generally, among other things, depend on:

1   (International) tax considerations

2   Size, nature and (financial) organization of activities

3    Inter-company relations

4    External relations (liabilities)

5    Auditing and publication requirements

6    Applicable legislation

Every enterprise must be registered in the Trade Register of the Chamber of Commerce in the district where the business is carried out. Additionally, corporate entities must be registered in the district where their legal registered office is located (if in another district).

Third parties may rely on the registration at the Trade Register and also can obtain information from the Register on the type of legal business entity involved, the authorized capital, the powers of the management, the corporate registered office, etc.

All enterprises are entitled to operate under the name of their owners or of their head office, or under almost any invented name as long as the name does not confuse the public, and the trade name or trade mark rights of others are not infringed. A *trade mark* applies both to products and to services, according to the 1971 Uniform Benelux Act on Trademarks. A *trade name* is the name under which the business activity of an enterprise is wholly or partly conducted (see the 1971 Trade Names Act, 'Handelsnaamwet', mentioned below).

The choice of legal business entity is also important in determining the amount of social security payments and insurance premiums which employers and employees must pay under the Dutch tax system. Social security payments and the Dutch insurance schemes for employed persons will be explained in greater detail in subsequent paragraphs (see p. 296). At this point suffice it to say that the insurance schemes ('ZW/WAO/WW') are applicable to those persons working in the Netherlands who may be designated as 'employees'. The owner of a one-man business and the partners of unincorporated legal business entities cannot be described as employees and, accordingly, are excluded from this insurance.

It is an entirely different situation, however, for the corporate business entities such as the N.V. (Dutch legal abbreviation for a public company with limited liability or corporation), or the B.V. (Dutch legal abbreviation for a private company with limited liability or a closed corporation). But even here, the director will not be insured under the social security insurance scheme if, in fact, he only has control of the N.V. or B.V., or if he occupies a position of power within the company (for example, as a director-controlling shareholder). However – as the other employees – aside from these types of situations, the director of the N.V. or B.V. will be insured under the Social Security Acts.

Finally, any business entity in the Netherlands, regardless of its legal form, which employs a certain number of employees is obliged to establish a works council (ondernemingsraad) in order to facilitate deliberation and consultation with representatives of its employees. If an enterprise has branches in several municipalities, each branch is considered a separate enterprise for the purpose of determining the number of employees.

## One-man business

*Definition* The law regards a one-man business as an autonomous entity. A one-man business can only be regarded as such if it accounts for its own profits and losses. If not, then the entity will not be regarded as a one-man business but rather as a branch establishment.

*Formation and representation* In a one-man business, the owner operates or trades under his own name and for his own account. For this purpose he can be a natural legal person as well as a legal entity, or may also possess the legal status of an incorporated company. A one-man business must be registered in the Trade Register pursuant to the Trade Register Act.

*Liability* Even if an owner of a one-man business has contributed only part of his private capital to his business, he is held personally liable to the extent of his private capital for legal acts which he performs in furtherance of his business.

## Unincorporated legal business entities
### Partnerships and general partnerships
*Definition*
From a legal perspective, the partnership and the general partnership form of legal business entities are very similar. For instance, both are based on an agreement between two or more partners (individuals or corporations) with the purpose of co-operating in order to make a profit. The law requires that these partners contribute capital, property, labour or goodwill. A purely nominal contribution will suffice.

One difference between the partnership and general partnership is a formality in that the agreement between the partners in a general partnership must stipulate that the co-operative effort will be carried out under a joint name. In practice, however, the partners in a partnership also work together under a joint name.

*Formation and representation*
An agreement between the partners is sufficient to form a (general) partnership. This 'deed of partnership' must specify whether or not, and in what way and to what extent, one or more of the partners is entitled to act in the name of and on

behalf of the (general) partnership. The other partners are not legally responsibl if one or more partners act on their own behalf, or if they fraudulently purport t act on behalf of the (general) partnership. To avoid this situation the Trad Register Act (Handelsregisterwet) also requires that the authority representin the (general) partnership be registered.

### Liability

Unless otherwise stipulated in the deed of the general partnership (and registere at the Trade Register), third parties may hold all partners jointly and severall liable for any act a co-partner performs on behalf of the partnership, whether o not it is performed pursuant to the partnership objective. The same is applicabl to the partners of a partnership, provided that they can only bind each other fo certain obligations. If the partnership declares bankruptcy and an attachment i made, the business creditors of the general partnership have priority over th personal creditors of the individual partners, but only to the extent that partner ship assets are involved. All creditors of a partnership have equal rights.

### Alienation, dissolution

It is often very difficult to determine the value of the shares of an individua partner of the (general) partnership. Among other factors, the value is influence by those provisions which govern the termination of an individual partnership. / (general) partnership terminates:

1   At the expiration of the deed of partnership

2   When the objective of the partnership has been accomplished or is no longe feasible

3   Upon the death, insanity or bankruptcy of one of the partners

4   Upon notice (according to prescribed formalities)

5   By court order

### Miscellaneous

A (general) partnership is suited mainly for small business, or as a legal form fo co-operation between enterprises. Apart from tax considerations, a (general partnership is generally impractical for an enterprise which experiences growth because of the financial risks inherent in the (general) partnership form.

### Limited partnerships
#### Definition

A limited partnership is basically the same as a general partnership, except that a limited partnership has one or more partners whose liability is limited to thei capital contribution ('stille vennoten' or 'commanditaire vennoten').

*Formation*
A limited partnership is formed in the same way as a general partnership.

*Representation, liability*
The limited partnership is represented by one or more so-called managing partners (beherende vennoten). The liability of the managing partners is the same as that of a general partner, i.e. unlimited. If one or more of the 'sleeping' partners (the limited partners) are in any way involved in the management, directly or by proxy, their liability will be unlimited, even if third parties are aware of their status as limited partner(s).

To avoid the potential adverse effects of unlimited liability in a limited partnership, the managing partner often forms a company with limited liability (N.V. or B.V.), the shares of which can be held by the limited partners.

The liability of the limited partners is restricted to the amount of their capital contribution to the limited partnership.

*Alienation, dissolution*
The same applies as in the general partnership.

*Miscellaneous*
The names of limited partners are not required to be registered at the Trade Register (only their number, their nationality, the country in which they live and the total value of the contribution). However, for managing partners, full names and addresses must be registered.

## Incorporated business entities: public companies with limited liability and private companies with limited liability
*Definition (general)*

1    A public company is an incorporated business entity with an authorized capital divided into freely transferable shares. The corporation is an autonomous legal entity that can enter into contracts and sue and be sued. The N.V. (Dutch legal abbreviation for a public company or with limited liability) is favoured by large enterprises with high capital stock requirements since its shares can be traded on the stock exchange upon application. The shares, however, do not have to be listed. The N.V. parallels the American corporation (Inc.), the British public limited liability company (PLC), the French Société Anonyme (SA) and the German Aktiengesellschaft (AG).

2    A private company is an incorporated enterprise with an authorized capital divided into shares which, in principle, cannot be freely transferred. The B.V. (Dutch general abbreviation for a private company with limited

liability or closed corporation) parallels the American close corporation, the British private limited liability company (Ltd), the French Société à Responsabilité Limitée (SàRL) and the German Gesellschaft mit beschränkter Haftung (GmbH).

## Formation

1    An N.V. and a B.V. are in principle formed in the same way. The company is formed by a legal act of the founders. Since 1 January 1987 this 'foundation' can be performed by one person (Dutch or non-Dutch individual or company). Incorporation takes place by means of an official deed, executed by a public notary (a quasi-legal official whose duty it is to handle such tasks). This deed must be in the Dutch language. It contains the articles of association (statuten) and the by-laws, if any.

The articles of association set out the identity of the company and must contain the name, the registered office and the objectives of the company. In addition, information concerning the capital and the shares must be recorded.

The articles of association must be submitted to the Ministry of Justice, which ensures that all the legal requirements have been met before giving approval. This approval takes the form of a certificate with a 'statement of no objection' ('verklaring van geen bezwaar'), and enables the company to be effectively incorporated. Ministerial approval is also required for changes in any of the provisions of the articles of association.

2    *Share capital.* Book II of the Dutch Civil Code stipulates the minimum capital for an N.V. and a B.V. The capital in the company is held in the form of issued shares. At the present time, a minimum capital of Dfl 100 000 is required for an N.V.; the paid-in capital should amount to at least Dfl 100 000. Minimum capital required for a B.V., both issued and paid-in, equals Dfl 40 000. The articles of association state the value of the authorized capital and the number and value of the shares. The company should amend its articles of association if it wishes to issue shares.

The Minister will refuse to give his approval at the time of the formation if the company does not fulfil its financial obligations. The Minister can also refuse to give his approval if the capital of the company and its other financial sources are not proportionate to the company objectives. The Public Prosecutions Department can also demand the dissolution of the company if, after the formation of the company, the capital requirements stated above can no longer be met.

3    *Pre-formation transactions.* The founders and their representatives may enter into contractual arrangements on behalf of the company prior to its incorporation. To avoid the appearance that the founders are acting on their own

behalf, it is customary to add the initials 'i.o.' (which means 'in the process of incorporation') to the name of the future company. A preliminary investigation as to possible trade name infringements is advisable. These pre-formation transactions will bind the company, once incorporated, only if it ratifies every such act. Normally, the relationship between the founders is defined in a pre-formation agreement.

*Representation* The general meeting of the shareholders of the company was riginally the highest authority. More recently, however, companies have often ut limitations on the powers of the shareholders' meeting. All powers not dele-ated by law or the articles of association to the other corporate organs are etained by the shareholders.

In the Netherlands, a general meeting of the shareholders must be held at ast once a year, within six months of the end of the fiscal year. The articles may ncrease the number of meetings if desired. If the managing or supervisory lirectors fail to convene a required meeting, then any shareholder may request he permission of the president of a district court to convene the meeting himself. hareholders with 10% of the issued capital may also make such a request for a on-stipulated meeting, if their request has been ignored by the corporate fficials.

The daily business affairs of a N.V./B.V. are managed by one or more nanaging directors (bestuurders) who may be either natural or legal persons and eed not be shareholders or Dutch citizens, unless so stipulated in the articles. Normally, the managing directors represent the company in and out of court. The managing directors are, in most cases, appointed at the general meeting of hareholders. The powers of management must be stated in the articles of associa-ion, as well as the limitations of their powers.

*Liability* The liability of the shareholders of a public company with limited iability is limited to the nominal value of their shares. The same applies to the hareholders of a B.V.

*Dissolution* The company is dissolved:

1    In circumstances defined in its articles

2    By a resolution of the general meeting of the shareholders

3    In the case of insolvency after having been declared bankrupt

4    By a court order in circumstances defined by law

The liquidation resolution must be registered in the Trade Register and pub-lished in the Official Gazette and one other newspaper. During the period of

winding up, the designation 'in liquidation' must be added to the name of th
company.

The company will not cease to exist until all the accounts payable an
receivable have been settled. The shareholders are entitled to what remains afte
the claims of the creditors have been settled.

### Choice of the type of business entity

The choice of one of the previously described legal forms will depend on the posi
tion that the individual entrepreneur has in the production chain, i.e. producer
wholesaler–retailer.

The Dutch manufacturer who operates within the franchise system as
producer of products intended for franchising will, in all probability, form hi
enterprise into a public or private limited company, while the retailer within th
franchise system will prefer, for example, the one-man business entity. Thus, a
already noted, the type of business entity chosen is of less importance to th
franchise organization.

## LEGAL ASPECTS

### Introduction

The franchise contract is not specifically mentioned in Dutch legislation. It
separate contractual elements are, however, specifically provided for by impera
tive legal rules. These 'designated contracts', from which the franchise contrac
as a whole is composed, include a contract of sale, a lease agreement, a contract o
employment, and a licensing agreement. Furthermore, because the Netherland
is a member of the EC, other European legal rules may apply, particularly in th
area of free competition.

Thus, in order to determine the consequences for the contracting/fran
chising parties, each of these contractual elements must be repeatedly examinec
and a determination must be made as to what extent they apply to a specific fran
chise agreement. Since the franchise agreement, by its nature, has the ability tc
influence free competition, this aspect will be examined first, in light of the pos
sible applicable legislation.

### Competition and restrictive trade practices

*General* Theoretically, a system of free competition exists in the Netherlands.
The government, in the person of the Minister for Economic Affairs (MEA), may
under certain circumstances intervene in some sectors of business if it believes
that certain restrictive trade agreements conflict with free competition or with the
public interest.

*The Economic Competition Act* The Economic Competition Act of 1956 (ECA)
serves as an instrument of economic policy. The ECA has a two-sided formal

urpose. First, it is intended to monitor co-operation in order to prevent the gative consequences of unrestricted competition. Second, it is designed to strict this co-operation in the event that it conflicts with the public interest. 'ith this Act, the Minister for Economic Affairs has secured a form of control.

The ECA applies to two components of the area of free competition. First, forceable agreements or decisions between or among owners of legal enter- ises will be subject to scrutiny. Second, and similarly, ECA review of dominant )sitions will occur. These dominant positions are defined as the factual or legal lationship in trade or industry which entails the predominant influence by one more owners of enterprises in a particular market of goods and services in the etherlands.

Trade agreements which potentially may have a 'restrictive effect' on trade ust be reported to the Minister for Economic Affairs within one month after e agreement takes effect. Failure to do so is a criminal offence. This govern- ental unit will review the agreement by applying the underlying theories out- ned in the ECA. A determination of the agreement's compliance with the ECA ll then be made. If the Minister for Economic Affairs finds that a specific agree- ent (or any action) conflicts with the public interest, he can declare it to be com- etely or partially inoperative. A specific agreement, or entire category of greements, which has been declared inoperative, is null and void and therefore nenforceable.

Pursuant to the ECA, a variety of different types of retail price maintenance also under the control of the Minister for Economic Affairs. An example of one pe of retail price maintenance is a vertical retail price maintenance – the obliga- on of retailers to sell goods at prices which have been fixed either by the supplier the goods or by preceding suppliers.

Vertical retail price maintenance may be either *individual* or *collective*. *Individ- ıl* vertical retail price maintenance is involved whenever the pricing obligations, ıd the supervision of delivery of the goods, are solely the concern of the supplier who has fixed the price) and the committed retailer(s). In contrast, *collective* ertical retail price maintenance occurs when the supplier is not autonomous, ut has obligations to third parties (associates of the buyer) in connection with ıe price maintenance. Collective vertical price maintenance is divided into two pes: *collective application* of vertical price maintenance and *collective upholding* of ertical retail price maintenance.

In applying the provisions of the ECA, the Minister for Economic Affairs as taken a position on these three types of vertical price maintenance. For the ıost part, individual vertical price maintenance is permitted, but the Minister as also determined that vertical retail price maintenance is forbidden for durable onsumer goods (radios and televisions, motor cars, washing-machines, etc.) omplete freedom of trade therefore exists for permitted goods, subject to the mitation that the Minister may determine several categories of forbidden goods. n contrast, *collective upholding* of retail price maintenance is not enforceable egardless of what type of goods are involved.

Although the Dutch regulations are not insignificant, European legislation
becoming increasingly influential, even though it has the potential for infringir
the jurisdiction of Dutch legislation. A group exemption concerning categories
franchise agreements was adopted on 30 November 1988. These European reg
lations allow retail prices to be recommended as long as no pressure is exerted
actually enforce final prices.

The Dutch legislature has adopted this provision, and the Supreme Court
the Netherlands has held that a recommended retail price must not be viewed as
binding price. The assumption is that the public will not be misled by recom
mended price-fixing unless a comparison between an individual selling price an
an unrealistically high recommended retail price is advertised. Accordingly,
appears that by adopting this provision, the Dutch legislation has put an end
the various ways in which the vertical retail price system has been judged in th
past.

Articles 85 and 86 of the EC treaty have had an immediate effect on th
Dutch legal system. European legislation is of a higher order of law; howevei
there is some discussion as to whether a place has been reserved for the Dutc
national legislation alongside that of the European legislation in this field.

There is essentially a split of opinion on this issue. One view stems from th
notion that restrictive trade agreements need only be opposed at a Europea
level. In contrast, the other faction takes the position that resistance to restraint
on economic competition is precisely the area where a place must be reserved fo
the national legislation.

The European Commission has recommended that a national judge activel
apply European legislation in a national judicial procedure. A Dutch judge wi
therefore directly test the restrictive trade provisions against articles 85 and 86 c
the EC treaty.

## Liability

*General* A franchisor must be aware that he can be held liable to the consumer o
the basis of unreliable functioning of or damage to the product which the fran
chisor has put on the market (the section 'Product liability' below) as well as to th
franchisee on the basis of the provisions of the franchise contract (section on 'Con
tractual liability').

*Product liability* The Dutch legislature has recently drawn up special legislatior
in the area of product liability based on the EC directive concerning produc
liability. In this legislation, product liability can result in strict liability. The legis
lature, however, takes the view that strict liability is insurable.

The EC product liability directive stipulates that a consumer can choos
whether to hold the manufacturer or the supplier liable for damages caused by
imperfect products, as long as their business is established inside the EC.

*Contractual liability* In a franchise agreement the franchisor may guarantee the franchisee exclusivity concerning a product, area, or a length of time. The franchisor is in principle liable to the franchisee if these guarantees are violated. In many cases, the franchisor will attempt to exclude any liability on his part, through contractual provisions. A means by which the franchisor can preclude liability towards the franchisee is by including the so-called 'exoneration clauses'. However, good faith – which has previously been discussed and which is quite characteristic of the Dutch legal system – is influential in the relationship of the franchisor and the franchisee. Jurisprudence has stipulated that, under certain circumstances, an appeal to certain specific exoneration clauses by a producer is in conflict with good faith, and therefore is not permitted. In addition, gross culpability and intent cannot be excluded from the contract.

In the same way, good faith can influence the contractual relationship of the franchisee and the consumer. The consumer can hold the franchisee liable for infringing the provisions of their contract, although 'exoneration clauses' are included in the contract.

Next to these 'exoneration clauses', the contract between the franchisee and the consumer will often contain general conditions, by which the franchisee restricts or excludes the rights and claims of the buyer.

The new Dutch Civil Code, previously mentioned, is becoming increasingly influential. A new regulation recently came into force which concerns the inclusion of stipulations for general conditions. In the new General Conditions Act, two lists have been included: the 'black list' and the 'grey list'. The 'black list' sets forth stipulations which can never be included in an agreement with a consumer. If included, they are considered to be null and void. The stipulations included on the 'grey list' are those which are considered to be unreasonably onerous for the consumer. It is the entrepreneur's responsibility to prove that the stipulation in question is not unreasonably onerous, given the specific circumstances of the case.

## Intellectual property

*General* One of the significant concepts behind the system of franchising is the image or business concept which the franchisor is able to offer to the franchisee. The term 'image' includes all colour combinations, slogans, approaches to selling, methods of approaching the customer, uniforms, training of staff, suggestions for the layout of the business, specifications for the establishment of the business, definite instructions for the operation of the business and any other advice the franchisor can give. Stated more generally, the know-how at the franchisee's disposal – includes all the functions to be carried out in the operation of the franchisee's enterprise.

It is important to the franchisee that the business concept given him by the franchisor remains intact. The franchisor who has developed a specific business concept also wants certain parts of that concept protected by industrial rights of ownership.

***Trade mark rights*** It is prudent for a franchisor to register his trade mark with the Benelux Trademarks Office; only by being registered and by continuous use are the trade mark rights obtained and preserved. The franchisor subsequently can authorize the use of the trade mark by the franchisee under licence.

The trade mark used in a franchise system can often be a service mark since its function is to distinguish the services uniformly rendered in the system.

The registration of a trade mark with the Benelux Trademarks Office only provides the trade mark protection in the Benelux countries; any entrepreneur must search the trade marks which have been registered in the Benelux, in order to see whether he is free to register his own trade mark without infringing the rights of anyone else. In the Netherlands, this can be accomplished by a so-called authorized trade mark representative.

***Trade name rights*** Within a franchise chain, the trade mark will often be the same name as the trade name. As with the trade mark, the franchisor who wishes to enter the Benelux market should investigate whether his trade name has previously been used. Furthermore, it should be noted that a trade name can only be transferred to another enterprise based on and together with a conveyance of that enterprise.

***Used models, copyright and slogans*** Under certain circumstances, models, copyrights, and slogans can be protected. Registration is a precondition to protection. The requirements for registration differ, and are stricter than the formality of registering a trade mark with the Benelux Trademarks Office.

It is also possible to license the use of an industrial title of ownership. With this licence, the licensee becomes entitled to use an industrial title of ownership.

Finally, it must be mentioned that if an industrial title of ownership is not protected by specific legislation, and thus cannot be enforced by that legislation, action can still be taken against possible infringements. Such an infringement is actionable as a wrongful act pursuant to the Dutch Civil Code.

## Real estate leasing

***General*** The franchisee can conduct his business or trade on business premises. Naturally, he can rent or buy these premises himself, but usually it is the franchisor who, within the framework of the franchise agreement, puts the business premises at the disposal of the franchisee. The franchisee pays a fee to the franchisor for the use of the premises. This fee may or may not be included in the total franchise fee.

The stringency of the Dutch rent legislation which will apply to the franchisee is contingent on the type of business he conducts on the premises. The most extreme mandatory legislation is that which applies when the business premises are intended to be used to run a retail business or trade, and the business space is accessible to the public so that goods and services can be supplied directly (B.W. Article 1624, business space; cited in Dutch as Article 1624 BW, 'bedrijfsruimte'). Since most franchise chains are involved in the retail sector, these provisions will be applicable to the majority of franchisees who lease business properties from franchisors.

*Business space* A variety of regulations are set out in Articles 1624ff. of the Dutch Civil Code, whose purpose is to protect the lessee of the business space. The Articles provide, with a few exceptions, that a lease agreement should always have a minimum term of ten years. A term of this length provides the lessee with the opportunity to build up a solid business structure, while allowing him to make decisions concerning investments and to facilitate long-term forecasting and plans. It is very rare for the lessee to prematurely terminate the term lease agreement.

Accordingly, an incongruity can exist between the parties: the desired length of the franchise agreement may conflict with the mandatory legally enforced period of the lease agreement as provided for in the Articles.

It is very important for the franchisor that on termination of the franchise agreement the leased premises be vacated by the franchisee. Problems may arise if the franchise agreement has a shorter term than the ten-year lease mandated by the Code. It is highly questionable whether, in the case of a termination of the franchise agreement before the expiration of the ten-year period, the franchisor can legally force the franchisee to vacate the premises prematurely.

Dutch courts have been frequently called upon to decide in which instances the aforesaid mandatory provisions may be set aside. For example, court review of the relationship between putting the business space at the disposal of the lessee and other stipulations involving joint co-operation has occurred.

When a 'combination' of legal relationships results from the franchise contract, a Dutch court may hold that certain mandatory provisions will prevail. For example, in the areas of 'leasing and letting' of office space, as found in Article 1624 of the Civil Code, the Dutch Supreme Court has ruled that where a contract defines a leasing and letting relationship as well as other legal relationships, i.e. is 'combined', the provisions concerning leasing and letting prevail.

Only once has such a case, in the context of a franchise agreement, been brought before a (lower) court. In this particular case, a franchisee had grossly violated its franchise agreement, giving the franchisor grounds for terminating the franchise relationship. The question put before the court was whether the franchisee could be ordered to vacate the leased premises at that time, even though the ten-year lease term had not expired.

The court ruled that this franchisee could not in good faith appeal to the protective stipulations of Article 1624ff. of the Civil Code, and the court decided that the franchisee had to vacate the leased premises.

In view of the specific circumstances of this case it is difficult to draw general conclusions concerning this issue.

In the future, all the circumstances of each case must be carefully considered, including: the amount paid by the franchisee for the use of the business premises, the extent of default by the franchisee, the importance to the franchisor of acquiring this business space and, naturally, the contractual obligations of the parties pursuant to the franchise agreement.

The resulting problems are produced by the fact that the ten-year term is mandatory by law. There is a way of avoiding this mandatory term: *before* a leasing or letting agreement with a different period is concluded, both franchisor and franchisee must ask the district judge permission for this different period. In such a case, the duration of the leasing or letting agreement must be made identical to the duration of the franchise agreement.

Thus, the franchisor must take into account the inherent risks, advantages and disadvantages of letting business space to the franchisee when making his decision.

### Foreigners working or establishing a business in the Netherlands
*General* One who wishes to establish or run a business or enterprise in the Netherlands must comply with various regulations governing, among other things, the employment of foreign workers in the Netherlands, the establishment of the business or enterprise, and the usage, renovation or construction of buildings used in the business or enterprise.

*The employment of foreign workers in the Netherlands* One who decides to employ foreign workers in a Dutch business within the framework of the franchise agreement will encounter a large number of regulations which control the length of stay of the worker in the Netherlands as well as conditions of his employment. These regulations can be found in the Aliens Act 1965, the Stipulations Concerning Aliens 1966, the Circular Concerning Aliens 1982 and the Employment of Foreign Workers Act.

It is apparent from this legislation that a foreign worker who wishes to be legally employed in the Netherlands must first secure both a work permit and a residence permit.

*Work permit*
A Dutch employer is not permitted to employ an unlimited number of foreign workers. The starting premise, found in the Employment of Foreign Workers Act (WABW), is that an employer is altogether prohibited from employing foreign workers. An exemption from this ban may be granted by way of a work permit. In the Netherlands, this work permit is granted by a regional job centre. The regional job centre must refuse to issue a work permit if either:

1    The employee concerned does not possess a residence permit, or

2    A limit has been imposed on the employer as to the number of foreign

workers he may employ, and this limit will be exceeded by the issuance of a work permit.

In addition, a work permit can be refused on the ground of incidental circumstances. Such circumstances include the supply of workers on the Dutch labour market, the way in which the employer has approached the foreign worker and circumstances which concern the accommodation of the worker. At present, the unemployment rate in the Netherlands is high; a work permit, therefore will not be readily granted.

*Residence permit*
Every foreign worker is permitted to enter the Netherlands if he or she possesses a visa and a valid passport or, depending on the nationality, possesses a valid passport only. These documents give the foreigner the opportunity to stay in the Netherlands for three months. After three months, a residence permit is required to enable a foreign worker to remain legally in the Netherlands.

This period of three months is reduced to eight days after arrival in the Netherlands if circumstances arise which prove that the employee intends to remain in the Netherlands longer than three months. Such circumstances include the purchase of a house, entering into an employment agreement or entering into any other type of long-term obligations. In such a case the person concerned must immediately report to the Dutch police authorities to obtain a temporary residence permit.

The application for a (temporary) residence permit is granted or denied based on the criteria of the 'common good'. If the criteria are met, a residence permit will be granted. However, a number of conditions will probably be imposed on the foreigner, including the provision of a financial guarantee in regard to the expenses of the employee while in the Netherlands, as well as a guarantee over the cost of return to the foreigner's country of origin.

Thus, anyone who wishes to employ foreign workers in the Netherlands should consider whether the required permits can be obtained. In the franchisor-franchisee context, it goes without saying that residence and work permits need not be obtained if either the franchisor or franchisee employs only residents of the Netherlands.

**Establishment Acts** The requirements which apply to a Dutch person who wishes to establish a business also apply to a foreigner who wants to start up a Dutch business (see p. 278), provided that a 'statement of no objection' will be obtained only after a strict examination that all legal requirements have been met.

Since 1937, regulations governing the establishment of a business in the Netherlands have been aimed at increasing the standard of business practices and preventing irresponsible establishments. The most important Act in this area is the Establishment of Business Act (Vestigingswet Bedrijven). The framework of this Act is elaborated on further in various General Administrative Orders.

### Establishment of Business Act

Administrative orders, referred to as Establishment of Business Orders, have now been specified for nearly all branches of industry. Pursuant to these orders, it is forbidden to carry on a business without having first obtained a licence from the Chamber of Commerce and Industry. The Chamber of Commerce and Industry will issue such a licence only if requirements of creditworthiness, business knowledge, and competence of the manager or executive manager have been met.

The requirements of creditworthiness and business knowledge have been drawn up in detail together for all businesses in the so-called Basic Decree. The requirements for competence, on the other hand, have been separately drawn up for each branch of industry.

One must realize that the Establishment of Business Act distinguishes between the requirements that are made of the manager and those required of an executive manager of an establishment. The manager actually manages the running of the business and the staff employed in the business; the executive manager runs the business as a whole. The manager, for example, can be the owner, branch manager or head of a department. An executive manager, on the other hand, can manage a number of branches. The distinction between manager and executive manager is important in assessing which licensing requirements must be complied with.

Since the General Administrative Orders, and thus the requirements for the establishment of a business, are repeatedly subject to amendments, it is advisable to obtain up-to-date detailed information from an expert before establishing a business.

### Retail Sector Licensing Act

Some business activities do not fall within the provisions of the previously mentioned legislation but rather come under the Retail Sector Licensing Act. This Act requires an establishment to obtain a licence from the Chamber of Commerce and Industry. Since the Act regulates businesses which specialize in the retail sector, the majority of franchise establishments are governed by its provisions. The licence will be issued only if the executive manager fulfils the requirements of competence for the retail sector. The requirements of competence are enumerated in detail in the General Administrative Order which, and similarly to the Establishment of Business Act, is amended regularly.

### Town and Country Planning and the Nuisance Act

In the Netherlands, the use, renovation, and construction of buildings is regulated to a large extent by legislation from central and local government. The use and construction of buildings are regulated by the zonal plan as well as by the relevant planning regulations connected with the zonal plan.

The planning regulations explicitly stipulate which building uses are permitted for certain types of establishments, thereby guaranteeing that the inconvenience inherent in operating such establishments will be concentrated within specific areas. Zones have been created for catering establishments, for the retail sector, for trade in bulky goods and for industrial companies.

Local governments in the Netherlands may use police restraint to prevent the construction or use of buildings in violation of the applicable zonal plan. In practice, this means that both the use and the building activities must be suspended.

Due to stringent legislation in this area, information should be obtained before purchasing real estate for the purpose of establishing a business. Current local zonal plans, and the possibilities the plan offers, must be investigated in advance.

Finally, it should be noted that one who is planning a franchise business may also be confronted with the provisions of the Nuisance Act. The Nuisance Act requires particular types of trading and catering establishments to secure licences. Before a licence will be granted, the licensee must stipulate certain restrictions on nuisance, hazards and inconvenience to the surrounding area. Restrictions are therefore often imposed on routing to the establishment as well as on any negative effects which may be associated with the establishment such as parking inconvenience, annoyance resulting from shopping trolleys, and visual nuisance from illuminated advertising.

It is clear that a plethora of detailed and complex legislation, subject to regular amendment, is encountered when starting up a business in the Netherlands.

## Provisions on employment agreements

*General* The franchisee, in his or her role of employer, will in almost all cases enter into employment agreements. The content of typical employment agreements, usually evidenced by a written contract, will be influenced by Dutch employment laws. This body of law contains regulations for the making, the content, and the termination of the employment agreements. Implicit in all contracts of employment is the principle of 'freedom of contract'. As mentioned previously, the parties to an employment agreement are free to determine its contents.

The four elements (mandatory legislative stipulations, stipulations by parties, supplementary stipulations and good faith) will probably be applicable to the employment agreement. It should be noted that the legal regulations concerning the employment agreement are much more comprehensive than those regulations applicable to and governing other types of agreements. Regulations applicable to and governing the employment agreement are sometimes merely supplementary law. However, mostly these regulations will be of a mandatory nature. The mandatory nature results from the desire of the law to protect and benefit the employee, who is frequently viewed as the weaker party in an employment agreement.

In addition to the above-referenced general regulations, the employment agreement law will include the Collective Employment Agreement Law, the Dutch legal abbreviation of which is 'CAO'.

As a result of the existence of the above regulations, little flexibility exists for application of the so-called principle of 'freedom of contract'.

*The drafting of the employment agreement* The employment agreement can be in the form of a written document, or can be merely an oral agreement. However, the law requires that, certain regulations be in writing, which may be also facilitated by publication by the employer of a code of rules. If such regulation or rules must be incorporated into an agreement, it is strongly advisable to have the entire agreement in written form.

*The content of the employment agreement* In all cases, the employment agreement must contain a provision that obliges the employer to pay the employee wages. In the absence of this provision, no employment agreement will exist.

In principle, the parties to an employment agreement are free to determine the wage rate. In practice, the wage rate is established in the CAO.

In the Netherlands, the right to an obligatory minimum wage is enjoyed by all male and female employee from 23 to 64 years of age. In the event the employee earns less than the minimum wage, he or she is entitled to claim payment of the deficiency from the employer.

In addition to the minimum wage law, employers in the Netherlands are subject to EC regulations which provide that wages be paid equally to male and female employees. The policy behind these regulations is that equal pay must be received by male and female employees engaged in equal work. However, in general, Dutch law obliges an employer to treat male and female employees equally in all respects.

Finally, the employer in the Netherlands is required to uphold the following general objectives in the relationship with the employee:

1    To conduct his business operations as a fair employer

2    To provide for employee safety while the employee engages in work

3    To provide the employee with employment

*Termination of employment* Termination of the employment agreement can occur in four different ways. Distinctions in termination exist as follows:

1    By contract

2    By giving notice

By court order

By operation of law

*ermination by contract*

n light of the above-mentioned principle of 'freedom of contract', consent by
oth employer and employee to termination of the employment contract will see it
ome to an end. However, because of the severe consequences experienced by an
mployee who voluntarily terminates the contract of employment, i.e. disqualifi-
ation for unemployment benefits, an employee will usually seek voluntary ter-
nination in conjunction with some 'justifiable' grounds (for example, see 'Ter-
nination by court order', below).

*ermination by giving notice*

n the area of termination of employment agreements, Dutch legislation begins
·y recognizing the freedom of the parties to terminate their employment agree-
nent whenever a mutual desire to do so exists. However, when termination of the
greement is at issue, the parties must take into account specific regulations.
ermination in breach of these regulations may result in severe consequences.
he party at fault in improper termination may be held liable for resulting
lamages, and a court may require restoration of the parties' relationship and
tatus to that of the pre-termination period, including the right of the employee to
eceive back wages.

Many complex and detailed regulations for termination of an employment
greement exist under Dutch law. For example, there is a prohibition against dis-
nissing an employee without the previous consent of the director of the Regional
abour Agency. Until such consent is obtained, and where the termination is in
reach of his employment obligations, the employer is obliged to continue pay-
nent of wages, as long as the employee is willing to perform his work.

In addition to the general prohibition against termination without approval,
pecific prohibitions against termination will be encountered. A dismissal in
·iolation of these specific prohibitions will be void, and the employee will con-
inue to receive his or her pay, though not engaging in any work activity.

*Termination by court order*

3oth the employer and employee can request the court to dissolve the employ-
nent agreement on the basis of extraordinary and compelling reasons. Should
he plaintiff in such action succeed, the court can dissolve the employment agree-
nent immediately, or at some future date. Further, the court can award the
:mployee a compensation indemnity, which is frequently the case.

*Termination by operation of law*

Termination of the fixed-term employment agreement occurs automatically by
)peration of law, and without court declaration. Termination shall also occur by
)peration of law upon the decease of one of of the parties.

*The Collective Employment Agreement (CAO)* In the Netherlands, Collective Employment Agreements (CAOs) are concluded mainly by negotiations between employers and various employee representative organizations such as employees unions and federations of trade unions.

The CAO will operate only to regulate the conditions of employment which necessarily exist during the individual employer–employee relationship. Accordingly, where the employer–employee relationship is connected by one of the above representative organizations, the CAO regulations must be taken into account.

Conditions of employment stipulated in the CAO are automatically and imperatively included in the employment agreement between the connected employer and employee. In principle, provisions to the contrary are void.

Where a specific employer is bound by a CAO, but an employee is not, conditions of employment must be incorporated into the employment agreement unless the CAO provides otherwise. In such instances, the parties must make special arrangements, since conditions of employment will not become automatically and imperatively part of the employment agreement.

Finally, an employer not connected to any employers' representative organization by CAO negotiations is not bound by the CAO, unless the Minister of Social Affairs declares otherwise. If such declaration is made, it will result in application of some or all of the CAO provisions. These types of declaration are referred to as those of 'commonly binding force'.

In the Netherlands, most CAOs are declared commonly binding. Consequently, even employers not currently subject to union membership are bound by the provisions of these CAOs.

### Termination of the franchise agreement

In a franchise agreement, the parties are free to establish their mutual legal relationships. This is also the case in the event of dissolution or termination of the relationship. As previously mentioned, a franchise agreement is composed of various separate agreements, each of which is regulated by law. Thus when the entire franchise agreement is terminated, the regulations governing each of its separate components must also be taken into account.

## TAX AND FINANCIAL CONSIDERATIONS

### The Dutch fiscal system

The tax laws, such as the Company Tax Act, the Income Tax Act, the Wage Tax Act, the Value Added Tax Act, and the Wealth Tax Act, are all subject to the broad provisions of the General Act Concerning Public Taxation (AWR). Basic requirements for the levying of taxes are stipulated in the AWR. For example, the AWR mandates rules for:

1    Making a tax declaration (Article 8, AWR)

2    The tax assessment (Article 10, AWR)

3    The information which must be provided by the business entity subject to
     taxation, including allowing the inspection of its accounts (Articles 47 to 50,
     AWR)

4    The objection to and appeal against a tax assessment (Articles 23 to 30,
     AWR)

## Applicable legislation

This section briefly describes the following in light of the various Dutch fiscal acts:

1    Those persons and entities subject to taxation

2    The object of taxation

3    The applicable taxing rate

*Company Tax Act (VPB)* According to the Company Tax Act, those entities
subject to taxation are divided into the following groups:

1    Those with domestic tax liabilities. In principle, tax liability is based on total
     income, in the Netherlands as well as abroad.

2    Those with tax liabilities abroad. This group is only liable to pay taxes
     on income acquired within the Kingdom of the Netherlands ('internal
     income').

The Act also makes a distinction between entities with unlimited tax liabilities
and those with limited tax liabilities. Those with unlimited tax liabilities are:

1    Public limited companies, private limited companies, general partnerships
     and other partnerships in which the capital is totally or partially divided into
     shares (i.e. a company with share capital)

2    Co-operative associations

3    Mutual insurance companies

To this group with unlimited tax liability, the legal fiction applies that such businesses are deemed to be run with their total capital.
     Those with limited tax liabilities are:

1    All the corporate bodies under private law not mentioned above

2      Associations without a legal status

3      Enterprises of public bodies or bodies controlled by statutory legal bodies

Those with tax liabilities in the last-mentioned group only have a subjective tax liability if and insofar as they are running a business. The capital of these bodies is accordingly divided into *company* and *private* capital. Company tax is obviously only levied on the returns from the enterprise.

Company tax rates vary according to the amount of taxable returns; a tax rate of 40% is applied to taxable returns up to Dfl 250 000, while taxable returns above this amount are subject to a 35% tax rate.

***Wealth Tax Act (VB)*** The Wealth Tax Act imposes tax liability on the following persons:

1      Natural persons who are living in the Kingdom of the Netherlands at the beginning of the calendar year

2      Natural persons with tax liabilities abroad but with capital within the Netherlands

The tax rate in general which applies is 80%. The Wealth Tax Act also provides for a so-called 'anti-accumulation' regulation. This regulation requires those who are liable to pay income tax, as well as wealth tax, to pay a *maximum* of 80% of their taxable income in income tax and wealth tax together.

***Income Tax Act (IP)*** The following persons are required to pay income tax pursuant to Article I of the Income Tax Act:

1      Natural persons who are living in the Netherlands and have an income

2      Natural persons who are living *outside* the Netherlands and who have an income from *within* the Netherlands

Income tax is levied on:

1      Returns from a business

2      Income from employment

3      Income from capital

4      Income in the form of a regular payment (dividend)

5      Returns from substantial interests

Obviously, various deductions are available to those persons with tax liabilities under the Income Tax Act.

The tax rate under the Act is determined by a person's relevant 'tax bracket'. Specific income classes are fixed annually, on which specific percentages are levied for taxation.

The tax rate for the highest income bracket is 60%, in accordance with recent changes in the law (the Oort Plan).

*Value Added Tax (OB)* The entrepreneur is liable to pay taxes according to the Value Added Tax Act. The Value Added Tax Act defines an entrepreneur as 'a person who independently runs a business, also understood as the independent practising of a profession'.

According to the Value Added Tax Act, actual entrepreneurship occurs if:

1  A business is being 'conducted', i.e., there is organized participation in the social and economic life by means of organization of capital and work, and enduring, sought-after needs of society are satisfied.

2  There is autonomy, i.e., no relationship of authority exists.

Value added tax is levied on the supply of goods and services. The applicable rates are 0%, 6% and 18.5%. The 0% rate is applied to the *export* of goods; exported goods are thus tax-exempt from the value added tax. The 6% rate applies generally to goods and services which are considered the 'essentials of life'. The 18.5% rate applies to all other goods and services.

N.B. An entrepreneur within the meaning of the Value Added Tax Act is required to organize his administration so that the applicable rates can be determined from his method of administration.

*Wage Tax Act (LB)* Employed persons are required to pay taxes pursuant to the Wage Tax Act. When a 'state of employment' exists, the Wage Tax Act requires the employer to deduct the tax from the employee's wages and transfer the tax to the tax authorities. When such a state of employment exists, the employee must pay premiums and social security payments in addition to the wage tax. This topic will be further dealt with in the next section.

The wage tax rate is to a large extent determined in conjunction with the Income Tax Act.

## Fiscal consequences for franchisor and franchisee

Aside from the implications arising from the legal form in which the franchisor and franchisee choose to operate their business, various fiscal consequences should be taken into account if one is intent upon running a business in the Netherlands. For example, the Dutch system requires the franchisor who supplies goods and services to the franchisee to comply with tax requirements under the Value Added Tax Act. The same applies to the franchisee who supplies goods and services to the consumer. Additionally, when a contract of employment or contract of services exists between the franchisor and franchisee, the 'employer' must make the necessary deductions for the wage tax or social security premiums.

Moreover, the various adverse tax consequences under the Dutch tax system as found, for example, in the levying of the accumulation of wealth tax and the income tax, can largely be avoided by careful consideration of the remuneration of natural persons employed in the enterprise.

Therefore, before establishing a franchise chain and similar businesses it is necessary to seek advice concerning all problems and possibilities arising under applicable corporate and fiscal legislation.

## Social security payments

*General* In the Netherlands, a comprehensive system of regulations provides benefits for every Dutch person who, because of various circumstances, is not in a position to provide for his or her own maintenance. Under this system, such a person receives a benefit which is paid and granted by the Dutch state or by agencies created on behalf of the Dutch state. These benefits serve to guarantee to every Dutch citizen a certain minimum level of existence, so that he or she is protected against the adverse financial consequences of unemployment, disability, illness, old age, etc.

The money for these benefits is acquired partly from general resources (thereby provided by all tax-paying citizens) and partly from the resources of 'national insurance contributions'. There exist a great number of Acts which stipulate through mandatory legislation that citizens, employees, enterprises and companies are obliged to pay insurance contributions. These various Acts always state who must pay the premiums and in what amount. In addition, the Acts stipulate which persons are entitled to receive a benefit and under what circumstances the benefits accrue.

These Acts can be divided into two categories:

1    National insurance applicable to every citizen, such as the General Disability Act, the General Retirement Act, etc.

2    The employed persons insurance schemes, such as the Unemployment Act, the Health Act, the Act Concerning Disability, etc.

The Bedrijfsverenigingen are the bodies responsible in the Netherlands for the implementation of the appropriate legislation. It is they who decide whether, under the appropriate legislation, there is an obligation to pay the premiums pursuant to a relationship between two parties.

There are 26 Bedrijfsverenigingen in the Netherlands, each of which is responsible for the administration of premiums under the Acts. A separate Bedrijfsvereniging regulates each branch of industry. The Bedrijfsverenigingen believe that it is a worthwhile aim to have as many employed people as possible insured within the framework of the insured persons insurance schemes.

*The employed persons insurance scheme* Pursuant to the employed persons insurance scheme, insurance premiums must be paid when an employer–employee relationship is found to exist between the parties. Whether or not such a relationship exists between a franchisor and its franchisee is open to debate. On the one hand, it is obvious that when entering a franchise agreement, the franchisor and franchisee intend to create a relationship in which both parties are independently practising a profession or operating a business and also that the parties involved do not intend there to be an employer–employee relationship between the parties. On the other hand, however, the parties cannot by agreement deviate from the provisions of this legislation or exclude its applicability; the law is to be regarded as mandatory and the franchisor and franchisee will be subject to its provisions.

It is clear that if a franchisee operates his business in the form of an incorporated enterprise he will be considered in the service of the enterprise. For this reason, the insurance premiums will be paid by the enterprise. If, however, a franchisee operates his business in the form of an unincorporated business, he will not be directly insured within the context of this legislation, and will be subject to all the consequences stemming from such an 'independent entrepreneurship'.

The aim of the franchisor and the franchisee in negotiating an agreement is centred on establishing the franchisee's independence. Accordingly, disagreements often arise with the Bedrijfsvereniging over who is required to pay premiums, particularly in regard to the employed persons insurance schemes. On the one hand, the franchisor and the franchisee argue that the franchise is an independent business or profession. On the other hand, the executive body of the Bedrijfsvereniging frequently takes the position that an employer–employee relationship exists between franchisor and franchisee, so that the 'employer' and also the 'employee' have to pay premiums on account of the insured persons insurance schemes. Dutch legislation, and corresponding jurisprudence, indicate when an employer–employee relationship exists; such a relationship is readily assumed.

In any case, an employee is defined as someone who is employed on the basis of an employment agreement, an arrangement for which the regulations are laid down separately by law. Generally, such an employment agreement is thought to exist between 'employer' and 'employee' if a relationship of authority prevails and, during a certain period of time, work is carried out for a specific wage.

Obviously, doubtful cases exist in defining the employer–employee relationship and the dividing line is not always easily drawn. Dutch legislation therefore regards even those who are not employed on the basis of an employment contract as employees subject to the employed persons insurance schemes. A premium

must therefore be paid for and by such persons. In the Netherlands, such a
employment relationship is generally called a fictitious employer–employee
relationship.

***The fictitious relationship*** There are no specific legislative rules defining whethe
a contract of employment, and thus an employer–employee relationship, exists i
the context of franchising. The question of whether the so-called fictitiou
employer–employee relationship exists must be determined by the facts of eacl
case.

The content of the written contracts between parties is therefore not of overriding importance in defining this relationship. Rather, the actions of the partie
and the implementation of their relationship are the determining factors. Thus,
in the context of franchising, the independence of the franchisee in conducting
his business and the degree of control exerted by the franchisor over the franchisee, along with numerous related circumstances, will be determinative on this
issue.

Additional factors relevant to this issue have been recorded by means of a
checklist drawn up by the Social Security Council, an advisory body of the
Bedrijfsvereniging. The checklist mainly focuses on the overall way in which the
franchisee manages his business. Relevant inquiries include whether the franchisee manages the business capital, has staff in his service, has creditors and
debtors, runs the risks related to ownership, is economically independent of his
buyers and/or customers or works without inspection or control of the progress
over and above his own system. Additional considerations include whether the
income from the business or profession is built up from the payments of many
customers or buyers, the party involved trades under his or her own name or
trade name, the franchisee is the entrepreneur with respect to VAT, whether
competition is encountered, etc.

If the majority of these questions can be answered in the affirmative, then a
fictitious employer–employee relationship will generally not be found to exist.
Accordingly, the franchisor and the franchisee will not be required to pay the
national insurance contributions.

In the last few years in the Netherlands, many cases have gone to court on
this issue and, at the present time, many such cases are pending, particularly with
respect to franchise relationships. Clearly, the matter has not been completely
resolved. A great deal of caution is therefore required in drafting franchising
agreements, as well as in the way in which the business is actually carried out.

As has been previously indicated, it is the Bedrijfsvereniging who first
decides whether, in a franchisor–franchisee relationship, one is required to
pay national insurance contributions in the context of the employed persons
insurance schemes. If, after an investigation, a Bedrijfsvereniging is of the
opinion that premiums must be paid, an assessment will be made retrospectively
over the previous three years for all contributions due. In this case, the franchisor
is assessed for all his franchisees, resulting in enormous financial consequences

to the franchisor. The franchisor who disagrees with the decision of the Bedrijfsvereniging, and this is frequently the case, can appeal to the Court of Appeal, which can then decide whether the Bedrijfsvereniging has mistakenly imposed the national insurance contributions on the franchisor. If the Court of Appeal also reaches a judgment which is unacceptable to one of the parties, the case can be brought finally before the Central Court of Appeal, which has the final word on the matter.

These legal proceedings, including all requests for appeal, can take many years to complete. During this time, a great deal of uncertainty exists with respect to the franchisor's and franchisee's possible liability to pay national insurance contributions. Serious financial consequences are at stake, such that one should seriously consider in advance the issues concerned. To the greatest extent possible, franchising organizations should be formed as independent enterprises by the terms of the franchise agreement as well as by the implementation of the franchise agreement. It is also important that the control exerted by the franchisor over the franchisee should not be disproportionate to the object of the franchise.

Naturally, the franchisor has the option to submit the contract in advance to the Bedrijfsvereniging, to explain the actual relationship between franchisor and franchisee and to ask the Bedrijfsvereniging to declare that the relationship between parties will not be regarded as a (fictitious) employer–employee relationship when the work is executed according to this contract and according to the actual circumstances, and thus to declare that mandatory national insurance contributions will not be imposed.

However, such a decision of the Bedrijfsvereniging will always be granted conditionally, in such a way that the Bedrijfsvereniging will always reserve the right to modify its decision. Complete security will therefore not be obtained with such a decision of the Bedrijfsvereniging.

## CONCLUSION

Franchising, as a method for expansion of business operations, is currently enjoying success in the Netherlands. Both large and small franchise operations have recognized the profit potential resulting from business expansions through this method.

The number of franchisee establishments connected to multinational franchising operations continues to grow. The trend is apparently for expansion, not only for fast-food establishments, but also for an array of all types of goods and services.

The services sector seems especially promising at this time. Currently, this sector is in the early stage of development, and, accordingly, opportunities for expansion are available. The first dental service franchise was recently announced, and it is anticipated that financial and insurance service operations will soon follow.

Whether expansion through the franchise system is sought by large or small businesses, both types of entities should be appraised of the various Dutch regulations which have direct and/or indirect implications for their plans. While no 'franchise law' as such is currently in force, many aspects of Dutch legislation will require strict compliance on the part of both franchisor and franchisee. Familiarity with laws governing trade practices, industrial property, employer-employee relations, tax issues and various licensing requirements is necessary.

# CHAPTER 14
# PORTUGAL

*Manuel P. Barrocas*

## AN OVERVIEW OF FRANCHISING IN PORTUGAL

As in many other EC countries, franchising has grown substantially in Portugal during the last few years, mainly since 1986. As a matter of fact, there were about 500 franchisees in 1986, which increased by 1988 to about 620 and in 1989 to 1100. The number of franchisors was 35 in 1986, 60 in 1987 and 100 in 1989. It is expected that these figures will grow considerably over the next few years.

For this reason, a franchise association, the Associação Portuguêsa de Franchising, was set up in 1989 which aims to promote franchising.

The Portuguese government has not adopted any specific attitude towards franchising. Although in some EC member states the commercial banks have made loans available to franchisees on special terms and have established franchise departments, this has not yet occurred in Portugal.

## STRUCTURE OF A VENTURE IN PORTUGAL

### Advantages and disadvantages
There are two types of Portuguese company:[1]

1   A private company (so-called 'sociedade por quotas')[2]

2   A public company (so-called 'sociedade anónima')[3]

The 'sociedade por quotas' and the 'sociedade anónima' are similar in general terms, in that they are both companies with limited liability, i.e. the shareholders are only liable to the extent of their contribution towards the share capital, and the creditors of the company cannot call upon them for the payment of debts. Both entities have, of course, legal personality separate from the shareholders.

### Best choice
The 'sociedade por quotas' (S.p.Q.) is a very popular type of company in Portugal,[4] because it is suitable for a small number of shareholders (two is the

301

minimum) and for setting up of firms of small or medium-size businesses which do not involve public subscription of capital. The minimum share capital is 400 000 escudos and contributions in kind are allowed.

The 'sociedade anónima' (S.A.) is a type of company which is normally used by investors when there is need for a greater financial capacity. It requires the minimum share capital of 5 million escudos and at least five shareholders.

If the business is to be developed with less than five shareholders an S.p.Q. is the best choice. On the other hand, if the business is to be carried out on a larger scale, i.e. demanding a more complex company having a larger number of shareholders than five, the S.A. will be more suitable. It will be appreciated that the choice of company type will be made after consideration of all relevant factors.[5]

Both types of company are subject to the same tax regime, including the tax rates as well as the annual examination of accounts and rules on publicly recorded legal information. Financial information is required to be publicly recorded with an S.A. An S.p.Q. is obliged publicly to record financial information only where the profit and loss account total of revenues is more than 180 million escudos, or the net sales and other income is more than 370 million escudos or the number of employees is 50 or more.

The transfer of shares in an S.A. is easier than in the S.p.Q., as in the case of the latter prior authorization of the general meeting of shareholders is required (except where provided otherwise in the articles of association) and the intervention of a public notary. Transfer of shares in an S.A. is also exempt from capital gains tax up to 1992 if they have been held by the seller for more than one year. The same tax benefit is not applied to the transfer of shares in an S.p.Q. The law is more rigid with respect to the auditing requirements of an S.A., since there is an obligation to have a supervisory board which should include a chartered public accountant. This requirement is not obligatory for an S.p.Q. except where the company, during two consecutive financial years, achieves two of the three requirements mentioned above, i.e. the figures concerning the total of revenues, net sales and number of employees. Apart from these aspects there are no other significant differences between an S.p.Q. and an S.A. Alternatively, the foreign investor can decide to set up a branch in Portugal rather than a subsidiary. Unlike the subsidiary, the foreign investor operating through a branch will be directly involved in the business in Portugal.

There are no substantial differences between a branch and a subsidiary, as Portuguese law is applicable, in general, to the activities of both. However, there is a difference concerning taxation since the branch is subject to a global rate of 40.15% of corporate tax, including direct profits, capital gains and municipal taxes, and the subsidiary is subject to a higher global rate of 52.65% due to a tax on the distribution of shareholders' profits.

For further remarks about branch operations see pp. 321–325.

# Formation

Firstly, it should be appreciated that the incorporation of a company is a complex matter. Therefore, it is essential to obtain legal advice about the articles of association and to deal with formalization and registration.

Secondly, instead of incorporating a company, a company investor may decide to take over an existing company registered in Portugal.

*Formation of an S.p.Q.* The main requirements for the formation of an S.p.Q. are:

1   There must be at least two shareholders.

2   The minimum share capital must be 400 000 escudos divided into 'quotas' (shares) whose minimum amount is 20 000 escudos each.

3   Apart from the general meeting of shareholders the company must have at least one director (called a 'gerente'). The existence of a supervisory board is not obligatory.

4   The by-laws (memorandum and articles) should indicate at least the following matters: identification of the shareholders and number of shares held by them, name and objects of the company, place of the registered office and how the company is bound. They may indicate conditions for transfer of shares between the shareholders or in favour of third parties, pre-emption clauses, any special majorities in certain matters, special provisions on distributions of profits, etc.

5   Once a name is chosen and before the by-laws are drafted, a request for the acceptability of the intended name should be presented to the regulatory authority concerned.

6   Application should be made for foreign investment authorization whenever a non-resident of Portugal intends to participate in a company (see p. 313).

7   After the above items are dealt with, a bank account should be opened in order to deposit the amount of the share capital which is to be paid up pursuant to the incorporation deed (the law requires that at least 50% of the share capital should be paid up at that time).

8   Incorporation of a company takes place before a public notary with the execution of a notarial deed of incorporation which comprises the memorandum and articles of association.

9   Registration of the company with the registrar.[6]

10   Notification to the tax office of the date of commencement of business.

11   This process takes between three to four weeks, not including the time needed to obtain documents relating to foreign investors in their country where the company is formed by non-residents (see p. 313).

12   The legal costs will not exceed 2% of the amount of the share capital, including notary's and registrar's fees and expenses of official publications.

### Formation of an S.A.

1   The company must have at least five shareholders.

2   The minimum share capital is 5 million escudos, which is divided into 'acções' (shares) whose usual nominal value is 1000 escudos each.

3   The company must have at least one director ('administrador' or 'director') if the share capital does not exceed 20 million escudos and three or more (but always an odd number) if the share capital is higher.

4   Apart from the general meeting of shareholders the company must also have a supervisory board comprising at least three auditors. One of them should be a chartered public accountant unless the share capital is no more than 20 million escudos when one auditor will be sufficient.

5   The articles of association should deal with at least the same issues as apply to an S.p.Q.

6   The minimum amount of 30% of the share capital must be paid up at the notarial incorporation date and deposited at a bank.

7   The other requirements relating to an S.p.Q. apply equally to an S.A.

### Statutory requirements
The statutory requirements may be summarized as follows:

1   Name of the company.

2   The company's registered office.

3   The objects of the company.

4   The amount of share capital (including if the capital, or part of it, is paid up in kind, a description of assets contributed and their respective values). Kinds of shares in an S.A. (for instance, ordinary shares, non-voting shares, redeemable shares, shares which have been fully reimbursed, so-called

'acções de fruição' and, of course, nominative, bearer shares and registrable bearer shares, etc.

5   Transfer of shares.

6   Pre-emption clauses.

7   Transmissibility *mortis causa*.

8   Management:

  (a)   number of directors

  (b)   how the company is bound

  (c)   appointment of managers (alternatively this subject can be reserved for the general meeting of shareholders)

9   Shareholders' meetings:

  (a)   special provisions regarding notice of meetings, if any

  (b)   any special majorities in certain matters, if at all

0   Profits and reserve funds:

  (a)   any special provisions about distribution of profits

  (b)   creation of special reserves, if appropriate

## Directors: appointment, duties and responsibilities

The directors are the legal officers and representatives of the company. They are usually appointed in the incorporation deed (memorandum and articles of association) which in the case of an S.p.Q. may be for an indefinite period of time. This is not usually the case with an S.A., where a general meeting of shareholders is convened forthwith after incorporation, although directors can be appointed at the time of incorporation. In the case of an S.A. there is a time limit for holding office which has a maximum extension of four renewable years.

The directors may not be employees depending on whether there is a pre-existing or current employment contract governed by the labour law. However, if an employment contract exists at the beginning of the director's period of office it will be suspended whilst the office is held.

Directors are appointed in the articles of association or by the general meeting of shareholders. Their appointment must be notified to the registrar as well as their removal from office which can be the decision of the shareholders or automatically at the end of the period of the appointment.

The directors are bound to the company by a duty of diligence and must have due regard for the shareholders and employees of the company.

Loans to directors of an S.A. are prohibited and agreements between the company and the directors are null and void if the board of directors has not given prior consent without the opposition of the supervisory board. This regime is not applied to an S.p.Q. However, in both types of companies the directors may not develop any business whose object will involve it in competing with the company. The directors are responsible for keeping the books and records of the company, and for preparing and filing the annual accounts.

Finally, in both types of companies the directors are personally liable *vis-à-vis* claimants if they have performed their duty negligently and led the company to a position in which there is an insufficiency of assets to pay the debts.

## LEGAL CONSIDERATIONS

### Introduction
Any of the traditional methods of international franchising arrangements can be developed under Portuguese law.

Portuguese law does not contain any specific laws relating to franchise agreements, which are therefore subject to the general contractual law. Every usual provision and covenant of a master franchise agreement will normally be permitted provided that it is not against the law, i.e. the freedom of the parties to contract and to engage in a lawful business is respected.

Since there is no legislation specific to franchising and the practice of this type of contract only has a recent history in Portugal, no jurisprudence exists and only a few comments by legal commentators are available. Therefore, experience in other countries, together with the domestic law, jurisprudence and comments upon matters relevant to the franchise agreement (for instance, about the law of contract in general, competition law, intellectual property, etc.), have to be borne in mind. Since they do not infringe Portuguese law, franchise agreements commonly used by international franchise companies are fully accepted.

A final word about the contractual franchise relationship in case of bankruptcy of the franchisee: Portuguese law allows the franchisor to terminate the contract for fair cause if the franchisee is bankrupt, and the franchisor is not bound to deal with the trustee in bankruptcy of the franchisee.

### Antitrust considerations
Portuguese antitrust law currently in force dates back to 1983 and is contained in two main separate statutes, which are Decree-law no. 422/83, dated 3 December 1983 and the more recent Decree-law no. 428/88, dated 19 November 1988. These laws are not so stringent as those which are in force in other countries, such as the USA. Generally, Portuguese antitrust law is rather early in its development.

Decree-law no. 422/83 considers the following as restrictive trade practices:

Price fixing

Price recommendations

Discriminatory prices and sale conditions

Refusal to supply

There are a certain number of requirements to be considered in each case as follows:

Price fixing is forbidden for goods and services. Consequently, minimum price fixing is not allowed except by operation of law, e.g. with respect to various printed materials or whenever the government exempts some goods or services, as can be the case with luxury products or where there is a patent conferring exclusivity.

Price recommendations are not prohibited, except in the following circumstances:

(a) Where they are practised on an individual basis by an enterprise which has a dominant position in the market concerned.

(b) If the recommended price is generally followed by dealers in a way that effectively makes the price uniform in the market. When the market is not considered to be competitive enough, price recommendations may be considered as unlawful.

(c) If the price recommendation results from an agreement between enterprises or association of enterprises.

(d) A price recommendation might be forbidden even if it is within the scope of an EC Block Exemption Regulation as the Cartel Authority (Conselho da Concorrência) has held that EC antitrust law only prevails over the domestic law where trade between member states is significantly affected by any practice. Where the fair competition and free trade between the member states is not involved the domestic law is applied.

Discriminatory practices as to prices and sale conditions are *inter alia* those applying different terms for satisfying an order and different kinds of packaging delivery, transport and payment where they are not justified by the

differences in cost of supply. Every producer, importer, distributor an
other supplier is obliged to produce price lists by reference to sale condition
and to disclose them to the dealer and or end user if requested by them.

4    Refusal to supply.

There may be individual or concerted practices wherein there is a dominant posi
tion which in an uncompetitive market prevents, restrains or distorts fair com
petition. There is deemed to be a dominating position where:

1    An enterprise holds a share equal to or higher than 30% of the domesti
     market and does not suffer any significant competition.

2    Two or more enterprises do not have significant competition between then
     or where there is no significant competition from third parties where the
     hold a share equal or higher than 50% (if there are not more than thre
     enterprises) or 65% (if there are not more than five enterprises) of th
     domestic market.

Decree-law no. 428/88 has implemented the system of prior notification o
any intended merger or concentration of enterprises whenever one of the follow
ing circumstances exists:

1    The annual sales volume resulting from the merger or concentration will b
     equal to or higher than 5000 million escudos.

2    The market share for the product concerned will equal or be higher than
     20% of the market as a result of the merger or concentration (or 5% of th
     EC market).

3    The merger or concentration of the enterprises will modify substantially th
     competitive framework.

It is assumed that there is always a concentration of enterprises in the case of
merger or concentration of two or more companies or if an enterprise obtain
significant influence over other enterprises, as can be the case with a group o
companies. It is necessary for proposed mergers or concentrations to be notifiec
to the Minister of Commerce, or they will be null and void.

Agreements giving effect to restrictive trade practices are null and void anc
parties to those which are in violation of the law are subject to fines.

There is no system of notification of agreements.

The Cartel Authority (Conselho da Concorrência) is entitled to judge in th
first instance any claim that there is a restrictive trade practice and to declarc
specific agreements or practices as lawful or unlawful which have been submittec
to it by the government or any enterprise or interested party.

## Restraint of trade

The basic rule is that a provision concerning a restraint of trade is lawful whenever it is not against the principle of good faith (bona fide) and does not represent an unreasonable violation of the principle of freedom of trade. The positions of franchisor and franchisee as well as of employer and employee are considered.

Restraints of trade can be imposed either during the performance of the agreement concerned (franchise or employment) or after their termination (*post pactum finitum*). As for the relations between the franchisor and the franchisee, there is no legal obstacle to imposing a requirement that the franchisee should carry on no other business than the franchise. Covenants imposing post-termination restraints against conducting a similar business are not expressly provided for in the law. In the writer's opinion, such covenants are valid and enforceable in principle if confined to what is stringently required to protect the know-how or other essential interests of the franchisor's business. Therefore, a prohibition against conducting the same business is only valid to the extent necessary to protect such know-how and essential interests and for a limited period of time which must be reasonable. A similar regime is found in relation to the performance by an employee of an employment contract. However, in this case there is a specific provision contained in Article 36 of the basic law of the employment contract approved by the Decree-law no. 49408. In principle, such covenants are void unless for a maximum period of three years after the termination of the contract and provided that there is potential damage to the employer arising out of the performance by the employee of a competing activity and provided that compensation is paid to the employee for the acceptance of such limitation.

Penalty clauses may be agreed to reinforce the effectiveness of the restraints with pre-fixed amounts of compensation.

There is no rule of law limiting the length of the term during which a tied sale of products from franchisor to franchisee may be permitted. The rules concerning the *doctrine of good faith* are dominant in this matter. According to such rules the contract may create a long-term binding tie but not a perpetual one. What should be the length of the *long-term link* is not defined at law and only very serious reasons affecting the freedom of the parties may be a sufficient ground to terminate a legally binding contract, especially in the case of a franchise which subjects the franchisee to an exclusive activity in performing the agreement.

## Liability of franchisor

As there is no franchise legislation in Portugal the general principles on civil liability laid down in the Civil Code are applied both so far as liability in contract and liability in tort are concerned.

The areas where liability for damages can be considered concern the relations between the franchisor and the franchisee, on the one hand, and the franchisee and/or the franchisor *vis-à-vis* third parties on the other hand.

Both parties to an agreement are obliged to observe the following rule as to performance provided for in Article 762 of the Civil Code:

> In fulfilling obligations as well as in exercising the correspondent rights, both parties are bound to act in accordance with principles of the *good faith*.

The same doctrine is applied to precontract negotiations even after termination of the contract. Good faith has two features which are both integrated into the rule of law: firstly, honesty of intention, the absence of malice and the absence of design to defraud or to seek an unconscionable advantage; and secondly, the duty to supply to the other party all information and co-operation which is needed for the performance of the agreement and discharge of the obligations by and of the other party. Of course, that rule of *good faith* is applicable beyond the *prima facie* obligation of both parties to fulfil the express or implied duties they have agreed.

Apart from the termination of the contract for cause, any contract may be declared null and void by reason of an *error in fact* under very limited conditions and also may be compulsorily revised or terminated in the event of a serious and abnormal change of the circumstances upon which the agreement has been based and entered into in such a manner:

1   That the demanding of the fulfilment of the contract by one party against the other party is not in accordance with the principles of *good faith*; and

2   Such demand is not covered by the provisions of the contract.

It should be said that, in practice, cases involving annulment or revision/termination of the contract are very seldom used and limited to very few cases.

As far as liability *vis-à-vis* third parties is concerned, Portugal has already implemented the EC Council Directive of 25 July 1985 on liability for defective products. These are the basic provisions of Portuguese law in this respect:

1   The producer is liable under the law for the defective product even where there is no negligence (indirect legal liability or vicarious liability).

2   The producer shall not be liable if he proves (a) that he did not put the product into circulation, (b) the defect did not exist at the time when the product was put into circulation by him, (c) the product was neither manufactured by him for sale or any form of distribution for economic purpose nor manufactured or distributed by him in the course of his business (d) the defect is due to compliance of the product with mandatory regulations issued by the public authorities, (e) the scientific and technical knowledge at the time when he put the product into circulation was not such as to enable the existence of the defect to be discovered, (f) in the case of a manufacturer of a component, that the defect is not attributable to the design of the product in

which the component has been fitted or to instructions given by the manufacturer of the product.

Joint and several liability where two or more persons are liable.

Relevant damage: personal injury or death as well as damages to property if and to the extent that the loss exceeds 70 000 escudos. No limit of liability.

Limit of liability: 10 000 million escudos, as to the producer's total liability for damage resulting from a death or personal injury and caused by identical items with the same defect (see Article 16(1) of the EC directive on Product Liability of 25 July 1985).

Contractual limitation of liability is forbidden.

Time limit for making a claim is three years from the date the plaintiff becomes aware or should reasonably have become aware of the damage, the defect and the identity of the producer.

The rights conferred upon the injured person shall be extinguished upon the expiration of a period of ten years from the date on which the damage was caused, unless the injured person has in the meantime instituted proceedings against the producer.

The Portuguese law which implements the EC Directive does not apply to products put into circulation before the date on which it entered into force (12 November 1989).

Legislation relating to protection of the consumer has also been enacted recently.

Liability can arise from a simple recommendation or advice provided that there is a contractual or legal duty to render the recommendation or advice.

In general, limitation of liability is not permitted, except in the case of liability in contract concerning the damages caused by the representatives, employees or other auxiliary people.

A claim in tort is barred after three years. A claim in contract is barred after 0 years.

## ntellectual property
Trade names, trade or service marks, copyrights, industrial or intellectual property rights are registrable in Portugal. The registration bodies which record such rights are the INPI (Instituição Nacional da Propriedade Industrial) for trade names, service marks and other industrial and intellectual property, and the Conservatoria da Propriedade Literária, Científica e Artística, which is administered by the Sociedade Portuguesa de Autores, a private association, for copyright.

Portugal is a founder member of the International Union for the Protection

of Patents and Trademarks established under the Convention of Paris in 189
and has subscribed to all subsequent revisions. Protection afforded under Portu
guese law is as follows:

1    Patents – 15 years

2    Industrial drawings and models – renewable periods of five years

3    Trade marks and service marks – renewable periods of ten years

4    Business names and emblems – 30 years

Patents and trade marks registered or pending in any of the countries in the
Union have a priority for 12 months and six months, respectively, which is recog
nized on making applications for registration in Portugal.

Portugal has also ratified the 1948 revision in Brussels of the Berne Conven
tion, the 1952 Geneva Convention, and the 1967 Stockholm Convention regu
lating author's rights, which are protected for 50 years following death or, in th
case of foreign publications, such lesser period as may be established in th
country of origin.

The EC Council Regulation no. 3842/86 dated 1 December 1986 concern
ing counterfeit goods is in force in Portugal since it is directly applied as an EC
regulation.

### Real estate and leasing
Portugal recognizes freehold and leasehold interests in land or buildings. A free
hold interest may subsist over the whole land or building or only over a separat
and independent unit integrated into a *condominium* (for instance in an offic
building, shopping centre, mall, etc.). A lease is the most common way to acquir
premises, particularly as Portuguese law provides for substantial protection to th
tenant *vis-à-vis* the landlord.

It is not possible to establish a yearly term for a business lease contrac
('contrato de arrendamento'). It is usual to agree an initial period of time (usuall
6 or 12 months) which is renewable by operation of law except if the tenan
terminates it at the end of any period.

The landlord is entitled to terminate the lease contract only through ar
action instituted in the civil court where he is required to prove and convince th
judge that one or more breaches of the lease contract by the tenant has occurred
Those breaches would involve serious default and include failure to pay ren
which is usually payable monthly.

As far as the acquisition of premises under a lease contract is concerned, i
can be made in one of two ways:

1    By direct negotiation and conclusion of a lease contract ('contrato de
     arrendamento') with the landlord

By a 'contrato de trespasse', i.e. the acquisition of the tenant's rights together with the assets, goodwill, etc. forming part of the premises or establishment where the business is conducted

ne landlord has no right to oppose the 'contrato de trespasse' because the free ssignment of the lease contract is afforded by law to businesses so that the cation where the business is developed and to which goodwill attaches can freely  sold to a third party. An important exception should be made, however, amely that the execution of a 'contrato de trespasse' must be notified to the ndlord within 15 days after the applicable notarial deed has been executed. therwise the transmission of the new tenant's right as to the leasehold may be pposed by the landlord and the latter will be entitled to demand the termination  the lease contract based on the transmission of the leased premises to an authorized third party. It should also be noted that the landlord has a pre- nption right to acquire the location, the establishment and the goodwill in case  a 'contrato de trespasse'. However, the landlord would not have the right to quire the goodwill where the tenant is a franchisee since in such a case the anchisor owns the goodwill, over which the tenant/franchisee has no right of sposition.

Another way to transfer the possession of a leasehold interest, but only mporarily, is the so-called 'contrato de cessão de exploração', i.e. an agree- ent which transfers only the exploitation of an establishment (consisting of the sets, goods, goodwill, usually the employment contracts relating to the respec- ve employees, rights and obligations vis-à-vis third parties, etc.). However, this ntract is only efficaceous vis-à-vis the landlord if he has authorized the transfer  possession of the leasehold interest. If such transfer is made without the land- rd's consent, the landlord may apply to the court to terminate the lease contract.

The 'contrato de cessão de exploração' is distinguished from the 'contrato  trespasse' not because of the legal impossibility of the landlord's opposition, hose consent for the transmission of the leasehold interest is not required, but so because the title of the establishment (i.e. the business unit represented by sets, goods, goodwill, credits and liabilities, etc.). is transmitted to the pur- aser in the case of 'trespasse'. In the 'contrato de cessão de exploração' such tablishment is only temporarily leased to the third party on a basis which does ot involve any transfer of title.

Finally, the law provides for an annual increase of rent which entitles the ndlord, through a written notice, to demand from the tenant, one year after the st increase, an updated rent in accordance with the percentage established by e government every year which takes into account the inflation rate. During the st few years the annual average increase of rents has been approximately 7%.

## oreigners working or establishing a business in Portugal

**Vork permits** Foreigners in Portugal benefit from practically the same rights as ortuguese citizens except for political rights and, in general, the rights within the

Constitution of the Portuguese Republic reserved for nationals. Foreign citizei are allowed free access into Portugal. Exceptions apply to those who have r means of subsistence or who have no entry visas (in cases where these are nece sary) or to those who come from foreign countries which do not have diplomat relations with Portugal. Since Portugal joined the EC a differentiation has bee made between EC nationals and others with regard to residence and work pe mits. Special mention should be also made of the fact that Brazilian nationa have a right to apply for Portuguese nationality and to maintain dual nationalit As a general rule, foreigners who do not intend to reside in Portugal can stay fe three months, whether or not they need a visa for entry. If their stay is for longe than three months they are obliged to obtain a residence permit.

***Non-EC nationals*** Foreigners who are not EC nationals wishing to take up res dence in Portugal must apply to the Serviço de Estrangeiros (Immigration Offic either when in Portugal or while still abroad. In the latter case, it is more cor venient to make applications through the local Portuguese consular office. Res dence permits depend on the activity proposed to be exercised in Portugal or o retirement, or similar. If carrying out a professional activity, the registration contracts signed with a local registered company must be made at the Ministry Labour, and only after this procedure is completed can permission for work and residence permit be issued. This rule is not applicable to liberal professions.

EC residents benefit from special rules, namely the guarantee that their res dence permit will not be cancelled and that they have freedom of movement in E( countries in the circumstances provided for in the EC legislation (see Articles 4 and 56 of the EC Treaty).

***Right of establishment*** The right of establishment is one of the fundamenta rights set forth in the EC legislation and it can be exercised either through th establishment of a one-person business or through the setting up of a Portugues company.

We have considered work permits; now we shall consider the establishmen takeover or merger with an existing business or self-employment.

The concept of 'foreign investment' should be borne in mind in considerin these matters. Foreign investment is the term given to operations which ar carried out in order to create stable and long-lasting economic ties with an estab lished enterprise (or one which is being established) in Portugal, thus gaining direct or indirect control over it. Investors can be either foreign individuals o companies or Portuguese residents who are considered by the authorities to b economically linked to foreigners. The following operations are considered a foreign investments when they are made by these classes of investors:

1    Setting up or expansion of branches and subsidiaries

2    Total or partial takeover of pre-existing enterprises registered in Portugal

Acquisition of share capital and the holding of shares in companies or groups of companies either already existing or being set up in Portugal

Drawing up or amending consortia contracts (contratos de consórcio) or widening the scope of joint venture contracts (contratos de associação em participação and others)

Total or partial acquisition of premises located in Portugal

Loans to, or other indirect holdings in the share capital of, a company

Acquisition of real estate located in Portugal which is directly connected with some of the above-specified operations

'oreign investment can be effected *inter alia* by transfer of funds from abroad, by mporting equipment, by utilizing credits and other funds in Portugal belonging o the foreign investor, by transfer of technology, etc.

Repatriation of capital proceeds of the investment and export of profits are ;uaranteed by law.

Foreign investment operations can be carried out either by direct foreign nvestment (IDE) or by an investment contract. In the case of IDE a prior leclaration must be made through a Portuguese resident (usually a lawyer) to the egulatory authority, the Institute of External Commerce of Portugal (hereafter eferred to as ICEP), which must include identification data and features of the iroject to be carried out in Portugal. The investments of particular interest are lealt with in an investment contract and they are those which create a large iumber of jobs or require a deeper study because of their importance and com-ilexity. Also of great interest are the investments which involve negotiations rela-ive to special tax incentives and easier access to internal credit facilities and the ike. The investment contract is negotiated with the ICEP and with other authori-ies and signed by the ICEP and the investor.

In the case of an IDE, the ICEP has two months to take a final decision about he investment project and the right of establishment. If no decision is reached vithin this period it is regarded as being tacitly approved and it is the duty of the nvestor to put his project immediately into effect. Upon the request of the nvestor and at his own risk, the ICEP can authorize interim activities to take ilace within the two-month notice period, if these be urgent and not capable of iostponement.

Investment projects can be rejected in the following cases:

I   If it is considered that the type of activity in Portugal is linked to the public authority.

!   If they affect public order, security or health.

3     If they are related to the production and selling of arms, ammunition or any weapons of war.

4     If they violate mandatory provisions.

Two principles apply in Portugal today. One is the principle of freedom of establishment by EC or non-EC residents, and the other is the principle of equality amongst them and between them and national investors. In the meantime investment projects presented by non-EC residents can at first be subject to evaluation and possible later negotiation, depending on the effect they have on the country's economy. This means that the ICEP can, at its discretion, decide against giving approval, if the project does not accord with the national interest.

On the other hand, investment projects presented by EC residents will always be approved because of the EC regulations. Exceptions to this rule are mainly those mentioned above. The principle of non-discrimination between investors applies, and the EC residents cannot be treated less favourably than residents of Portugal or non EC-residents.

Foreign investors have the right to transfer out of the country dividends, proceeds of investment and any other amount accrued from the investment.

The investment contract will be examined with special attention given to the following aspects:

1     Technical, economic and financial feasibility

2     The possibility of the investment being considered of greater interest for regional development and for the modernization of technology

3     Prediction of positive exchange rate effects, high added values and creation of jobs

4     Significant financial provision of capital belonging to the investor

5     High level of technology and good personnel training programmes

Special financial and tax incentives can be included in these investment contracts.

Transfer of shares, or contracts, or the assignment of rights concerning foreign investments (which have already been authorized and registered in Portugal) between non-residents is similarly subject to the regime of prior declaration and registration at the ICEP. Exceptions are:

1     Subscription or acquisition (on the stock exchange) of shares in Portuguese companies; the holding of the non-resident in the company's share capital should (as a result of that operation) remain no higher than 20% of the relevant share capital.

2     Transfers amongst investors who are EC residents.

The exceptions indicated in 1 and 2 do not need prior declaration to the ICEP but must be registered in the Company or in the Trade Registry within 30 days from completion.

Purchase and sale of shares of national companies by EC residents is free of control, if they are not classified as cases of foreign investment as defined above. The nature of the purchases must, however, be previously verified or checked in accordance with exchange control regulations by the Banco de Portugal (central bank). These operations are not, however, free of control for non-EC residents, who must have previous permission from the Banco de Portugal.

As for operations which fall into the category of foreign investment, the following should be noted:

Certain activities are unrestricted, and only depend upon the submission of a report to the Banco de Portugal, provided that they are carried out between EC residents and Portuguese residents:

(a)  real estate acquisitions which should not be integrated in foreign investment projects and not be intended to be sold for the purposes of accommodation, or for agricultural exploitation, or actual agricultural land, when previous permission must be obtained from the central bank

(b)  movements of capital for personal purposes, but subject to certain restrictions

(c)  payments in connection with the international supply of goods and services

(d)  direct guarantees, suretyships and other securities given by residents for financial credits or other commercial transactions

(e)  transfers concerning insurance contracts (premiums, indemnities, etc.)

(f)  indemnities for loss, damage or expenses

(g)  reimbursements for cancellation of contract or overdue payments

(h)  assignments and transfers of industrial property rights

(i)  operations concerning acquisition of shares and other securities

2     Acts or contracts which lead to activities of a nature referred to in 1, between non-EC residents and Portuguese residents, are restricted and dependent upon previous authorization from the Banco de Portugal.

3    Borrowing and lending through resident financing companies, and loans
     from residents in Portugal to non-residents and vice versa, require the
     consent of the Banco de Portugal.

4    Residents are not free to open bank accounts abroad. Any current account
     settlements with non-residents and settlement by way of inter-group clear-
     ings also require consent.

The time necessary for obtaining the Banco de Portugal's consent (via a commercial bank based in Portugal) in all cases referred to in 2, 3 and 4 above varies, but
as a rule it should not take more than 20 days, and could be less in urgent cases.
These restrictions will end or be reduced significantly by 1993.

### Employment law

Labour law in Portugal is based upon the principles of protection of the worker, in
regard to termination of the employment contract, although without affecting the
regular development of the employer's business whenever, for disciplinary reasons or due to economic or technical circumstances, it is necessary to dismiss
workers.

Therefore, except in certain cases, it is not possible to dismiss a worker
who is under contract for an indefinite term, unless there are fair reasons for
doing so, including the employee's failure to adapt to the job.

*Formalities*  No formalities are required in the case of a contract for an indefinite
term. It can be made in writing, or verbally, or by combination of these. A fixed-
term employment contract (a contract which terminates at the end of an agreed
period or at the end of an agreed time extension) must always be a written agreement. In the absence of a written agreement an indefinite-term contract is
regarded as existing. A contract is required to be set out in writing only where the
work is of an especially complex nature or where a fixed term of employment is
agreed.

*Legal requirements for employment contracts*  In addition, it should be noted that
the rights and duties of the contracting parties are the same for indefinite-term
and fixed-term work as for part-time work.

*Probationary period*  The law provides a period of 60 days as a trial period within
which either the employer or the employee can terminate the contract without
either a period of notice or a fair reason for dismissal. Where it is difficult to assess
the aptitude of the employee within 60 days owing to the complexity of the job or
the high degree of responsibility involved, a longer probationary period may be
agreed, either through a collective agreement or by written agreement of the
parties, but the limit for such an assignment is six months.

***Minimum statutory salary*** There is a minimum national monthly salary. Because of the traditional low level of salaries in Portugal it has become the practice to pay additional remuneration in the form of Christmas and holiday allowances (each, as a rule, equal to one month's normal wage), allowances for work in revolving shifts, length of service premiums and productivity premiums. The Christmas and holiday allowances are obligatory and are paid to most of the working population; other additional payments are optional and only some are set out in collective agreements.

***Different levels of fixed remuneration*** As far as salaries are concerned, there are many different arrangements: fixed salaries, variable salaries (depending on the productivity of the employee) or a mixture of both. Completely variable salaries, without a fixed basic sum, do not exist in practice. The employer and the employee are forbidden to come to any agreement by which the employer is to pay taxed and other legal charges which are strictly due from the employee.

***Social security*** The social contributions (payroll) are: employer, 24.5%; employee, 11%. Both are calculated on all remunerations and allowances paid by the employer. All employees as well as the members of the managing board are obliged to pay their contributions towards social security. Foreigners, however, who are temporarily working for a branch or subsidiary in Portugal, so long as they prove that in their country of origin they are subject to obligatory payments, do not need to make a contribution. However, they can opt to be covered by both social security regimes.

***Holiday allowance*** According to the present law, payment of a thirteenth and fourteenth month is obligatory (as mentioned above – Christmas and holiday allowances). These biannual additional salary payments are calculated on the basic salary, which does not include any additional remuneration or other payments based on uncertain factors (e.g. volume of sales in case of a salesman or productivity).

***Time limits of work – collective agreements*** Collective agreements set out the maximum work time per week for each sector of economic activity. It can be said that, on average, the maximum weekly total for industry is between 40 and 42 hours, and for administrative personnel 37.5 hours.

***Overtime*** The law only authorizes overtime in the case of increased workload, emergency or in exceptional cases. Overtime is paid at a minimum hourly rate of 1.5 times salary for the first hour and 1.25 times salary for each subsequent hour. Work done at weekends or on holidays has a special rate of remuneration (depending on each collective agreement, but is normally equal to a rate of double the salary per day) as well as conferring the right to a rest day on another working day.

*Illness* If the employee is ill he has no right to receive salary from the employer for the days he is ill since he will benefit from social security. His social security entitlement is to receive 60% of his salary after the third day of illness. Some collective agreements lay down, however, that the employer is obliged to pay the difference between the 60% payment from the social security and the total salary for a certain limited period.

## Termination
### Individual dismissal

Contracts made for an indefinite term cannot be terminated by the employer even when notice is given to the employee. The employer can only terminate the contract by means of a written disciplinary procedure proving that there exists 'fair reason' for the dismissal. The legal definition of 'fair reason' for the dismissal is: a fault on the part of the employee which, owing to its seriousness, impedes the continuation of work because it breaks the links of trust. The employer must send a written 'note of blame' (nota de culpa) to the employee, and the latter may answer it in writing within a certain predetermined time (at least five working days). If the employer sacks the employee without having carried out the disciplinary procedure and 'hearing' the employee in writing, or before the employee has presented his statement of defence in writing, or in case of an unfair dismissal, the dismissal is considered null and void. As a result the employee has the right to receive all the salary that he would receive in normal circumstances and to ask for reinstatement in the enterprise. Alternatively, he may prefer compensation for his dismissal which is a minimum of one month's salary for every year that he has worked for the employer. The employee has also the right to apply to the industrial court (within five days from dismissal date) for interim relief.

Reasons that are considered fair reasons for dismissal are laid down in the statute (including, amongst others, misconduct for disobeying orders, non-co-operation, drunkenness, violence and swearing, dishonesty and other offences, incompetence, lack of qualifications, poor time-keeping, abnormal reduction of the worker's productivity, the abolition of the work post by reason of economic or technological factors, etc.).

Contracts for a period of six months or less can be agreed if the nature of the work is considered temporary, i.e. special and transitional work, such as a seasonal job, the launch of a new business activity with an uncertain duration, etc. A fixed-term contract can be successively renewed for equal periods of time (as a rule every six months) up to a maximum of three years from the starting date.

Such a contract can be terminated as long as the employee is given at least eight days' written notice by the employer that his contract is no longer to be renewed. Any employment contract, other than a fixed-term contract, can be terminated at any time by agreement between the employer and the employee. Contracts can also be terminated when it becomes definitely and absolutely impossible for the employment to continue (because of unforeseeable reasons such as *force majeure*, winding-up of the company, bankruptcy, etc.) or for the employee to attend (for instance owing to an incurable illness) or for the employer to re-admit him. However, the employee can always and freely terminate an indefinite-term contract by giving two months' notice (or one month if the contract is less than two years old).

In the case of a fixed-term employment contract, the employee can end the contract under the same conditions as the employer, that is, up to eight days before the end of the initial term or any extension. If neither party gives such notice, then the contract is automatically renewed for the same term, and if it goes over the agreed periods, the contract automatically becomes a contract for an indefinite term.

### Redundancy and lay-off

The law permits some or all workers to be made redundant through a process of negotiation with the works council of the company or other workers' representatives with the assistance of the Ministry of Labour. This can be due to the closing down of the company, or the closing down of one or a number of its production or service departments, because of the need to reduce staff for structural, technical or market reasons or for a mixture of these. Compensation corresponding to one month per year worked, with a minimum of three months, is due to each dismissed worker.

Lay-offs are also provided for in Portuguese law. These have more or less the same procedure as redundancy. Lay-offs must be backed by market reasons, by economic or technical reasons or by other occurrences seriously affecting the normal activity of the company. A lay-off may consist of a temporary suspension of work or of the interruption of work for one or more normal work shifts or in reduction of the normal number of working hours.

## TAX CONSIDERATIONS

### Corporation tax

The 'Imposto sobre o Rendimento de Pessoas Colectivas' (IRC) is the corporate income tax which is due in respect of each fiscal year which coincides, in general, with the calendar year. However, branches of a non-resident company may have a different fiscal year.

*Collective entities subject to tax and computation of profits* Companies, co-operatives and other collective entities with their head office or effective management control in Portuguese territory and whose principal activity is of a commercial, industrial or agricultural nature.

*Taxable profit/taxable income* These entities are obliged to keep proper accounts and the taxable profit is the net profit of the trading year adjusted as provided for in the law. The taxable income which is actually subject to taxation is determined by deducting from taxable profit the fiscal losses during the previous five years and the available fiscal benefits.

*Business profits* The following are *inter alia* considered as business profits: profits arising from sales of goods or services; discounts and commissions; financial profits such as interest, dividends, discounts, profits on foreign exchange, etc.; profits deriving from real estate or industrial rights, value added, etc.

*Business expenses* The following are *inter alia* considered as business expenses since they are considered by the tax authorities as necessary to produce the taxable profits or to maintain the producing source: expenses incurred in production or acquisition of any goods or services such as raw materials, labour, energy and other general expenses of manufacture, maintenance and repairs; expenses incurred in distribution and sale; expenses incurred in collecting debts; costs relating to rationalization of production, research and consultancy; tax and social security contributions; depreciation and amortization provisions; indemnities; travel; entertainment and similar expenses are accepted provided that they are reasonable.

*Depreciation and amortization* The law provides a complex regime for calculating the depreciation and amortization of tangible assets. Depreciation is accepted as a deduction and the straight-line method should in principle be followed. Rates of depreciation and amortization of different assets are fixed by law, and only in exceptional circumstances (as a tax benefit investment) can they be accelerated.

*Provisions, elimination of double taxation and deduction of losses* Provisions can be made for the following items: bad debts, devaluation of merchandise in stock, legal fees concerning pending claims and some others. Ninety-five per cent of dividends received from an entity with its head office or effective management control in Portugal is deducted in order to *eliminate double taxation* and only the remaining 5% is treated as a taxable profit, provided the taxpayer holds at least 25% of the share capital of that entity and has been its shareholder for two consecutive years or from the date of setting up of the entity and remains a shareholder for two consecutive years.

*Deduction of losses* Losses relating to a specific trade year may be carried forward for five years. There is no carry back.

Collective entities with their head office or effective management control in Portuguese territory and which do not exercise, as a principal function, an activity of a commercial, industrial or agricultural nature.

These entities are not obliged to keep proper accounts unless they also exercise a commercial, industrial or agricultural activity as a secondary function. Their revenues should, however, be duly recorded as well as expenses and investments. Taxable income is calculated on the net total revenue.

A permanent establishment (the branch) in Portuguese territory which has
the aim of exercising a commercial, industrial or agricultural activity of an entity
that does not have its head office or effective management control in Portugal.

The branch is considered as such for these purposes provided that employees
or other staff have an activity, continuous or not, for more than 120 days a year.
They are obliged to keep accounts and the taxable profits and taxable income are
computed in accordance with the same rules as set forth above for trading entities
based in Portugal.

Companies and other entities which do not have their head office or effective
management control in Portuguese territory and which have revenues not attrib-
table to a permanent establishment.

A specific regime for these non-resident entities is provided in the law. They
have occasional or regular activity in Portugal, but not on an established or
resident basis. Consequently, they must appoint a representative in Portugal and
are subject, in general, to the same fiscal procedures as explained above *mutatis
mutandis*.

*Groups of companies*  The holding company may apply to the Minister of Finance
for authorization for the taxable profits to be assessed for all the companies of the
group by consolidation of their balance sheets and profit and loss accounts.

*Special situations*  The Economic European Interest Grouping and the similar
domestic organization Agrupamento Complementar de Empresas are subject to
the so-called regime of 'transparência fiscal' (fiscal transparency). Their main
activity is not included in those agreements whereby the 'group' has been set up;
for these reasons the profits and losses are attributed to the participating parties
and not to an organizational entity.

*Rates of tax*  The rate of IRC is 36.5%[7] except in the following cases: the taxable
income of a non-resident entity, which is not attributable to a permanent establishment (branch), is subject to a rate of 25%, except profits arising from:

Copyrights; royalties and revenues derived from the use of equipment,[8,9]
15%

Remuneration of directors and other revenues resulting from the application
of capital, 20%

In the case of the non-trading entities based in Portugal mentioned above, the
rate is 20%.

**Dividend payments**
Dividends are subject to income tax and form part of the total revenue the taxpayer receives in each fiscal year. Attention is drawn to the different rates of the

tax as explained above, depending on whether the taxpayer is or is not resident i
Portugal. Attention is also drawn to the elimination of double tax, which is als
referred to above.

## Indirect taxation

Of all indirect taxes, IVA (Imposto sobre o Valor Acrescentado), i.e. the valu
added tax (VAT) is the most significant. It closely follows the sixth EC Directiv
and is charged on the transfer of assets and on services rendered. The standar
rate is 17%; there is a reduced rate of 8% for certain food products, transpor
electricity supply, restaurants, hotels, lawyers fees, etc. and a higher rate of 30%
for certain luxury products.

Customs and excise duties are levied on the value of goods at the time c
entry into Portugal or the EC. The rates of duty vary depending on the good
imported and the country from which they are imported. Portugal is entitled t
apply customs duties in relation to EC origin goods at an annual regressive rate a
from 1986 up to January 1993, although the rates are not, in general, ver
significant.

Stamp duty is also an indirect tax which covers a large range of contracts an
is payable when they are executed.

## Individual income tax

The IRS (Imposto sobre o Rendimento das Pessoas Singulares) is applied to a
individuals residing in Portuguese territory and to those, although not residen
there, who have obtained taxable income in Portuguese territory. The earnings c
a family subject to IRS are treated as one taxable income only, and the taxpayer i
the head of the family. Residents in Portuguese territory are those who hav
stayed longer than 183 days or, if for a lesser time, have a regular place of habita
tion in Portuguese territory on 31 December in the relevant year.

According to the OECD model followed in the bilateral double-taxatio
treaties to which Portugal is a signatory, earnings from employment are taxed i
the country of residence, or in the country of origin of the revenue if the taxpaye
has a permanent establishment there. If he is employed, the earnings are taxed i
the country where the work is carried out. However, if the employee is resident i
the country of the other state party to the treaty and does not stay for more tha
183 days of the fiscal year in the country of origin of the revenue, or if the paymen
of wages comes from an employer who is not resident in the country of the origi
of the revenue, then the country of residence of the taxpayer is the one which sha
charge the tax.

The IRS is applied to the income arising from employment contracts, libera
professions and others. This kind of income includes salaries and all earning
resulting from an employment contract either with a private or with a govern
ment employer. Therefore, salaries, subsidies, participations, commissions
premiums, percentages, travelling and representation allowances, company cars
school fees, home leave allowances, etc. are all considered as income.

Remuneration earned by company directors or other company officials, their travelling and representation allowances, etc. are also deemed as income.

Within limits provided for by law, certain subsidies from the social security, and travel expenses that are duly justified, are not usually taxed.

Average rates of tax range from 16% to 29.15%.

## Social security payments

Social security provides old-age (retirement) and invalidity pensions, medical and medicinal benefits, unemployment benefit, maternity and death benefits to all payers, all pensions for widowed spouses, etc. Both employers and employees are subject to payroll taxes ('seguirança social', i.e. social security) calculated according to salaries – the so-called 'taxa social única'. Payroll taxes (as well as IRS) are deducted at source by the employer who is responsible for them and for related interest and fines in the event of a claim by the authorities.

The 'taxa social única' is paid at 11% by the employees and at 24.5% by the employer and it is charged upon salaries and almost all other kinds of remuneration received by the employee and paid by the employer. To the percentage paid by the employer must be added another 0.5% on the total payments to employees which goes towards a professional sickness fund.

Not only do employees have to pay this tax, but so do independent self-employed people, professionals, and sole traders, in accordance with certain conditions, as well as directors and managers of any corporations or companies.

Foreigners working temporarily in Portugal are not obliged to pay this payroll deduction if they can prove that they are only temporarily in Portugal and that they pay social security contributions in their country of origin. However, they can opt to make contributions to both social security regimes. Complementary pension schemes and pension funds are also available.

## Tax incentives, financial aids and internal credit access

Portuguese law provides a set of tax incentives and financial aids which either are already laid down in the statutes or may be negotiated with the authorities for larger investments in the country. Internal credit access is free for the resident companies and individuals.

*Notes*

1  There are also other forms of business activity ('sociedade em nome colectivo', equivalent to the partnership, and 'sociedade em comandita', equivalent to the limited partnership). However, they have disadvantages for the business since the partners are personally liable on a joint and several basis for the liabilities of the partnership.

2  Equivalent to private limited company and 'Gesellschaft mit Beschrankter Haftung (GmbH)'.

3  Equivalent to public limited company, or stock corporation, or the 'Aktiengesellschaft' and the 'société anonyme'.

4  Below are the figures corresponding to the different types of companies in Portugal in the year of 1985:

    (a)  sociedades anónimas,                                              3 331

    (b)  sociedades por quotas,                                        128 827

    (c)  sociedades em comandita,                                     7

    (d)  sociedades em nome colectivo,                              1 025

5    A 'sociedade anónima' may also be set up with the participation of four shareholders who hold one share each only and a fifth shareholder holding all the remaining share capital.

6    The company acquires legal personality with the completion of registration only. In order to save time and avoid delays in the commencement of business the law allows the provisional registration to be done before the execution of the notarial deed and, therefore, before the presentation of the application for the definitive registration. Under the circumstances, the legal setting up is related back to the provisional registration date.

7    A municipal surcharge, the so-called 'derrama', should be added, whose rates are not the same for all municipalities. For Lisbon it is 10% of the IRC (i.e. an effective rate up to 3.65%, which makes a total of 40.15%).

8    The rate applied to residents for Portugal for these kinds of revenue is 16%.

9    See also double-taxation treaties on this matter.

# CHAPTER 15
# SPAIN

*Gonzalo de Ulloa*

## AN OVERVIEW OF FRANCHISING IN SPAIN

There is no specific regulation related to franchising in Spain, since this contract form was nearly unknown in Spain until the 1970s–1980s. Before this, there were only very exclusive business chains which sold cosmetic products on a non-exclusive distribution basis.

Since 1980 franchising has developed considerably in Spain, principally in the clothes, fast food, pottery and crystal objects and perfumes markets. There are still very important fields, however, where franchising distribution systems remain hardly exploited, as in the financial services area.

On the other hand, several businesses, such as Spanish hotels, are already exploiting external franchising, with the support of the new regulation concerning franchising recently passed by the Spanish Parliament. There is still no specific franchising regulation and, generally speaking, the franchising contract is based on the provisions of the Civil Code relating to the conclusion of agreements, and in particular on Article 1255, which provides autonomy to the contracting parties as regards the content of the agreement. More recently, longer and more detailed franchising agreements, following the model of typical American franchising agreements, are being considered by large Spanish firms.

For franchising, the following legislation has to be taken into account, depending on the juridical nature of the business and of the franchisor as concerns franchising contracts in Spain:

1    Law 26/1984 of 19 July, relating to the defence of consumers and users

2    Law 32/1988 of 10 November, relating to trade marks

3    Law 11/1986 of 20 March, relating to patents

4    Law 22/1987 of 11 November, relating to intellectual property

5    Law 16/1989 of 17 July, on the defence of competition

6    Regulation 4087/88/EEC of 30 November, relating to the application of
     Article 85 of the Treaty to certain categories of franchising agreements

7    Royal Decree 1750/1987 of 18 December, relating to transfer of technology.
     It is in this Royal Decree where the concept of franchising agreement
     appears for the first time, correctly placed alongside transferable industrial
     property rights.

8    Unfair Competition Law of 10 January 1991

Since the decree of 18 December 1987, franchising agreements in Spain have
begun to acquire the same features as in other Community countries.

## STRUCTURE OF SPANISH VENTURE

### Advantages and disadvantages
Franchising is a form of commercial marketing whereby goods and/or services
are distributed at a retail level under the same trade mark or trade name through
a network of similar, economically independent, outlets. Franchisors generally
furnish initial and continuing training, guidance and other assistance to their
franchisees, thus enabling inexperienced businessmen, who are relatively numerous in Spain, to compete in the market. Many franchisors also provide access to
capital assistance to franchisees with insufficient capital resources of their own,
and, to this extent, franchising helps to eliminate one of the principal causes of
business failure.

Low entry barriers make franchising an attractive method of business
expansion in Spain, where large capital outlays are not required and start-up
costs may quickly be recovered.

The notion that franchisees are totally independent businessmen has been
overemphasized. No businessman is totally independent and free of controls,
since all businesses are subject to controls imposed by government, suppliers,
creditors, and accounting rules. In no other method of doing business are controls more necessary than in franchising. Successful franchising depends upon
the development and maintenance of uniform specifications, standards and
operating procedures in the franchisee's business. These ensure uniform quality
throughout the franchise system.

### Types and formation of business entities
Entities which will usually sign franchising agreements are merchants, defined in
Article 1 of the Commercial Code as:

1    Those with legal capacity to engage in commerce and who habitually dedi-
     cate themselves to the same.

2     Mercantile or industrial companies which are established according to the Commercial Code. The Commercial Code defines a company or corporation contract as one in which two or more persons undertake to put into a common fund money or property for profit-making purposes and which, regardless of its form, will be commercial in nature, provided that it has been established in accordance with the provisions of the Commercial Code. Once the mercantile company has been set up, it will have a legal personality for the purpose of all its acts and agreements.

The capacity to engage in commerce is dependent upon two factors according to Article 4 of the Commercial Code: (a) being of legal age (which is 18 years of age), and (b) having authority to dispose of goods.

By their nature, Spanish companies may be either civil or mercantile. Mercantile companies may be collective, limited partnerships or partnerships based on shares, limited liability companies, or joint stock companies.

Civil and mercantile companies are distinguishable both by their form and by their aims. As to form, a company which is set up by public instrument and which is registered in the Mercantile Registry is a mercantile company. Those which are 'freely established' are civil companies. Mercantile companies are those whose aims are commercial operations, that is, those who carry out a business activity. Civil companies are those which are not dedicated to business and therefore do not enter into franchising agreements.

Among the mercantile entities the Spanish Commercial Code establishes the following.

*Collective entity (general partnership)* According to Article 125 and the following provisions of the Commercial Code, this is the type of enterprise where all the partners, collectively and under a firm name, undertake to participate in the same rights and obligations in proportions which they establish. The creation or constitution of a general partnership is governed by the rules relating to mercantile companies in general. The contract must be executed in a public instrument and the document must be registered in the Mercantile Registry.

The main obligations of the partners can be set out as follows:

1     To contribute completely according to their commitment in the partnership agreement

2     To indemnify damage caused to the firm due to malice, abuse of power or gross negligence on their part

3     To bear losses in the proportion agreed to, or, in the absence thereof, on a pro rata basis to the portion of interest of each partner in the firm

4     Not to compete against the firm

5    Not to remove or deduct from the common assets more than the amount
     assigned to each for personal expenses and drawings

The following are the most important rights of the partners:

1    To participate in the firm's management and to obtain information concern-
     ing the accounts and operations of the firm

2    To participate in the profits, as provided for in the agreement or, if not so
     provided, on a pro rata basis in proportion to the interest of each partner in
     the firm

*Commandite entity (limited partnership)* These are companies established in
accordance with Article 145 and the following provisions of the Commercial
Code in which several parties contribute with a given capital to the common fund,
without involvement in the firm's operations, which are carried out exclusively
by others under a collective name. This type of company may be 'simple' in
nature or it may have shares. In the former case, the capital is formed as for a
collective company. In the latter, the capital is divided into shares. The constitution of limited partnerships is governed by general rules. A public instrument and
the registration in the Mercantile Registry are required.
    The obligations of partners in a limited partnership are essentially the same
as those of the partners of a general partnership:

1    To contribute the capital promised in the agreement (in the case of a part-
     nership by shares, the capital shall be represented by shares and may not
     exceed 50 million pesetas)

2    To indemnify the firm for damages caused by malice, abuse of power, or
     gross negligence on their part

3    To bear the losses, although each partner's liability is limited to the funds he
     or she contributed to the firm

There is no obligation not to compete with the company, since the partners are
not involved in its management.
    Each partner in a limited partnership enjoys the following rights:

1    To be informed as to the running of the firm's business

2    To participate in the profits in the manner provided for, and, failing that, on
     a pro rata basis, in proportion to his interest or the shares held in the firm

3    In a limited partnership by shares, the partner may transfer title, without

requiring the consent of the remaining partners, since the shares are negotiable instruments

*Limited liability company* This is a commercial company with capital stock divided into 'participations' of equal value. Participations are much like the shares of a joint stock company, but there are no certificates and they are not transferable on the stock exchange. It operates under a company business name.

The personal elements of the company are members or partners, and cannot exceed 50. The law describes managing members as being those who are charged with establishing the company. In respect of their actions, it must be said that the validity of contracts executed on behalf of the company prior to its inscription in the Mercantile Registry is dependent upon their being 'ratified' by the company within three months of its official constitution.

Appointment of directors must be set out in the incorporation documents. Appointment becomes effective from the moment it is accepted. Details of the appointment must be filed for registration in the Mercantile Registry, within ten days following acceptance. The name, age, address and nationality of each director must be stated.

Directors represent the company in all matters relating to its business or trade and their acts and agreements bind the company. They may not work on their own account or on account of another in the same type of business as that conducted by the company.

The directors are liable to the company for damages and losses caused by fraud, abuse of power, or gross negligence. Legal action by the company to impose liability on the directors requires the previous approval of members representing a majority of the capital.

*Public limited company (sociedad anónima)* According to Section 4 of the first Title of the Spanish Code, this is the type of company in which the capital stock is divided into shares. It is composed of contributions made by the partners who are not personally responsible for the company's debts. The 'sociedad anónima' is the usual company form for entities seeking to limit liability and having a capital stock of more than 50 million pesetas.

Besides the Commercial Code, a new Law of 22 December 1989 implements all EC directives concerning public companies and sets out significant changes, especially as regards the responsibilities of directors (see below).

The company acquires legal personality upon registration in the Mercantile Registry.

Spanish legislation establishes possible forms of managing a public limited company:

1    Sole administrator

2    Several administrators, appointed in such a way that each one can operate

independently, and may validly bind the company (this is not common practice)

3    Several directors, individually appointed (the board of directors is the typical form)

4    Managing directors

5    Representatives, appointed for specific and definite responsibilities

From this wide list of management styles, the most common one is through a board of directors ('consejo de administración').

The appointment of directors (and fixing of their number in those cases where by-laws give a maximum or minimum number) is a task of the general meeting of shareholders. In addition, the meeting may fix guarantees to be required of directors, provided there is nothing to the contrary set out in by-laws.

The board of directors is considered to be validly constituted when more than half of its members are present or represented at the meeting. Resolutions are passed by absolute majority vote of the directors present at the meeting, which must be convened by the chairman, or by a person acting in his place. Voting by signature and without a meeting is allowed only when no member opposes this procedure.

The new revised text of the Law on Public Limited Companies, which was passed on 22 December 1989, states that directors should be efficient, dedicated and loyal to the company in performing their duties. Likewise, following the criteria provided by the former law of 1951, it also requires that directors should not disclose any confidential information to which they may have access as a result of their position. This obligation remains even when the directors no longer occupy this position in the company.

The obligations of every director could therefore be summarized in three categories: loyalty, dedication and discretion of action. Directors are responsible to the company, shareholders and creditors for any damage caused as a result of acts which breach the law or by-laws and have been performed without the due care which should have been taken in the course of their duty.

All members of the directorate who have acted to the detriment of the company or have entered into any harmful agreement are jointly liable. The only exception to the above is when a member can prove that he did not take part in the agreement or action, knew nothing of this agreement or action, did everything possible to avoid the harm arising, or, at the very least, clearly expressed his opposition.

Article 133 states that the fact that the detrimental act or agreement has been adopted, authorized or ratified by the board of directors will not under any circumstances lead to exoneration from any liability.

The new provisions established by Law 19/1989 place on the directors the

nus of proving that the work has been carried out diligently. They also have the
esponsibility of proving the validity of their claim that they either knew nothing
f or opposed the adoption or execution of any adverse agreement.

Shareholders who attend the board meeting and express their opposition to
he agreement, those absent and those unlawfully deprived of their vote, as well as
ompany administrators, are authorized to challenge agreements harmful to the
ompany and to the advantage of others.

## LEGAL CONSIDERATIONS

### General legislation applying to franchising

The franchise contract in Spain is characterized by being governed, in general
erms, by the principle of contractual freedom established in Article 1255 of the
Civil Code, which states that contracting parties are free to establish contracts
ccording to their own interests.

However, there are two main laws in Spain to take into account when
ssessing the juridical nature of the franchise contract: the new Trade Marks Law
2/1988 of 10 November 1988, and the EC Regulation 4087/88 of 30 November
988. The latter refers to the application of Article 85.3 of the Treaty of categories
f franchise agreements.

These statutes deal with certain partial aspects of franchising. The former
reates several property rights which are often the object of franchising agreements, such as trade marks, commercial names and signs. The latter, in force
hroughout the EC since February 1989, regulates agreements directly from the
oint of view of competition law. The combination of these two provisions is very
seful as regards the drafting of the clauses of a franchising agreement.

It is necessary to point out here that the Spanish legislation, like most other
European legislation, has traditionally considered the doctrine of the exhaustion
f rights as far as intellectual and industrial property rights are concerned.
Spanish courts have, for example, declared several times that trade mark rights
annot be used to draw up vertical distribution agreements incompatible with the
air appliance of competition law.

In accordance with the trade mark law, the first step to be taken by the
ranchisee is to assure himself that the trade mark, which is the object of the
ontract, effectively belongs to the franchisor. One of the new provisions estab-
ished in the recent law is that trade mark ownership is acquired through registra-
ion. The franchisee has therefore to confirm the ownership of the franchisor in
he Industrial Property Register. Well-known marks do not need to be registered
n Spain, for their owners to have the right to judicially oppose third parties
ttempting to register marks which could lead to confusion with their marks. To
void any doubt, however, as to whether a mark is well-known or not, the
ranchisee's best course of action is to oblige the franchisor to register the mark,
efore signing the contract. It is also advisable, particularly as regards inter-
ational franchise agreements, to require the franchisor to confirm that there is

no conflict with third party rights in relation to the franchisor's trade marks and trade name.

In the same way, it is also advisable to register other industrial property rights of a more technical nature, such as patents and utility models. The registration does not, in itself, affect the validity of the contract, but the law provides certain incentives for the inscription of licences and cessions. In this context, the licence has to be registered to be sustained against third parties.

### Law of competition

With regard to the law of competition, insofar as it affects franchising, an analysis of the following statutes is necessary:

1   Act on Protection of Competition no. 16 of 17 July 1989 (published in the Official State Gazette no. 170 of 18 July)

2   Unfair Competition Bill no. 121/107 (Gazetted on 2 February 1989 in issue no. 106)

The aim of both statutes, which closely follow the EC provisions on competition in Articles 85 and 86 of the Treaty of Rome, is to introduce a radical change in the conception of the law dealing with competition in Spain. This is no longer conceived as being chiefly aimed at settling conflicts between competitors, but rather as a means of organizing and controlling market behaviour. The notion of competition, which is given the sufficient substantive and procedural mechanism in the former Act to ensure adequate market discipline, thus becomes the specific object of protection.

Franchising is considered to be within the scope of both Acts as a part of competition legislation, and, while not referred to expressly, is given the same necessary protective framework as in the EC Treaty.

In the first place, the Protection of Competition Act creates a general prohibition on any agreement, collective recommendation, decision or practice arranged, or of a consciously parallel nature, aimed at, or with the effect of preventing, faking or limiting competition in all or part of the domestic market. It then lists, albeit not exhaustively, the practices which are particularly prohibited. For example, the first of these practices is the direct or indirect fixing of prices or other commercial or service conditions.

Article 1, paragraph 2, provides that agreements, decisions and recommendations which are prohibited by paragraph 1 are null and void as a matter of law unless covered by the exemptions in Article 2, which are solely as follows:

1   Agreements, decisions or recommendations and practices which are the result of the application of an Act or of the regulations passed in the implementation of an Act.

**2** Reasoned proposals from the Defence of Competition Tribunal to the government, through the Ministry of Economy and Finance, to amend or eliminate restrictive competitive situations, as established in the legal provisions.

For its part, Article 3 sets out the cases in which it may be possible to authorize, for example, agreements, decisions, recommendations and practices as referred to in Article 1, or categories thereof, if they contribute to improving the production or marketing of goods and services, or if they promote technical or economic progress. This authorization is, however, subject to the following conditions:

That such practices allow consumers or users to participate adequately in the benefits therefrom

**2** That they do not impose restrictions which are not indispensable for the attainment of those objectives on the enterprises concerned

**3** That they do not enable the participating enterprises to eliminate competition in a substantial part of the products or services concerned

Moreover, according to Article 3, paragraph 2, authorization may be given for the agreements, decisions, recommendations and practices referred to in Article 1, or categories thereof, if this is justified by the general economic situation or the public interest, and if:

They are intended to defend or promote exports, insofar as compatible with the obligations arising from the international agreements ratified by this country.

**2** They are intended to adjust supply to demand when there is a consistent market demand downturn or when the excess of productive capacity is clearly anti-economic.

**3** They produce a sufficiently significant rise in the social and economic standards of depressed zones or sectors.

**4** Because of their reduced significance, they will not affect competition.

Likewise, Article 5 provides for the drafting of exemption regulations which refer to the types of agreements, decisions, recommendations, and arranged or consciously parallel practices that are referred to in Article 3.1 and which also cover franchising agreements when:

**1** Only two enterprises are involved and they impose restrictions on the distribution and/or supply of certain products for sale or resale, or in connection with the acquisition or use of industrial or intellectual property rights or secret industrial and commercial know-how; or

2   They are intended only for the preparation and uniform application of standards or types, or for specialization in the manufacture of certain products, or for joint research and development; or

3   They are aimed at, or have the effect of, increasing the enterprises' rationalization and competitiveness, above all in the case of small and medium-sized enterprises.

The Act also provides for the drafting of exempting regulations on the types of agreements, decisions, recommendations, and practices which are referred to in Article 3.1, if a mandatory report of the Competition Defence Tribunal has been issued.

In line with this objective, Article 1 considers the purpose of the Act, which enshrines the protection of competition in the interest of everyone participating in the market and, to this end, places a ban on acts of unfair competition.

For its part, Article 2 defines what are understood to be acts of unfair competition, bearing in mind that the act is deemed to be competitive when, given the circumstances in which it is done, it is objectively seen to be suitable for promoting or ensuring the distribution on the market of one's own services or those of a third party (the draft of the Unfair Competition Bill of 31 January 1989).

Article 17 provides that discriminatory treatment of the consumer in matters of prices and other sales terms is, in the absence of justified cause, unfair. Article 18 enshrines the principle of the prohibition on price fixing, establishing that prices will be freely fixed unless there is a provision to the contrary in an Act of Parliament or in regulations.

To recapitulate, we can say that, to a large extent, the new Spanish legislation is adjusted to EC law on competition, providing prohibitions and exemptions of similar scope to those considered in Articles 85 and 86 of the Treaty of Rome.

## Liability of the franchisor
The liability of the franchisor for infringement of competition laws will depend on the circumstances. Apart from the general sanctions provided for in the Civil Code, there is a range of pecuniary sanctions.

According to Article 10 of the Protection of Competition Act, the Tribunal of the Defence of Competition can impose fines ranging from Pts 150 000 up to 10% of the turnover of the relevant undertaking in the financial year prior to the resolution of the tribunal. The fines can be imposed on those economic agents, undertakings, associations or groups of undertakings which, deliberately or negligently, breach the provisions set out in the Act.

The establishment of the amount of the fine varies in accordance with the following factors:

The effects of the restriction on competition

The size of the affected market

The market share of the undertaking

The duration of the restriction on competition

The effect of the restriction on effective or potential competitors, on the economic development and on users and consumers

Whether the infringement is an isolated case or has occurred repeatedly

Managers and directors can be also subjected to fines of up to Pts 5 000 000. Undertakings can also be subjected to fines from Pts 10 000 up to Pts 150 000 periodically until the cease of the breach.

On the other hand, General Law 26/1984 of 19 July (BOE no. 176 of 24 July) on the defence of consumers and users provides guarantees and responsibilities which can be enforced in case of breach of the protection granted by the Law. Actions and omissions which may cause harm and prejudice to users and consumers also fall under the scope of the Law.

Chapter IX of the Act sets out a wide range of sanctions for breaches of the Law and establishes fines going from Pts 500 000 up to Pts 100 000 000, or even up to five times the value of the goods or services which are the object of the breach. The Council of Ministers can likewise determine the temporary closure of the undertaking, establishment or service for a maximum period of five years.

All the aforementioned legislation can influence franchising agreements. There are two main laws applicable to product liability in this respect, the Consumers' Law, from now onwards referred to as CL ('Ley General para la Defensa de los Consumidores y Usuarios'), and the EC directive on product liability, which is also fully applicable in Spain.

As Lucan says in her book *Daños por Productos y Protección del Consumidor* (Damages for products and consumer protection):

> Unlike the EEC Directive on liability for damages caused by faulty products, Chapter VIII of the CL does not specify who must assume liability.

She continues as follows: 'Article 26 speaks in general terms of "those who produce, import, provide or supply products or services to consumers or users". Article 28, on the other hand, does not even make mention of this and simply affirms that "liability is assumed". It is in Article 27 where we apparently find the criteria for defining to whom liability corresponds. In this respect the following general definition is given: ''The manufacturer, importer, seller or supplier of products or services to consumers or users, is answerable for the origin identity and fitness of the same, in accordance with their nature and purpose and the norms which regulate them.'' The article goes on to establish that, in the case of loose products, the liability is of the holder, without excluding the possibility of identifying and proving the liability of the previous holder or supplier (Article 27.1.b). When the products are packaged, labelled or closed ''the firm or trade name which features on the label, presentation or publicity has liability'' (Article 27.1.c).

'Before beginning an analysis of the concrete problems found in this area, a few clarifications may be of use. First of all, in spite of the terminological confusion and ambiguity found in Chapter VIII, here, as in other matters, the interpreter must overcome the obstacles and the legislation's deficient wording. For example, the impression is given here that produce, manufacture, supply, provide and sell, can be used interchangeably. In this way, the parties mentioned in Article 26 (. . . those who produce, import, provide or supply . . .) are identified with those mentioned in Article 27.1 (the manufacturer, importer, seller or supplier).

'Article 26 of CL establishes a system of liability through default by inversion of the burden of proof. This does not mean, however, that a claim can be filed, successfully, against anyone.

'The precept speaks of ''the actions and omissions of those who produce, import, provide or supply products or services to consumers or users, which cause loss or damages to the same.'' This means that the victim must not only prove the damage suffered and that this damage was caused by the product, but also that it was the defendant who produced, imported, provided or supplied the product. The latter can be exonerated from liability if he can prove that he took all the care and diligence which the nature of the product required. As a consequence, the victim should choose with care against which member of the production and distribution chain to file his claim.

'This choice cannot be taken arbitrarily. Depending on the kind of defect the product has, it may prove more advisable to bring action against one or other of the parties involved. For example, if the product caused damage because its design was faulty, the retailer, given the present structure of the production system, would have no great difficulty in proving that he acted with all due diligence. If, however, he had not fulfilled certain control, revision or inspection requirements, or had contributed towards the appearance of the defect by inadequate storing or installation, it would be a completely different state of affairs.

'Our case law and its application of Article 1.591 of the Civil Code is relevant here: all those who intervene independently, together with the promoter, in the construction of a building are equally liable for the possible defects of the same. For each of the defendants, the only way of escaping this responsibility is to prove that they had nothing to do with these defects.

'Therefore, given the similarity between the damages caused by the

ruining'' of a building (in the all-embracing interpretation given by our courts)
ad damages caused by products, it is probable that Article 26 of CL may be
pplied in a similar manner.

'The victim may therefore file claims against all the parties who intervened
the production and distribution of the product. If a claim is filed against one of
e parties only, there will exist no possibility of opposing it, with the exception of
assive *litis consorcio*. The victim may, however, find himself in the position of
aving to reinitiate legal proceedings should the defendant manage to prove that
e acted with diligence.

'For this reason, it is advisable to file the claim against all those who partici-
ated in the production and distribution process. In this way the participants who
o not prove their diligence will all be liable. Provided it is not clearly obvious that
e liability corresponds to one party in particular, all parties concerned will be
onsidered equally liable.

'In principle, therefore, each of the members of the production and distribu-
on chain of a product is liable only for the damages caused by action or omission
n his part, but the burden of proving the contrary is his. On the other hand,
epending on each individual case, determining who must pay compensation can
rove complex.

'The first point to consider is that a modern production process does not
onsist of a single, isolated act. The complexity of production systems means that
wide variety of parties are involved in the elaboration and commercialization of
product. Goods are not usually elaborated entirely by the ''manufacturer'', nor
e they simply put at the disposal of the public by ''the seller''. On the contrary,
whole series of activities, and consequently of parties who carry them out, are
volved. They are so interrelated that the party who launches the product on the
arket is merely the last link of a long chain. Together with him are to be found,
the production phase, the manufacturer of the raw materials and the various
omponent parts, materials or substances which make up the product. Moreover,
e product may well be elaborated by one party, although another puts his
ctory mark or distinguishing sign on it, and presents himself as the manufac-
rer. In the distribution phase, several intermediaries may appear, who may
ave, by their behaviour, spoilt the product or contributed to the appearance of
s damaging potential.

'If the product causes damages because the manufacturer committed an
rror in the assembling of the various parts which made up the finished product,
is will not present many problems. He will be liable because it will be almost
mpossible to prove that, in spite of the error, he acted with the due diligence
xacted by the nature of the product. The question here is whether the manufac-
rer of the finished product acted with sufficient diligence, in spite of his not
iscovering the damaging potential of certain components or raw materials used
his product. Even when the behaviour determining the damages caused to the
onsumers is precisely the fact of having commercialized a faulty product, it is
easonable to think that this is a question which our courts would have to decide

on, bearing in mind the nature of the product and the fault, its complexity and whether or not it was possible to detect this fault beforehand.

'On the other hand, if the manufacturer or one of the intermediaries through his behaviour, caused the faulty characteristic of the goods, is it possible for the seller or manufacturer to prove that he did not neglect any control or inspection obligations? It is also necessary here to refer to the concrete circumstances of each case according to the practical possibility of verifying the product control.'

## Industrial and intellectual property
First of all it should be pointed out that Spanish trade mark law is strongly based on registration. The steps to follow in applying for a trade mark are as follows:

1   Filing of the trade mark application before the Trademark Office (prior investigation is, in most cases, advisable).

2   Said application will be published in the Official Gazette of the Trademark Office (BOPI), and the parties interested have a term of two months in which they can file opposition before the Trademark Office. The Trademark Office can *ex officio* oppose the application based on a prior similar or identical existing registered trade mark.

3   The Trademark Office will decide on the opposition filed by third parties and against said decision the aggrieved party can file a Reconsideration Appeal, also before the Trademark Office. The appeal will be decided by the Office in the term of one year as from the filing.

4   Against the decision issued by the Trademark Office on the Reconsideration Appeal, the aggrieved party can file a Contentious-Administrative Appeal before the Provincial Court, and finally against the decision taken by this court, an appeal can be filed before the Supreme Court.

A trade mark is granted for a term of 20 years, and can be renewed for successive periods of 20 years. The trade mark covers the whole of the Spanish territory.

Other traits of the Spanish trade mark law are as follows.

This Law follows the International Nomenclature, which has 34 classes for trade mark products and eight (35–42) for service marks.

The trade mark should be used and, if in the term of five years it has not been used, it can be cancelled.

Rights that a trade mark which has been granted confers to its owner are mainly the ones defined under Article 31.1: 'The owner of the registered trade mark may exercise the actions prescribed in Article 35 of this Law against third parties who use for economic purposes, without his consent, an identical or similar trade mark or sign to distinguish identical or similar products or services when the similarity between signs and the similarity between products and services could give rise to errors.'

As far as legal actions against the violation of a trade mark are concerned, Article 35 of the Law establishes that: 'The owner of a registered trade mark may bring before the courts the corresponding civil or criminal actions against anyone who prejudices his right and may demand that the necessary measures be taken to safeguard them.'

The civil actions derived from the violation of trade mark rights prescribe five years from the date on which they could have been exercised.

In accordance with Article 41, for the purposes of the assignment or the taxation of a trade mark registration, the trade mark is considered indivisible although it may be jointly owned by various persons.

As far as assignment or licence of a trade mark is concerned, Articles 42 and 43 establish as follows.

## Article 42

'1　Both a trade mark registration application and a trade mark may be subject to licences for all or part of the products or services for which it is registered and for all or part of Spain. The licences may be exclusive or non-exclusive.

2　The rights conferred by the registration of a trade mark or by its application may be exercised against any licensee who violates any of the limits of his licence as set out in his contract or by virtue of the provisions of the previous number.'

## Article 43

'For the assignment or licence of a trade mark to be effective it must be presented in writing and inscribed in the trade mark register.'

The international registration of a trade mark carried out in accordance with the Madrid arrangement will be effective in Spain.

Finally, Articles 76 and 77 of this law define commercial names (business names) in the following way.

## Article 76

'1　A commercial name is understood to be the sign or denomination used to identify an individual or legal entity in the exercise of his business activity and which distinguishes his activity from identical or similar activities.

2　In particular, the following may constitute commercial names:

    (a)   Patronymic names, registered names and the denominations of legal entities.

    (b)   Fantasy names.

    (c)   Names which allude to the purpose of the business activity.

    (d)   Anagrams

    (e)   Any combination of the signs mentioned above.'

### Article 77

'A commercial name will be protected in the conditions prescribed in article 8 of the current Minutes in Spain of the Paris Union Convention for the protection of industrial property of the 20 March 1883, provided the owner demonstrates that he has used it in Spain. When the owner of a commercial name initiates proceedings to declare null a subsequently registered trade mark or commercial name or business sign, he must provide proof of the use mentioned above and initiate the action before five years have elapsed from the date of publication of the corresponding concession.'

## Real estate and leasing

The normal way to acquire real property in Spain is through a purchase-sale contract. This is a contract for which the parties appear before a notary to make the declarations for the sale and purchase. A public document is then granted and the contract is registered in the Property Registry. In the absence of agreement to the contrary, the notarial charges are paid by the seller. Fees for additional copies are charged to the buyer. Article 1462 of the Civil Code provides that when a sale is made by a public document the granting of the same is equivalent to the delivery of the subject matter of the contract, unless expressly stated to the contrary in the document or otherwise clearly understood.

Some brief comments regarding Spanish legislation on leasing are as follows.

The leasing of commercial locales is governed by the Urban Lease Law of 6 November 1964. This Law requires that, upon entering into a contract, the lessee place a deposit equal to two months' rent with the lessor. This deposit does not earn interest for the lessee. The lease period must be set by contract. The lessee may terminate the lease by giving 30 days' notice and paying rent for the period left in the lease agreement.

According to the Law, repairs necessary for the conservation of the property are the responsibility of the lessor. If the lessor does not fulfil his duty under the law, the lessee may demand that the former make the necessary repairs or terminate the contract, and, in either case, claim compensation for damages.

The Law provides the lessee with a preferential purchase right in the case of a sale of the leased property by the owner. Many times this right is waived under the terms of the contract.

The lessee also has a right under the Law to assign the rights and obligations f the lease to a third party. However, if this assignment is not carried out in strict ccordance with the Law, the lessor may impede the assignment. The lessor may lso exercise preferential rights and has a right to increase the rent in the case of an ssignment. The increase can be mutually agreed to or limited to 15% of what the ssignor paid as rent.

The lessor may terminate the lease agreement for many reasons according to he Law, including transfers not in accordance with the law and sublets for more han is legally permitted. The lessee may terminate the contract for failure by the essee to effectuate necessary repairs in the locality, its installations and services or hings of necessary use or common to the property in order to fulfil the purpose of he contract.

## Right to establishment and employment laws

The basic rules in this area are set out in the Organic Law 7/1985 of 1 July 1985 oncerning rights and liberties of foreigners in Spain and complemented by Royal Decree 1119/86 of May. The Constitutional Court case 115/87 of 7 July, owever, declared unconstitutional certain articles of the Organic Law 7/85 egarding the rights of foreigners to gather publicly, associate or appeal against dministrative resolutions.

Royal Decree 1099/86 of 26 May 1986 governs the entry, residency and mployment in Spain of citizens of EC member states.

Foreigners may be legally resident in Spain under the following regimes: on  temporary visit or in permanent residence. No formalities other than normal passport and/or visa controls are required for a visit of up to 90 days. It is ometimes possible to obtain an extension of a temporary visit.

Residency requires official authorization. A residence permit will normally not be issued if adequate means of support are not proved to be available. The duration of residence permits varies according to circumstances. However, except in unusual circumstances, residence permits (including any extension which may have been authorized) will have a maximum duration of five years.

Foreigners who wish to pursue business activities in Spain, whether on their own account or on behalf of others, must first obtain a special entry visa at the Spanish Embassy of the country of origin, and apply for work and residence permits. The granting of such a visa depends upon whether or not treaties exist between Spain and the applicant's home country. Political and economic factors may also come into play.

There are numerous types of work permit, and the formalities vary from one to another. In general terms, to obtain a permit for an 'ordinary' job, an application should be submitted to the Office of the Director of National Security (Dirección General de Seguridad del Estado). From here an application for a work permit will be passed on to the Ministry of Labour and Social Security, and one for a residence permit will be processed by the Ministry of the Interior. Applications may be also processed by local authorities through police stations.

Additionally, it should be noted that there are numerous special provisions applying to different classes of workers. For example, there are special procedures for artists, executives, professors under contract to Spanish universities, technicians contracted by the Spanish government, persons intending to work in more than one province, etc. In the case of an executive (one whose position involves high management functions, special responsibilities, or the representation of enterprises with a share capital in excess of 25 million pesetas), the application for a work permit and residency authorization is submitted directly to the Ministry of Labour and Social Security. There are also special provisions for workers from certain regions, particularly Latin America.

The granting of work and residency permits is not only dependent on the applicant's characteristics and general good citizenship. It is also dependent upon the local labour conditions. In general terms, if the position sought by the foreigner could be filled by an unemployed Spaniard, the work permit will be denied. Both permits are either granted or denied simultaneously and, if granted, are valid for the same period.

An initial work permit is generally granted for a period of one year. It is possible to obtain an extension, provided the circumstances remain the same as those in effect when the permit was granted. The same office or body which issued the permit grants or denies the extension. If circumstances vary, a new permit cannot be valid for more than five years.

### Foreign investments

Royal Decree 2077/1986 of 25 September 1986 provides the legal framework applicable to foreign investments in Spain and adapts Spanish regulations on this subject to the requirements of the EC. The law, in general, is designed to permit foreign investors to operate under the same conditions as Spanish residents. The new law creates four categories of foreign investments which are controlled in various ways, according to their financial characteristics and economic effects on the domestic market.

Royal Decree 2077/1986 also dictates who may make the foreign investment and the procedure involved. Only persons with certain characteristics can be holders of foreign investments. Article 1 indicates that entities and branches in Spanish territory of private foreign legal persons or natural persons not resident in Spain may hold foreign investments. Foreign legal persons, foreign natural persons and Spaniards not resident in Spain may also be holders of foreign investments.

Spanish companies with a certain percentage of foreign interest can make foreign investments through the creation of other Spanish companies or by acquiring shares or other interests.

Foreign investments are made by the use or contribution of foreign capital. This may be done at the exchange rate value in pesetas of the currency as quoted on the Spanish currency market. Cash contributions can also be made in pesetas from foreign accounts in convertible pesetas or in any other rm which regulations covering transactions and transfers abroad permit.

Direct contributions to a business of foreign capital equipment is another rm of foreign investment. The maximum value of the equipment contributed to e Spanish business will be equal to the taxable base for the purpose of value lded tax upon importation.

The third class of foreign-origin capital contributions involves providing chnical assistance, patents and licences of foreign manufacture to the business. rior government approval is required for these contributions and will depend on e nature and value of the contribution.

The fourth class of contributions is described in the legislation as 'any other leans of investment, that is subject to administrative authorization'. A method reseen by the law is the use of domestic capital. However, both Spanish com- anies with foreign interest, as well as branches or establishments of foreign ompanies, can use, without needing authorization, their ordinary accounts in esetas to make foreign investments.

## ermination

ontracts lapse under Spanish legislation, contained in the Civil Code, as a result f one of the following causes: payment or completion, loss of property or npossibility of performance, confusion of the rights of creditor and debtor, ompensation or novation. All the causes could apply to a franchising agreement, king into account their special nature.

### ayment or completion

#### apacity to make or receive the payment

1 payments or delivery obligations, the obligations made by parties without legal uthority to dispose of or capacity to transfer the subject matter, are considered oid. However, no claim can be made against a creditor who has spent or onsumed it in good faith.

Normally, creditors or their representatives may receive payment or deliv- ry. However, the law establishes a series of special rules, so that a payment or elivery made to a person without capacity to administer the creditor's property ill be valid in the extent to which it has been converted to his use.

#### ime and place of payment

n the case of a 'pure obligation', payment is due when the obligation is born. If 1e obligation is subject to a pending condition, the time for payment is when the ondition is met.

Payment must be made in the place designated in the contract. If no place vas stipulated, and there is a specific object to be furnished, delivery must be 1ade where the object was located at the time the obligation was created. In any ther case, the place of payment or delivery shall be that of the domicile of the erson obligated to pay or to deliver.

Performance requires that the obligation meets precisely what the contract calls for, and nothing else. Payments of debts in money must be made in the currenc agreed upon. Where the contract is silent on this matter, payment is presumed to b in pesetas. The furnishing of negotiable notes or bills of exchange, or of other men cantile documents, will only satisfy payment when actually paid, unless, of course non-payment is the fault of the creditor.

Pending payment of the note, the action derived from the original obligation i suspended. In the absence of special provisions, creditors are not compelled t accept partial performances of the principal obligation. However, when the debt i partly liquid and partly non-liquid, the payment of the first, without liquidation c the second, may be sought by creditors and made by debtors.

**Loss of the property or impossibility of performance** The law provides that an obligation consisting of a concrete delivery will lapse when the object of the con tract is lost or destroyed, provided there is no fault by the debtor. Debtors wil also be released from the obligation to act in the face of legal or physical impos sibilities. In this respect, the Code establishes the following special rules:

1    The obligation must involve the delivery of something specific.

2    The obligation will not lapse as a result of loss of the property, regardless of wha caused the loss, when the debt or obligation arises from an offence or crime.

3    If the obligation lapses as a result of loss of the property, any actions which the debtor may have against third parties as a result of the loss will, by operation o law, be transferred to the creditor.

**Confusion of rights** A confusion of rights occurs when the debtor and creditor are the same person. Since it is legally and logically impossible for a person to be debtor to himself, the obligation is deemed to be extinguished. However, an exception is made in the case of such confusion arising as a result of transfer of titles by inherit ance, if the heir or beneficiary accepted the inheritance 'on benefit of inventory'. The use of this device serves to maintain the complete separation of hereditary property and the property of the inheritor.

*Pardon*
A 'pardon' is the waiver of the right to collect by the holder, that is to say, by the creditor. The forgiveness of the main debt will extinguish any accessory obligations, but the extinction of the latter is always dependent upon that of the former.

*Offset*
Offset occurs when two persons, acting in their own right, are both creditors and debtors to each other. By operation of law, each debt is extinguished by the concur- rent amount of the credit even though debtors and creditors may not be aware of this fact.

If the debts are payable in different places, the parties may be compensated
y indemnification for the transport costs or costs resulting from the change of
lace of the payment. If one person has several debts owing, the priority for offset
, as follows: (1) the debt indicated by the debtor; (2) that indicated by the
reditor; (3) the interest before debt principal; (4) the most onerous debt; all debts
ro rata.

*Iovation* Novation as termination of a contract takes place when one of the
ɔllowing causes occur:

The subject matter of the obligation or the main conditions of the obligation
are varied by agreement;

Another person is substituted for the debtor; or

There is substitution of a third party in respect to the rights of the creditor.

panish law does not foresee any special rules for franchise agreements in
eneral. They therefore, in general terms, follow the rules established for dis-
ribution contracts. My following comments on distribution contracts are thus
lso applicable to franchise agreements.

It is important to make some brief remarks about the termination of fran-
hise agreements in the Spanish legal system and case law.

There is no provision in Spanish law for general contracting conditions.
'he principle of bona fides in the Spanish Civil Code is thus the applicable rule
n connection with Articles 1258 of the Civil Code and 56 of the Commercial
Code.

*A contract of duration* Distribution contracts are, by their very nature, for a
luration in which the parties' interests depend, within a framework of certain
tability, directly on the fact of the prolongation in time of the services.

There are two aspects to the problems of these contracts: the legal limit
ɔn the duration of the obligatory relation with lasting services – definitive or
ɔtherwise – and the form in which the duration affects the terms of the bilateral
elation, particularly cancellation.

*Contracts of indeterminate duration*
The basic question here is a possible unilateral cancellation of the contract by the
ɔroducer-wholesaler. This faculty is recognized in all legal systems in principle
ɪnd is based on the impossibility of infinite or life-long legal relations. In return, a
ɔeriod of notice, to be observed by the cancelling party, is usually established.
The aim here is to prevent losses which may be caused to the other by the termina-
ion of the relation.

In Spanish law, in the absence of specific rules governing the distribution agreement, the discipline on contracts of duration must be extracted from the specific cases legally typified (work and services leases, mandate, commission, company). On the basis of the provisions for these types, the principle of *ad nutum* cancellation of contracts concluded for an indeterminate time is admitted (Article 1586 of the Civil Code *sensu contrario* and Article 302 of the Business Code). The frame of reference to be used when interpreting this period of notice is the normal business practice of wherever the distributor operates.

The decision of the Supreme Court of 14 February 1973 admitted the unilateral termination of an exclusive sales contract with a clause according to which both parties could end the relation with no requirement other than notification. According to the court, this is not in conflict with Article 1256 of the Civil Code. It is based on the nature of the contract *intuitu personae* and on the effect on the assets of each party which may be caused by the other's inactivity or lack of diligence.

The case law is not unequivocal on the distributor's right to indemnification for notice, even where the party cancelling the contract does not respect this notice.

Any possible indemnification must, in any case, include loss of profits in terms of the products to which the distributor may not have had access, and the consequential damages from the costs caused by the cessation of the relation and the very unavailability of the products.

### Contracts of definite duration

These contracts end with the expiration of the period of the effective term set by the parties: in principle, there is no right to indemnification of any sort, except in hypothetical cases of provision for renewal clauses.

In Spanish law, the principle of the independence of private volition would appear to exclude any renewal not provided for in the agreement. Given the state of the question in Spanish law and the lack of doctrine and case law on the matter, the only resort available, as far as possible, is the principle of bona fides in the performance of contracts (Article 1258 of the Civil Code and Article 57 of the Business Code).

**Protection for the distributor and complementary indemnification** The Spanish courts have established that if one of the parties terminates the agreement without legal cause, the other party is entitled to ask for indemnification for the losses and damages suffered.

Some areas of the doctrine seek to establish a right to complementary indemnification. The basic elements of such compensation would be the costs caused to the distributor by the cancellation of the relation and the clientele contributed by it to the producer-wholesaler's establishment during the period of the contract.

# TAX AND FINANCIAL

## Introduction

In Spain, taxes are imposed both nationally and municipally. The regional governments (Comunidades Autónomas, see below) also have the right to levy taxes. Municipal taxes may include the following: fiscal licence (licencia fiscal), rural property taxes (contribución territorial rústica), urban property tax (contribución territorial urbana), ground tax (impuestos sobre solares), occupancy tax (impuesto sobre la radicación), tax on increased land value (incremento sobre el valor de los terrenos), proprietor's luxury tax (impuesto sobre gastos suntuarios), advertising tax (impuesto sobre la publicidad), and motor vehicle circulation tax (impuesto sobre circulación de vehículos).

National taxes include the following: personal individual income (impuesto sobre la renta de las personas físicas), net worth tax (impuestos sobre patrimonio), corporation tax (impuesto sobre sociedades), inheritance tax (impuesto sobre sucesiones), tax on property transfers and documentary legal acts (impuesto general sobre transmisiones y actos jurídicos documentados), value added tax (VAT) (impuestos sobre el valor añadido, IVA), customs duties (renta de aduanas), special taxes (e.g. alcohol, beer, petroleum products, tobacco).

Consideration will be given to the general outlines of the most relevant taxes.

## Corporation tax

*Concept and applicability* Legislation in force on this matter is contained in the Law 61/1978 of 27 December 1978 and in the Regulation 2631/1982 of 15 October 1982. This tax involves a direct and personal tax levied on the income of companies and other legal entities, in accordance with the provisions of the Regulations.

The income of the taxpayer includes the following:

1    Earnings from economic operations of all types, and those derived from professional and artistic activities

2    Earnings from any asset not connected to the above-mentioned activities

3    Increase in the value of assets determined in accordance with the provisions regulating this tax

This tax is levied upon all entities having juridical character and not subject to individual income tax. It is levied throughout Spain, independently of regional government tax systems, international treaties or agreements.

The national and regional governments are exempted from corporation tax. The autonomous administrative bodies – Banco de España; territorial public administrative bodies, apart from those of the state and regional governments; the Roman Catholic Church, and the non-Catholic confessional associations; pension and mutual associations and the Spanish Red Cross – are also exempted from corporation taxes. However, the exemptions referred to here do not apply to the earnings which these bodies obtain from their assets dedicated to commercial pursuits, nor to increases in these assets.

**Attribution of income** Taxpayers subject to corporation tax by virtue of a personal obligation are assessed on the basis of all the earnings and increases in assets, irrespective of the place where they occurred and the residence of the payer. Those taxpayers subject to payment of corporation taxes under a 'real' obligation (i.e. based on ownership of property in Spain, or receipt of payments from Spain) are only subject to tax on earnings and increases in assets obtained in Spain.

The tax address of taxpayers resident in Spain is deemed to be that of the head office, provided that it is there where the administrative management and direction of the business are effectively centred. The fiscal address of taxpayers resident in other countries is that of the place where effective management and direction of the business in Spain are carried out. An entity is deemed to be resident in Spain if it meets any of the following requirements:

1    It was incorporated or established in accordance with Spanish law;

2    Its head office is in Spanish territory; or

3    The headquarters of the effective management are in Spanish territory.

**Taxable base** The taxable base is the amount of the taxpayer's income during the assessment period. There are three systems for fixing the taxable base: through income, through assets, or through indirect assessment. If the taxable base turns out to be negative under the method selected, this 'loss' may be carried forward during the five succeeding financial years.

*Taxable base assessed on the basis of income*
The taxable base may be fixed by means of the positive or negative evaluation of earnings, expenses, increases and reductions in assets. Several factors are taken into account, as follows.

*Assessable and non-assessable income* Assessable income includes, among other items, income from the pursuit of an entrepreneurial or professional activity, and the value of profit-making acquisitions which are not subject to inheritance gifts or subsidies of any type. Contributions made by company owners or corporation shareholders during the financial year (e.g. share issue premiums and contributions made by the members for the reinstatement of capital in cases of loss,

eferred to in Article 99 of the Public Companies Act) are treated as positive items
f capital and, thus, are not considered assessable.

*Deductible and non-deductible items* Deductible items include, for example, non-
governmental tributes and surcharges, social security contributions made by the
axpayer, amounts paid as legal items for company purposes, and amounts
assigned by the taxpayer for personnel accident insurance. Examples of non-
deductible items are participation in profits, payment of fines and sanctions
established by a public body.

*Increases and reductions of assets* These are variations in the value of the assets of
he taxpayer, as a result of any change in their composition. No increase or reduc-
ion of assets is deemed to occur in the case of the division of joint property, dissolution of communities or selling-out by a co-owner. Differences of net worth,
as a result of any profit-making transfer, are treated as increases and reductions of
assets and, as such, shall be assessed as part of the income of the transferring
party. The amount of the increase or reduction of assets, in the case of valuable or
gratuitous alienation, is the difference between acquisition and alienation values
of the asset.

*Evaluation of income and expenses* Income and expenses are assessed at their accounting value, as long as accountancy reflects the true situation of the assets of the
company.

*Other methods to determine the taxable basis*
The Spanish corporation tax regulation sets out two different methods to determine the taxable basis. Under the first method, the taxable base is determined by
*assets*. The taxable base is fixed at the difference between the value of financial
capital at the beginning and at the end of the period of assessment. The second
method is by *indirect assessment*, according to the Law for the Review of Taxation
Procedures of 21 June 1980. The indirect assessment procedure is intended as a
back-up method for the determination of the taxable base. It is designed for cases
where the taxpayer offers resistance, excuses, or refusal to tax inspectors; or significantly breaches his accounting obligations or any obligations which make the
government unable to obtain the required data for the assessment of the taxable
base. In these cases, the government may use any kind of available or background
data relevant for this purpose, including information about other contributors
with a similar position.

## Value added tax
*Concept and applicability* The value added tax originated with Spain's entry into
the EC on 1 January 1986, and applies to 'consumption'; that is to say, to the
delivery of goods and services effected by companies and professionals, as well as
to the importation of goods into the Spanish peninsular territory and Balearic

Islands. (The value added tax does not apply to operations carried out in the Canary Islands, or in Ceuta and Melilla.)

According to the Law 30/1985 of 2 August and to its regulation 2028/85 of 30 October, the tax applies to both habitual and occasional deliveries of goods and services made by companies or professionals on their own account, and carried out in the course of their business or professional activity. Also included are some deliveries of goods and services carried out without retribution, such as the use of one's own goods or services. Certain services are deemed exempt from this tax, i.e. public postal services, health services rendered by public or certain legally recognized private bodies with authorized prices, social services for the handicapped and for drug addicts, and services related to education.

This tax will generally be paid when goods are delivered, services rendered or a taxable operation carried out. Individual or legal entities carrying out the business, professional activity or delivery of goods or services subject to the tax are liable. With some exceptions, the tax debt must be passed on to the person for whom the taxable operation is carried out. The latter is then obliged to pay the tax, regardless of any agreements which may exist between the two parties.

*Special regulations for imports* Imported goods are subject to VAT. For the purposes of this tax, importation is defined as the entry of goods into the Spanish peninsular territory or Balearic Islands, whatever the destination of the goods or the condition of the importer may be. The following are recognized as exceptions to the VAT applicability to importation: Ships to be used for maritime navigation (except warships and recreational craft), share certificates and original paintings and sculptures imported directly by their creators. The obligation to pay this tax arises at the time the importer requests customs to dispatch the merchandise, after the verification of compliance with customs regulations. The individual or entity carrying out the importation is liable for the tax. The tax base is determined by adding customs duty, commissions, transport and insurance to the 'value in customs'.

*VAT calculation* Taxpayers liable for payment of VAT may deduct from the VAT received by them, the amount equal to the VAT they were required to pay in the acquisition or importation of goods and services. To be eligible for such a deduction, the taxpayer must provide the tax authorities with documented proof of claimed VAT payments. In general, the regulations regarding infractions and sanctions, established in the General Tributary Law (in section 14.01(2)), are applicable to VAT. However, VAT legislation does contain a few peculiarities of its own in this respect. A taxpayer who carries out differentiated business or professional activities must maintain separate 'deducted accounts' for each one of them.

There are separate tax scales for VAT. The basic VAT tax rate is 12%. There is a reduced rate of 6% for certain basic items such as books, housing, etc., and a special rate of 33% for luxury items such as vehicles, jewellery or pleasure craft.

The VAT legislation provides for various special regimes. These include a simplified regime for operations which do not exceed a value of 50 million pesetas in a year. There are also special regimes for agriculture, livestock and fisheries, for second-hand goods, for objects of art, antiques and collectors items, for travel agents and for retailers. Each of these has several regulations which differ from those of a general nature, mentioned above.

## Withholding tax

The Law 14/1985 of 29 May on taxation of financial activities sets out a withholding tax system in Spain and ensures the taxation of the income of financial assets. We can make a classification to limit the concept of income on capital assets:

1    Dividends, associations and co-operatives (the returns of co-operatives' gains according to the Spanish legislation), premiums for having attended general meetings and participations in the profits of undertakings, as well as the use or the utilization of goods and services on a gratis basis or at prices notably inferior to the ones of the market can result in the party being considered an associate, shareholder or participant.

2    The gains obtained independently of the juridical concept when they do not come from participation in the social capital nor from the direct remuneration of services rendered to the society by directors, advisors, administrators or employees. This concept makes reference to founders' rights, enjoyment bonds or similar assets:

   (a)   The first are nominative assets, different from shares, which allow founders of undertakings to reserve for themselves remuneration and advantages with a maximum of 10% of the net capital gains for a period of up to 15 years.

   (b)   The second refers to assets given to the owners of redeemed shares, as a result of operations of reduction of capital. They include the right to participate in benefits and liquidation quotes but without having the right to vote or receive information. It is important, however, to make clear here the difference (as regards taxation) between the receipt of the asset and its enjoyment, since the former gives rise to income gain and the latter to capital gain.

3    Specific incomes. In this classification interest and, generally speaking, all payments expressly due to the utilization and addition of foreign capital to the undertaking, including issuing and redemption bonuses, are considered.

The difference between the amount payable at the issuing, or endorsement, and that to be paid when an exchange bill, a porteur bill, a treasury bill, bonds or other assets become demandable is also considered as a capital gain. Gains obtained in this way will be part of the taxable basis either under the regime of the physical persons' income tax or corporation tax.

On the other hand, payment of interest is subjected to a withholding tax of 25%, on the difference between acquisition or subscription of financial assets and the corresponding alienation values.

Finally, Spanish law provides for a withholding tax of 55% on incomes obtained from the discount of certain financial assets.

### Miscellaneous taxes

Until very recently, the basic regulations relating to special taxes were traditionally contained in Law 39/1979 of 30 November 1979, and the Decree of 4 November 1980. The legislature enacted a new law on this matter, Law 45/1985 of 21 December 1985, under which special taxes are imposed on:

1    Alcohol and alcoholic beverages

2    Beer

3    Hydrocarbons

4    Manufactured tobacco

The former law had also provided for special taxes on telephone usage and soft drinks. These were omitted in the new law since they are at present only subject to VAT.

The new law is applicable throughout the Spanish mainland and the Balearic Islands. For historical reasons, the special taxes on alcohol and alcoholic beverages, as well as on beer, are also applicable in the Canary Islands.

### Customs duties

The basic legislation on this matter is the Decree of 17 October 1974 approving the recast text of integrated taxes as regards customs duties. There are other rules relating to particular aspects of customs, such as: the Law on the System for Active Improvement Operations, regulated by the Decree of 30 June 1964; and the Recast Text on Temporary Admissions, approved by a Decree of 25 October 1969.

It must be pointed out that, in principle, all imports, whether intended for consumption or re-exportation (that is, whether definitive or temporary) are subject to tax. The tax is applicable throughout mainland Spain and the Balearic Islands. It is not applied in the Canary Islands, nor in Ceuta or Melilla.

The tax for compensation for internal levies is a sort of countervailing duty. It takes effect upon the entry of foreign goods into Spanish customs territory. It is intended as a tax on imported goods to compensate for the fiscal treatment of domestic goods. The taxable base results from the addition of import duties to customs value, as defined in the Agreement on Customs Value of Goods, signed in Brussels on 15 December 1950.

The tax is levied in accordance with rates in force at the imposition period. This tax has been derogated by the value added tax, at least insofar as EC goods are concerned.

In addition to this basic system for import taxation, there is another system which allows temporary importation to be free from import duties and other levies. There is a time limit, fixed by customs authorities, inherent in this latter system. Once the limit has passed, imported goods or objects must be re-exported.

This special import system involves three other ones: temporary importation, transit and active improvement operations.

Since the exportation of goods is a beneficial activity for the country, it is understandable that the state should promote it and that only few exports are subject to tariff levies and other taxes. The tariff law establishes duties only in special cases or for very particular circumstances. At present, tariff duties are levied for the exportation of hide for tanning and of untreated red iron (ferric oxide).

Spain's policy of exports promotion takes the following forms: fiscal measures, such as credit for export, credit insurance for export and assistance in the opening up of new markets. The so-called 'exporter's letter' is the instrument containing these advantages intended to encourage businessmen to undertake export operations. One should also point out the improvements introduced by the Ministry of Economy and Finance, which return to exporters all or part of the indirect taxes subject to taxation, as a consequence of double-taxation agreements signed by Spain.

## Local taxes

***Regional government taxation*** The Kingdom of Spain is divided into different communities, called 'comunidades autónomas', which are as follows: Andalucía, Aragón, Asturias, Baleares, Canarias, Cantabria, Castilla-La Mancha, Castilla-León, Cataluña, Extremadura, Galicia, Madrid, Murcia, Navarra, País Vasco, La Rioja and Valencia.

Article 133 of the Constitution provides that regional governments ('comunidades autónomas') and local corporations may establish and levy taxes, in accordance with the Constitution and the law. Article 157.1 of the Constitution sets out the resources of the regional governments as follows:

1    Taxes transferred wholly or partially by the state; surcharges on national state taxes and other participation in national income

2    Their own taxes, fees and special contributions

3    Transfers from an inter-territorial compensation fund, and other allocated sums charged to the general national budget

4    Earnings from their assets

5    The proceeds of credit transactions

The Organic Law on the Financing of Regional Governments delimits the specific economic competence of the communities.

***Provincial and municipal taxation*** Apart from regional governments, the other local bodies with capacity to impose tax obligations are provincial and municipal authorities, and local municipal corporations. Among the various local taxes and fees, the most important are: municipal ground tax; tax on increased land value and capital gains; municipal luxury tax; and municipal advertising tax.

Of particular importance is the tax on increased land value or capital gain. This tax is levied on the increase in the value of land whose ownership is transmitted by any title, or in respect of which any property right of limited ownership is established or transferred, and on land belonging to legal entities. In transfers by purchase, the transferor is subject to the tax. However, as a practical matter, the holder of the property, i.e. the transferee, will be held responsible for tax payment. He may seek reimbursement from his predecessor in title. This issue of who shall pay the tax is a customary practice, provided for in the purchase-sale contract.

The taxable base is made up of the difference between the market value of the land at the time of acquisition and alienation. The tax accrues when the ownership of the land is transferred, whether by valuable or gratuitous title, whether *inter vivos* or by succession. The rate is fixed in accordance with a scale, which may not exceed 40% of the increase in value in the case of individuals, or 5% in the case of legal entities.

## Social security obligations

Social security in Spain is compulsory and therefore all employers must register their employees as well as themselves in the social security general regime. For this purpose, an employer is any natural or juridical person, private or public, who carries on an activity, even on a free basis.

The registration of employees in the social security system is a prerequisite to the beginning of any activity and can take place through the requirement of the worker or of the social entity of affiliation.

Contributions to the social security are normally provided by employees and employers, the latter being obliged to pay for the regime of work accidents and professional diseases and the guarantee salary fund on their own.

Employers are legally obliged to provide for the accomplishment of all payments. That is to say, they are responsible for the payment of both parts of the contribution: the employer's and the employee's. For this purpose they will deduct the employee's contribution from his salary, when monthly payments of the same are made. If they do not make the deduction in this period they will not e able to charge it afterwards and will themselves be liable for the debt with the ocial security.

Also, the employer who, having made the deduction, does not pay it to the ocial security within the period established by law, will be responsible before the orresponding social entities and before employees, without prejudice to his riminal and administrative responsibility.

Finally, any agreement, either individual or collective, by means of which an mployee assumes the obligation of payment of the employer's social security ability, or intends to vary the lawful payment bases, is void.

# CHAPTER 16
# UNITED KINGDOM

*Martin Mendelsohn*

## OVERVIEW OF FRANCHISING IN THE UK

In the widest sense, franchising has been evident in the UK as a trading format for many years. There are those who describe the 'tied' public house system as a franchise, although it is doubtful whether its legal structure is such as to justify that nomenclature.

The principles upon which franchising is based are evident in non-trading practices of the very distant past. The baronial system, dating back as far as the England of Norman times, possessed many of the elements which are common in franchising today. The barons, having been granted territories by the king, represented him in their areas and collected and paid royalties, as well as meeting many other requests from the monarch. Indeed, the USA cannot even claim originality in class actions because the barons indulged in such a strategy nearly eight hundred years ago. The terms of the settlement are enshrined in that most famous of historical documents, the Magna Carta.

### In the beginning

As in the USA, the early stirrings of business format franchising in the UK took place in the mid-1950s with the establishment of the Wimpy hamburger franchise.

The growth rate of UK franchising, however, has been much slower than in the USA and perhaps in many other countries, due to the effect early on of pyramid selling schemes and other fraudulent practices which became associated with franchising and gave it a bad reputation.

Although there were some attempts during the early 1970s to establish a franchisors' trade body, it was not until 1977 that the British Franchise Association (BFA) was formed when eight franchise companies joined forces to found the association.

### Pressures

The existence of legislation in the USA must not be regarded as conclusive evidence that it is needed elsewhere. Considerations differ from country to country. The pressures in the UK are different from those in the USA. In the UK, legisla-

on will only be introduced to regulate franchising if there are abuses by franchisors not covered by existing laws to a sufficient degree that they come to the
attention of the government and merit their imposition on a whole business sector.

The government would have to resolve that it had to respond and if it
decided to do so it would be able to ensure the passage into law of its proposals. At
the present time, the government has no intention of introducing legislation
directly affecting franchising.

Indeed, the government expects the franchise industry, in the form of the
BFA, to regulate itself and control and eliminate any abuses which become
apparent.

## Expansion

The expansion of franchising as a marketing method is very evident and the
growth in interest since 1977 when the BFA was formed, and, in particular, over
the last five years has been considerable.

## Government attitude

The UK government has for some time been encouraging the development and
growth of small businesses, and it has indicated that it sees franchising as being
capable of making an increasingly significant contribution. There has already
been an extension to an incentive scheme to accommodate franchise operations
and it is clear that ethical franchising has government support.

The establishment of an all-party committee on franchising by Members of
Parliament as a result of BFA lobbying has involved MPs of all political persua-
sions in positive support for franchising. This support will be reflected in the
future in the way in which Parliament deals with measures affecting franchising.
There are also now civil servants in various departments who have a familiarity
with franchising.

## Future developments

The increasing attendance at BFA seminars of representatives from major UK
companies indicates interest in investigating the scope for growth using the franchise method of marketing. The flow of developing franchises to the market-place
is a slow process because it can take up to two years from the time positive interest
is established to the point at which the first franchise sales are made, and thereafter from three to five years for the franchise to grow to a significant size. There is
a real interest in master franchise arrangements. An inhibiting factor frequently
to be found is the difficulty in obtaining commercial properties for occupation by
franchised outlets.

## Bank support

The major banks in the UK all provide positive support for franchising. The
National Westminster Bank was the first to establish a franchise manager at head
office in June 1981. The other banks with franchisee managers and specialist

departments include Barclays Bank (since August 1981), the Royal Bank of Scotland, the Midland Bank and Lloyds Bank. All the banks have been very supportive of franchise development and have sponsored various projects primarily for the BFA.

The National Westminster Bank has recently sponsored the NatWest Centre for Franchise Research at the City University Business School in London which provides the first full-time franchise research centre in the world. The Business School has appointed a Professor of Franchising and will be running a number of courses and developing a post-graduate diploma in franchising.

## Trade associations

There are two complementary recognized trade associations in UK franchising – the British Franchise Association (BFA) for franchisors, and the Franchise Consultants' Association (FCA) for consultants.

The BFA has three classes of membership: full membership, associates, affiliates. Full membership is open to those who have been in business as franchisors for a period of two years with four successful franchisees operating during that period.

Associate membership is open to companies which are developing new franchise systems. The criteria for this category are: (a) disclosure to the BFA of any material information relating to the franchisor and the franchise; (b) at least one successful pilot scheme in operation for at least one year (financed and managed by the applicant); and (c) evidence of success with at least one franchisee over a period of one year, unless the applicant is a substantial company (i.e. with more than 25 company-owned operations) which runs its franchise as a separate division. There is also a Code of Ethics which has to be observed by members and which follows the form adopted by the European Franchise Federation.

Affiliate membership is open to those providing services to franchisors and it includes the following categories: accountants, banks, design consultants, franchise consultants, insurance brokers, solicitors and surveyors.

## STRUCTURE OF A UK VENTURE

A prime consideration is the type of structure of the UK operation. Either a limited company or a partnership could be established to control the operations. There are a number of advantages and disadvantages in both cases which should be examined.

### Advantages and disadvantages
*Advantages of a limited company*
1   The liability of the shareholders is limited to the full nominal value of share capital for which they have agreed to subscribe.

2   The company is a separate legal entity from the shareholders.

3   The tax on company profits is currently restricted to a level of 34%. There is a lower rate for small companies.

4   Personal higher rate tax for individuals can be avoided if profits are retained by the business (individuals pay income tax which is levied on salaries and benefits).

5   Greater pension benefits can be obtained.

6   Finance can be raised under the Business Expansion Scheme, in some cases.

7   The spread of ownership can be wider.

### Disadvantages of a limited company

1   Legal and financial information is filed on public record.

2   The company must comply with statutory legislation laid down by the companies legislation, including the requirement for an annual audit.

3   Loans to directors are generally prohibited.

4   Loans to shareholders can give rise to tax consequences.

5   Personal guarantees are often required to be given by directors which diminish the value of the limited liability status.

6   National insurance contributions can be significantly higher.

7   Tax is payable on amounts withdrawn in the form of dividends or extra remuneration.

8   There may be a double charge to capital gains tax in the event of the sale of the business.

### Advantages of a partnership

1   Flexibility of actions which are governed only by the partnership agreement.

2   Greater confidentiality because information does not have to be filed on public record.

3   Losses from the business may be offset against other income, thus reducing tax liabilities.

4   Partnerships are given a longer period in which to pay partners' tax and national insurance contributions.

5    It is relatively easy to transfer the business to a limited company in the future.

### Disadvantages of a partnership

1    The partners are personally responsible on a joint and several basis for all the liabilities of the partnership.

2    There is less flexibility in transferring the ownership because a change in the partners entails dissolution of the old partnership and the setting up of a new partnership, unless certain procedures are followed.

**Best choice**  The choice of structure will depend on a number of specific factors, but in general a limited company is viewed as the best choice in an international framework. There are two alternatives to consider if a limited company structure is chosen. The company can either be established from scratch, or purchased as an existing shell company (known as an off-the-shelf company).

### Formation of company

**From scratch**  Professional advice should be sought when adopting this approach. It takes about six weeks to finalize arrangements after the initial application has been made. It tends to be a relatively costly exercise, the major elements being registration and professional fees. A name for the company must be chosen and agreed with the Registrar of Companies. The name must not be the same as that of an existing company, and not contravene the various rules governing the choice of names. A memorandum and articles of association must be drafted which set out the objectives and scope of the business of the company and the rules regulating the shareholders and its management. Standard documents are available as a guide, but these may need to be amended to suit the particular requirements of the company. All constitutional documents must be lodged with the Registrar of Companies. When he is satisfied that all requirements have been complied with, a certificate of incorporation will be issued. Business can then commence.

**Off-the-shelf company**  This is a much quicker exercise in that business can commence almost immediately. Professional advice should again be sought. An existing company which has never traded can be purchased for a relatively modest sum, and the change of name process takes about four weeks. The constitution documents (memorandum and articles of association) may require amendment, and, as before, all documents have to be lodged with the Registrar of Companies. The Registrar will then issue a certificate of incorporation on change of name. The total cost of acquisition and of the changes will probably be similar to the cost of the 'tailor-made' company but without the disadvantage of delay.

***Statutory requirements*** The Companies Act has the following requirements which apply when forming a new private company in the UK. As a brief guide:

1   The company must have at least two shareholders and one director on incorporation.

2   If there is only one director of the company, another person must be appointed as company secretary.

3   If there are two or more directors, any director can fulfil the role of company secretary, or another person can be appointed.

4   An initial board meeting must be held to deal with the following matters:

   (a)   appoint additional or new directors

   (b)   appoint auditors to the company for the following year

   (c)   determine the financial year end of the company

   (d)   determine banking arrangements for the company

   (e)   allot shares and approve any transfers of the subscribers' shares

   (f)   make arrangements for the keeping of the statutory books

   (g)   establish the place of the registered office of the company

5   The Registrar of Companies must be notified on the appropriate statutory forms of details relating to directors, shareholders, the financial year end, and the registered office.

6   The notification of the financial year end must be sent to the Registrar within six months of the date of incorporation. If this is not done, the year end will be fixed at 31 March in each year. The first financial period will normally exceed six months, but must not exceed 18 months.

### Directors: appointment, duties and responsibilities

The directors are the legal officers of the company and as such are governed by the Companies Act.

***Appointment and removal*** The first directors of the company are appointed by the subscribers to the memorandum and articles of association (i.e. the initial shareholders). The directors are not automatically employees of the company, but an employee may be appointed as a director. Further directors are appointed by the directors, but must be approved by the shareholders at the next annual general meeting and details must be notified to the Registrar. Directors may be removed from office by the shareholders passing an ordinary resolution in general meeting. This must also be notified to the Registrar.

*Duties and responsibilities* The directors are bound by a duty of good faith to the company and must have due regard for the employees of the company. They are required to exercise due skill and care in fulfilling the directors' role. They also have a duty not to trade if the company is insolvent, and may be deemed to be acting fraudulently and incur personal liabilities if they do so. There are strict rules governing loans to directors, and normally they are prohibited from accepting loans from the company. The directors are responsible for keeping the books and records of the company, and for preparing and filing the annual accounts of the company.

*Statutory books* The statutory books of the company should include the following: register of the shareholders and share transfers; register of the directors and the company secretary; register of the directors' interests (i.e. any beneficial shareholding which they may have); register of mortgages and charges on the assets of the company.

## LEGAL CONSIDERATIONS

Franchising in the UK differs from that in many countries in that there are not only no specific franchise laws, but there are also no reported decisions of the courts dealing with disputes between franchisors and franchisees. That is not to say that there is a lack of legal involvement because franchise transactions, like any other commercial contractual arrangements, are affected by the general commercial law.

A number of pyramid selling schemes were introduced in the UK in the late 1960s. Their impact was such that, following a court decision ordering the compulsory liquidation of one of the pyramid companies, legislation was introduced to regulate pyramid and similar trading schemes.

So far as litigation is concerned, there appear only to be two reported decisions involving a franchise company and they only deal with the enforcement by injunction of post-termination covenants in restraint of competition. There have been some unreported decisions, but they have dealt with the same issue without any analysis of franchising, which was not necessary at the interlocutory stage of the proceedings. There are disputes between franchisors and franchisees, but so far it appears that in the main they are settled before or during the formal hearing.

Experience shows that the pattern of litigation can be summarized under the following headings:

Termination disputes

Misrepresentation claims

Enforcement of post-termination non-competition covenants

Non-payment of franchise fees

Attempts by franchisees to break away

It is proposed in this chapter merely to highlight those areas where the application of a particular legal principle or statute affects franchise transactions. The treatment of each topic is of necessity brief.

## Pyramid selling

The regulation of pyramid selling is legislated for in Part XI of the Fair Trading Act 1973, which defines such schemes. The fact that a franchise system is within the definition does not cause a problem. The problem arises if there is non-compliance with the regulations which have been made under the provisions of the Act.

Regulations have been made under the Act which exempt those trading schemes under which the prospect of payments or benefits are held out to only one participant in the UK or, alternatively, under which the only prospect of benefit is the receipt of a sum not exceeding £75 in respect of the introduction of other participants.

The exclusion of one participant is intended to permit franchising of the UK by an overseas franchisor to a master franchisee.

The regulations contain a number of requirements dealing with such matters as:

A limit of £75 on the value of goods to be supplied to a participant in a trading scheme

A prohibition on non-returnable deposits

A prohibition on charging for the provision of training or other services to a participant

The right for a participant to terminate without penalty at any time on 14 days written notice

The infringement of the regulations is a criminal offence. The civil consequences are that sums paid and accepted in contravention of the regulations are recoverable. No undertaking or liability to pay sums in contravention of the regulations is enforceable.

The provisions make it difficult if not impossible to divide the UK into marketing areas with area or development agreements involving sub-franchising. The UK government is considering this problem, which may in due course result in changes being made.

## Antitrust considerations

The UK antitrust laws are not so stringent as those which apply in the USA and it is not difficult for franchisors easily and legitimately to avoid their application. They are contained in three separate statutes – Restrictive Trade Practices Act 1976, the Competition Act 1980 and the Resale Prices Act 1976. As a result of an examination of the operation of these statutes the UK government has concluded that changes should be made which will be radically different in approach. The government's proposals are set out below after the existing law is explained.

*Restrictive Trade Practices Act 1976* This applies briefly to agreements between two or more persons carrying on business within the UK in the supply of goods or the provision of services, being agreements under which two or more parties accept restrictions in relation to certain matters listed in the Act. These matters include the following:

1    In relation to goods:

   (a)   prices to be charged or paid

   (b)   prices to be recommended or supplied

   (c)   the terms and conditions on which goods are to be supplied or required

   (d)   the quantities or description of goods to be produced

   (e)   processes of manufacture

   (f)   persons to or from whom or areas or places from which acquired goods are to be supplied or required

2    In relation to services:

   (a)   prices to be charged or paid

   (b)   the terms or conditions on or subject to which services are to be supplied

   (c)   the extent or scale to or on which designated services are to be made available, supplied or obtained

(d)  the form or manner in which designated services are to be made available, supplied or obtained

(e)  the persons to or from whom, or areas or places from which, designated services are to be made available or supplied

There are a number of requirements to be satisfied in both cases before the provisions can take effect:

1   There must be an agreement and it should be noted that the court has the power to declare whether an agreement is one to which the Act applies. Agreement is defined and includes arrangements which need not be enforceable.

2   It (the agreement) must be made between two or more persons carrying on business within the UK in the production or supply of goods or the application to goods of any process or manufacture or, as the case may be, the supply of services.

3   Two or more individuals carrying on business in partnership with each other are treated as a single person. Whether or not a person carries on business in the UK is a question of fact; representation by an agent in the UK does not for this purpose of itself mean that a person is carrying on business within the UK.

4   Restrictions have to be accepted by two or more parties in respect of the matters listed. Restriction includes a negative obligation whether expressed or implied and whether absolute or not.

In franchising there is no doubt that franchisees accept many restrictions in respect of the matters listed. The franchisor usually accepts none. However, there are two ways in which a franchisor commonly invites application of the Act to his agreement:

1   Where he grants exclusive territorial rights he will be accepting a restriction in the last of each of the categories above which applies to goods and services. In view of the restriction which the franchisee inevitably will be accepting this will require the agreement to be registered. In practice in the UK many franchisors do not grant exclusive territorial rights in order to avoid the need for registration. A foreign franchisor who does not carry on business within the UK who enters into a contract with not more than one person who does carry on business in the UK will not be affected.

2   Where the principal shareholder and/or director of the franchisee (being a company) is required to enter into the agreement not only to guarantee the

franchisee's performance of the contract but also to preserve the trade secrets etc. of the franchisor.

What one has is a three-party contract: franchisor (a), franchisee (b) and guarantor (director/shareholder) (c). Assuming the franchisor and the franchisee both carry on business within the UK as provided in the appropriate section, the first trigger has been squeezed. The next point to consider is whether two or more parties have accepted relevant restrictions. Again assume the franchisor has not accepted any restrictions; if the franchisee has accepted the usual spread of restrictions one has to consider whether the covenant by the guarantor amounts to the acceptance of a restriction within the framework of the relevant section.

If the covenant is so framed that the guarantor is prevented from making use of the know-how, trade secrets and confidential information acquired by him as director and/or shareholder in the franchise company there is no restriction accepted by him.

The basic reason is that the guarantor is not granted any rights under the franchise system entitling him to operate the franchise system or use any of the property rights associated therewith including know-how and trade secrets etc. On the other hand, by virtue of his position he has acquired knowledge of the franchisor's system, methods, know-how and trade secrets. He is not accepting any restrictions under the relevant provisions in the Act by covenanting not to use or disclose such information, since it was never his to make use of and nor has he ever been licensed to use it for his personal benefit.

There could be a tripartite agreement with two parties accepting restrictions which does not come under the Act: a franchisor who is a foreign company which does not carry on business within the UK, a franchisee who does, and the principal who is an employee or officer of the franchisee but who does not carry on business within the UK. In such a case, the franchisee and principal could accept otherwise registerable restrictions without the Act applying. The danger in such an arrangement is that if either the franchisor or the principal subsequently carry on business in the UK in the production or supply of goods or the provision of services, the Act could then apply.

Care must also be taken to ensure that the franchisor accepts no other restrictions, particularly where the supply of products is concerned.

There are also some exemptions which cover such matters as exclusive dealing, trade marks, patents and registered designs, exclusive supply of services, know-how about services and copyright, which are exempt from registration in limited circumstances specified in the Act. These exemptions are unlikely to be of any value in formulating a franchise agreement.

Having made the decision whether or not to become involved in a registrable agreement, the consequences of registration must be considered. Basically, the restrictions must be modified or abandoned or be so insignificant that the Director General of Fair Trading (DGFT) advises the Secretary of State that they should not be put before the court. If one does not agree to modify or abandon the restrictions and they are not considered insignificant then a reference is made to the court which has to be satisfied that the case comes within one of the tests laid down which are to ensure that the consumer interest is paramount. It should be appreciated that in practice the DGFT has been positive in his approach to franchise agreements.

The provisions are wide-ranging and if and when a franchise agreement is referred to the court the whole business practice of franchising is likely to be on trial, not merely the particular restrictions contained in the referred agreement. It is also significant for both franchisor and franchisee that the tests to be satisfied pay no heed to what is in their respective interests. Indeed, restrictions could be removed from an agreement which destroy the whole fabric of the franchise scheme and leave the franchisor without control over substantial areas of the system.

The risk of being involved in the heavy expenditure which would be incurred in a reference to the court with the uncertainty of its outcome does not justify the use of a registerable agreement. In addition, there are, of course, the unfortunate consequences which could follow an accidental omission to register any particular agreement. With a fast-growing franchise chain it would, of course, be quite easy for this to happen by simple clerical error or omission.

It should also be borne in mind that even if the agreement is registered and the restrictions considered to be insignificant at the time of registration, that does not end the matter. The Secretary of State may, if requested by the DGFT, withdraw his direction if there has been a material change of circumstances.

In the light of the adoption by the European Commission of the Block Exemption Agreement for categories of franchise agreements (see Chapter 2), it is unlikely that the DGFT would raise any issues about an agreement which complies with the regulation and benefits from its provisions. This is reinforced by the government proposals (see below) which will, when implemented, adopt the European Block Exemption Regulation.

*The Competition Act 1980* This Act has the potential to affect franchise companies. It is concerned with what are described as anti-competitive practices in the following terms.

A person engages in an anti-competitive practice if, in the course of business, that person pursues a course of conduct which, of itself, or when taken together with a course of conduct pursued by personnel associated with him, has, or is intended to have, or is likely to have, the effect of restricting, distorting or preventing competition in connection with the production, supply or acquisition of goods in the UK or any part of it or the supply or securing of services in the UK or any part of it. (The word 'person' includes a company or firm.)

If it appears to the DGFT that any person has been or is pursuing an anti-competitive practice he may investigate the position and publish a report. The

DGFT has the power to seek information and obtain documents relevant to his investigations. Time is given to allow for negotiation and the provision of undertakings as to future conduct, but if no negotiations take place or negotiations are not concluded, a competition reference may be made to the Monopolies and Mergers Commission. The Commission investigates and reports on whether the person was engaged in an anti-competitive practice and if such practice operated or might be expected to operate against the public interest.

Following the Commission's report there is a procedure whereby undertakings as to future conduct are sought, but if no agreement can be reached the Secretary of State may make an order prohibiting the continuation of the course of conduct which has been held to be anti-competitive.

There are five considerations:

1    Regulations have been made under the Act which *inter alia* exempt companies:

     (a)   with less than £5 million annual turnover in the UK

     (b)   who enjoy less than one quarter of a relevant market

     (c)   who are not members of a group of interconnected companies which have an aggregate annual turnover in the UK of £5 million or more or enjoy one quarter or more of a relevant market

2    An investigation under the Act is concerned with the practice engaged in by an individual person and not with all those who may be engaged in it or in a similar practice. There may be differences in the structure of the transaction and the economics of the particular market, which means that what is anti-competitive in one case may not be in another. Whatever these differences it would seem likely that there will emerge clear indications of the thinking of the Office of Fair Trading, the Secretary of State and the Monopolies Commission as cases are dealt with. None of the cases which have so far been dealt with involve franchising or franchise companies or appear to have any specific consequences for franchising.

3    The present attitude of the Office of Fair Trading appears to be that the members of a franchise chain are not competing intra-brand. Rather they are analogous to a multiple chain of stores or outlets and are competing inter-brand in the market. This should mean that the above practices utilized for the benefit and strength of the franchise chain and which strengthen its competitiveness in the market should be free from complaint under the Act.

4    It seems probable that a person is unlikely to be able to act anti-competitively

unless he enjoys market power. This does not mean that he need dominate the market but that his presence in the market is such that his behaviour can have the effect stipulated in the definition. It is recognized that in some circumstances practices which would be anti-competitive may be pro-competitive, for example when employed by a small firm fighting for entry into a market.

The views already expressed by the Monopolies and Mergers Commission in its report on full line forcing and tied sales are that in relation to franchising it did not consider that the public interest would be an issue.

*The Resale Prices Act 1976* This Act prohibits the enforcement by suppliers of goods to dealers of any condition establishing or providing for the establishment of minimum resale prices to be charged on the resale of the goods in the UK. Two factors are worth noting:

   The Act is concerned with the prohibition of *minimum* resale price conditions. It does not affect *maximum* resale price conditions unless there is collusive action by suppliers or dealers.

   The Act only applies to goods and thus does not apply to services. A question may arise if the provision of a service includes of necessity the inseverable sale of goods.

*Changes proposed* The UK government intends to introduce new competition laws when the parliamentary timetable permits. It is not known when these changes will take place. The government's legislative proposals are contained in a White Paper published on 18 July 1989.

The system of registration of agreements whose form falls within the provisions of the Restrictive Trade Practices Act 1976 will be dropped. The Resale Prices Act 1976 which prohibits the fixing of minimum resale prices (but which does not affect the fixing of maximum resale prices or the prices at which services should be supplied) will also be repealed.

These Acts will be replaced by a new law which will be similar to the EC Treaty (Article 85) and will prohibit agreements or concerted practices which have the effect or have the object of preventing, restricting or distorting competition in the UK or in a part of the UK and in particular:

   Those fixing pricing and charges, including any terms or conditions (e.g. resale prices, discounts, credit terms) which determine effective net prices.

   Those which may be expected to lead to the fixing of prices, such as price information exchange agreements and recommendations on fees.

3    Collusive tendering.

4    Those sharing or allocating markets, customers, raw materials or other inputs, production or capacity.

5    Collective refusals to supply or to deal with suppliers, collective discrimination in the terms on which different customers or classes of customer are supplied, and collective anti-competitive conditions of supply such as tie-ins aggregated or loyalty rebates and 'no competition' clauses.

In describing the proposals the government makes a number of points:

1    It is considering applying the prohibition to agreements wherever made which are implemented in the UK.

2    What is the 'relevant market' for a particular product or service will be established through economic analysis.

3    There will be *de minimis* provisions to permit parties to operate contracts without facing the risk of penalties unless the DGFT has declared the agreement anti-competitive. There will be two *de minimis* levels:

(a)   where the parties to the agreement have a combined turnover below £5 million; and

(b)   (in the case of vertical agreements) where no party has a turnover in excess of £30 million.

4    These figures may be adjusted up or down according to experience. The fact that an agreement comes below one of the *de minimis* levels will not offer protection against private action (concerning which see more below) but the burden of proving that the agreement could adversely affect competition in the relevant market taken as a whole is placed upon the plaintiff.

5    Even if neither *de minimis* level is exceeded, the parties could nevertheless apply for an exemption.

6    Unlike the EC rules, there will be no market share test in assessing the *de minimis* levels.

7    Price fixing will not benefit from the *de minimis* level.

8    There will be guidance notes issued by the DGFT, compliance with which will protect against penalties. The court will be able to have regard to guidance notes but will not be bound by them.

9    The prohibition in the law will not be intended to encompass agreements to grant licences for the exploitation of patents, know-how, plant variety rights and other intellectual property so long as they contain and go no further than the subject matter of the licence.

10   There will be financial penalties (see below).

11   There will be rights of private action (see below).

12   Company directors and managers who negotiate or operate prohibited agreements may be penalized.

*Exemptions*  The legislation will permit application to be made for exemption if it is claimed that agreements will 'make a sufficient contribution to the production or distribution of goods or the provision of services or to economic or technical progress, so as to countervail their restrictive effects and if consumers share adequately in the benefits'.

The government recognizes that provision should be made for block exemptions and in particular will provide that agreements which are exempt under Article 85(3) of the EC Treaty, whether individually or by falling within a block exemption, will be exempt under the new legislation without the need for separate application.

The grant of exemption on an individual basis or by application of a block exemption will ensure validity of the agreement and freedom from penalties and private action.

The DGFT will investigate and publish his conclusions in relation to agreements in respect of which a decision is sought, summarizing the nature and purpose of the agreement. If no objections are received, the conclusions will become the decision. If there are objections they will be referred to a new Restrictive Trade Practices Tribunal (RTP Tribunal) which will determine the issues.

The DGFT will also:

1    Investigate suspected infringements of the prohibition.

2    Issue complaint letters.

3    Have power upon a warrant being issued by a magistrate to enter premises to examine and remove business records.

*Financial penalties*  The DGFT will not have the power to impose civil penalties; that will be a function of the RTP Tribunal, which will be able to impose penalties of up to 10% of the UK turnover of the parties to the agreement or £250 000, whichever is higher, with a maximum of £1 million. For higher penalties and for those to be imposed on directors and executives, the High Court will decide and there will be appeals permitted against the level of penalties to the Court of Appeal.

There will also be a right of appeal to the High Court on a point of law or on the grounds that the RTP Tribunal's decision is not justified by the evidence.

*Private action*  Under the provisions of the Restrictive Trade Practices Act 1976 a person adversely affected by the operation of a registrable agreement which was not registered is entitled to bring a claim for breach of statutory duty. There is no information available to indicate the extent to which this remedy has been used, although it is believed to have been insignificant. In the White Paper the government suggests that there are signs of a growing interest in pursuing such a remedy.

The government intends to continue to make available a right of private action in addition to any penalties which may be imposed. It hopes that the part played by private action will grow over time to form a significant part in the enforcement system. The government is considering whether there are positive steps which could be taken to encourage the bringing of such actions.

There is unlikely to be such a significant impact on antitrust practices by private litigation as there is in the US since the UK system, like the EC system, will require action by the regulatory authority to condemn or exempt any practice which is allegedly anti-competitive. Indeed the new law will require the judge in a private action to order a stay in proceedings where an exemption decision is pending and the court will have a discretion to ask the DGFT to submit an opinion in a case involving private actions.

*Transitional arrangements*  The government has acknowledged that the changes will create uncertainty for business and will therefore delay the commencement of the prohibition to allow for the preparation of guidance notes and block exemptions. In addition, agreements entered into prior to the introduction of the new legislation into Parliament will benefit from a transitional period of one year after the commencement of the prohibition. If an application for exemption is made sufficiently before the end of the period of one year, the DGFT will have the power to extend the benefit of the transitional provisions in an individual case for six months at a time for up to a maximum of a further two years (i.e. three years in total).

During the operation of the appropriate transitional period the agreements will not be invalid for offending against the prohibition and nor will the parties be liable to penalties or third-party action.

For an agreement registered under the Restrictive Trade Practices Act 1976 but whose restrictions were considered sufficiently insignificant and therefore not referred to the Restrictive Practice Court, the transitional period will be five years from the date of application of the prohibition.

### Restraint of trade – common law rules

The basic common law rule is that a covenant in restraint of trade is void and unenforceable except to the extent that the person seeking to enforce it can demonstrate that it is reasonable with regard to time as well as area of operation in order to protect his legitimate interest.

There are two normal provisions in franchise agreements which may be said *prima facie* to have the capacity to be in restraint of trade. In a franchise involving the tied sale of products there may be a third.

The first provision is designed to ensure that the franchisor who is trained to the task and properly motivated will devote the whole of his time and attention to the franchised business and to no other. The franchisor is, of course, concerned also that the know-how acquired for the purpose of the operation of the franchised business is not being used to set up a competing business contemporaneously with the running of the franchised business.

The second provision covers restraint on the conduct of a similar business both while the contract is running and after termination. The franchisor has developed a sophisticated bundle of rights and know-how; he will have his own operations; he will have franchisees and he will wish to grant more franchises, particularly in an area where a franchisee has failed, or has had to be terminated or has withdrawn. His rights and know-how require protection from being gratuitously used by a former franchisee and he has the legitimate right to look for such protection. The question is to what extent does the law permit this?

As already mentioned, a covenant in restraint of trade is void at law unless the person seeking to enforce it can show that it is reasonable with regard to time as well as area of operation. The courts have not yet determined the approach to adopt to franchising. The normal post-contractual restraint provisions are found either in vendor and purchaser or employment servant cases. In the former case, the standard of reasonableness is easier to satisfy than in the latter.

In considering a franchise agreement two judges in the Court of Appeal have said different things: one said that franchising is in neither of the accepted categories, but is perhaps 'betwixt and between'. The other said that the franchisee was a 'cross-breed' but that for the purposes of that case he was prepared to assume he was an employee and apply the employee tests. In that case, which was concerned with an interlocutory application for an interim injunction which was granted to enforce a time and radius clause, the full case for franchising was not argued. If it is fully argued, one would hope that the courts will conclude that the same standard of reasonableness should be required as that which is required in vendor and purchaser cases.

The additional provision to which reference was made is where there is a tied sale of products from franchisor to franchisee. These types of arrangement are analogous to those which came before the courts involving the petrol companies' solus agreements. The courts appear in such cases to have reached the conclusion that a tied product sale for a period in excess of five years was unreasonable.

In franchising it is safe, therefore, to take the same view of the length of terms of the agreement as have been approved by the courts in the petrol company cases.

However, the courts have indicated that the acceptable length of the tie will depend on the circumstances in the particular trade and thus the whole franchise scheme should be looked at in the context of its place in the market. Franchising is different from the petrol company type of arrangement. The petrol company arrangement was dealt with on the basis that the garage proprietor owned his business before he struck the deal with the petrol company. In franchising, the franchisee does not. He receives a licence permitting him to trade using the franchisor's name, goodwill, system, methods and know-how. If the products which are an integral part of the scheme are trade marked or otherwise identified with the franchisor's trade name it must be legitimate to require that such goods are tied as part of the overall package; otherwise the franchisor's trade marks, trade name and goodwill will be adversely affected and ultimately lead to the devaluation of the franchise scheme to the detriment of all franchisees, as well as the franchisor.

If the goods are not trade marked by the franchisor the set-up of the business and franchise chain branding and goodwill will ultimately be affected and the integrity and value of the franchise system devalued if each store trades with a different range of stock. Invariably, it is the case that such arrangements provide for franchisees to effect purchases at advantageous prices.

Furthermore, the franchisee surrenders no freedom which he previously held. Prior to the grant of the franchise, the franchisee had no right to exploit the name and goodwill of the franchisor, or to make use of his system, methods and know-how. Since the grant of the right to do these things will be limited by the conditions laid down relating to the purchase of products, it is arguable that there is indeed not restraint at all, merely a limited right to conduct business under a licence. On the other hand, if there is held to be a restraint then perhaps the value of membership of the franchise chain could be regarded as sufficient justification for its imposition.

## Liability of franchisors

**Tort** As already pointed out, there are no franchise laws in the UK. One is left with the application of general principles to the transactions. While in the USA case law is abundant, there is none in the UK directly related to business format franchising. There are some cases which offer guidance because they relate to analogous transactions, and the most fertile sources of such authority are those cases involving the petrol companies, their leasing and licensing activities, and their tied sales arrangements.

The three areas in the field of tortious liability which are likely to cause most activity are negligence, misrepresentation and vicarious liability, i.e. negligence in advising the franchisee; misrepresentation in selling the franchise; and claims against franchisors by customers or franchisees.

So far as negligent advice is concerned, whether it be given in writing or orally, the general body of law would apply without any special consideration for the fact that the transaction is a franchise.

So far as misrepresentation is concerned, the scope is considerable. Negotiations which lead to the sale of a franchise can take a long time to conclude that a franchisee prospect is suitable; franchisees take time to decide that the franchise is viable and acceptable to them. Franchisees are usually able to see the franchise operation at work, having previously been supplied with a description of what is on offer. With negotiations spread over a lengthy period, the business capable of being looked at, and with so many areas of business activity where the franchisee relies upon the franchisor for guidance, the scope and incentive for misrepresentations to be made are considerable. The areas offering such scope include profit projections, site approval, setting-up advice, advice on procedures and so on.

In order that one can misrepresent, the statement made must express an existing fact. A statement of opinion by someone with particular knowledge (e.g. a franchisor) is factual in the sense that it imports that the person holds the opinion and has grounds for it. A franchisor is likely to be held by the courts to be a person professing particular skills owing a special duty of care and to be warranting that the advice given is sound.

This latter statement is drawn from a judgment of the Court of Appeal in a case involving a lease by a petrol company of a filling station. The petrol company assessed the likely throughput of petrol and failed to take into account adverse factors known to them, which arose after the initial assessment was made. There are so many parallels to be drawn between the issues in that case and franchising that it must be considered an important case for franchising. This case preceded the Misrepresentation Act 1967, which broadly speaking gave the same remedies for innocent misrepresentation as were available for fraudulent misrepresentation. A franchisor would be liable for an innocent misrepresentation unless he had reasonable grounds to believe and did believe when the contract was made that the facts represented were true.

**Contract** By virtue of the Supply of Goods and Services Act 1982 there is implied in a contract for the supply of a service, where the supplier is acting in the course of a business, an implied term that the supplier will carry out the service with reasonable care and skill.

Apart from this statutory provision and the implied warranty referred to above, the liability of a franchisor under contract will depend upon the nature and extent of his contractual obligations and his performance under the contract.

The question, however, arises of the extent to which a franchisor may be able in the franchise contract to limit the scope of any claim which may be made against him by the franchisee.

Any contract term which attempts to exclude liability for misrepresentation will be subject to the provisions of s. 1(1) of the Unfair Contract Terms Act 1977 which requires 'that the term shall have been a fair and reasonable one to be included having regard to the circumstances which were, or ought reasonably to have been, known to or in the contemplation of the parties when the contract was made.'

This same text is applied in the case of liability for loss or damage by negligence but does not apply to 'any contract so far as it relates to the creation or transfer of a right of interest in any patent, trade mark, copyright, registered design, technical or commercial information or other intellectual property or relates to the termination of any such right or interest.'

It is difficult in the absence of guidance from the court to know how far this exemption goes. The terminology for dealing with these proprietory interests does not appear to be compatible with either the way in which some of them are created or the manner in which they are dealt with. In particular, there must be some doubt as to whether the grant of a licence (so common in dealing with these interests) is intended to be and is covered by the wording of this exemption.

The Consumer Protection Act 1987 contains provisions under three headings: product liability, consumer safety, and misleading price indications.

*Product liability* This part of the Act introduces the EC product liability directive proposals, which are basically intended to make manufacturers liable for defective products without proof of negligence. The Act imposes civil liability for damage caused by a defective product. The liability falls upon the following:

1    The producer, i.e. the manufacturer

2    Anyone who holds himself out as being the producer by putting his name or make on the product

3    Anyone who imports a product into the community (i.e. the EC)

4    The supplier of a product if he is unable to identify the producer or importer or his own supplier

The following issues therefore arise. A franchisor who may have nothing whatever to do with the manufacture of the products is clearly at risk of being regarded as 'any person who, by putting his name on the product or using a trade mark or other distinguishing mark in relation to the product, has held himself out to be the producer of the product'. However, there is a defence available if the franchisor can show that he 'did not at any time supply the product to another'.

The word 'supply' is defined as including 'selling hiring and /or lending' the goods. The definition deals with other practices, such as hire purchase and even making gifts.

A franchisor who does not feature in the chain of supply of products to a franchisee would have this defence available to him. However, a franchisor who organizes global purchasing for franchisees in one of the many ways available may lose the benefit of this defence.

Insurance arrangements should be reviewed to ensure that they provide adequate cover against any product liability claims which may arise under the Act.

***Consumer safety*** This part of the Act introduces a criminal offence for supplying consumer goods which fail to comply with the general safety requirement. Goods fail to comply if they are not reasonably safe, having regard to all the circumstances, including whether they are defective (under Part 1 of the Act) and whether they conform to published standards of safety.

The danger of the proposals for franchisors will lie in those cases where the franchisor specifies products, supplies them, or nominates or approves sources of supply. A franchisee against whom proceedings are taken could put forward as a defence evidence that he took all reasonable steps and exercised due diligence to avoid committing the offence. In putting forward such a defence, the franchisee can allege that the offence was due to the act or default or in reliance on information given by another, i.e. his franchisor. The franchisee will also have to establish that 'it was reasonable in all circumstances for him to have relied on the information, having regard in particular to the steps which he took, and those which might reasonably have been taken, for the purpose of verifying the information' and 'to whether he had reason to disbelieve the information'.

The Act imposes a criminal sanction on the person whose act or default in the circumstances described above is responsible for the commission of an offence.

The effect of these provisions must be to make franchisors more aware of the risks they run in selecting products and suppliers, and may cause franchisees to question, with justification, the choices made in order to protect themselves from prosecution.

It should be noted that insurance will not protect against the commission of a criminal offence. Franchisors can only obtain protection by taking great care in the selection of products and suppliers.

The Act also provides a civil remedy for those who may be affected by a contravention of the obligations imposed by safety regulations. This may provide a cause of action for franchisees against franchisors, although the franchisor may have recourse to the manufacturer or supplier to him or his franchisees.

***Misleading price indications*** This part of the Act creates a criminal offence if, in the course of business, a person gives (by any means whatever) to a customer an indication which is misleading as to the price at which any goods, services, accommodation or facilities are available (whether generally or from particular persons).

This provision extends to services and thus is wider than the scope of the Resale Prices Act. Franchisors will have to be careful in advertising prices in national (or even local) advertising, and in their marketing and promotional endeavours on behalf of the network. Also, care will have to be taken in the production of point-of-sale and other material which may bear price indications.

## Industrial and intellectual property

*Trade names* It is not possible to register a trade name in the UK unless it is a trade mark or service mark (see below). A franchisor may be able to secure the use of the trade name by registering it as a corporate name, thereby preventing a third party from using the same or very similar trade name as part of its corporate name.

The owner of a well-established trade name may be able to protect it by preventing a third party from using it. The prevention would take the form of bringing a passing-off action at common law against the infringer. To succeed, the owner would have to show that the third party is copying his name or using one which is confusingly close to it and in a manner in which the public is being confused or deceived into thinking that it is trading with the real owner.

*Trade marks/service marks* The role of trade marks and service marks in franchising is fundamental. Franchisees rely on the goodwill, good reputation and wide recognition of the franchisor's trade names, trade marks and service marks. The stronger the brand name or mark, the greater will be the value of membership of the franchised network.

Any person claiming to be the proprietor of a mark used or proposed to be used by him in the UK, whether or not a British subject, may make an application to the Trade Marks Registry for the registration of a mark in the UK. There are 42 classes, each itemizing a range of products or services, and a separate application has to be made for each class or, as is not uncommon, the relevant part of a class.

Registration of a mark confers on the owner a legal monopoly in the use of that mark in relation to the goods or services for which it is registered and the owner of a registered mark has the right to sue in the courts for infringement of his mark.

Because registration confers this legal monopoly, care is taken to ensure that registration is not granted for marks which are identical to, or which can readily be confused with, words or symbols which other people should be free to use in the ordinary course of a business in respect of the class of goods or services for which registration is sought. For this reason, the law sets out the criteria by which marks must be judged if they are to qualify for registration.

The Trade Mark Register is in two parts: Part A and Part B. The former is used for distinctive marks, while a mark registered in the latter need not be distinctive in use. While one can sue for infringement of a mark registered in Part A or Part B, it is a defence to an action based upon alleged infringement of a Part B mark to show that the action complained of will not confuse or mislead the public.

The Registrar of Trade Marks may object to registration on the following grounds:

1   The mark is not distinctive. The Registrar may require evidence of distinctiveness. Distinctive means suitable for distinguishing the applicant's

goods or services from the goods or services of others. Invested words or designs are presumed to be distinctive unless they are proved to be in common use or are too like existing marks. Some words can never be distinctive, e.g. place names, or laudatory epithets.

The mark is descriptive. It is a common mistake to seek to use a mark which is descriptive of the goods or services to which it relates. It is not possible to register such a mark in the UK, where the rule seems to be enforced far more strictly than in the USA.

The specification of goods or services is too wide.

The mark is immoral, illegal, improper, scandalous or misleading.

After searching the Register the mark is too like others on the Register or in use.

here is an appeal procedure. Once the Registrar's objections (if any) are dealt ith, the application is advertised in the *Trade Mark Journal* and will be registered nless objections are raised within the period allowed for that purpose. The egistrar will allow the applicant and any opponent to argue the case, and there is right of appeal to the High Court. The Registrar can advertise a doubtful case efore being satisfied regarding the objections raised.

The registration procedure can take two years but the effective date of registration is the date that the application is lodged.

Failure to register a licensed user is not of itself fatal to the validity of the nark, although it is essential to register a licensed user if its use is to count to ie benefit of the proprietor of the mark in question. The Registrar has a discretion about registration of the user, and normally will allow it where the wner has the right to continuing control over the way in which the mark will e used.

*assing off* A similar cause of action exists in many jurisdictions. It is the means y which one protects that which cannot be protected by registration. In a House f Lords decision, it was said that five characteristics must be present to create a alid cause of action for passing off:

A misrepresentation

made by a trader in the course of trade

to prospective customers or ultimate consumers of the goods supplied

which is calculated to injure the business or goodwill of another trader and

5    which causes actual damage to the business or goodwill of the other trader

The case referred to goods but there is no reason to doubt that the principles would also apply to services.

**Patents**  Patented equipment or processes rarely form the central feature of a franchise. In some cases, they may be incidental, although important, elements of the franchise package. The main concern for the franchisor is to ensure that in the event of the termination of the franchise agreement the franchisee will not have the benefit of the continued use of the patented equipment or process. As the role of patent in franchising is limited it is not intended to deal with this aspect in detail.

**Know-how/trade secrets**  Know-how usually means the franchisor's particular business system and methods. A franchisor's know-how, trade secrets and confidential information can only be protected at common law by virtue of his contractual arrangements with third parties in the form of restrictions on use and disclosures and non-competition and restraint of trade clauses.

In theory, it is possible to contract to keep secret any information imparted by one party to another. In addition, it is also possible to enforce confidentiality where in the circumstances in which the information is imparted it is clear that a confidential relationship exists.

The real difficulty which arises for franchisors is that in many cases the 'trade secrets' are not secret in themselves. The various components of these 'trade secrets' are within the public knowledge. In these cases, the element which is 'secret' is the particular way in which these non-secret elements have been gathered together to produce the end product. This feature is recognized by the European Commission in the Block Exemption Regulation (see Chapter 2).

**Copyright**  Copyright protection can be a much more valuable weapon for the preservation of the franchisor's trade secrets and know-how than is commonly realized. There are many important elements in the franchise package which can be protected by copyright, such as operations manuals, price lists, menus, training, publicity and promotional material (including point-of-sale material), compilations, fabric designs, premises layout and design drawings of fixtures, fittings, equipment get-up and appearance, and floor and wall coverings.

The law relating to copyright in the UK does not require protection by registration.

Copyright in 'literary work' arises upon the creation of that work. 'Literary work' has been defined as 'work which is expressed in print or writing, irrespective of the question whether the quality or style is high . . .' There is a requirement for a literary work to be 'original' but only in the sense that the work must originate from the author and not be copied by him from another source.

Thus, copyright flows 'naturally' and without formality from the act of creation.

Since 1911 neither registration nor any formal notification of the claim to copyright on copies of a literary, dramatic, artistic or musical work has been a prerequisite either of copyright itself or the entitlement to institute proceedings for infringement. All the innocent party need prove is that the infringer has substantially copied his work. It is, therefore, important that the original work is retained and upon it should be noted the date of its creation and details of its creator.

There is no requirement to exhibit any symbol in connection with copyright work in the UK, such as there is in the USA. However, the 'copyright notice' ©, name of copyright owner and year of first publication) on published works appears in order to attract copyright in countries which are not signatories to the Berne Convention – notably the US – which accept this as sufficient formality because they belong to the Universal Copyright Convention.

Before any matter can attract copyright, it must exist in some permanent form. Thus, it is not possible to obtain copyright protection for a particular idea. Only when written expression has been given to that idea does copyright protection become available, but only in respect of the way in which the idea is expressed.

*Industrial designs* Articles employed in the franchised business may be capable of protection as registered designs. Protection for designs by means of registration is available in most countries and in the USA as design patent. British law is unique in this respect, in that there has evolved the concept of protection for the design' in question.

As registered designs do not play a significant role in franchising, the information given here is limited.

## Real estate and leasing

Land in England and Wales (it should be noted that Scotland and Northern Ireland have their own quite separate systems) may be owned in two ways.

The acquisition of a freehold title affords an absolute right of ownership. This should be contrasted with the acquisition of a lease, which will grant exclusive possession to a tenant for a finite number of years in return for which the tenant will pay a rent and agree to perform other stated obligations (often quite onerous) to his landlord.

*Freeholds* A franchisor entering the English market may wish to acquire some freehold sites to assist in the establishment of the business free from interference by third parties. This may have the virtue of yielding some investment profit as time goes on and once the franchisor's covenant is well established the possibility of a sale and leaseback with an English institutional landlord may arise. There is, of course, a considerable cost factor to be borne in mind if this course is adopted.

***Leaseholds*** The alternative way to acquire trading sites is to choose to take a lease. It should be understood that, on the whole, desirable property sites are in heavy demand and that competition for them is very keen. Scarcity of property is a common delaying factor for franchise systems.

The typical lease of premises in prime and good secondary locations will usually be granted by a property investor and typically for a term of 25 years (although periods of 15 years are not uncommon) at a commercial rent reflecting the market value of the building. In many cases, an assignment will be taken of an existing lease. The rent will be subjected periodically to revision (typically upwards only) at stated intervals. The property market has for some years past favoured reviews of rent every five years.

It is likely that such a lease will be granted on a 'full repairing and insuring' basis which will oblige the tenant to be responsible for the maintenance of the building (including the structure if the building is self-contained) and for refunding to his landlord the cost of insuring the building against damage by fire and other insurable risks. If the premises form part of a larger building (for instance a unit in a shopping centre or mall) the lease will provide for the tenant to maintain the interior of the property and to make a contribution towards the maintenance of the exterior and structure of the whole building or complex. Well-drafted leases will also contain provisions requiring the tenant to obtain his landlord's consent prior to the disposal of the lease or to the carrying out of alterations to the premises, and provisions regulating the use of the premises. It would be usual to require the landlord to act reasonably in dealing with such matters, but sometimes it becomes a question of negotiation.

The underlying principle of the English leasehold property market is the concept of the 'clear lease'. In other words, the property investor simply seeks a return from his building and requires the tenant to assume complete responsibility for its maintenance and the cost thereof.

A trading company entering the English market, unless it is substantial in its home market (and perhaps also already has an international reputation), will find it difficult to acquire leases of prime and semi-prime properties without the provision of some form of guarantee (be it by locally based directors, bank bond, or form of rent deposit). A franchisee (often entering business on his own account for the first time) may find it difficult to acquire the lease of such a property without some form of support from his franchisor. A good retained estate agent (real estate broker) specializing in the relevant commercial sector can often assist the approval process for a company entering the English market.

***Planning laws (Zoning)*** Another major consideration for the franchisor is the question of the authorized use for the purposes of English town planning legislation. Local authorities (which, broadly speaking, run the second tier of government in towns and cities, or in particular areas of larger cities) have powers to approve the way in which land is used. Central government (by regulation made pursuant to a statute) has laid down certain classes of use, and local authorities are responsible for the implementation and mixture of such uses in the towns and cities themselves.

For planning purposes, commercial uses broadly fall into retail and non-retail categories. The retail category comprises shops for most purposes, although there are one or two notable exceptions. Interpretations of the legislation may sometimes vary from authority to authority. For instance, a bakers' shop with an in-store bakery may need a separate permission for the baking operation since experience shows that some authorities will view it more as a light industrial function than retail.

Restaurants were excluded from the definition of 'retail shop' some years ago, resulting from a deliberate policy move to try to discourage a proliferation of restaurants at the expense of retail shops in high street locations. In consequence it often became difficult to obtain a specific planning permission for use as a restaurant and many local authorities actively discouraged such a use. However, the law was reviewed in 1987 with a view to liberalizing local authority planning attitudes towards restaurant use. A separate use class comprising restaurants (including take-away units) was created with the intention of facilitating a more sympathetic attitude by planners to restaurants in high street shopping locations. In practice this has not worked quite as well as was intended, although there is certainly now a more positive attitude towards restaurants than was the case in 1987.

Non-retail commercial uses are discouraged from town centres. Municipal authorities have actually encouraged the growth of industrial estates on the fringe of towns and cities which can be the focal point for a manufacturing and wholesale distribution network.

*Security of tenure* Legislation passed in 1927 and 1954 provides commercial tenants with a considerable degree of protection from unreasonable actions by their landlords. At the expiration of a lease of commercial premises, a tenant in occupation for the purpose of a business carried on by him is given the right to renew his lease.

The terms of the new lease (including a new rent) will be determined by the court if the parties themselves cannot reach agreement. The right can only be defeated if the landlord can justify certain specified grounds, the most important being that he wishes to redevelop, that he wishes to occupy the premises for his own use (when he must have owned the reversion to the property for five years), or that the tenant has persistently failed to honour his obligations. In practice, terms are agreed, but the tenant has to be aware of his rights and take certain steps within the time limits specified in the legislation, otherwise the rights can be lost.

In the event that a landlord is allowed to regain possession for redevelopment or because he wishes to use the premises for the purposes of his own business, the tenant will be entitled to a measure of compensation (although it must be said that in many cases such compensation is unlikely to be commercially adequate). In certain cases, a tenant may also be able to obtain compensation for improvements which he has made to the premises. The legislation also seeks to prevent a landlord from unreasonably withholding his consent to a tenant's application to assign his lease or to carry out alterations. This legislation is hardly foolproof (and in certain respects can be excluded by agreement between the parties) and instances may still arise where a landlord may frustrate (no matter how unreasonably) the tenant's objective.

The landlord and tenant legislation can also provide a trap for the unwary franchisor. In circumstances where a franchisor takes a lease of premises and underlets to a franchisee, the franchisor may wish to prevent the franchisee from renewing the underlease when the term comes to an end. Where the franchisor's own lease is significantly longer than the underlease granted to the franchisee it is possible (by excluding with the agreement of the court the provisions of the 1954 Act which provides security of tenure to the tenant) to prevent the franchisee from acquiring the right automatically to renew his lease.

However, because of the impact of the legislation, it becomes more difficult to achieve this aim where the franchisor's lease is not significantly longer than the franchisee's underlease. Indeed, there is little settled law on this issue and it may even be impossible to prevent a right of renewal of the franchisee's underlease in these circumstances. The franchisor may also find himself in a position where he is denied the right to renew his own lease, if it is the franchisee who is in actual occupation of the premises at the end of the term granted by the franchisor's lease. These difficulties all flow from the intention of the legislation to protect the person in actual occupation of the premises.

*Tenant's continuing liabilities* A problem which can be significant arises from the fact that the original tenant who enters into a lease remains liable throughout the duration of that lease, even after he has assigned it and severed all connection with the premises. In effect, therefore, such a tenant guarantees the performance by his successors in title of the tenant's obligations throughout the duration of the lease.

The original tenant can, therefore, be obliged to make good repairs to the premises (or to pay the landlord the costs of doing so) many years after the lease has been sold. He can also be called upon to pay rent (even at a revised level over which he has had no influence) may years later. Even if a lease has been acquired after the original tenant has sold his interest, that subsequent tenant many still remain liable to cure the defaults of his own successors in title if a covenant given to that tenant's landlord is drafted in a certain way.

This contingent liability should be considered carefully, particularly as English leases are generally longer in duration than those in many other countries and do not usually contain clauses which permit the tenant to terminate the lease. Also, the practice which is, for example, common in the USA, allowing franchisors to remedy breaches of covenant in leases entered into by franchisees and also providing for an automatic assignment of a franchisee's lease to the franisor without landlord's consent, will probably be unacceptable to English land-rds. In many cases, the franchisor will be taking over an existing lease and will ot be able to influence its provisions.

## oreigners working or establishing a business in the UK

*Vork permits* In general, people seeking to enter the UK for employment must ave work permits. These permits are issued by the Department of Employment respect of a specific employ and only to individuals aged between 23 and 54 ars. Work permits must be obtained before arrival in the UK and applications r them must be made by prospective employers.

Representatives of foreign companies which have no branch subsidiary or her representatives in the UK and persons in certain other categories (such as inisters of religion), although coming for employment, do not need work per-its and may be admitted for an appropriate period not exceeding 12 months if ey hold a current entry clearance granted for the purpose (see below) or, where try clearance is not mandatory, other satisfactory evidence to show that they do ot require a work permit.

There is also an exception for Commonwealth citizens if they can prove that e of their grandparents was born in the UK and islands and for nationals of the ember states of the EC.

It should be noted that the possession of a work permit does not absolve the older from complying with visa requirements. The holder of a work permit is ormally admitted for a maximum of 12 months. At the end of the first year of the older's stay, the permit may be extended if he is still engaged in the employment ecified in the permit or other employment approved by the Department of mployment, and the employer confirms that he wishes to continue to employ m. Where appropriate a corresponding extension will be granted to the appli-nt's wife and children.

If the work permit was originally issued for less than 12 months the approval the Department of Employment will be necessary before the original permit n be extended.

Not every type of job will qualify for the issue of a permit. There are eight tegories, and a permit will only be issued for jobs requiring working in these tegories. The eight categories are:

Those holding recognized professional qualifications

Administrative and executive staff

Highly qualified technicians having specialized experience

Other key workers with a high or scarce qualification in an industry or occu-pation requiring specific expert knowledge or skills

5    Highly skilled and experienced workers for senior posts in hotel and catering establishments who have successfully completed appropriate full-time training courses of at least two years' duration at approved schools abroad, or exceptionally, have acquired other specialized or uncommon skills and experience relevant to the industry

6    Entertainers and sportsmen/women who meet the appropriate skills criteria (professional sportsmen/women taking part in competitions of international standing do not normally require permits)

7    People coming for a limited period of training on the job or work experience approved by the Department of Employment

8    Other persons only if, in the opinion of the Secretary of State for Employment, their employment is in the national interest

*Entry clearance*  Individuals who wish to transact business in the UK are treated as visitors and will be granted entry into the country provided that they meet the UK requirements relating to visitors. Those, other than EC nationals, who wish to establish themselves in business or self-employment or to take over or join an existing business have to satisfy the rules relating to businessmen and self-employed persons. These provisions apply to all forms of business and self-employment, whether on the applicant's own account or in partnership, the only exception being writers and artists, who are treated as a separate category.

An applicant must obtain a current entry clearance issued for this purpose. In order to do so, he must satisfy the entry clearance office that:

1    He will be bringing in money of his own to put into the business; his level of financial investment will be proportional to this interest in the business; he will be able to bear his share of the liabilities; he will be occupied full time in the running of the business; and there is a genuine need for his services and employment. All these requirements must be fulfilled and not merely some of them.

2    The amount to be invested by him will not be less than £150 000. He must provide evidence that this amount or more is under his control and disposable by him in the UK.

3    He meets the additional requirements set out below relating to those intending to take over or join as a partner in an existing business or those wishing to establish a new business in the UK on their own account or to be self-employed.

An applicant intending to take over or become a partner in an existing business must:

Show that his share of the profits will be sufficient to maintain and accommodate himself and his dependants.

Produce audited accounts of the business for previous years in order to establish the precise financial position.

Provide a written statement of the terms upon which he is to enter the business.

Show that his services and investments will create new, paid full-time employment in the business for personnel already settled in the UK.

Satisfy the entry clearance officer that the proposed partnership or directorship does not amount to disguised employment and that he can earn a living without supplementing his business activities by employment of any kind or by recourse to public funds.

An applicant seeking to establish a new business in the UK must show that:

1 He will be bringing into the country sufficient funds of his own to establish the enterprise.

2 He can realistically be expected to maintain and accommodate himself and any dependants without recourse to employment of any kind (other than his self-employment) or to public funds.

3 The business will provide new, paid full-time employment in the business for persons settled in the UK.

An individual who has been admitted as a businessman or self-employed person will not obtain entry clearance if he fails to meet any of these requirements. If he is given leave to enter, he will be admitted for a period not exceeding 12 months, provided that there are no general grounds for justifying refusal. However, a condition restricting his freedom to take employment will be attached.

There are provisions for applications or extensions to be granted if the applicant continues to meet all the requirements which he had to meet in order to obtain entry. Documentary evidence of the same nature as that of the original application will be needed in support of the application for extension. Extensions are usually granted for a maximum period of 12 months with conditions restricting employment.

On the completion of four years as a businessman or self-employed person, indefinite leave to remain in the UK may be obtained.

## Employment laws

With few exceptions, every employee who has been in his job for two years has the right not to be unfairly dismissed. The employer must have a prescribed reason for and be reasonable in dismissing an employee within the meaning of the Employment Protection (Consolidation) Act 1978. If these requirements are not met, the aggrieved employee can apply to an industrial tribunal within three months from the date of dismissal to be reinstated or to be awarded compensation.

Where an employee terminates the contract himself, either with or without notice, in circumstances such that he is entitled to terminate it without notice by reason of the employer's conduct, he can claim to have been constructively dismissed by his employer. This provision is aimed at employers whose behaviour towards the employee is such that the employee cannot reasonably be expected to continue in that employment.

There is a 'deemed' dismissal when an eligible woman is denied her right to return to work after maternity leave. In these circumstances, she is treated as having been dismissed from the notified day of return.

There is statutory provision for employers to make lump sum redundancy payments to employees dismissed for reasons of redundancy. Redundancy in practice means dismissing employees, with or without notice, if the reason for dismissal 'is attributable wholly or mainly to:

> the fact that his employer has ceased, or intends to cease, to carry on the business for the purposes for which the employee was employed by him, or has ceased, or intends to cease, to carry on that business in the place where the employee was so employed; or
>
> the fact that the requirements of that business for employees to carry out work of a particular kind, or for employees to carry out work of a particular kind in the place where he was so employed, have ceased or diminished or are expected to cease or diminish.'

Minimum periods of notice required to be given by an employer to terminate the contract of employment of a person who has been continuously employed for one month or more have been established. These range from one week's notice to 12 weeks' notice in the case of a person who has been employed for 12 years or more.

Employees may enjoy additional forms of protection during their period of employment by virtue of the provisions of various other statutes, including measures designed to afford protection when a business is sold. These statutes include those which deal with issues of sex discrimination, race relations, equal pay, and measures relating to health and safety at work.

## Foreign investment

There are no restrictions on foreign investment.

### Terminations

There are no special laws which apply to the termination of franchise agreements. The franchise relationship is contractual and the normal laws of contract apply. It invariably the case that the contract will lay down the rights of termination, the grounds upon which termination may take place and the consequences thereof. In the absence of provision for termination, a party wishing to terminate will have to either rely on the breach of the contract by the other or risk being in breach himself.

If the contract is of an intermediate period and makes no provision for termination, the law will require that a notice which is given is reasonable in length (bearing in mind the circumstances) and clear and unambiguous.

## TAX AND FINANCIAL CONSIDERATIONS

### Corporation tax

The profits of companies resident in the UK are subject to corporation tax at a rate of 34% unless the company is eligible for the small company rate.

The tax payable is calculated on the adjusted profits, including capital gains, for each accounting period of the company and is usually payable nine months after the close of the period. If the accounting period is longer than 12 months, it will be split into the first 12 months, and the remaining months, and profits will be apportioned on a time basis. Interest is charged on any tax which is not paid by the due date.

There is a reduced rate of corporation tax of 25% for small companies. These are defined as companies whose profits plus capital gains are £250 000 or less. There is tapering relief on profits between £250 000 and £1 250 000. Where two or more companies are under common ownership, the limits of £250 000 and £1 250 000 are divided between the total number of active companies, even if not all the companies are UK resident.

### Adjustment to accounting profits

Under UK tax legislation there are a number of significant adjustments which must normally be made to accounting profits in order to determine profits for taxation purposes.

*Allowable expenditure* Only revenue expenditure incurred wholly and exclusively for the purposes of trade is an allowable deduction for calculating trading profits, while expenditure incurred in acquiring or improving assets is usually allowable in computing any capital gain or loss on their subsequent disposal. Other expenditure is disallowed.

*Capital allowances* The depreciation and amortization of fixed assets is normally disallowed in calculating trading profits, and special 'capital allowances' are substituted. These are given as a writing-down allowance, calculated on the cost

in the first year and on the unallowed portion of cost left over from the previou
year (declining balance). There are different rates of allowance on different type
of assets (e.g. buildings excluding land, plant and equipment, cars, patents, etc.

***Dividend receipts*** A major adjustment between accounting and tax profits relate
to dividends passing between two UK resident companies; such dividends ar
exempt from corporation tax in the hands of the recipient company.

Dividends receivable from overseas by a UK resident company are subjec
to corporation tax in the normal way. Relief is normally obtained for oversea
taxes borne on such dividends.

***Capital gains*** For UK taxation purposes, a capital gain is usually calculated a
the amount by which the sale proceeds of an asset exceed the original cost to th
person disposing of it. The gain is reduced by an indexation allowance to giv
relief for the inflationary element since 1982 included in the gain. For UK resi
dent companies, corporation tax currently stands at 35%. Capital gains tax is nc
generally levied on non-residents.

## Dividend payments and advance corporation tax (ACT)

While withholding tax is not deducted from dividends, a UK resident company i
required to make an advance payment of corporation tax (ACT) when a dividen
is paid. The amount of the payment is calculated (at present) as 25/75ths of th
dividend, and is payable whether or not the company has profits for the purpose
of corporation tax in the year in which the dividend is paid. If the company ha
taxable profits, ACT paid in the year can be offset against the corporation ta:
payable in respect of those profits, subject to the overriding condition that th
amount of ACT offset cannot exceed 25% of the taxable profits. Any ACT lef
unrelieved because of this restriction (or because the company had no taxabl
profits in the relevant period) may be carried back to reduce the corporation ta
liability for the previous six years, or carried forward indefinitely, again subject t
the restriction.

There are arrangements for transferring unrelieved ACT from parent com
panies to subsidiaries within UK groups and for paying dividends within group
without ACT payments (51% ownership in both cases). Moreover, a UK com
pany receiving dividends which have borne ACT will be able to set such ACT
against that payable on its own dividends.

A UK resident individual receiving a dividend from a UK resident company
will pay tax on the amount of the dividend plus the ACT applicable to it but wil
receive a tax credit for the amount of the ACT. The tax credit is not available as a
matter of course to non-residents receiving dividends from UK companies. How
ever, some of the UK's more recent double-taxation treaties have included provisions to extend the benefit of the credit, or part of the credit, to certain categorie
of shareholder resident in the treaty country. Such treaties commonly allow ar
individual shareholder to recover the whole of the tax credit. Some, but not all, o

those treaties which allow a tax credit to an individual shareholder also allow a corporate shareholder who controls 10% or more of the voting power of the UK company to recover half of the tax credit, less a 5% withholding tax on the sum of the dividend and recoverable credit.

Although branches of non-resident companies are liable to corporation tax, they have no liability to ACT in respect of dividends paid by the non-resident company.

### Close companies

Close companies are, in general, UK resident companies controlled directly or indirectly by five or fewer 'persons', and for this purpose an individual and his near relations and certain other associates are regarded as one person. A UK subsidiary of a non-resident company which would itself have been close if it had been a UK company is deemed to be a close company.

In general, a close company is obliged to pay by way of dividend (or it and its shareholders will be treated for UK tax purposes as though it had done so) the whole of its investment income after deducting corporation tax. Its trading profits need not be distributed. Where the company is a trading company, or a member of a trading group (as defined), regard can be given to the requirements of the company's business in determining whether investment income need be treated as paid out.

The definition of 'distributions' which are not allowed as 'expenses' in calculating taxable profits and which result in an ACT payment is widened to cover, for example, certain expenses incurred by the company for its shareholders.

Tax (at the same rate as ACT, i.e. 25/75ths) is payable by the company on loans made to individual shareholders, although the tax is repaid when the loan is repaid.

### Trading with associated companies overseas

Transactions between UK companies and their associates overseas should be on a commercial basis. If a transaction takes place on unreasonable terms entered into because of common control over the two companies, the Inland Revenue has power to assess the UK company on the profits that would have been made on a commercial basis.

The law on this point is commonly referred to under the expression 'arm's length trading'. It is normally good evidence that a transaction is on an arm's length commercial basis if it can be shown that similar deals take place at a comparable price with third parties not connected with the group. Where such evidence is not available, it may be necessary to show that the UK company gets a reasonable profit according to the trade usage, or alternatively, that it gets a reasonable share of the total group profit.

In particular, service charges made to a UK subsidiary or associated companies for administrative and other help provided by non-UK companies will be allowed by the Inland Revenue provided that the amount of such charges can be shown to be reasonable and fair for the services provided. Equally, the Inland Revenue will expect UK companies to make charges for the services which they render to overseas group companies.

### Indirect taxation

*Value added tax (VAT)*  This tax is applied on the sale of goods and services in the UK in the course of business and also applies to imports of goods and certain services. There is a single positive rate of 17.5% although certain transactions are zero-rated or exempt.

New businesses (whether operating by way of a branch or local company) should register with HM Customs and Excise if they expect their sales in any year to exceed £35 000. There are severe financial penalties for a number of VAT offences, including failure to register for VAT purposes when required to do so.

The tax is effectively borne only by the ultimate consumer of goods, and most traders, manufacturers, wholesalers and retailers will act as collectors of VAT, paying over to Customs and Excise the tax recoverable from their customers and being credited with tax payable on their expenses (including capital expenses). They will, therefore, bear no final tax charge themselves. Exceptions to this general rule will apply in the case of businesses undertaking exempt transactions, and in the case of purchases of private motor cars and most entertaining expenses where the VAT element will not be recoverable.

Some of the more important exempt transactions (no tax is chargeable on the sale, but no VAT is recoverable on related purchases) are rents on short leases, interest on loans, transfers of money, stocks and securities, and insurance. In addition, the tax is not charged by small traders with an annual turnover of under £35 000 who are not registered for VAT.

Some of the more important zero-rated items (no tax is chargeable on sale, but VAT is recoverable on related purchases) are most foods (other than purchased in a restaurant or a fast food outlet), transport other than of goods within the UK, power and fuel (but not road fuel), books and periodicals, and all goods for export.

Problems may arise over VAT chargeable on services, particularly where these are rendered to overseas companies. Charges for services include such things as management charges, know-how payments, royalties and any other payments other than for goods. Most services are zero-rated when made to overseas companies, but the detailed rules are complex, and professional advice should be sought.

*Customs and excise duties*  These duties are levied on the 'dutiable value' of goods at the time of their entry into the UK or the EC. The rates of duty vary quite considerably depending on the item imported and the source country from which the goods are received.

The dutiable value of goods in normal circumstances where the transaction

, at arm's length between independent parties is the purchase price of the goods lus the related charges of bringing the goods to the port of entry in the UK (e.g. ·eight and insurance).

It should be noted that all charges which may be related to the goods, other ¬an UK inland charges, are dutiable. Thus where a royalty is payable on the oods, it must be declared at the time of entry and duty paid on that element as ·ell.

Where the transaction is an independent one, the goods will be 'cleared' ¬mply by the importer completing the necessary documentation and paying the ppropriate duty. These formalities are often carried out by an agent on behalf of ¬e importer.

In the case of a UK subsidiary, it is important to establish that it is acting ¬dependently; otherwise, the authorities may contend that it is merely acting as ¬n agent for its foreign patent company, and as such, subject to duty computed on ¬e selling prices to its UK customers. To avoid this contention, it must be shown, ¬mong other things, that the UK company holds inventories and fixes its own ¬lling prices.

## ¬mployee-related taxes

*ay As You Earn (PAYE)* In most cases, for employees working in the UK, the ¬hole of the earnings of each tax year (including benefits-in-kind) are assessable ¬ income tax, and the tax must be deducted or withheld by the employer from ¬lary payments, under the PAYE scheme.

Any UK subsidiary, branch or establishment may be required by the Inland ¬evenue to provide the name and address of employees assigned to them by a ¬on-resident employer for a continuous period of 30 days or more.

There are two rates of tax: 25% on the first £23 700 of taxable income and ¬0% on the balance.

The PAYE method of collecting tax applies to foreign nationals even though ¬heir earnings may be paid overseas by a non-resident company. If the overseas ¬ompany has a branch in the UK or if the employee works under the manage- ¬ent and control of a UK company, the onus is upon that branch or company to ¬ollect tax under PAYE and pay it over to the collector of taxes on a regular basis. ¬here are provisions whereby the UK company can obtain the necessary details ¬f the individuals concerned and their emoluments and can reimburse itself for ¬he tax suffered where the overseas employer makes payments of remuneration ¬irect to the employees.

Where there is no UK branch or company which can operate PAYE, the ¬nland Revenue may ask the overseas employer to account for the tax, if neces- ¬ary with the assistance of agents in the UK.

Where PAYE is in operation, an annual return is required to be made to ¬he Inland Revenue showing the total remuneration paid to each employee, ¬ncluding all expenses and benefits.

It is also the duty of every employer to make an annual return to the Inland

Revenue showing the total remuneration paid to each employee, including all expenses and benefits:

1    Every director, whether paid or not; and

2    Other employees, where their salary together with all expenses and benefits-in-kind exceeds £8500 per annum.

If an individual is appointed as a director of a subsidiary company in the UK, that company must make a return of any expenses which it pays on his behalf, even though no fees or salary are receivable by the individual in the UK in respect of his directorship. Similarly, the provisions may apply in respect of any individual from overseas although not appointed a director, if the subsidiary paid expenses to or for him or provides him with benefits or facilities and the aggregate of his salary and such expenses and benefits amount to £8500 or more in a tax year.

*Social security contributions* Social security contributions are part of the state-administered social security scheme providing for pensions, sickness, industrial injury, unemployment and other benefits. Both the employee and the employer make contributions based wholly on the employee's earnings. There is a sliding scale of rates.

Special rates for 'contracted out' employees apply where the employer has his own pension scheme providing benefits at least matching the state scheme and has chosen to contract out of the second-level state scheme. The Occupational Pensions Board requires to be satisfied that the employer's scheme meets certain minimum requirements before permission to contract out can be given.

### Investment incentives
*Enterprise zones* Enterprise zones have been established in various parts of the country since 1981 to encourage industrial and commercial activity by removing certain fiscal burdens and statutory or administrative controls. The main benefits, which are available only to businesses and commercial enterprises located in the zones, are 100% relief from rates (local property taxes), 100% capital allowances (for corporation and income tax purposes) for commercial and industrial buildings, and deemed town planning permission for most buildings and activities. The reliefs apply for ten years from the designation of a zone.

*Regional selective assistance* Grants are available on a selective basis for manufacturing and service projects in specified areas of Great Britain known as assisted areas. There are two main types of grants – project grants and training grants. To be eligible, projects must either create new employment or safeguard existing employment in assisted areas and bring an identifiable regional and national benefit. The amount of support granted will be the minimum necessary to ensure the project goes ahead.

***Area-specific regional loans and grants*** Regional loans and grants are available from the EC in certain specified areas in Great Britain. Loans are available from the European Investment Bank for projects which create or safeguard employment in the assisted areas and from the European Coal and Steel Community for projects which create new employment opportunities for redundant coal and steel workers. The European Regional Development Fund offers a wide range of grants in areas affected by job losses in the steel, shipbuilding, textile and clothing industries to help new businesses start up and existing small firms grow.

***Loan guarantee scheme*** This scheme is intended primarily to help the small businessman who has a viable business proposition but is unable to obtain any conventional lending. By guaranteeing 70% of the loan, the government encourages banks and financial institutions to lend money in support of viable business propositions. A premium of 2.5% on the guaranteed proportion of the loan is payable by the borrower. Loans are made for smaller amounts. They are repayable over two to seven years.

***Application procedures*** For enterprise zones, the applicant applies through the Department of the Environment, for regional and European loans and grants through the Department of Trade and Industry, and for the loan guarantee scheme through participating lenders (mainly banks).

***Agency or ministry administering grant of incentives*** The Department of Trade and Industry administers the granting of regional and European incentives, the Department of Employment the loan guarantee scheme, and the Department of the Environment the enterprise zones.

***Applicant's obligations*** The applicant's obligations vary considerably and are wholly dependent on what type of grant is made. If the applicant's circumstances subsequently change within the specified period, certain grants will have to be repaid.

# APPENDIX A
# EC TREATY

*Article 85*

1. The following shall be prohibited as incompatible with the common market: all agreements between undertakings, decisions by associations of undertakings and concerted practices which may affect trade between Member States and which have as their object or effect the prevention, restriction or distortion of competition within the common market, and in particular those which:

a) directly or indirectly fix purchase or selling prices or any other trading conditions;

b) limit or control production, markets, technical development, or investment;

c) share markets or sources of supply;

d) apply dissimilar conditions to equivalent transactions with other trading parties, thereby placing them at a competitive disadvantage;

e) make the conclusion of contracts subject to acceptance by the other parties of supplementary obligations which, by their nature or according to commercial usage, have no connection with the subject of such contracts.

2. Any agreements or decisions prohibited pursuant to this Article shall be automatically void.

3. The provisions of paragraph 1 may, however, be declared inapplicable in the case of:

- any agreement or category of agreements between undertakings;

- any decision or category of decisions by associations of undertakings;

- any concerted practice or category of concerted practices;

which contributes to improving the production or distribution of goods or to promoting technical or economic progress, while allowing consumers a fair share of the resulting benefit, and which does not:

(a)  impose on the undertakings concerned restrictions which are not indispensable to the attainment of these objectives;

(b)  afford such undertakings the possibility of eliminating competition in respect of a substantial part of the products in question.

# APPENDIX B

COMMISSION REGULATION (EEC) NO 4087/88
of 30 November 1988
on the application of Article 85 (3) of the Treaty to categories of franchise
agreements

THE COMMISSION OF THE EUROPEAN COMMUNITIES,

Having regard to the Treaty establishing the European Economic Community,

Having regard to Council Regulation No 19/65/EEC of 2 March 1965 on the application of Article 85 (3) of the Treaty to certain categories of agreements and concerted practices,[1] as last amended by the Act of Accession of Spain and Portugal, and in particular Article 1 thereof,

Having published a draft of this Regulation,[2]

Having consulted the Advisory Committee on Restrictive Practices and Dominant Positions,

Whereas:

(1) Regulation No 19/65/EEC empowers the Commission to apply Article 85 (3) of the Treaty by Regulation to certain categories of bilateral exclusive agreements falling within the scope of Article 85 (1) which either have as their object the exclusive distribution or exclusive purchase of goods, or include restrictions imposed in relation to the assignment or use of industrial property rights.

(2) Franchise agreements consist essentially of licences of industrial or intellectual property rights relating to trade marks or signs and know-how, which can be combined with restrictions relating to supply or purchase of goods.

(3) Several types of franchise can be distinguished according to their object: industrial franchise concerns the manufacturing of goods, distribution franchise concerns the sale of goods, and service franchise concerns the supply of services.

(4) It is possible on the basis of the experience of the Commission to define categories of franchise agreements which fall under Article 85 (1) but can normally by regarded as satisfying the conditions laid down in Article 85 (3). This is the case for franchise agreements whereby one of the parties supplies goods or provides services to end users. On the other hand, industrial franchise agreements should not be covered by this Regulation. Such agreements, which usually govern relationships between producers, present different characteristics than the other types of franchise. They consist of manufacturing licences based on patents and/or technical know-how, combined with trade-mark licences. Some of them may benefit from other block exemptions if they fulfil the necessary conditions.

(5) This Regulation covers franchise agreements between two undertakings, the franchisor and the franchisee, for the retailing of goods or the provision of services to end users, or a combination of these activities, such as the processing or adaptation of goods to fit specific needs of their customers. It also covers cases where the relationship between franchisor and franchisees is made through a third undertaking, the master franchisee. It does not cover wholesale franchise agreements because of the lack of experience of the Commission in that field.

(6) Franchise agreements as defined in this Regulation can fall under Article 85 (1). They may in particular affect intra-Community trade where they are concluded between undertakings from different Member States or where they form the basis of a network which extends beyond the boundaries of a single Member State.

(7) Franchise agreements as defined in this Regulation normally improve the distribution of goods and/or the provision of services as they give franchisors the possibility of establishing a uniform network with limited investments, which may assist the entry of new competitors on the market, particularly in the case of small and medium-sized undertakings, thus increasing inter-brand competition. They also allow independent traders to set up outlets more rapidly and with higher chance of success than if they had to do so without the franchisor's experience and assistance. They have therefore the possibility of competing more efficiently with large distribution undertakings.

(8) As a rule, franchise agreements also allow consumers and other end users a fair share of the resulting benefit, as they combine the advantage of a uniform network with the existence of traders personally interested in the efficient operation of their business. The homogeneity of the network and the constant cooperation between the franchisor and the franchisees ensures a constant quality of the products and services. The favourable effect of

franchising on interbrand competition and the fact that consumers are free to deal with any franchisee in the network guarantees that a reasonable part of the resulting benefits will be passed on to the consumers.

(9) This Regulation must define the obligations restrictive of competition which may be included in franchise agreements. This is the case in particular for the granting of an exclusive territory to the franchisees combined with the prohibition on actively seeking customers outside that territory, which allows them to concentrate their efforts on their allotted territory. The same applies to the granting of an exclusive territory to a master franchisee combined with the obligation not to conclude franchise agreements with third parties outside that territory. Where the franchisees sell or use in the process of providing services, goods manufactured by the franchisor or according to its instructions and or bearing its trade mark, an obligation on the franchisees not to sell, or use in the process of the provision of services, competing goods, makes it possible to establish a coherent network which is identified with the franchised goods. However, this obligation should only be accepted with respect to the goods which form the essential subject-matter of the franchise. It should notably not relate to accessories or spare parts for these goods.

10) The obligations referred to above thus do not impose restrictions which are not necessary for the attainment of the abovementioned objectives. In particular, the limited territorial protection granted to the franchisees is indispensable to protect their investment.

11) It is desirable to list in the Regulation a number of obligations that are commonly found in franchise agreements and are normally not restrictive of competition and to provide that if, because of the particular economic or legal circumstances, they fall under Article 85 (1), they are also covered by the exemption. This list, which is not exhaustive, includes in particular clauses which are essential either to preserve the common identity and reputation of the network or to prevent the know-how made available and the assistance given by the franchisor from benefiting competitors.

12) The Regulation must specify the conditions which must be satisfied for the exemption to apply. To guarantee that competition is not eliminated for a substantial part of the goods which are the subject of the franchise, it is necessary that parallel imports remain possible. Therefore, cross deliveries between franchisees should always be possible. Furthermore, where a franchise network is combined with another distribution system, franchisees should be free to obtain supplies from authorized distributors. To better inform consumers, thereby helping to ensure that they receive a fair share of the resulting benefits, it must be provided that the franchisee shall be obliged

to indicate its status as an independent undertaking, by any appropriate means which does not jeopardize the common identity of the franchised network. Furthermore, where the franchisees have to honour guarantees for the franchisor's goods, this obligation should also apply to goods supplied by the franchisor, other franchisees or other agreed dealers.

(13) The Regulation must also specify restrictions which may not be included in franchise agreements if these are to benefit from the exemption granted by the Regulation, by virtue of the fact that such provisions are restrictions falling under Article 85 (1) for which there is no general presumption that they will lead to the positive effects required by Article 85 (3). This applies in particular to market sharing between competing manufacturers, to clauses unduly limiting the franchisee's choice of suppliers or customers, and to cases where the franchisee is restricted in determining its prices. However, the franchisor should be free to recommend prices to the franchisees, where it is not prohibited by national laws and to the extent that it does not lead to concerted practices for the effective application of these prices.

(14) Agreements which are not automatically covered by the exemption because they contain provisions that are not expressly exempted by the Regulation and not expressly excluded from exemption may nonetheless generally be presumed to be eligible for application of Article 85 (3). It will be possible for the Commission rapidly to establish whether this is the case for a particular agreement. Such agreements should therefore be deemed to be covered by the exemption provided for in this Regulation where they are notified to the Commission and the Commission does not oppose the application of the exemption within a specified period of time.

(15) If individual agreements exempted by this Regulation nevertheless have effects which are incompatible with Article 85 (3), in particular as interpreted by the administrative practice of the Commission and the case law of the Court of Justice, the Commission may withdraw the benefit of the block exemption. This applies in particular where competition is significantly restricted because of the structure of the relevant market.

(16) Agreements which are automatically exempted pursuant to this Regulation need not be notified. Undertakings may nevertheless in a particular case request a decision pursuant to Council Regulation No 17[3] as last amended by the Act of Accession of Spain and Portugal.

(17) Agreements may benefit from the provisions either of this Regulation or of another Regulation, according to their particular nature and provided that they fulfil the necessary conditions of application. They may not benefit

from a combination of the provisions of this Regulation with those of another block exemption Regulation,

HAS ADOPTED THIS REGULATION:

### Article 1

1. Pursuant to Article 85 (3) of the Treaty and subject to the provisions of this Regulation, it is hereby declared that Article 85 (1) of the Treaty shall not apply to franchise agreements to which two undertakings are party, which include one or more of the restrictions listed in Article 2.

2. The exemption provided for in paragraph 1 shall also apply to master franchise agreements to which two undertakings are party. Where applicable, the provisions of this Regulation concerning the relationship between franchisor and franchisee shall apply *mutatis mutandis* to the relationship between franchisor and master franchisee and between master franchisee and franchisee.

3. For the purposes of this Regulation:

(a) 'franchise' means a package of industrial or intellectual property rights relating to trade marks, trade names, shop signs, utility models, designs, copyrights, know-how or patents, to be exploited for the resale of goods or the provision of services to end users;

(b) 'franchise agreement' means an agreement whereby one undertaking, the franchisor, grants the other, the franchisee, in exchange for direct or indirect financial consideration, the right to exploit a franchise for the purposes of marketing specified types of goods and/or services; it includes at least obligations relating to:

   – the use of a common name or shop sign and a uniform presentation of contract premises and/or means of transport,

   – the communication by the franchisor to the franchisee of know-how,

   – the continuing provision by the franchisor to the franchisee of commercial or technical assistance during the life of the agreement;

(c) 'master franchise agreement' means an agreement whereby one undertaking, the franchisor, grants the other, the master franchisee, in exchange of direct or indirect financial consideration, the right to exploit a franchise for the purposes of concluding franchise agreements with third parties, the franchisees;

(d) 'franchisor's goods' means goods produced by the franchisor or according to its instructions, and/or bearing the franchisor's name or trade mark;

(e) 'contract premises' means the premises used for the exploitation of the franchise or, when the franchise is exploited outside those premises, the base from which the franchisee operates the means of transport used for the exploitation of the franchise (contract means of transport);

(f) 'know-how' means a package of non-patented practical information, result-ing from experience and testing by the franchisor, which is secret, substan-tial and identified;

(g) 'secret' means that the know-how, as a body or in the precise configuration and assembly of its components, is not generally known or easily accessible; it is not limited in the narrow sense that each individual component of the know-how should be totally unknown or unobtainable outside the fran-chisor's business;

(h) 'substantial' means that the know-how includes information which is of importance for the sale of goods or the provision of services to end users, and in particular for the presentation of goods for sale, the processing of goods in connection which the provision of services, methods of dealing with custom-ers, and administration and financial management; the know-how must be useful for the franchisee by being capable, at the date of conclusion of the agreement, of improving the competitive position of the franchisee, in par-ticular by improving the franchisee's performance or helping it to enter a new market;

(i) 'identified' means that the know-how must be described in a sufficiently comprehensive manner so as to make it possible to verify that it fulfils the criteria of secrecy and substantiality; the description of the know-how can either be set out in the franchise agreement or in a separate document or recorded in any other appropriate form.

*Article 2*

The exemption provided for in Article 1 shall apply to the following restrictions of competition:

(a) an obligation on the franchisor, in a defined area of the common market, the contract territory, not to:

   – grant the right to exploit all or part of the franchise to third parties,

   – itself exploit the franchise, or itself market the goods or services which are the subject-matter of the franchise under a similar formula;

   – itself supply the franchisor's goods to third parties;

(b)  an obligation on the master franchisee not to conclude franchise agreement with third parties outside its contract territory;

(c)  an obligation on the franchisee to exploit the franchise only from the contract premises;

(d)  an obligation on the franchisee to refrain, outside the contract territory, from seeking customers for the goods or the services which are the subject-matter of the franchise;

(e)  an obligation on the franchisee not to manufacture, sell or use in the course of the provision of services, goods competing with the franchisor's goods which are the subject-matter of the franchise; where the subject-matter of the franchise is the sale or use in the course of the provision of services both certain types of goods and spare parts or accessories therefor, that obligation may not be imposed in respect of these spare parts or accessories.

### Article 3

1. Article 1 shall apply notwithstanding the presence of any of the following obligations on the franchisee, in so far as they are necessary to protect the franchisor's industrial or intellectual property rights or to maintain the common identity and reputation of the franchised network:

(a)  to sell, or use in the course of the provision of services, exclusively goods matching minimum objective quality specifications laid down by the franchisor;

(b)  to sell, or use in the course of the provision of services, goods which are manufactured only by the franchisor or by third parties designed by it, where it is impracticable, owing to the nature of the goods which are the subject-matter of the franchise, to apply objective quality specifications;

(c)  not to engage, directly or indirectly, in any similar business in a territory where it would compete with a member of the franchised network, including the franchisor; the franchisee may be held to this obligation after termination of the agreement, for a reasonable period which may not exceed one year, in the territory where it has exploited the franchise;

(d)  not to acquire financial interests in the capital of a competing undertaking, which would give the franchisee the power to influence the economic conduct of such undertaking;

(e)  to sell the goods which are the subject-matter of the franchise only to end users, to other franchisees and to resellers within other channels of distribution supplied by the manufacturer of these goods or with its consent;

(f)   to use its best endeavours to sell the goods or provide the services that are the subject-matter of the franchise; to offer for sale a minimum range of goods, achieve a minimum turnover, plan its orders in advance, keep minimum stocks and provide customer and warranty services;

(g)   to pay to the franchisor a specified proportion of its revenue for advertising and itself carry out advertising for the nature of which it shall obtain the franchisor's approval.

    2. Article 1 shall apply notwithstanding the presence of any of the following obligations on the franchisee;

(a)   not to disclose to third parties the know-how provided by the franchisor; the franchisee may be held to this obligation after termination of the agreement;

(b)   to communicate to the franchisor any experience gained in exploiting the franchise and to grant it, and other franchisees, a non-exclusive licence for the know-how resulting from that experience;

(c)   to inform the franchisor of infringements of licensed industrial or intellectual property rights, to take legal action against infringers or to assist the franchisor in any legal actions against infringers:

(d)   not to use know-how licensed by the franchisor for purposes other than the exploitation of the franchise; the franchisee may be held to this obligation after termination of the agreement;

(e)   to attend or have its staff attend training courses arranged by the franchisor;

(f)   to apply the commercial methods devised by the franchisor, including any subsequent modification thereof, and use the licensed industrial or intellectual property rights;

(g)   to comply with the franchisor's standards for the equipment and presentation of the contract premises and/or means of transport;

(h)   to allow the franchisor to carry out checks of the contract premises and/or means of transport, including the goods sold and the services provided, and the inventory and accounts of the franchisee;

(i)   not without the franchisor's consent to change the location of the contract premises;

(j)   not without the franchisor's consent to assign the rights and obligations under the franchise agreement.

3. In the event that, because of particular circumstances, obligations referred to in paragraph 2 fall within the scope of Article 85 (1), they shall also be exempted even if they are not accompanied by any of the obligations exempted by Article 1.

## Article 4

The exemption provided for in Article 1 shall apply on condition that:

(a)  the franchisee is free to obtain the goods that are the subject-matter of the franchise from other franchisees; where such goods are also distributed through another network of authorized distributors, the franchisee must be free to obtain the goods from the latter;

(b)  where the franchisor obliges the franchisee to honour guarantees for the franchisor's goods, that obligation shall apply in respect of such goods supplied by any member of the franchised network or other distributors which gives similar guarantee, in the common market;

(c)  the franchisee is obliged to indicate its status as an independent undertaking; this indication shall however not interfere with the common identity of the franchised network resulting in particular from the common name or shop sign and uniform appearance of the contract premises and/or means of transport.

## Article 5

The exemption granted by Article 1 shall not apply where:

(a)  undertakings producing goods or providing services which are identical or are considered by users as equivalent in view of their characteristics, price and intended use, enter into franchise agreements in respect of such goods or services;

(b)  without prejudice to Article 2 (e) and Article 3 (1) (b), the franchisee is prevented from obtaining supplies of goods of a quality equivalent to those offered by the franchisor;

(c)  without prejudice to Article 2 (e), the franchisee is obliged to sell, or use in the process of providing services, goods manufactured by the franchisor or third parties designated by the franchisor and the franchisor refuses, for reasons other than protecting the franchisor's industrial or intellectual property rights, or maintaining the common identity and reputation of the franchised network, to designate as authorized manufacturers third parties proposed by the franchisee;

(d)  the franchisee is prevented from continuing to use the licensed know-how after termination of the agreement where the know-how has become generally known or easily accessible, other than by breach of an obligation by the franchisee;

(e)   the franchisee is restricted by the franchisor, directly or indirectly, in the determination of sale prices for the goods or services which are the subject-matter of the franchise, without prejudice to the possibility for the franchisor of recommending sale prices;

(f)   the franchisor prohibits the franchisee from challenging the validity of the industrial or intellectual property rights which form part of the franchise, without prejudice to the possibility for the franchisor of terminating the agreement in such a case;

(g)   franchisees are obliged not to supply within the common market the goods or services which are the subject-matter of the franchise to end users because of their place of residence.

### Article 6

1. The exemption provided for in Article 1 shall also apply to franchise agreements which fulfil the conditions laid down in Article 4 and include obligations restrictive of competition which are not covered by Articles 2 and 3 (3) and do not fall within the scope of Article 5, on condition that the agreements in question are notified to the Commission in accordance with the provisions of Commission Regulation No 27[4] and that the Commission does not oppose such exemption within a period of six months.

2. The period of six months shall run from the date on which the notification is received by the Commission. Where, however, the notification is made by registered post, the period shall run from the date shown on the postmark of the place of posting.

3. Paragraph 1 shall apply only if:

(a)   express reference is made to this Article in the notification or in a communication accompanying it; and

(b)   the information furnished with the notification is complete and in accordance with the facts.

4. The benefit of paragraph 1 can be claimed for agreements notified before the entry into force of this Regulation by submitting a communication to the Commission referring expressly to this Article and to the notification. Paragraphs 2 and 3 (b) shall apply *mutatis mutandis*.

5. The Commission may oppose exemption. It shall oppose exemption if it receives a request to do so from a Member State within three months of the forwarding to the Member State of the notification referred to in paragraph 1 or the

communication referred to in paragraph 4. This request must be justified on the basis of considerations relating to the competition rules of the Treaty.

6. The Commission may withdraw its opposition to the exemption at any time. However, where that opposition was raised at the request of a Member State, it may be withdrawn only after consultation of the advisory Committee on Restrictive Practices and Dominant Positions.

7. If the opposition is withdrawn because the undertakings concerned have shown that the conditions of Article 85 (3) are fulfilled, the exemption shall apply from the date of the notification.

8. If the opposition is withdrawn because the undertakings concerned have amended the agreement so that the conditions of Article 85 (3) are fulfilled, the exemption shall apply from the date on which the amendments take effect.

9. If the Commission opposes exemption and its opposition is not withdrawn, the effects of the notification shall be governed by the provisions of Regulation No 17.

### Article 7

1. Information acquired pursuant to Article 6 shall be used only for the purposes of this Regulation.

2. The Commission and the authorities of the Member States, their officials and other servants shall not disclose information acquired by them pursuant to this Regulation of a kind that is covered by the obligation of professional secrecy.

3. Paragraphs 1 and 2 shall not prevent publication of general information or surveys which do not contain information relating to particular undertakings or associations of undertakings.

### Article 8

The Commission may withdraw the benefit of this Regulation, pursuant to Article 7 of Regulation No 19/65/EEC, where it finds in a particular case that an agreement exempted by this Regulation nevertheless has certain effects which are incompatible with the conditions laid down in Article 85 (3) of the EEC Treaty, and in particular where territorial protection is awarded to the franchisee and:

(a) access to the relevant market or competition therein is significantly restricted by the cumulative effect of parallel networks of similar agreements established by competing manufacturers or distributors;

(b) the goods or services which are the subject-matter of the franchise do not face, in a substantial part of the common market, effective competition from goods or services which are identical or considered by users as equivalent in view of their characteristics, price and intended use;

(c) the parties, or one of them, prevent end users, because of their place of residence, from obtaining, directly or through intermediaries, the goods or services which are the subject-matter of the franchise within the common market, or use differences in specifications concerning those goods or services in different Member States, to isolate markets;

(d)  franchisees engage in concerted practices relating to the sale prices of the goods or services which are the subject-matter of the franchise;

(e)  the franchisor uses its right to check the contract premises and means of transport, or refuses its agreement to requests by the franchisee to move the contract premises or assign its rights and obligations under the franchise agreement, for reasons other than protecting the franchisor's industrial or intellectual property rights, maintaining the common identity and reputation of the franchised network or verifying that the franchisee abides by its obligations under the agreement.

## Article 9

This Regulation shall enter into force on 1 February 1989.

It shall remain in force until 31 December 1999.

This Regulation shall be binding in its entirety and directly applicable in all Member States.

Done at Brussels, 30 November 1988.

*For the Commission*
Peter SUTHERLAND
*Member of the Commission*

*Notes*
1   OJ No 36, 6. 3. 1965, p. 533/65.
2   OJ No C 229, 27. 8. 1987, p. 3.
3   OJ No 13, 21. 2. 1962, p. 204/62.
4   OJ No 35, 10. 5. 1962, p. 1118/62.

# APPENDIX C
# EUROPEAN CODE OF ETHICS FOR FRANCHISING

## PREFACE

The European Franchise Federation, EFF, was constituted on 23rd September 1972.

Its members are national franchise associations or federations established in Europe.

The EFF also accepts affiliates, i.e. non European franchise associations or federations, and other professional persons, interested in or concerned with franchising. Affiliates have no voting rights and cannot be appointed officers of the EFF.

The objects of the EFF are, among others, the ongoing unbiased and scientific study of franchising in every respect, the co-ordination of its members' actions, the promotion of the franchise industry in general and of its members' interests in particular.

The EFF also comprises a Legal Committee, composed of two lawyers from each national member association or federation and highly qualified in franchise matters.

The EFF has, furthermore, installed a Franchise Arbitration Committee which is at the disposal of parties preferring to submit their disputes to the latter's determination.

The evolution and the ever growing importance of franchising in the EC economy as well as the EC Block Exemption Regulation for franchise agreements, entered into force on 1st February 1989, prompted the EFF to revise its existing *Code of Ethics*.

This *Code of Ethics* is meant to be a practical ensemble of essential provisions of fair behaviour for franchise practitioners in Europe, but not to replace possibly related national or EC law.

This *Code of Ethics* is the end-product of work carried out by the European Franchise Federation and its member associations (Austria, Belgium, Denmark, Germany, France, Italy, the Netherlands, Portugal and the United Kingdom) in conjunction with the Commission of the European Community. It shall replace the previous *European Code of Ethics* as well as all national and regional Codes existing at that time in Europe.

By subscribing to the EFF, its members accept the *European Code of Ethics* a undertake not to delete or amend it in any way. It is, however, recognised th national requirements may necessitate certain other clauses or provisions an providing these do not conflict with or detract from the Code and are attached t the Code in a separate document, permission to do this will not be withheld b, the EFF.

By adhering to the EFF its members commit themselves to impose on their own members the obligation to respect and apply the provisions of this *Code of Ethics for Franchising*.

## 1  DEFINITION OF FRANCHISING

Franchising is a system of marketing goods and/or services and/or technology, which is based upon a close and ongoing collaboration between legally and financially separate and independent undertakings, the Franchisor and its Individual Franchisees, whereby the Franchisor grants its Individual Franchisees the right, and imposes the obligation, to conduct a business in accordance with the Franchisor's concept. The right entitles and compels the individual Franchisee, in exchange for a direct or indirect financial consideration, to use the Franchisor's trade name, and/or trade mark and/or service mark, know-how*, business and technical methods, precedural system, and other industrial and/or intellectual property rights, supported by continuing provision of commercial and technical assistance, within the framework and for the term of a written franchise agreement, concluded between parties for this purpose.

* 'Know-how' means a body of non patented practical information, resulting from experience and testing by the Franchisor, which is secret, substantial and identified;

- 'secret', means that the know-how, as a body or in the precise configuration and assembly of its components, is not generally known or easily accessible; it is not limited in the narrow sense that each individual component of the know-how should be totally unknown or unobtainable outside the Franchisor's business;

- 'substantial' means that the know-how includes information which is of importance for the sale of goods or the provision of services to end users, and in particular for the presentation of goods for sale, the processing of goods in connection with the provision of services, methods of dealing with customers, and administration and financial management; the know-how must be useful for the Franchisee by being capable, at the date of conclusion of the agreement, of improving the competitive position of the Franchisee, in particular by improving the Franchisee's performance or helping it to enter a new market.

- 'identified' means that the know-how must be described in a sufficiently comprehensive manner so as to make it possible to verify that it fulfils the criteria of secrecy and substantiality; the description of the know-how can either be set out in the franchise agreement or in a separate document or recorded in any other appropriate form.

## GUIDING PRINCIPLES

. The Franchisor is the initiator of a franchise network, composed of itself and its Individual Franchisees, of which the Franchisor is the long-term guardian.

2 **The obligations of the Franchisor:**
The Franchisor shall

- have operated a business concept with success, for a reasonable time and in at least one pilot unit before starting its franchise network;

- be the owner, or have legal rights to the use, of its network's trade name, trade mark or other distinguishing identification;

- shall provide the Individual Franchisee with initial training and continuing commercial and/or technical assistance during the entire life of the agreement.

3 **The obligations of the Individual Franchisee:**
The Individual Franchisee shall

- devote its best endeavours to the growth of the franchise business and to the maintenance of the common identity and reputation of the franchise network;

- supply the Franchisor with verifiable operating data to facilitate the determination of performance and the financial statements necessary for effective management guidance, and allow the Franchisor, and/or its agents, to have access to the individual Franchisee's premises and records at the Franchisor's request and at reasonable times;

- not disclose to third parties the know-how provided by the franchisor, neither during nor after termination of the agreement;

4 **The ongoing obligations of both parties:**
Parties shall exercise fairness in their dealings with each other. The Franchisor shall give written notice to its Individual Franchisees of any contractual breach and, where appropriate, grant reasonable time to remedy default;
Parties should resolve complaints, grievances and disputes with good faith and goodwill through fair and reasonable direct communication and negotiation;

## 3 RECRUITMENT, ADVERTISING AND DISCLOSURE

3.1  Advertising for the recruitment of Individual Franchisees shall be free
ambiguity and misleading statements;

3.2  Any recruitment, advertising and publicity material, containing direct
indirect references to future possible results, figures or earnings to
expected by Individual Franchisees, should be objective and capable
verification;

3.3  In order to allow prospective Individual Franchisees to enter into any bin
ing document with full knowledge, they shall be given a copy of the prese
*Code of Ethics* as well as full and accurate written disclosure of all informati
material to the franchise relationship, within a reasonable time prior to tl
execution of these binding documents;

3.4  If a Franchisor imposes a Pre-contract on a candidate Individual Franchise
the following principles should be respected:

-   prior to the signing of any pre-contract, the candidate Individual Fra
    chisee should be given written information on its purpose and on a
    consideration he may be required to pay to the Franchisor to cover tl
    latter's actual expenses, incurred during and with respect to the pr
    contract phase; if the Franchise agreement is executed, the said co
    sideration should be reimbursed by the Franchisor or set off against
    possible entry fee to be paid by the Individual Franchisee;

-   the Pre-contract shall define its term and include a termination clause

-   the Franchisor can impose non-competition and/or secrecy clauses
    protect its know-how and identity.

## 4 SELECTION OF INDIVIDUAL FRANCHISEES

A Franchisor should select and accept as Individual Franchisees only those wh
upon reasonable investigation, appear to possess the basic skills, educatio
personal qualities and financial resources sufficient to carry on the franchis
business.

## 5 THE FRANCHISE AGREEMENT

5.1  The Franchise agreement should comply with the National law, Europea
community law and this *Code of Ethics*.

The agreement shall reflect the interests of the members of the franchised network in protecting the Franchisor's industrial and intellectual property rights and in maintaining the common identity and reputation of the franchised network. All agreements and all contractual arrangements in connection with the franchise relationship should be written in or translated by a sworn translator into the official language of the country the Individual Franchisee is established in, and signed agreements shall be given immediately to the Individual Franchisee.

5.3  The Franchise agreement shall set forth without ambiguity, the respective obligations and responsibilities of the parties and all other material terms of the relationship.

5.4  The essential minimum terms of the agreement shall be the following:

-   the rights granted to the Franchisor;

-   the rights granted to the Individual Franchisee;

-   the goods and/or services to be provided to the Individual Franchisee;

-   the obligations of the Franchisor;

-   the obligations of the Individual Franchisee;

-   the terms of payment by the Individual Franchisee;

-   the duration of the agreement which should be long enough to allow Individual Franchisees to amortize their initial franchise investments;

-   the basis for any renewal of the agreement;

-   the terms upon which the Individual Franchisee may sell or transfer the franchised business and the Franchisor's possible preemption rights in this respect;

-   provisions relevant to the use by the Individual Franchisee of the Franchisor's distinctive signs, trade name, trade mark, service mark, store sign, logo or other distinguishing identification;

-   the Franchisor's right to adapt the franchise system to new or changed methods;

-   provisions for termination of the agreement;

    –    provisions for surrendering promptly upon termination of the franch
             agreement any tangible and intangible property belonging to the Fra
             chisor or other owner thereof.

## 6  THE CODE OF ETHICS AND THE MASTER-FRANCHISE SYSTE

This *Code of Ethics* shall apply to the relationship between the Franchisor and its
Individual Franchisees and equally between the Master Franchisee and its Individual Franchisees. It shall not apply to the relationship between the Franchisor
and its Master-Franchisees.